HISTORICAL DICTIONARIES OF RELIGIONS, PHILOSOPHIES, AND MOVEMENTS

Jon Woronoff, Series Editor

1. *Buddhism*, by Charles S. Prebish, 1993
2. *Mormonism*, by Davis Bitton, 1994. *Out of print. See no. 32.*
3. *Ecumenical Christianity*, by Ans Joachim van der Bent, 1994
4. *Terrorism*, by Sean Anderson and Stephen Sloan, 1995. *Out of print. See no. 41.*
5. *Sikhism*, by W. H. McLeod, 1995. *Out of print. See no. 59.*
6. *Feminism*, by Janet K. Boles and Diane Long Hoeveler, 1995. *Out of print. See no. 52.*
7. *Olympic Movement*, by Ian Buchanan and Bill Mallon, 1995. *Out of print. See no. 39.*
8. *Methodism*, by Charles Yrigoyen Jr. and Susan E. Warrick, 1996. *Out of print. See no. 57.*
9. *Orthodox Church*, by Michael Prokurat, Alexander Golitzin, and Michael D. Peterson, 1996
10. *Organized Labor*, by James C. Docherty, 1996. *Out of print. See no. 50.*
11. *Civil Rights Movement*, by Ralph E. Luker, 1997
12. *Catholicism*, by William J. Collinge, 1997
13. *Hinduism*, by Bruce M. Sullivan, 1997
14. *North American Environmentalism*, by Edward R. Wells and Alan M. Schwartz, 1997
15. *Welfare State*, by Bent Greve, 1998. *Out of print. See no. 63.*
16. *Socialism*, by James C. Docherty, 1997. *Out of print. See no. 73.*
17. *Bahá'í Faith*, by Hugh C. Adamson and Philip Hainsworth, 1998. *Out of print. See no. 71.*
18. *Taoism*, by Julian F. Pas in cooperation with Man Kam Leung, 1998
19. *Judaism*, by Norman Solomon, 1998. *Out of print. See no. 69.*
20. *Green Movement*, by Elim Papadakis, 1998. *Out of print. See no. 80.*
21. *Nietzscheanism*, by Carol Diethe, 1999. *Out of print. See no. 75.*
22. *Gay Liberation Movement*, by Ronald J. Hunt, 1999
23. *Islamic Fundamentalist Movements in the Arab World, Iran, and Turkey*, by Ahmad S. Moussalli, 1999

Historical Dictionary of Mormonism

Third Edition

Davis Bitton and Thomas G. Alexander

*Historical Dictionaries of Religions,
Philosophies, and Movements, No. 89*

The Scarecrow Press, Inc.
Lanham, Maryland • Toronto • Plymouth, UK
2008

SCARECROW PRESS, INC.

Published in the United States of America
by Scarecrow Press, Inc.
A wholly owned subsidiary of
The Rowman & Littlefield Publishing Group, Inc.
4501 Forbes Boulevard, Suite 200, Lanham, Maryland 20706
www.scarecrowpress.com

Estover Road
Plymouth PL6 7PY
United Kingdom

British Library Cataloguing in Publication Information Available

Library of Congress Cataloging-in-Publication Data

Bitton, Davis, 1930–
  Historical dictionary of Mormonism / Davis Bitton and Thomas G. Alexander.
  — 3rd ed.
    p. cm. — (Historical dictionaries of religions, philosophies, and movements ;
no. 89)
  Includes bibliographical references.
  ISBN-13: 978-0-8108-5814-5 (hardcover : alk. paper)
  ISBN-10: 0-8108-5814-2 (hardcover : alk. paper)
  eISBN-13: 978-0-8108-6251-7
  eISBN-10: 0-8108-6251-4
  1. Mormon Church—Dictionaries. 2. Mormons—Biography—Dictionaries.
I. Alexander, Thomas G. II. Title.
  BX8605.5.B558 2008
  289.303—dc22   2008014759

∞™ The paper used in this publication meets the minimum requirements of
American National Standard for Information Sciences—Permanence of Paper
for Printed Library Materials, ANSI/NISO Z39.48-1992.
Manufactured in the United States of America.

Contents

Editor's Foreword

The Church of Jesus Christ of Latter-day Saints, or Mormonism as it is widely known, is one of the younger religions. To the surprise and sometimes consternation of many outside the Church, it did not wither and die. To the contrary, it has grown at an exceptional pace, taking root in many different settings—the majority of its members are currently outside of the United States. Whether it will eventually join the select circle of "world religions," as many of its adherents hope, remains uncertain. At any rate, it is well on its way.

The story of Mormonism is gripping when you consider the efforts of its founders and leaders over more than a century and a half. But it is just as important to consider the present to understand why the Church has retained its vitality and achieved record growth. For this, it is necessary to examine, in addition to Mormonism's religious precepts and practices, it social, economic, and cultural activities as well as its ability to keep abreast of the times. An impressive amount of information on both the past and the present, the essential religious concepts, the work in many different fields and countries, and the role of leaders as well as ordinary members is provided in this volume, mainly in the introduction and the dictionary section. It is supported by a helpful chronology and a selective bibliography for those who want to do further reading.

This third edition of the *Historical Dictionary of Mormonism* was compiled and mostly written by Davis Bitton, who also produced the first two editions. Alas, before he could finalize the manuscript he passed away, and the completion and updating had to be undertaken by Thomas G. Alexander. Dr. Bitton was emeritus professor of the University of Utah, where he taught history for several decades. He wrote and lectured extensively on Mormon history, including such publications as *Guide to Mormon Diaries and Autobiographies* and *The Mormon*

Experience: A History of the Latter-day Saints. Dr. Alexander is the Lemuel Hardison Redd Jr. professor emeritus of western American history at Brigham Young University. Along with lecturing, he has also authored, coauthored, edited, or coedited an impressive number of articles and books; those most relevant to Mormon history include *Mormonism in Transition: A History of the Latter-day Saints, 1890–1930* and *Things in Heaven and Earth: The Life and Times of Wilford Woodruff, a Mormon Prophet*. Both authors were founders and past presidents of the Mormon History Association. They were also close friends and associates. Their combined knowledge and experience will provide answers that are comprehensible to Mormons as well as non-Mormons.

Jon Woronoff
Series Editor

Preface to the Third Edition

From one point of view, Mormons are but one relatively small group within the contemporary religious spectrum. They see themselves as "God's chosen people," as the "only true and living church," not unlike several other religious groups. Those curious about such a religion might need no further excuse for reading about it. But since its formal organization in 1830, Mormons have had a colorful, exciting history. In the 20th century, while melding into the larger society and achieving respectability in the eyes of most people, Mormonism continued to grow. Especially during the past 30 or 40 years, that growth has been dramatic, which not surprisingly has evoked opposition and denunciation from some quarters. This is not a quiet, dull religion undifferentiated from the many Christian denominations.

Other works of reference exist, but they are pitched exclusively to the Mormon audience or are, in the case of older biographical and historical encyclopedias or the five-volume *Encyclopedia of Mormonism*, library works of reference rather than a handbook that can be easily carried and used. We have benefited from these other works and have supplied a bibliography for those wishing more, but the current dictionary should be more than sufficient as a preliminary orientation to Mormon history, beliefs, practices, and terminology.

We are all familiar enough with encyclopedias arranged in the irrational but convenient alphabetical order that little explanation is required. Part of the fun is in random browsing. At the same time, readers new to the subject might want an overview of Mormon history. Other than the chronology and introduction in the beginning of this book, the entries on New York Period, Ohio Period, Missouri Period, Illinois Period, Exodus, Utah Period, and Colonization can be read in order. Alternatively, the biographical sketches of the presidents of the Church from the beginning can be read in sequence: Joseph Smith, Brigham

Young, John Taylor, Wilford Woodruff, Lorenzo Snow, Joseph F. Smith, Heber J. Grant, George Albert Smith, David O. McKay, Joseph Fielding Smith, Harold B. Lee, Spencer W. Kimball, Ezra Taft Benson, Howard W. Hunter, Gordon B. Hinckley, and Thomas S. Monson. Other articles often include historical information.

In the preface to the second edition of this book, Davis Bitton wrote, "I wish to thank my wife, JoAn, who encouraged me in this project; librarians who assisted me in finding specific details; and general editor Jon Woronoff, whose kindly supervision has made this series the valuable resource it is." After Davis died, JoAn asked me to complete the work that he had so ably begun. I agreed to do this. I thank her for trusting me with the task. I also thank Lyn Clayton for previous help on some of the biographies he prepared for an earlier work.

Most especially, I thank my wife, Marilyn, whose unflagging support for a life that is far too full of projects in various states of completion has added to the joy of nearly a half century of marriage.

Thomas G. Alexander

List of Acronyms and Abbreviations

AML	Association for Mormon Letters
BYU	Brigham Young University
CEBA	Centro Escolar Benemerito de las Americas
CPART	Center for the Preservation of Ancient Religious Texts
FARMS	Foundation for Ancient Research and Mormon Studies
JST	Joseph Smith Translation
JWHA	John Whitmer Historical Association
LDS	Latter-day Saint, often used as a substitute for Mormon or for Church of Jesus Christ of Latter-day Saints in English-speaking countries
LDSSA	Latter-day Saint Students Association
METI	Middle Eastern Text Initiative
MHA	Mormon History Association
MIT	Massachusetts Institute of Technology
MYSC	Mormon Youth Symphony and Chorus
NRI	Nauvoo Restoration, Inc.
RLDS	Reorganized Church of Jesus Christ of Latter Day Saints
UCLA	University of California at Los Angeles
YMMIA	Young Men's Mutual Improvement Association, superseded by Young Men
YWMIA	Young Women's Mutual Improvement Association, superseded by Young Women

Chronology

1805 23 December: Joseph Smith Jr. born in Sharon, Windsor County, Vermont.

1830 26 March: The *Book of Mormon* published in Palmyra, New York. **6 April:** Joseph Smith organized the Church of Christ in Fayette, New York. **30 December:** Church members instructed to gather in Ohio (*Doctrine and Covenants*, section 37).

1831 2 August: Missouri dedicated as the Land of Zion.

1833 20 July: Mob destroyed Mormon printing office in Independence, Missouri. **November:** Mormons left Jackson County, Missouri, due to mob opposition.

1834 8 May: Small "army" known as Zion's Camp began its march from Ohio to Missouri to assist beleaguered Mormons. **30 June:** The group dispersed.

1835 14 February: Quorum of Twelve Apostles organized. **28 February:** First Council of the Seventy organized. **17 August:** Meeting agreed on contents to be included in the *Doctrine and Covenants*, which became the third book of scripture (the "standard works"). **September:** *Doctrine and Covenants* published. **14 September:** Emma Smith appointed to select hymns.

1836 27 March: Kirtland (Ohio) Temple dedicated.

1837 13 June: Two Mormon apostles left Ohio on mission to England, the first proselytizing outside North America. **30 July:** Nine persons baptized in the River Ribble at Preston, England.

1838 6 July: Most Mormons depart from Kirtland, Ohio. **27 October:** Missouri governor Lilburn W. Boggs ordered extermination or expulsion of the Mormons from the state. **30 October:** Seventeen Mormons killed at Haun's Mill in Missouri.

1839 **January:** Exodus of Mormons from Missouri began. **25 April:** Land purchased in Illinois at site soon renamed Nauvoo. **8 August:** John Taylor and Wilford Woodruff left for mission to England.

1840 **6 June:** Forty-one converts set sail from England. **15 August:** Baptism for the dead officially announced. **16 December:** Nauvoo Charter signed by Illinois governor.

1841 **24 October:** Palestine dedicated for the return of the Jews by Apostle Orson Hyde.

1842 **1 March:** Articles of Faith written by Joseph Smith in letter to John Wentworth and published in Nauvoo newspaper. **17 March:** Female Relief Society organized.

1843 **23 May:** Missionaries left Nauvoo for Pacific islands. **12 July:** Revelation on marriage recorded, instituting the possibility of plural marriage, or polygamy.

1844 **27 June:** Joseph and Hyrum Smith killed by a mob in Carthage, Illinois. **8 August:** Leadership of the Church by the twelve under Brigham Young approved by vote in a large conference in Nauvoo.

1846 **4 February:** Evacuation of Nauvoo began. **1 May:** Nauvoo Temple dedicated. **13 July:** Volunteers began to enlist in the Mormon Battalion of the U.S. Army.

1847 **22–24 July:** Pioneer company under Brigham Young arrived in the Salt Lake Valley. **5 December:** First Presidency reorganized with Brigham Young as president of the Church.

1848 **June:** Crops saved when flocks of gulls devour crickets.

1849 **6 October:** Missionaries called to preach in Continental Europe.

1850 **28 February:** University of Deseret, predecessor of University of Utah, founded. **15 June:** *Deseret News* began publication. **9 September:** Congress organized Utah Territory. **20 September:** Brigham Young appointed governor of Utah Territory.

1851 **11 July:** *Pearl of Great Price* (fourth volume of scripture) published as a pamphlet in England.

1852 **28–29 August:** Plural marriage first publicly announced.

1857 **24 July:** Definite news received that a U.S. Army regiment had been ordered to Utah. Rumors had reached Utah earlier. **7–11 September:** Mountain Meadows Massacre.

1858 **11 June:** Peace commissioners resolved dispute and brought an end to the Utah War.

1859 **10–17 July:** Horace Greeley interviewed Brigham Young.

1860 **24 August–10 September:** English explorer Richard F. Burton visited Utah.

1861 **18 October:** Telegraph line reached Utah.

1862 **8 July:** Lincoln signed Morrill Anti-bigamy Act, prohibiting polygamy and limiting property ownership by religious organizations in the territories.

1869 **10 May:** Transcontinental railroad completed.

1870 **12–14 June:** Rev. J. P. Newman and Mormon apostle Orson Pratt debated the question "Does the Bible sanction polygamy?"

1874 **23 June:** Poland Act passed by Congress, restricting local government in Utah.

1875 **3 October:** U.S. president Ulysses S. Grant began visit to Utah. **16 October:** Brigham Young Academy founded in Provo, Utah (predecessor of Brigham Young University).

1877 **1 January:** St. George Temple dedicated. **29 August:** Brigham Young died. **4 September:** Twelve apostles under President John Taylor presided over the Church.

1878 **25 August:** Primary organization for children founded by Aurelia Spencer Rogers.

1879 **6 January:** Reynolds decision handed down. U.S. Supreme Court upheld constitutionality of the Morrill Anti-bigamy Act and confirmed conviction of polygamist George Reynolds. **21 July:** Joseph Standing, Mormon missionary, killed by a mob in Georgia.

1880   19 August: Mormon missionaries arrested for preaching in Berlin and ordered out of Germany. **5–6 September:** U.S. president Rutherford B. Hayes and party visited Utah. **10 October:** *Pearl of Great Price* officially accepted as a standard work. First Presidency of the Church reorganized with John Taylor as president.

1882   22 March: Edmunds Act against polygamy passed by Congress.

1887   3 March: Edmunds-Tucker Act, intensifying penalties for polygamy and allowing for confiscation of LDS Church property, became law without presidential signature. **25 July:** Death of Church president John Taylor. Twelve apostles presided over the Church.

1888   21 May: Manti (Utah) Temple dedicated.

1889   7 April: Wilford Woodruff became president of the Church.

1890   24 September: Manifesto issued by Church president Wilford Woodruff. **6 October:** Manifesto approved by vote in general conference.

1891   9 May: U.S. president Benjamin Harrison and party visited Salt Lake City.

1893   6 April: Salt Lake Temple dedicated. **8 September:** Mormon Tabernacle Choir won second prize at Chicago World's Fair (the Columbian Exposition).

1894   13 November: Genealogical Society of Utah organized.

1895   8 May: Constitutional convention completed its work in drafting a state constitution for Utah.

1896   4 January: Utah became a state.

1897   24 July: Fiftieth anniversary of entrance of Mormon pioneers into Salt Lake Valley celebrated. **November:** *Improvement Era* began publication.

1898   2 September: Church president Wilford Woodruff died. **13 September:** Lorenzo Snow sustained by apostles as president of the

Church. **9 October:** Lorenzo Snow and other authorities sustained by vote of general Church conference. **8 November:** B. H. Roberts elected Utah's congressman (he was accused of polygamy and not allowed to take his seat).

1903 **15 October:** Brigham Young Academy became Brigham Young University.

1904 **5 April:** "Second manifesto" ended plural marriage.

1913 **21 May:** Boy Scout program officially adopted for boys of the Church.

1915 **January:** *Relief Society Magazine* for women began publication.

1929 **15 July:** Mormon Tabernacle Choir started weekly radio broadcast.

1930 **6 April:** Centennial of the organization of the Church celebrated.

1933 **5 November:** Chapel in Washington, D.C., dedicated.

1936 **7 April:** Welfare program introduced.

1937 **July:** Outdoor pageant, "America's Witness for Christ," began at Hill Cumorah in New York.

1947 **24 July:** Centennial of the arrival of pioneers in the Salt Lake Valley celebrated.

1954 **July:** Indian Placement Program inaugurated. **21 July:** Church College of Hawaii announced.

1963 **12 October:** Polynesian Cultural Center dedicated in Laie, Hawaii.

1966 **1 May:** First stake in South America organized in São Paulo, Brazil.

1969 **3–8 August:** World Conference on Records took place in Salt Lake City.

1970 **15 March:** First stake in Asia organized in Tokyo. **22 March:** First stake in Africa organized in Transvaal, South Africa.

1971 **January:** New Church magazines began publication: *Ensign* (for adults), *New Era* (for youths), and the *Friend* (for children).

1972 **14 January:** Establishment of the Historical Department of the Church announced, replacing the Church Historian's Office.

1974 **1 September:** Church College of Hawaii renamed Brigham Young University–Hawaii campus.

1975 **19–21 June:** Open house for new 28-story Church office building in Salt Lake City.

1976 **25 June:** Missouri governor Christopher S. Bond rescinded 1838 extermination order.

1978 **9 June:** First Presidency announced that worthy men of all races would be eligible to receive the priesthood. **9 September:** Missionary Training Center replaced Mission Home in Salt Lake City and Language Training Mission.

1979 **29 September:** New edition of the King James Version of the Bible published.

1980 **6 April:** Centennial of the organization of the Church.

1981 **26 September:** New editions of *Book of Mormon*, *Doctrine and Covenants*, and *Pearl of Great Price* published.

1982 **1 April:** Church membership reached 5 million. **3 October:** New subtitle announced for *Book of Mormon*: *Another Testament of Jesus Christ*.

1984 **28 October:** The 1,500th stake organized: the Ciudad Obregon Mexico Yaqui Stake.

1985 **27 January:** Church members participated in a fast in order to raise funds ($11 million) for famine victims in Africa. **2 August:** Revised hymn book published. **23 October:** Family History Library dedicated. **10 November:** Ezra Taft Benson became 13th president of the Church.

1988 **12 November:** Centennial of Ricks College, Rexburg, Idaho.

1989 **16 May:** Brigham Young University Jerusalem Center dedicated.

1991   26 May: San Francisco de Macoris Dominican Republic Stake organized as the 1,800th stake of the Church. **31 May:** Church membership reached 8 million. **8–29 June:** Mormon Tabernacle Choir toured Eastern Europe. **December:** *Encyclopedia of Mormonism* published by Macmillan.

1992   30 August: The 1,900th stake created: Orlando Florida South Stake. **26 December:** Mormon Tabernacle Choir began tour of Israel.

1993   1 January: India Bangalore Mission opened, with Gurcharan Singh Gill as president. **6 January:** Mormon Tabernacle Choir concluded tour of Israel.

1994   5 June: Howard W. Hunter became 14th president of the Church. **17 November:** Future Church president Thomas S. Monson honored by Catholic Community Services of Utah for humanitarian care. **3 December:** More than 20,000 food packages prepared for families in Bosnia, Croatia, and Albania. **11 December:** Church's 2,000th stake created in Mexico City.

1995   21 February: Gordon B. Hinckley honored for promoting high moral values by National Conference of Christians and Jews (Utah Region). **12 March:** Gordon B. Hinckley becomes 15th president of the Church. **1 April:** Position of regional representative replaced by new position of area authority. **23 September:** Proclamation on the family issued by the First Presidency. See appendix 2. **18 December:** President Gordon B. Hinckley interviewed for the CBS television program *60 Minutes* by Mike Wallace.

1996   18 January: General authorities announced withdrawal from boards of directors of business corporations. **28 February:** More than half of Church membership lived outside the United States. **29 June:** President Gordon B. Hinckley awarded the Golden Plate Award for exceptional accomplishment in public service by the American Academy of Achievement.

1997   April: Organization of Third, Fourth, and Fifth Quorums of the Seventy announced. **19–21 April:** Mormon Trail Wagon Train departed from Iowa and Nebraska to reenact the overland journey to the Salt Lake Valley that occurred in 1847. **28 May:** New nine-story headquarters building for the *Deseret News* dedicated in Salt Lake City, Utah. **9**

July: Smithsonian Institution's National Museum of American History at Washington, D.C., opened an exhibit on the Mormon Pioneer Trail. **4 October:** Plan announced to construct "small" temples in areas whose population would not justify larger ones.

1998 February: President Gordon B. Hinckley toured Nigeria, Ghana, Kenya, Zimbabwe, and South Africa and announced plans to construct a temple in Ghana. **26 April:** President Gordon B. Hinckley addressed 20,000 people in Madison Square Garden, New York City. **7–10 June:** Dedication of temple in Preston, England, site of first English baptisms in 1837. **14 June–2 July:** Mormon Tabernacle Choir toured England, Belgium, Switzerland, Italy, France, Spain, and Portugal. **28 June:** First meetinghouse dedicated in Ukraine at Donetsk. **8 September:** President Gordon B. Hinckley interviewed on the network TV show *Larry King Live*.

1999 9 February: Deseret Management Corporation, the Church's holding company for commercial entities, acquired Bookcraft, Inc. **11 February 1999:** Leonard J. Arrington, the Church's most prolific and respected historian, died. **1 April:** Sesquicentennial of organization of the Sunday school celebrated. **25 April:** President Gordon B. Hinckley addressed 57,500 in Santiago, Chile. **29–30 April:** Women's Conference at Brigham Young University attended by 20,000 women. **13 May:** President Gordon B. Hinckley addressed Los Angeles World Affairs Council. **24 May:** Free website for genealogical research, familysearch.org, launched. **25 September:** Relief Society declaration on roles and values of women announced. **26 November:** *American Prophet: The Story of Joseph Smith*, a television documentary, made its national debut over the Public Broadcasting System. **24 December:** President Gordon B. Hinckley interviewed again on *Larry King Live*.

2000 8 March: President Gordon B. Hinckley addressed National Press Club Newsmakers Luncheon in Washington, D.C. **22 April:** The 100 millionth copy of the *Book of Mormon* printed. **21 June:** Announced that Ricks College would become a four-year institution and would be renamed Brigham Young University–Idaho. **7–8 October:** New 21,000-seat Conference Center in Salt Lake City, Utah, dedicated.

2001 20 January: Mormon Tabernacle Choir sang at the inauguration of President George W. Bush.

2002 **22 May:** First Missionary Training Center in Africa opened in Ghana. **27 June:** Rebuilt Nauvoo Temple dedicated in Nauvoo, Illinois. **8 December:** Hispanic Christmas fireside held in the Conference Center for 13,000 Spanish-speaking members.

2003 **12 November:** Mormon Tabernacle Choir was awarded the National Medal of Arts by President George W. Bush at the White House in Washington, D.C.

2004 **24 March:** Illinois House of Representatives passed a resolution expressing regret for the expulsion of the Latter-day Saints from Illinois following the murder of Joseph and Hyrum Smith in June 1844. **29–30 April:** Annual Women's Conference at Brigham Young University attended by 17,000 women. **27 May:** Elder Russell M. Nelson addressed an international conference on religious freedom in Kiev, Ukraine. **23 June:** President Gordon B. Hinckley received the Presidential Medal of Freedom at the White House in Washington, D.C. **19 October:** First Presidency issued a statement defending the definition of marriage as the union of a man and a woman. **26 December:** President Gordon B. Hinckley was interviewed for the third time on the television talk show *Larry King Live*.

2005 Bicentennial year of Joseph Smith's birth on 23 December 1805. Throughout the year programs, pageants, plays, and concerts commemorated his life and ministry. The Museum of Church History and Art offered an exhibit on "Joseph Smith: Prophet of the Restoration" attended by some 430,000 visitors during the year. **1 January:** More than 70 tons of relief supplies sent (in partnership with Islamic Relief Worldwide) to Indonesia to assist victims of tsunamis in southern Asia. Later additional containers of supplies were sent to Indonesia and Sri Lanka. **6–7 May:** Academic conference, "The Worlds of Joseph Smith," was held at the Library of Congress in Washington, D.C. **31 March:** Perpetual Education Fund announced to assist young people in selected countries complete an education leading to satisfactory employment. **July:** Website, josephsmith.net, launched by Family and Church History Department. **10 August:** Ricks College, in Rexburg, Idaho, was officially renamed Brigham Young University–Idaho, a four-year university. **September–October:** To aid victims of hurricanes Rita and Katrina, the Church sent 200 truckloads of supplies; 300,000 hygeine kits; and

60,000 cleanup buckets. Volunteer hurricane relief work on site totaled 35,000 man days. **17 December:** Release of film *Joseph Smith: Prophet of the Restoration* for showing in visitors centers.

2006   February: American Red Cross gave the Church its Circle of Humanitarians award for substantial aid to the Measles Initiative in Africa, where local members assisted in vaccinating millions. **30 April:** Mormon Tabernacle Choir performed its 4,000th broadcast. **May–August:** Church celebrated 50 years on Taiwan with concerts, youth conference, and 50-mile bike ride. **21–15 August:** Brigham Young University Education Week offered more than 200 classes to thousands of participants; many of the classes were disseminated worldwide through the Church's satellite system. **September–December:** Museum of Church History and Art held exhibit honoring Willie and Martin Handcart companies. **September:** Spanish edition of LDS scriptures released on the Internet. **21 October:** Annual Latino cultural celebration in Conference Center for Spanish-speaking members included songs and folk dancing. **November:** Mormon Tabernacle Choir received Mother Teresa award from St. Bernadette Institute for Sacred Art.

2007   4 February: Fireside service for young adults broadcast or rebroadcast in up to 32 languages. **10 February:** Worldwide leadership training session broadcast over the Church's satellite system. **31 March:** Salt Lake Tabernacle rededicated after several years of restoration and seismic stabilization. **31 March 2007–January 2011:** Museum of Church History and Art exhibit documented the Salt Lake Tabernacle. **Spring:** Members provided charitable assistance by responding to disasters including a flood in Argentina, tornadoes in the central and southwestern United States, landslides on the island of Hispaniola, an earthquake in Japan, and flooding in Jakarta. **30 April–1 May:** *The Mormons*, a four-hour documentary by Helen Whitney that examined the history, beliefs, and practices of the Church of Jesus Christ of Latter-day Saints, broadcast on PBS. The broadcast elicited considerable discussion and commentary. **25 June:** Church membership reached 13 million members. **26 June:** Announcement that the 1 millionth missionary since 1830 had been called. **10 August:** President James E. Faust died in Salt Lake City. **7 September:** Elder Marlin K. Jensen participated in a memorial service for those murdered by southern Utah Mormon militiamen in 1857. **2 October:** Church held its first online news conference. **6 October:** Henry B. Eyring sustained as second counselor in the First Presidency. Elder Quentin L. Cook sustained as a member of the Quorum of Twelve Apostles. **15 December:** Elder M. Russell Ballard urged members to use new media such as Internet blogs to defend the church.

2008 **27 January:** President Gordon B. Hinckley died at his home in Salt Lake City. **4 February:** Thomas S. Monson called as president of the Church with Henry B. Eyring as first counselor and Dieter F. Uctdorf as second counselor. **10 February:** Rexburg Temple in Idaho dedicated by President Thomas S. Monson.

Introduction

Many people have heard of Mormonism, if only vaguely. They may have seen Mormon missionaries with white shirt and tie and identifying name tags. A newspaper headline or a television news item tells of a Mormon politician. Perhaps one discovers that a classmate at school or a colleague at work belongs to this religion. But many know nothing at all about Mormonism. Sociologists conducting interviews or producers of documentaries asking questions of people on the street demonstrate rampant ignorance and misinformation. Even those with no particular bias in favor of or against Mormonism often understand virtually nothing about its beliefs, the obstacles it has faced, and its achievements.

Compared to other world religions, Mormonism has a short history. Members celebrated the Church's centennial in 1930. Not until 2030 will it reach its bicentennial. But those few generations covering less than two centuries compress a tremendous amount of human experience, with a cast of colorful characters and a series of dramatic confrontations. Like it or not, agree or disagree with its beliefs, one who seeks to understand Mormonism, its beliefs, its leading people, its way of looking at life—in short what makes it tick—must first have at least a general sense of its history.

THE 19TH CENTURY

The Church of Jesus Christ of Latter-day Saints—the official name, Mormonism being a nickname—was organized on 6 April 1830 in western New York. The religious toleration of early America allowed a multiplicity of competing churches. One strain of thinking about Christianity in the early 19th century was restorationism—essentially the idea that Christianity needed to return to the norms and usages of the primitive church. Not the only church grounded in such thinking, Mormonism was, at least in part, based on this understanding. It was also a prophetic religion. Those who joined the Church accepted its founder, Joseph Smith, as a prophet of God in the same way that Jeremiah and Ezekiel were prophets of God. Not claiming to be divine or to displace Jesus Christ as redeemer, Joseph mediated God's will to his followers. Such a claim made the new religion appear ominous. Who could know what he might say or do or what his followers might do under the assumption that they were performing God's will?

Like other Christians, Mormons believed the Bible. But they also accepted other books as scripture, most particularly the *Book of Mormon*. Without question, such an open-ended view seemed dangerous to many. Who knew how far it would go? Was there any limit? "Give me that old-time religion. . . . It's good enough for me." This refrain from a popular religious song expressed a common feeling. Never mind that it was directed against modernist impulses in Protestantism or that "old-time religion" might require careful defining. In this instance, the attitude simply meant that the Bible was inerrant and sufficient. There was no need, most people thought, for any other book to home in on the unique territory already occupied by the Holy Bible.

A third feature of the new religion was its missionaries. Those who believed carried the word to others. Mormon missionaries would hit the road and preach wherever they could. They called on friends and neighbors, relatives, and anyone who might listen. Full of conviction, they saw themselves as continuing the injunction of Christ to go into all the world and preach the gospel. Not surprisingly, many spurned their overtures. Those who did looked on the missionaries as disturbers of the peace. Pastors of existing churches saw them as "sheep stealers."

A fourth feature of Mormonism was the doctrine of gathering, preached in the 19th and early 20th centuries. As people joined the new church, they moved to join their fellow believers in covenant communities. A declared gathering place brought converts from near and far. By coming together, Mormons gathered in sufficient numbers to seem a threat to others. The older inhabitants would see the newcomers arrive individually, in families, in small wagon companies. When, the old settlers wondered, would the Mormons outnumber the others? When would they dominate the economy and the politics of the city or county?

Such fearful reactions led to street meetings, demonstrations, riots, and eventually mobs who burned the barns and homes of Mormons. This drama replayed itself in Ohio, Missouri, and Illinois. Finally, on the dark night of 27 June 1844, amid the shrieks and yells of a militia turned into a lawless mob, the founding prophet, Joseph Smith, and his brother, Hyrum—while incarcerated in jail awaiting trial—fell dead in a hail of bullets. Those who committed the brutal murders saw them as a justifiable lynching, perfectly consistent with the traditions of 19th-century America. The Mormons, stunned and grief-stricken, saw it as martyrdom.

In less than two years, still the victims of persecution, Mormons fled their cities, crossed the Mississippi, and headed westward into the Iowa territory. A bird's eye view during the next months would have seen wagon trains of refugees slowly moving westward, with camps established at intervals for rest, resupplying, and regrouping. It was another exodus. Fighting weather conditions and a lack of supplies, fearful of their persecutors, these "displaced persons" were strung out over several hundred miles. After a halt for the winter of 1846–47, they pushed on to the Great Basin on the western slope of the Rocky Mountains—a journey that required several months of painful, persistent travel across a wilderness with no cities along the way to serve as supply stations.

The geographical scope of the Mormon movement was vast. In addition to many believers who stayed where they were in Illinois, Iowa, Ohio, and other states, hundreds organized in wagon-train companies moved along the trail from Illinois to Utah. At the same time another company under Samuel Brannan sailed from New York around the southern cape of South America and then northward to Yerba Buena (later San Francisco) in California. And the federal government recruited 500 Mormons into the U.S. Army during the Mexican-American War. They marched as an infantry battalion on a seemingly interminable journey to Kansas, New Mexico, and across the dry wastes of Arizona to the Southern California coast at San Diego.

The refugees arrived in Utah beginning in late July 1947. They came from different directions. The main group crossed the plains through what is now Nebraska and Wyoming. Some came eastward from California. Others from the South crossed to what is now Colorado, then struck north to the California-Oregon-Mormon trail. Interrupted briefly by a clash with federal troops in 1857, the refugees embarked on an ambitious program of colonization, founding settlement after settlement—more than 500—throughout an immense empire that stretched from southern Canada to northern Mexico and from Colorado to California. The pioneering so central to the American experience as part of the great westward movement was inescapably part of what it meant to be Mormon in the 19th century.

What is amazing, perhaps, is that the Mormon religion continued to attract followers. Joining it meant unpopularity, sacrifice, and perhaps even death. In the face of such a stark reality, why did people flock to Mormonism at the beginning and why did they continue to declare their allegiance to it right through the times of troubles? Motives are not easy to decipher, but let us recognize the explanations that have been offered.

First, Mormons themselves said quite simply that they knew the Church was true and was guided by God's prophet. Therefore they had to follow it, whatever the cost. Such is the faith and testimony of religious believers.

Second, quite a few people in America and Europe were dissatisfied with the established churches. They longed for something different. Some of them were disaffiliated, unchurched "seekers." Others were still members of the existing churches but reluctant and dissatisfied communicants. Whether on the level of beliefs or mode of worship or organizational forms, they hoped and prayed for a change. When the Mormon missionaries came along, such people were ready to listen and respond. This was not the attitude of everybody, to be sure, or even a majority of Christians, but some people constituted a prepared audience, receptive to the new message.

Third, some joined the Mormons because they wanted to improve their situation. Bored or lacking opportunity where they were, they signed on in anticipation that moving to the place of gathering would give them a fresh start. Leaving the streets of industrial England, for example, people saw themselves as prosperous farmers or shop owners in America. Theology may have been secondary to these folks. Although they did not necessarily reject the new beliefs, their interest was more practical. Such workings of the human mind are difficult to measure even among contemporaries.

Fourth, Mormonism satisfied many human needs. In 1830, 1880, 1930, and right up to the present, there are people abroad in the land—all lands—who are hurting, depressed, very much alone, down in their luck, needing human contact. Maybe all of us fall into these categories at different times. Mormonism is not the only religion to provide for such needs, but from its beginning the Church has been very good at it. One could receive a helping hand, a leg up, an arm around the shoulder. What the Church provided was not simply a handout, for sacrifice and unpopularity came with the package. In addition, perhaps more important, Mormonism offered involvement, a feeling of doing something that mattered, a chance to help others even worse off than oneself—one of the best remedies known to health care professionals. For many, the Church congregation became the primary locus of interaction with others.

However the conversions are explained, people continued to join up. And since members of the Church tended to have many children, high birth rate played a part in Mormonism's growth. Six members formed the initial membership in 1830. By 1840 there were 16,000; by 1850, 51,000. By the end of the 19th century the Church had 283,000 members.

From 1841 on, something new was added—the practice of polygamy. Practiced by perhaps a quarter of the families, it was kept quiet at first, although rumors circulated and exposés were written. In 1852, ensconced in their new home in the Rocky Mountains, Church leaders publicly acknowledged and defended polygamy as a biblical practice that was part of the restoration of all things. Many considered it essential for the ultimate degree of salvation. Not normally justified, they said, the unusual marriage arrangement had been permitted by God under special circumstances, as with the patriarchs Abraham, Isaac, and Jacob, and now themselves. Since marriage was a religious sacrament, Church leaders also thought they were protected by the First Amendment.

For one man to have two or more wives at the same time was, to say the least, a departure from the norm in Western society. Polygamy was something one read about in *Arabian Nights* but did not witness in real life; it was not the prosaic monogamous marriage of Christian tradition. For several decades polygamy was the publicist's "hook," the feature of the Mormon religion that could be counted on to attract interest. Lacking the stimulation of today's explicit television and movie fare, many let their imaginations run wild. Appealing to prurient interest, polygamy became the most sensational thing about Mormons. It defined their public image.

With practically all of its leading men being polygamists, the Church was most easily caricatured in marital terms. Yet even for the half century of its practice in the Mormon community—roughly the second half of the 19th century—polygamy was a minority phenomenon. Anything less than half is a minority, and certainly less than half of Mormons lived in polygamous marriages or were the children of such marriages. Yet it was prominent, especially among the leaders, and attracted shocked attention.

Opponents mounted a national campaign. They denounced the Church in the press, from the pulpit, in the halls of Congress. The antipolygamy crusaders were, in their own view, simply defending the American home. If there were not laws sufficiently explicit to bar polygamy, they argued, let them be passed. Anti-polygamy statutes appeared on the books, reaching a culmination in the 1880s. Then those laws had to be enforced, which required decisions by the courts. Especially after 1884, hundreds of Mormon husbands and a few plural wives were hauled off to prison. The government dissolved the Church as a corporation and in large part escheated its property. In Idaho, a test oath was imposed to disenfranchise not only polygamists but all Church members.

Mormons living during the second half of the 19th century could not help but be aware of the strident negative press. Superstitious, contemptible lawbreakers, followers of a religion that was patently absurd—this was the verbal labeling followers were subjected to. Not distinguishing between the practice of polygamy and the entire community, some blunt preachers called for Mormonism's extermination. Naturally, especially within their own ranks, Latter-day Saints spoke back, defended themselves, and accused their enemies of hypocrisy.

EARLY 20TH CENTURY

Then everything changed. The transformation did not occur suddenly in the year 1900. It started a few years earlier and required the first decade of the 20th century to run its course. But transformation did take place.

The Church abandoned polygamy, ceasing to promote the practice. Those who know only what they read in the newspapers or see on television may be surprised at this, for occasional cases of polygamy continue to attract public attention. Those who still practice polygamy, however, have abandoned the Church; such marriages are performed by dissidents who have rejected the Latter-day Saint tradition. Nevertheless, for the Church, such cases are a public relations nightmare. Church members wince and feel they are being wrongly represented to the public, tarred for a practice long ago forsaken. For more than a century the Church itself has not advocated, taught, or performed such illegal marriages. Continuing to the present, no Church president or general authority, no local leader, no missionary is involved in the practice. In its 20th-century embodiment and up to the present, Mormonism has been a strong advocate of monogamy and traditional morality.

Economic and political practices of the past also faded. With the coming of the national political parties to Utah in the 1890s, the political stand-off based on religion disappeared, for both Republicans and Democrats courted both Mormons and non-Mormons. Differing religiously, they cooperated politically.

In many respects, Mormonism had become respectable. This is not to say that Mormon theology was accepted by others. But the Latter-day Saints appeared to follow a middle-class morality. They attended the same sports and recreational events as other people. They demonstrated their patriotism over and over again. Side-currents and subsurface eddies complicated this cheerful picture, but for six or seven decades, as we can verify by an analysis of press reports, a general spirit of good feelings prevailed. In some ways this attitude continues.

During the same years, through natural increase as well as conversions, the Church continued to grow. From 283,000 in 1900, membership ascended to 1 million by 1947. Membership doubled to 2 million by 1963 and to 4 million by 1979.

LATE 20TH AND EARLY 21ST CENTURIES

As always in the history of nations and institutions, we find both continuity and change. In noticing some distinguishing characteristics of the generation leading up to the present, we acknowledge that these individuals had raised their heads earlier, with hints of what was to come. Nevertheless, in attempting to understand the recent past and the present, the following deserve specific mention.

Burgeoning Growth

The Church continued to grow in number of members and also according to other important indices. In 1947, it was 1 million; 1963, 2 million; 1979, 4 million; 1991, 8 million. Just when the 16 million figure will be reached is unknown, but at the end of 2007 total membership was 12,868,606. During the same time period, from 1947 to 2007, the number of stakes (comparable to dioceses) grew from 169 to 2,745. A stake offers the complete program of the Church. The number of congregations, known as wards and branches, grew from 1,425 to 27,475. The number of missionaries out preaching to those willing to listen grew from less than 5,000 to 53,164.

Globalization

Raw membership figures fail to reveal some important facts. One is the movement of Mormonism into new countries. Missions are not established where forbidden by the government. The Muslim world has not been receptive to Christians of any kind, and the huge country of China places stringent limitations on worship and proselytizing. But where possible the Church has sent its missionaries, divided among 347 missions as of 2007. All missions succeed in converting people, but such success varies greatly from country to country. Especially fruitful mission fields have been Mexico, Central America, South America, Africa, and the Philippines. Although headquarters remained in the United States, at Salt Lake City, Utah, the Church membership became steadily more diverse. On 28 February 1996, a milestone was reached with more than half of all members living outside the United States, and that trend has continued.

Militating against establishing strong congregations around the world during the early decades of the Church's history was the doctrine of gathering. Small congregations were routinely depleted of their most committed members who emigrated to Utah. Then, starting early in the 20th century, or even before, those contemplating emigration were reminded of the limited employment opportunities that might await them. Discouragement of gathering was made stronger after World War II. On 1 December 1999, repeating advice uttered several times before, the

Church's First Presidency again stated that members should "remain in their homelands rather than immigrate to the United States."

Not well understood by many people are Mormon temples, edifices that are not ordinary meetinghouses but instead sacred spaces for the administering of ordinances to Church members. Throughout much of its history, the Church's temples were very few and confined to North America. Then temples were dedicated in England and Switzerland. The generation leading up to the present has been a generation of temple building. As temples have increased in number, all the ordinances have become more accessible to people in all parts of the world. From the 1980s to the present, temples have been erected every year until the number passed 100 and then 120. In simple terms, the construction of temples is institutional evidence of maturity, of putting down roots in many states and countries.

Opposition

We have noted the persecution of the 19th century. During the closing decades of the 20th century, after a half century or more of relative quiescence and presumably provoked by the growth and expansion already described, opposition by foes of the Church resumed. Attacking the Mormons were radio programs, newspaper and magazine articles, movies, and books carried by Christian bookstores. Some respectful dialogue occasionally occurred when spokesmen for Mormonism and conventional Christianity clarified their respective positions and even noted areas of agreement. But the name-calling was widespread. Anyone wishing to bash the Church had ample opportunity and ample resources. In its most repellant form, the opposition waved signs, desecrated sacred symbols, and shouted epithets at peaceable people attending conferences, pageants, and even weddings. Relying on law enforcement officers for protection, Mormons simply continued their activities and moved forward.

Increasing Prominence

Occupying headlines and being mentioned by news commentators is not a goal pursued by the Church. But increasing visibility is indicated by documentary television programs, movies produced by Latter-day Saint cinematographers, sports stars, popular entertainers, and politicians. At this writing, a Mormon, former governor Michael Leavitt of Utah, is secretary of health and human services. Another, Senator Harry Reed of Nevada, is majority leader of the U.S. Senate. Another, former governor Mitt Romney of Massachusetts, was a contender for the Republican nomination for president of the United States. The former president of the Church, Gordon B. Hinckley, appeared on national radio and television shows to explain the position of the Church. His successor, President Thomas S. Monson, indicated in an interview following his call that he would continue to meet with the press. Many Church members no doubt would prefer the quiet of obscurity, but the Church of Jesus Christ of Latter-day Saints will presumably continue its dynamic growth and be considered newsworthy, even if only as a decidedly non-trendy example of a group that stands athwart many of the trends of the age.

After all this time—after all the supposed accommodation and middle-class respectability of many members—Mormons continue to be a counterculture. In an age of increasing secularism in the Western world, Mormons believe in God. In a cynical age, they are idealistic. They scorn the values of the Hollywood elite and the mass media. Traditional morality remains their commitment. While some conservative Christians and Jews, or other believers in natural law and traditional values, might find their presence uncomfortable, in Mormons they have allies on these basic matters. Resisting the spirit of the age, Mormons continue to advance their religion. Finding themselves at odds with the larger culture is not a new experience for them.

The Dictionary

– A –

AARONIC PRIESTHOOD. The lower of the two major divisions of **priesthood**, the other being the **Melchizedek Priesthood**. As part of the **restoration**, the Aaronic Priesthood was conferred upon **Joseph Smith** and **Oliver Cowdery** by the resurrected John the Baptist (*Doctrine and Covenants*, section 13). The offices within the Aaronic Priesthood, from the bottom, are **deacon**, **teacher**, and **priest**.

ABEL, ELIJAH (1810–1884). African American member, **priesthood** holder, **missionary**. Born 25 July 1810 in Washington County, Maryland, he was baptized in 1832, one of a small number of African Americans who joined the church in the 19th century. He was ordained an **elder** in 1836 and ordained a member of the Third **Quorum** of the **Seventy** in Kirtland, Ohio, the same year. He served a mission in Canada and New York in 1838. He served as undertaker for the city of Nauvoo, Illinois, in 1840, and became a partner in the House Carpenters of Nauvoo in 1841. Married to Mary Ann Adams, he served as manager of the Farnham Hotel in Salt Lake City, Utah, from 1853. He served again as a missionary in Canada from 1883 to 1884. He died in Salt Lake City in 1884.

ABORTION. The following statement by the **First Presidency** was issued in 1973: "The Church opposes abortion and counsels its members not to submit to or perform an abortion except in the rare cases where, in the opinion of competent medical counsel, the life or good health of the mother is seriously endangered or where pregnancy was caused by rape and produces serious emotional trauma in the mother. Even then it should be done only after counseling with the local presiding priesthood authority and after receiving divine confirmation through prayer."

ACTIVITY. Regular participation in church worship and **callings**. In common usage, an "active" **member** is one who faithfully attends meetings, pays **tithing** and makes fast offerings, follows the **Word of Wisdom**, and in all respects tries to exemplify the standards of the Church. Obviously, there are degrees of activity. *See also* INACTIVITY.

ADOPTION. Young single mothers are encouraged to place newborns in a stable, two-parent home. **LDS Family Services** assists in making adoptive arrangements and provides counseling for the mother. The decision is the mother's. Adopted children may be sealed to parents in the **temple**, thus becoming permanent members of the **family** not only in this life but eternally. *See also* SEALING.

AFRICA. At the end of 2005 there were 237,401 Mormons and 42 **stakes** in sub-Saharan Africa. (The countries of North Africa have not proved congenial to Christian proselytizing.) South Africa contributed early converts and, after a 40-year hiatus, **missionary** proselytizing was resumed there in 1903. Since 1978 missionary work has been promulgated in other African countries where possible, with the greatest success in Nigeria, Ghana, and the Democratic Republic of the Congo. The first black African stake was created at Aba, Nigeria, in 1988. At the end of 2005 there were 11 stakes and 62 **wards** in South Africa, 14 stakes and 109 wards in Nigeria, and 5 stakes and 41 wards in Ghana. Also considered part of the African area for administrative purposes are Madagascar, Mauritius, and Reunion. **Temples** in Africa have been dedicated at Johannesburg, South Africa (1985), Accra, Ghana (2004), and Aba, Nigeria (2005).

AFRICAN AMERICANS. Standard designation for Americans of African ancestry. Since the term obviously does not include the millions who live in Africa or who have emigrated from **Africa** to **Europe** and other countries, or people of African ancestry born in Brazil and elsewhere, the encompassing racial label is **blacks**.

AFTERLIFE. *See* PLAN OF SALVATION.

AMADO, CARLOS H. (1944–). General Authority. Born on 25 September 1944 in Guatemala City, Guatemala, he was 11 when his parents joined the Church. He graduated from a technical college and then worked as a draftsman for four years. From 1965 to 1967 he served as a **missionary** in Peru, then served as branch **president**, **bishop**, **stake** president, and mission president in both Guatemala and El Salvador. He was a **seminary** teacher and then director for the Church Educational System in **Central America**. In 1989, he became a member of the Second **Quorum** of the **Seventy** and in 1992 a member of the First Quorum of the Seventy. He and his wife, Mayavel, have six children.

ANDERSEN, NEIL L. (1951–). General authority. Born on 9 August 1951 in Logan, Utah, he graduated with a bachelor's degree from **Brigham Young University (BYU)**. He earned a master's degree in business from Harvard University. In Florida his business interests included advertising, real estate development, and health care. He served as **stake** president and **president** of the France Bordeaux Mission. In 1993 he was called to serve in the First **Quorum** of the **Seventy** and in 2005 became a member of its presidency. He and his wife, Kathy Sue, are parents of four children.

ANDERSON, RICHARD LLOYD (1926–). Missionary, lawyer, historian. Born in Salt Lake City, Utah, on 9 May 1926, Anderson completed his early education in Utah, became a Navy radioman during World War II, and from 1946 to 1949 served as a missionary in the Northwestern states. Anderson authored *A Plan for Effective Missionary Work*, known as the Anderson Plan, which was widely used in many of the Church's missions in the early 1950s. After receiving a B.A. in History at **BYU** in 1951, Anderson attended Harvard Law School, earning the J.D. degree in 1954. After one year as a **seminary** and **institute of religion** teacher he entered the graduate program in ancient history at the University of California at Berkeley, completing the Ph.D. in 1962. At BYU, Anderson was named honors professor of the year. Teacher of the New Testament, he cultivated a special interest in Paul, leading to a book, *Understanding Paul* (1983). The acknowledged authority on the **witnesses of the** ***Book of Mormon***, he published many articles and in 1981 a book entitled *Investigating the* Book of Mormon *Witnesses.* He and his wife, Carma, have four children.

ANTHON TRANSCRIPT. Characters copied from the original ***Book of Mormon*** plates shown by **Martin Harris** in February 1828 to Professor Charles Anthon, of Columbia College (later University) in New York City. Anthon declared the characters genuine but, when told of their miraculous origin, recanted his authentication. He later gave two contradictory accounts of the interview. Whatever was said, Harris was sufficiently convinced that he put up most of the funds for the publication of the first edition of the *Book of Mormon* in 1830. The characters of the transcript, as they survive in a handwritten version, have been ridiculed as clumsy scrawls, but parallels have been found in Demotic Egyptian, Old South Arabian, Old North Arabian, Micmac, and a script carved on Olmec baked clay seals.

ANTI-MORMONISM. Rejection of Mormonism's claims is not anti-Mormonism, but militant, repeated, and organized opposition is. The earliest examples occurred just before and soon after the inception of the Church in 1830. Public demonstrations against the early Mormons often degenerated to looting and lynching. Many publications denouncing Mormons were filled with inaccuracies, oversimplification, and stereotyping typical of hate movements in general.

Publications and lectures against the Church can be found during every decade of Mormon history. Showing renewed vigor since the 1960s, anti-Mormonism at its worst is shamefully inaccurate and irresponsible, willing to use any means to accomplish its ends. When anti-Mormons try to document their assertions, they tend to ignore context and the question of typicality. They seem determined to portray Mormons and Mormonism in the worst possible light. In a similar vein, students of anti-Semitism have delineated all the key features of this mentality: scapegoating, obsession, stereotyping, caricaturing, overgeneralizing, and so forth.

Consider the many bases for anti-Mormonism. Atheists and foes of organized religion; those who dislike the Judeo-Christian ethic or belief in God; those who regard all Christians as unacceptable; **Catholics** who reject those outside their own faith; **Protestants**, especially evangelicals, who disapprove of Christians who are not "born again"; ex-Mormons who lash out at the religion they once embraced—from all these groups and sometimes from interaction between them ridicule and hatred gush forth. Short of ceasing to exist, the Latter-day Saints can do nothing that would satisfy their opponents.

A key factor in provoking such opposition is the success, or expansionist thrust, of Mormonism. A religion that was static or dwindling would more likely be ignored. A few individual Mormons have written and spoken out in defense of their faith, and some websites attempt to counter defamation and misrepresentation. However, the Church as such seldom responds to anti-Mormons, preferring to keep attention focused on its positive goals.

APOCRYPHA. The 14 books included in Catholic Bibles but excluded from most Protestant versions. They were included in the original edition of the King James Version as a separate section but later removed. A larger definition of the term would include extra-canonical works produced by early Christians, for which the term *pseudepigrapha* is more commonly used. Since they do not believe in a closed canon, Mormons have been interested in these works. "There are many things contained therein that are true, and it is mostly translated correctly," wrote **Joseph Smith** of the Old Testament apocrypha. "There are many things contained therein that are not true, which are interpolations by the hands of men. . . . Therefore, whoso readeth it, let him understand, for the Spirit manifesteth truth" (*Doctrine and Covenants*, section 91).

APOSTASY. Sometimes called the Great Apostasy. The falling away from the truths, principles, and authority of original **Christianity**. In the Mormon view, the beginnings of this process are discernible in the New Testament itself. At some point, probably as early as the second century, the Christian church no longer adequately represented God's work on earth. Of the multiple "Christianities" none remained pure or true to the original teaching. None had unqualified divine endorsement. Despite their claims, none possessed authority from God.

Any digressions from the teachings of **Jesus Christ**, whether theological under the influence of Greek philosophy or organizational under the influence of Roman law, are seen as manifestations of apostasy. Christians of the late Roman Empire and the Middle Ages were the victims of this process, not necessarily its perpetrators. Despite some individual lives of sincerity and even faithfulness, the Church as an institution was devoid of divine authority. The changes in teachings and ordinances were not minor but fatal.

Protestants of the Reformation era had a similar view of Christian history, differing on their dating of the process and their prescription for a remedy. For Mormons the Great Apostasy preceded the church councils and creeds of the patristic era. Therefore they do not regard those doctrinal pronouncements as authoritative or consistent with the New Testament norm. Most importantly, the loss of the true church in doctrine, organization, **sacraments**, and authority necessitated not a reformation but the **restoration** that occurred beginning with God's call to **Joseph Smith**.

APOSTATE. Someone who has abandoned the faith, especially one who has become belligerent or teaches doctrines condemned by the Church. An "inactive" **member**, one who does not participate in the meetings and programs of the Church, is not so described, and more than a few Church members, after spending some months or even years in **inactivity**, resume participation. The apostasy *from* the Church of an apostate is not the same as the **apostasy** *of* the Church, or the Great Apostasy. *See also* ACTIVITY; APOSTASY.

APOSTLE. *See* TWELVE APOSTLES, QUORUM OF THE.

AREA. Since 1984 the Church has been divided into geographical "areas" for administrative purposes. Division into geographical areas was a response to the growth of Church **membership** in different parts of the world and to the difficulty of coordinating everything from Church headquarters in Salt Lake City, Utah. Presidencies for areas outside the United States and Canada live in their areas, where they devote full time to planning, calling of leaders, training, and supervision.

Areas at the end of 2005 were Africa Southeast, Africa West, Asia, Asia North, Philippines, Pacific Islands, Australia New Zealand/Pacific Islands, South America South, Chile, South America West,

Brazil North, Brazil South, South America North, Central America, Mexico North, Mexico South, Europe West, Europe North, Europe East, North America Northwest, North America Southwest, North America West, North America Central, North America Northeast, North America East, North America Southeast, Utah North, Utah South, Utah Salt Lake City, Idaho, Europe West, Europe East, and Europe Central areas. Rather than having separate articles on each of these, the present dictionary groups them as follows: **North America**, **Central America and Mexico**, **South America**, **Europe**, **Africa**, **Asia**, and the **Pacific**. The presidency over an area is made up of three members of the **quorums** of the **seventy**. On 1 April 1995 the new administrative position of **area authority seventy** was created and the position of **regional representative** discontinued.

AREA AUTHORITY SEVENTIES. Experienced Church leaders who are members of the third and subsequent **quorums** of the **seventy**. Not designated as **general authorities**, they continue their regular employment and reside in their own homes. They train **stake** presidencies, serve in **area** presidencies, tour **missions**, train mission **presidents**, and complete other assigned duties (*Ensign*, 2004).

ARRINGTON, LEONARD J. (1917–1999). Historian, economist, intellectual leader. Born on 2 July 1917 on a farm near Twin Falls, Idaho, Arrington received a B.A. at the University of Idaho, joined the U.S. Army during World War II, serving in North Africa and Italy, and after the war earned a Ph.D. in economics at the University of North Carolina. His academic appointments were at Utah State University and **BYU**. He had appointments as visiting professor at the University of Bologna and the University of California at Los Angeles (UCLA). Arrington has served as president of the Western History Association, the Agricultural History Society, and the Pacific Coast Branch of the American History Association. In 1986 he was named a fellow of the Society of American Historians.

A leader among loyal Mormon intellectuals, Arrington was founding president of the **Mormon History Association (MHA)** in 1965 and from 1966 was an advisory editor of *Dialogue: A Journal of Mormon Thought*. In 1972 he was appointed Church historian, serving until

1982 (with a change of title in 1977 to director of History Division), and for 10 years supervised a team of professional historians who produced books, articles, oral histories, and working papers. When this History Division was abolished in 1982, Arrington and his team of historians were transferred to the **Joseph Fielding Smith Institute for Church History** at BYU, which he directed until his retirement in 1987. After 12 more years of productivity, he died in 1999. Arrington influenced a generation of historians working on the Mormon past. See his bibliography as compiled by David J. Whittaker in *Journal of Mormon History* 25 (Fall 1999): 11–45.

ART. Not possessed of elaborate meetinghouses and with a worship service that is simple rather than highly symbolic or liturgical, the Church would not appear to be a likely patron of the arts. Mormon artists, like others, make their way by seeking commissions or selling their work in the private sector. Still, in the visual arts there have been occasions when the Church has been a sponsor. First, architects have designed **ward** meetinghouses and especially **temples**, some of which are architecturally significant. Sculptors have produced works displayed on **Temple Square** or at historic monuments. A series of sculptures known as the Relief Society Monument to Women can be seen in a garden adjacent to the visitors' center at Nauvoo, Illinois. Paintings and murals have been important in the temples. At the end of the 19th century, several Mormon painters were sent to study in France in order to prepare them for this task. Other paintings hang in meetinghouses and visitors centers.

In 1984 the **Museum of Church History and Art** was dedicated in Salt Lake City, Utah. In addition to historical exhibits, it has both standing and temporary exhibits of Mormon art and intermittently holds Church-wide competitions. Hundreds of submissions of paintings, bas-reliefs, weaving, metalwork, and so on are submitted on Mormon religious subjects. Some of the most interesting of these come from areas of the world where the Mormon presence is relatively recent, such as Indonesia or Haiti, where native artistic traditions are employed to convey concepts of the Mormon religion. Besides overtly religious subjects, of course, Mormon artists do portraits, landscapes, pottery, and the like. *See also* LITERATURE; MUSIC.

ARTICLES OF FAITH. Thirteen statements of belief that appeared in an 1842 letter from **Joseph Smith** to John Wentworth, editor of the *Chicago Democrat*. While similar listings had been drafted earlier by **Orson Pratt** and others, this 1842 version became authoritative, as it was later incorporated into the *Pearl of Great Price* and thus canonized. For many years Mormon children have memorized these statements as part of their **Primary** training. Often printed on small cards and distributed as a means of introducing Mormonism to interested parties, the Articles of Faith are technically not considered a creed.

1. We believe in God, the Eternal Father, and in His Son, Jesus Christ, and in the Holy Ghost.
2. We believe that men will be punished for their own sins, and not for Adam's transgression.
3. We believe that through the Atonement of Christ, all mankind may be saved, by obedience to the laws and ordinances of the Gospel.
4. We believe that the first principles and ordinances of the Gospel are: first, Faith in the Lord Jesus Christ; second, Repentance; third, Baptism by immersion for the remission of sins; fourth, Laying on of hands for the gift of the Holy Ghost.
5. We believe that a man must be called of God, by prophecy, and by the laying on of hands by those who are in authority, to preach the Gospel and administer in the ordinances thereof.
6. We believe in the same organization that existed in the Primitive Church, namely, apostles, prophets, pastors, teachers, evangelists, and so forth.
7. We believe in the gift of tongues, prophecy, revelation, visions, healing, interpretation of tongues, and so forth.
8. We believe the Bible to be the word of God as far as it is translated correctly; we also believe the *Book of Mormon* to be the word of God.
9. We believe all that God has revealed, all that He does now reveal, and we believe that He will yet reveal many great and important things pertaining to the Kingdom of God.
10. We believe in the literal gathering of Israel and in the restoration of the Ten Tribes; that Zion (the New Jerusalem) will be built upon the American continent; that Christ will

reign personally upon the earth; and, that the earth will be renewed and receive its paradisiacal glory.

11. We claim the privilege of worshiping Almighty God according to the dictates of our own conscience, and allow all men the same privilege, let them worship how, where, or what they may.

12. We believe in being subject to kings, presidents, rulers, and magistrates, in obeying, honoring, and sustaining the law.

13. We believe in being honest, true, chaste, benevolent, virtuous, and in doing good to all men; indeed, we may say that we follow the admonition of Paul—We believe all things, we hope all things, we have endured many things, and hope to be able to endure all things. If there is anything virtuous, lovely, or of good report or praiseworthy, we seek after these things.

While some important aspects of theology are not included in these articles, which is consistent with article 9, the Articles of Faith provide a good point of departure for understanding the Mormon position. Books discussing each of these statements in detail have been published by **James E. Talmage** and **Bruce R. McConkie**.

ASIA. Although there were **missionaries** in India during the 1850s, virtually all progress in Asia has occurred since World War II. At the end of 2005, the Asia and North Asia **areas** had 330,770 Mormons, with 63 **stakes**; Taiwan had 42,881 Mormons, 9 stakes, one **temple**; Hong Kong had 22,263 Mormons, 5 stakes, one temple; India had about 6,000 **members** in 26 branches with no official prosleytizing activity; China had less than a thousand members.

The Asia North administrative area is comprised of Korea and Japan. Early missionary efforts in Japan started in 1901 but had negligible results. After World War II, conversions were more numerous, reaching 211 by 1949. Continuing expansion led to the organization of stakes and temples in Tokyo (1980) and Fukuoka (2000). Yoshihiko Kikuchi became a **general authority** in 1977. By the end of 2005 Japan had 121,068 members in 30 stakes and 167 **wards**.

Kim Ho Jik, studying for a doctorate at Cornell University, joined the Church in 1951 and upon returning to South Korea, helped lay the foundations for missionary work in his country. In 1956 two missionaries were sent from Japan. Growing rapidly, the Church in South Korea had its first stake in 1973, with Rhee Ho Nam as **president**. In 1985 a temple was dedicated at Seoul. Han In Sang became the first Korean general authority. At the end of 2005 there were 78,646 Korean members, divided into 17 stakes and 98 wards.

Perhaps the most striking Mormon success in Asia has taken place in the Philippines. The fact that most Filipinos were Christian and many spoke English facilitated proselytizing. The first mission was established in 1967 and the first stake founded in 1973. In 1984 a temple was dedicated in Manila. At the end of 2005 there were 553,121 members in 76 stakes and 466 wards. Over 80 percent of the missionaries in the Philippines are young Filipino men and women. After their missionary experience, they have been a major source of leadership for the Church in the Philippines.

ASSISTANTS TO THE TWELVE. A small group, starting in 1941 with five individuals called as **general authorities** to assist the Quorum of the **Twelve Apostles**. Under the direction of the twelve, they visited **stake conferences** and assisted in directing **missionary** activity. In 1976 this designation was terminated. The functions were assumed by the **quorums** of the **seventy**.

ASSOCIATION FOR MORMON LETTERS (AML). A private organization dedicated to the encouragement of Mormon **literature**. Founded in 1976, the AML holds an annual meeting with papers critically examining Mormon literature, sponsors readings, and gives awards in fiction, poetry, essay, and criticism. A newsletter and an annual publication are received by dues-paying **members**.

AUDITORS. A committee of professional auditors examines church financial records each year and issues a formal statement attesting to the fact that proper procedures are followed and accountability maintained. Businesses owned or controlled by the Church are audited by the Church's internal auditors, independent professional auditing firms, or government regulatory agencies.

AUSTRALIA. *See* PACIFIC.

AUXILIARIES. Organizations within the Church with programs for specific age or gender groups. Developed in response to perceived needs, mostly in the latter half of the 19th century, they have been modified as necessary in the 20th. In principle, the auxiliaries could be abolished, added to, or again modified, and the Church itself would go on. The principal auxiliary organizations are **Relief Society**, **Primary**, **Sunday School**, **Young Men**, and **Young Women**. The **priesthood** is not considered an auxiliary. Although the details of **quorum** organization and age-group divisions are subject to change as directed by **general authorities**, priesthood authority is prerequisite to the Church itself.

– B –

BABBITT, ALMON WHITING (1813–1856). Lawyer, politician, public official. Born in Cheshire, Massachusetts, Babbitt moved to western New York and joined the Church shortly after its organization in 1830. He served as a **missionary** for the Church in New York in 1831, married Julia Ann Hills Johnson in 1833, and served as a missionary for the Church in Canada in 1834, the same year he participated in **Zion's Camp**. Babbitt served as presiding **elder** for the Church in Kirtland, Ohio, in 1840–1841 and as lawyer for the Church in Nauvoo from 1843 to 1845. In 1842 Babbitt attended the University of Cincinnati and served as a member of the Illinois legislature in 1844. In 1945 he served as a member of the committee to petition the federal government on behalf of the Mormons in 1845. After the bulk of the members had evacuated Nauvoo in 1946, Babbitt remained in the city on assignment for the Church to help in selling properties. Chosen as congressional delegate for the provincial state of Deseret in 1849, he worked unsuccessfully for admission of the state into the union. After this service, Babbitt worked as an agent for the territory in Washington and was appointed secretary of Utah Territory, where he served from 1853 to 1856. He worked concurrently as a lawyer in Utah Territory from 1849 to 1856. Babbitt was killed by Cheyennes on his return to Utah in 1856.

BALLANTYNE, RICHARD (1817–1898). Teacher, **Sunday School** organizer. Credited with founding the first Sunday School in Utah at his home on 9 December 1849, Ballantyne was a convert from Scotland who emigrated to Nauvoo, Illinois, in 1843 and subsequently crossed the plains to Utah. In 1853–1854 he preached Mormonism as a **missionary** in Calcutta, India. An astute businessman and supporter of education, Ballantyne lived in Ogden, Utah.

BALLARD, M. RUSSELL (1928–). Businessman and **general authority**. Born in Salt Lake City, Utah, on 8 October 1928, Ballard attended primary and secondary schools as well as the University of Utah. From 1948 to 1950 he served in the British Mission. Outside the Church, Ballard acquired interests in automotive, real estate, and investment businesses, while his Church responsibilities included being a **counselor** in a bishopric, **bishop**, and **stake high councilman**. In 1974 Ballard became **president** of the Canada Toronto Mission. Two years later he was called to the First **Quorum** of the **Seventy**, of which he was a member of the presidency from 1980 to 1985. In October 1985 he became a member of the Quorum of the **Twelve Apostles**. He served on the Missionary Executive Council, Leadership Training, Personnel, and Information Communications Systems committees. He and his wife, Barbara, have seven children.

BAPTISM. Latter-day Saints regard baptism as an essential **ordinance** for entrance into the Kingdom of God, for **membership** in the Church, and as a condition for a remission of sins. Consistent with the original root meaning of the word and the symbolism of death and rebirth, baptism is by complete immersion in water. Infants, incapable of exercising faith, are not baptized. Adult converts who decide to accept Mormonism are baptized. Children who are raised by Mormon parents and instructed are baptized at age eight, considered the age of accountability.

BAPTISM FOR THE DEAD. Baptism of a living person who serves as a proxy for a deceased person. The practice is referred to in 1 Corinthians 15:29, where Paul cites it as evidence for the reality of the resurrection: "Else what shall they do which are baptized for the dead, if the dead rise not at all? why are they then baptized for the dead?" Reinstituted by a revelation to **Joseph Smith** in 1841, baptism for the dead is carried out only in **temples**. The rationale underlying the practice rests on the following propositions: that baptism is essential to salvation, that God would not be so unjust as to condemn someone for failing to accept a gospel never presented to him or her, that preaching and conversion go on in the spirit world, and that baptism, an earthly ordinance, can be accomplished vicariously. It is not believed that post-mortal spirits will be forced to accept immersion, as coerced baptism is contrary to agency, but for those who wish it, the means for satisfying all requirements is established. One result of belief in vicarious work for the dead has been much research in **genealogy** and the establishment of a notable Family History Library.

BATEMAN, MERRILL J. (1936–). Economist, educator, **general authority**. Born on 19 June 1936 in Lehi, Utah, Bateman served as a **missionary** in the British Mission. He earned a bachelor's degree in economics from the University of Utah and a Ph.D. from the Massachusetts Institute of Technology (MIT). After three years on the faculty of the Air Force Academy, he accepted a position as professor of economics and director of the Center for Business and Economic Research at **BYU** in 1967. He was then hired by Mars Corporation and simultaneously acted as consultant for the U.S. Departments of State and Commerce, the World Bank, and other agencies. In 1975 he became dean of the BYU Graduate School of Management and College of Business. He was president of BYU from 1996 to 2003. Bateman served as **bishop**, **stake president**, and **regional representative**. He was called to the Second **Quorum** of the **Seventy** in 1992, as **presiding bishop** in 1994, and to the First Quorum of the Seventy in 1995, becoming a member of its presidency in 2003. In 2007 he was called as president of the Provo Temple. He and his wife, Marilyn, are the parents of seven children.

BAXTER, DAVID S. (1955–). General authority. Born on 7 February 1955 in Stirling, Scotland, Baxter grew up in circumstances of poverty. When **missionaries** knocked on their door, the mother let them come in out of pity. Appreciating the spirit brought by the missionaries, the family studied and then joined the Church. David was not yet 13 when he was baptized in January 1968. The family moved to Surrey, England, and became active members of the **branch** there. David completed his primary education and then matriculated at the University of Wales, where he earned a bachelor's degree in business management in 1976. He was a missionary in Scotland from 1976 to 1978, serving for 10 months on the Shetland Islands. He became a senior executive for British Telecom. At the age of 25, he was called to be **bishop**. He was also **stake president**. From 2002 to 2006 he served as an **area seventy** and was second **counselor** in the presidency of the Europe West area. In April 2006, he was sustained a member of the First **Quorum** of the Seventy. He and his wife, Dianne, have four children.

BECK, JULIE B. (1954–). Counselor in **Young Women** presidency, **Relief Society** general president. Born on 29 September 1954, Beck attended Dixie College and **BYU** where she earned a degree in family science. She served as **ward** Young Women and **Primary** president and counselor in a **stake** Relief Society presidency. She was **called** in April 2007 as Relief Society general president. Julie married Ramon P. Beck in 1970 and they have three children.

BEDNAR, DAVID A. (1952–). Educator, **general authority**. Born on 15 June 1952 in Oakland, California, Bednar earned bachelor's and master's degrees from **BYU** and a Ph.D. from Purdue University. He has held faculty positions in business management at Texas Tech University and the University of Arkansas at Fayetteville, Arkansas. Author of books on organizational behavior, Bednar was named outstanding teacher by the College of Business Administration. He served as a **bishop**, **stake president**, **area authority seventy**, and **regional representative**. After serving as president of **BYU**–Idaho from 1997 to 2004, he became a member of the **Quorum** of the **Twelve Apostles**. He and his wife, Susan, have three sons.

BENNION, LOWELL L. (1908–1996). Educator, humanitarian. After growing up in the Salt Lake City, Utah, area, Bennion graduated from the University of Utah in 1928. He married Merle Colton and one month later departed for a **mission** to Germany. After his mission, joined by his wife, he remained to study at Erlangen, Vienna, and

Strasbourg, completing a doctoral dissertation under Maurice Halbwachs on the methodology of Max Weber.

He briefly worked for the Civilian Conservation Corps—jobs were not plentiful in 1934—before accepting the assignment as director of the **institutes of religion** adjacent to the University of Utah. He taught University of Utah students, ultimately thousands of them, on subjects ranging from the **scripture** to courtship and **marriage**, always with a strong emphasis on practical ethics.

Bennion authored many lesson manuals for use in **seminary** and institute classes, articles for Church magazines, a **Sunday School** manual, and an introductory book for college students entitled *The Religion of the Latter-day Saints*. In 1962 he became assistant dean of students and professor of sociology at the University of Utah. He founded a boys ranch in Idaho that provided a setting where urban youths could have a break from their stressful routine, learn to work in the outdoors, and come under the influence of a kindly mentor.

After retiring from the university, Bennion became executive director of the private Community Services Council, which aided hundreds of indigent and senior citizens. His favorite passage of scripture—Micah 6:8: "What does the Lord require of thee? But to do justly, to love mercy, and to walk humbly with thy God."—was placed on his grave after his death in 1996.

BENSON, EZRA TAFT (1899–1994). Agriculture leader, U.S. secretary of agriculture, **general authority**, Church **president**. Born on 4 August 1899 on a farm in Whitney, Idaho, Benson attended Utah State Agricultural College (now Utah State University), graduated from **BYU**, and earned a master's degree in agricultural economics at Iowa State College. He served as a county agricultural agent and was extension economist and marketing specialist for nine years in Boise with the University of Idaho.

His Church experience included service as a scoutmaster, **missionary** in England, **counselor** in the **stake** presidency, and from 1938 as a stake president in Boise. Becoming executive secretary of the National Council of Farmer Cooperatives in 1939, he moved to Washington, D.C., and became president of the Washington, D.C., Stake. In 1943 he was called to be a member of the **Quorum** of the **Twelve Apostles**. After the war he became president of the European

Mission and supervised a massive distribution of welfare supplies. He was a member of the national executive board of the **Boy Scouts** and received the Silver Beaver, Silver Antelope, and Silver Buffalo awards. After the election of Dwight D. Eisenhower as president of the United States in1952, Benson was named secretary of agriculture. Under constant criticism, he stayed in office for Eisenhower's two terms, the first clergyman to serve in a cabinet position. Back in full-time Church service, Benson supervised work in **Europe** (1964–1965) and **Asia** (1968–1971). In 1973, he became president of the Quorum of the Twelve Apostles. Known for his love of country, he warned of the dangers of Communism. When he became Church president in 1985, however, he studiously avoided making narrow political pronouncements. His presidency lasted until his death on 30 May 1994. He emphasized missionary proselytizing and the simplification of programs through **correlation**. He urged people to read the *Book of Mormon*.

BERNHISEL, JOHN MILTON (MARTIN) (1799–1881). Church leader, territorial delegate. Born in Perry, Cumberland County, Pennsylvania, Bernhisel received a medical certificate from the University of Pennsylvania in 1819. He graduated from the University of Pennsylvania medical department in 1827. He served as attending physician in Herculaneum, Missouri, in 1818 and 1819 and as a general practitioner in Pennsylvania from 1827 to 1832. In 1832, Bernhisel moved his medical practice to New York City and remained there until 1943, when he moved to Nauvoo. Bernhisel joined the **LDS** Church in 1837, during his time in New York. He became a member of the Council of Fifty in 1844. In 1845 he married Julia Ann Haight Van Orden. He remained in Nauvoo during the 1846 **exodus** to try to dispose of property left at the abandonment. He married plural wives Dolly Ranson, Catherine Paine, Fanny Spafford, Melissa Lott Smith, Catherine Burgess Barker, and Elizabeth Barker. He served as Utah territorial congressional delegate from 1851 to 1859 and again from 1861 to 1863. From 1859 through 1861 and from 1863 through 1879 he served as a general medical practitioner in Salt Lake City, Utah. He was also a vice president of Zion's Cooperative Mercantile Institution from 1868 to 1873.

BIBLE. Accepted as **scripture**, the Bible is one of the four standard works. The King James, or Authorized, Version is used in English-speaking countries. Other translations may be consulted for individual study and comparison. For non-English readers the Church decides on the best existing translation for its purpose. Mormons are quite traditional and even literal in their acceptance of the Bible as the word of God. Although scholars at **BYU** and others are familiar with biblical scholarship, they have been reluctant to accept any criticism that would undermine the authority of the sacred text. Young people study the Bible in **seminary** and **institute** programs. In the adult study course in **Sunday School** both the Old Testament and the New Testament are systematically read and discussed every four years.

During the early 1830s **Joseph Smith** prepared a revision of the Bible by going through a copy of the King James Version and making hundreds of changes and additions. The resulting work was first published in the 1860s. In the majoritarian Mormon Church the JST (Joseph Smith Translation) has never superseded the King James translation, but for comparison the current Church-sponsored editions of the Bible include many of the JST emendations in footnotes and an appendix.

Mormons find themselves in an isolated position. Their approach to the Bible is too literal and traditional for most modern Bible scholars and mainstream Christian churches. Yet **Protestant** evangelicals, themselves literalist and conservative, find it impossible to accept the Mormon concepts of an open canon, continuing revelation, or "inspired" improvements of the sacred text.

BICKERTONITES. After **Joseph Smith**'s assassination in June 1844, one who claimed the right to succeed him as **president** of the Church was **Sidney Rigdon**, a **counselor** in the **First Presidency**. When his proposal was rejected by a nearly unanimous vote of a conference of Church members on 8 August 1844, he moved to Pennsylvania and established his own church. By the time of Rigdon's death in 1876, he had only one disciple left, William Bickerton. Membership of the Bickertonites remained small and was threatened by internal dissension. Thirty-five or 40 families followed Bickerton to Kansas, where their settlement became the town of St. John. The church has continued to grow to approximately 15,000 members, of whom about 3,000 live in the United States. Rejecting not only the Church under **Brigham Young** but also the doctrines and **ordinances** introduced by Joseph Smith at Nauvoo, the Bickertonites accept as **scriptures** the **Bible**, *Book of Mormon*, and *Doctrine and Covenants* in their own edition, including later revelations that were pronounced legitimate by their own presiding authorities. Often designated as the Church of Jesus Christ (Bickertonite), the denomination's official name is "the Church of Jesus Christ with Headquarters in Monongahela, Pennsylvania." *See also* SCHISMS; SUCCESSION.

BIRTH CONTROL. Believing that preexistent spirits are waiting to be born into mortality, Mormon parents have historically had families larger than the American average. Decisions about **family** size are left up to parents, who consider among other things the family's financial resources and the physical and mental health of both the father and mother.

BISHOP. The head of a congregation, or **ward**, the bishop is closer to the level of a pastor or parish priest than to the bishops familiar to **Catholics**, Anglicans, and others. A layman called to preside over his congregation, the bishop is sustained by raised hand at a meeting of **ward** members. This call comes only to a male Latter-day Saint who has demonstrated faithfulness and who passes standards of **worthiness**.

The bishop calls **members** to fill the many lay positions in the ward; determines the worthiness of members for attending the **temple**; visits the sick; counsels; and in general concerns himself with the spiritual and temporal welfare of ward members. He has the assistance of two **counselors**, the three constituting a bishopric. Also assisting are an executive secretary, a ward clerk, and usually assistant clerks. Working in close conjunction with the bishop to meet the needs of ward members is the female president of the **Relief Society**.

Although men who serve are ordained as bishops, service as a bishop of a particular ward is temporary. Since the position pays no salary, a bishop continues his regular vocation. After a few years the bishop is released along with his two counselors, to be then replaced by another ward member called to this responsibility. *See also* CALLING; SUSTAINING.

BLACKS. In the 19th century, Mormons had little interaction with blacks. Although identified with abolitionism to some extent, which contributed to their persecutions by pro-slavery Missourians, Mormons did not take a consistent anti-slavery position, and among those who settled Utah before the Civil War there were a few slave holders. With few exceptions, **African Americans** were eligible for **membership** in the Church but not for **priesthood** and leadership. Only a few African Americans became Latter-day Saints during the first century and a half of the Church's history.

Although members speculated on the doctrinal reasons for the failure to ordain blacks, President David O. McKay said that it was a practice rather than a doctrine. Presently available evidence indicates that some **general authorities** like McKay's **counselor** Hugh B. Brown would like to have seen the policy changed. He gave talks indicating that the Church believed in full civil rights for all people, including blacks.

A great divide occurred in 1978, when President **Spencer W. Kimball**, with the support of his counselors and the **twelve apostles**, proclaimed that "every faithful, worthy man in the Church" (with no exclusion based on race) might hold the priesthood (*Doctrine and Covenants*, official declaration 2). Since then proselytizing has been carried out in several countries in **Africa**. In the United States, Brazil, Zaire, Nigeria, various European countries, and elsewhere, blacks have joined the Church, served as **missionaries**, participated in **ordinances** of the **temple**, and filled leadership positions. Since membership records do not indicate race, it is impossible to give the exact number of black members. *See also* GENESIS GROUP.

BLESSING OF INFANTS. An **ordinance** or ceremony in which the infant is brought to church by the parents and, during a Sunday meeting, given a name and a blessing. A group of **priesthood** holders form a circle, with one priest holding the baby, and a designated person, usually the father, formally declares the child's name and pronounces words of blessing to be enjoyed during the course of the child's life on condition of faithfulness. Infants are not eligible for **baptism**.

BONNEVILLE INTERNATIONAL CORPORATION. A corporation of Church-owned radio and television stations, including KSL in Salt Lake City, Utah. Other television and radio stations have been acquired and a production/advertising company created. As commercial enterprises, these all pay taxes. They do not proselytize but do broadcast public service announcements promoting **family** and community values.

BOOK OF COMMANDMENTS. First compilation of the **revelations** of **Joseph Smith** in published book form. A printing press had been established in Independence, Missouri, and in December 1832 the book was at press. Before the entire book could be printed, a mob stormed the printing office, destroyed the press and type, and scattered what had been printed. Some of the printed sheets were salvaged and later bound. Many of the revelations had already been published in *Evening and Morning Star*, a Church newspaper. In 1835, a larger collection of the revelations was published as *Doctrine and Covenants*.

BOOK OF MORMON. One of the four canonical or standard works of **scripture** of the Church. First published in 1830 in English, the *Book of Mormon* has since appeared in many editions, including translations into other languages (77 in its entirety, 28 others in an abbreviated version entitled *Selections*). Although listed on the 1830 title page as "author," **Joseph Smith** consistently declared that the work was a translation from hieroglyphic inscriptions on ancient metal plates. Since he made no pretense of understanding the "reformed," or modified, Egyptian language, the process was possible only "by the gift and power of God."

Recounting the experiences of an Israelite colony that migrated from Jerusalem around 600 BC, the *Book of Mormon* tells of their settlement in the Western Hemisphere; their divisions; their wars, prophets, and religious teachings. After his death and resurrection in Jerusalem, **Jesus Christ** appeared to these "other sheep" and gave them a condensed version of his ministry as recounted in the **Bible**. After a period of peace and harmony these people degenerated once again, participated in a series of bloody wars, and finally clashed in a struggle in which one major group was exterminated.

The survivors were among the ancestors of those later identified as the American Indians. One of the final **prophets, Mormon**, abridged a vast quantity of earlier records; it is the abridger's proper name that gives the title to the book as a whole. One of the "books" within the *Book of Mormon* also gives a highly compressed version of the history of an earlier colony that migrated to the Western Hemisphere as early as the third millennium BC.

On this historical framework, selective and "abridged" from more complete records, the *Book of Mormon* presents its religious message. At its heart is the repeated presentation, by anticipatory prophecy or later preaching, of Jesus Christ and his saving gospel as the divine means provided for human salvation. Looking forward to a future time, thought by Mormons to be the "dispensation" that started with Joseph Smith in the 19th century, the book also foretells the gathering of the Jews to Israel, the redemption of other tribes of Israel, and the **restoration** of the Christian gospel.

Critics began to ridicule the *Book of Mormon* even before it was published and continued afterward. It was denounced as a patent forgery, full of references to 19th-century concerns. Its use of an English style borrowed from the Authorized, or King James, Version of the Bible and undisguised lengthy quotations from Isaiah and the Sermon on the Mount were pointed to as obvious giveaways. References to horses, elephants, and steel were trumpeted as anachronisms. Mark Twain, unimpressed, called it "chloroform in print." Two major obstacles prevent many modern people from taking the book seriously. Those from Christian backgrounds, especially **Protestants**, proclaim the Bible to be unique as scripture and on the face of it cannot accept the claims of an additional scripture. Those of a secular bent, increasingly numerous, find it impossible to think in terms of prophets, angels, and an intervening God.

Such obstacles notwithstanding, the *Book of Mormon* has a rather impressive record. Those who read it prayerfully and carefully testify in large numbers that it teaches them, inspires them, and speaks peace to their souls. Their conviction that it is true, they say, comes from the Holy Ghost. It continues to be taught in adult **Sunday School** classes on a regular basis along with the other standard works.

Non-Mormon reaction continues, on the whole, to be negative. Archaeologists and anthropologists find no support for a Hebrew population in the Western Hemisphere. Other critics emphasize the environment of 19th-century New York as the formative matrix for the book. Against this, Mormon scholars continue their work on several parallel paths, including the Near Eastern setting of the first 40 pages of the *Book of Mormon*; the possible geographical fit of the book's account with actual places in the Western Hemisphere; refuting or explaining the claimed anachronisms; studying the book's proper names against their alleged background; discovering Hebraisms through analysis of the book's complex literary forms, including poetry, sermons, speeches, letters, typology, and others; and highlighting cultural and biological evidences of ancient contact between the earth's two hemispheres. Of particular interest has been the discovery of several outstanding examples of chiasmus (a parallel pattern of Near Eastern origins following the structure a-b-c-c-b-a). Defenders of the *Book of Mormon* find it implausible that a 23-year-old of Joseph Smith's minimal educational background could have produced such a work. *See also* INSTITUTES OF RELIGION; MAXWELL, NEAL A.; NATIVE AMERICANS.

BOOK OF REMEMBRANCE. A volume of **family** records containing **genealogy**, **patriarchal blessings**, personal histories, biographies, or autobiographies. Encouraged to keep such records, **members** of the Church are also motivated by an interest in genealogy.

BOY SCOUTS. In 1913, just a few years after the beginning of the Scouting movement, the Church began sponsoring troops. Soon the percentage of participation by Mormon boys in Scouting far exceeded the national average. In the United States Mormons arc a prominent and respected component of the Boy Scouts of America. In other countries, where possible, troops are sponsored in conjunction with the Scouting organizations there.

BRANCH. A congregation presided over by a branch **president** and two **counselors.** Either because the group is too small or because no **stake** has been organized in the surrounding area, a branch is not raised to the status of a **ward**. It is a ward in embryo, awaiting the necessary conditions.

BRANNAN, SAMUEL (1819–1889). Church leader, **apostate**, businessman. Samuel Brannan was an apostate Mormon who led a group to California, helping to found San Francisco. Born in Saco, Maine, Brannan was converted to Mormonism as a teenager and worked as a printer's apprentice in Kirtland, Ohio. In 1844 this early experience, which had been reinforced by work on newspapers, helped qualify him to assist in editing *The Prophet*, a Mormon newspaper in New York City. He got into trouble with Church authorities for the unauthorized, premature preaching of **polygamy**. After being disfellowshipped, he was reinstated and assisted **Parley P. Pratt** in editing *The Messenger*.

In 1846, while **Brigham Young** led the main body of Mormons overland to the mountain West, Brannan led 238 Mormons aboard the ship *Brooklyn*, which sailed around Cape Horn. On July 29 the *Brooklyn* arrived at Yerba Buena (San Francisco). Brannan and his group founded a community, which they called New Hope. He published the first newspaper and preached the first sermon in the new settlement. In June 1847 he received a letter from Brigham Young stating the intention of the Church leaders to establish a settlement in the Great Basin, not in California. Brannan traveled overland to meet Young and try to convince him of the advantages of the coastal location. Unsuccessful, he returned and used his powers of persuasion on discharged members of the **Mormon Battalion**, urging the advantages of the beautiful California location over the rigors of the Rocky Mountains.

In 1849 Brannan became a promoter of gold mining, thus contributing to the great Gold Rush. Investing in hotels, shipping, and construction, he became California's first millionaire. When asked for a generous contribution to Young and the Church, he refused. Two years later he was **excommunicated** for unchristianlike conduct and neglect of duty. Also cited as a cause of action was his active role in founding a vigilante committee in San Francisco.

In 1859 Brannan established Calistoga, a 2,000-acre ranch, in Napa Valley, California. In addition to raising Merino sheep and beautiful horses he distilled brandy from the harvest of the extensive vineyards. For a few years Brannan seemed to prosper, but he also appeared bent on self-destruction. In 1868 Brannan was wounded in a property argument. Then affairs provoked a divorce suit from his wife, which forced a liquidation of his property holdings. Brannan's alcoholism became more and more severe. After an ambitious plan to colonize Sonora in northern Mexico failed, Brannan became impoverished and spent his final years partially paralyzed and suffering from arthritis. In 1889 he died a pauper.

BRIGHAM YOUNG UNIVERSITY (BYU). Founded at Provo, Utah, in 1875 as the Brigham Young Academy, this institution was named a university in 1903. During the first half of the 20th century its growth was slow but steady. After World War II, BYU experienced spectacular growth, from 1,500 students in 1945 to 25,000 by 1970. A cap enrollment of 27,000 was then established, though the enrollment has reached more than 30,000.

Like other universities, BYU publishes a catalogue that describes its many colleges: Biology and Agriculture; Education; Engineering and Technology; Family, Home, and Social Sciences; Fine Arts and Communications; Humanities; Nursing; Physical and Mathematical Sciences; and Physical Education. There is also a law school and a school of management. BYU is accredited by the Northwest Association of Schools and Colleges. The special aura that sets BYU apart from most other universities is religious. Over 90 percent of the student body and faculty are Mormon. All faculty and students, Mormon and non-Mormon alike, are expected to adhere to an honor code that includes abstinence from tea, coffee, alcohol, and tobacco in keeping with the **Word of Wisdom**. Students are required to take classes in religion. In addition, student **wards,** organized for religious worship, also function as support groups.

Questions of academic freedom have arisen occasionally. One flurry occurred in 1910–1911 over the modernist views of a few professors, three of whom were forced to resign. In the early 1990s sociologists and historians raised questions about the attitude of the university toward their research and participation in certain popular organizations. A statement of the university's position on academic freedom sought to allay fears. The great majority of subjects—mathematics, agriculture, nursing, chemistry, foreign languages, management, and others—raise no problems. As for the rest, both students and faculty are fully aware before going there of BYU's basic commitment to the sponsoring Church. In addition to its on-campus programs, the university sponsors a large, successful distant learning program, with more than 600 courses for students in all parts of the world.

BRIGHAM YOUNG UNIVERSITY–HAWAII (BYU–Hawaii). Founded at Laie on the north shore of Oahu in 1955, the institution was known as the Church College of Hawaii until 1974. BYU–Hawaii offers bachelor's degrees in business, education, information sciences, social sciences, and psychology. Academic programs fall under the College of Arts and Sciences (in addition to traditional majors such as history, English, and political science, there are majors in exercise and sport science, Hawaiian studies, and social work); School of Business (including majors in accounting, hospitality and tourism, and international business); School of Computing; and School of Education (training primary and secondary teachers). In December 2006, BYU–Hawaii's total enrollment of 2,492 students included 1,141 international students, largely from the **Pacific** islands and **Asia**. A large percentage of students are able to pay tuition costs by part-time employment at the adjoining **Polynesian Cultural Center**. Students agree to follow a basic code of behavior and to take required religion classes. BYU–Hawaii is accredited by the Western Association of Schools and Colleges.

BRIGHAM YOUNG UNIVERSITY–IDAHO (BYU–Idaho). Formerly known as **Ricks College**, the institution adopted its current name on 10 August 2001. A four-year institution with degree programs, BYU–Idaho has a cap enrollment of 11,600 students at any one time but during the year serves 15,000 students, who come from all 50 states and more than 50 countries. Students may earn an associate's degree or a bachelor's degree. Most majors require an internship. Academic departments are divided into the following colleges: Agriculture and Life Sciences; Business and Communication; Education and Human Development; Language and Letters; Performing and Visual Arts; Physical Sciences and Engineering.

Restructuring in the interest of efficiency and cutting the cost of education, BYU–Idaho abolished its intercollegiate athletics programs. Instead students were to become participants in the Activities Program, with six core areas: outdoor, service, talent, fitness, sports, and social. A three-semester schedule was adopted to take advantage of campus facilities throughout the year. BYU–Idaho is accredited by the Northwest Commission on Colleges and Universities.

BRIGHAM YOUNG UNIVERSITY STUDIES. A refereed scholarly periodical established at **BYU** in 1959 and published quarterly. Usually called simply *BYU Studies*, this "voice for the community of **LDS** scholars" has included bibliographies, essays, poetry, fiction, and articles from the various disciplines of the humanities and social sciences. Especially prominent have been articles on Mormon history, including primary documents. The journal sponsors the website ldsfaq.byu.edu, which answers over 400 questions about Mormonism.

BROOKS, JUANITA (1898–1989). Folklorist, historian. Born in Bunkerville, Nevada, Brooks experienced the hardships of the frontier as well as the closeness to nature of her rural setting. She became a schoolteacher in Mesquite, an adjacent community, and in 1919 married Ernest John Pulsipher, who died in early 1921. Brooks attended **BYU**, graduating in 1925. She took a position at Dixie Junior College in St. George, Utah, where for a generation she taught English and debate. Later she earned an M.A. degree from Columbia University. In 1933 she married a widower, Sheriff Will Brooks.

As president of the **Relief Society** in her **stake**, Brooks supervised a project of typing early pioneer diaries for preservation. She became a field representative for the Huntington Library and was a major force in building up a Mormon collection there. Over a generation of productivity, often stealing time for writing from her household duties, Brooks produced biographies, a history of Jews in Utah, a memoir, and a thorough study of the **Mountain Meadows Massacre**. She received an honorary doctorate from the University of Utah and a distinguished service award from the Utah Academy.

BROTHER AND SISTER. In addition to the usual biological meaning of these terms, Mormons use them as forms of address for other members of the Church, as in "Brother Smith" or "Sister Hernandez."

The terms connote a feeling of fraternal closeness to fellow Church members. In the strict sense, as children of the one Heavenly Father, all humans are brothers and sisters. *See also* FORMS OF ADDRESS.

BROWN, HUGH B. (1883–1975). Lawyer, educator, **general authority**. Born in Utah on 24 October 1883, Brown was essentially a Canadian, for his family moved to Alberta when he was only six years old. He married Zina Young Card in 1908 and became a major in the Canadian Army during World War I. After studying law, Brown became a barrister and solicitor in Lethbridge, Alberta, as well as **president** of the Lethbridge **Stake**. In 1927 he moved his family to Salt Lake City, Utah, and joined a prominent law firm. Two years later he became president of the Granite Stake.

Politically, Brown was a Democrat. During the 1930s he served as state chairman of the Democratic Party and, after an unsuccessful bid for the U.S. Senate, was appointed chairman of the State Liquor Commission. In 1937 he was called as president of the British Mission. He supervised the downsizing of the mission during World War II, served as coordinator of **LDS** servicemen, and resumed presidency of the mission after the war.

In 1946 he took a position as professor of religion at **BYU**. In 1953 he was called to be one of the **assistants to the twelve**, and in 1958 was named to the **Quorum** of the **Twelve Apostles**. In 1961 he became a **counselor** in the **First Presidency**. An important participant in the expansion associated with the presidency of **David O. McKay**, Brown repeatedly emphasized Church support of civil rights for all Americans, though ordination of **blacks** to the **priesthood** came only later.

BROWN, S. KENT (1940–). Scholar. Born 1 October 1940 in Murray, Utah, Brown earned a bachelor's degree in classical Greek with a minor in Near Eastern languages at the University of California at Berkeley in 1967, followed by a Ph.D. in religious studies from Brown University. Since 1971 he has been a professor of ancient scripture at **BYU**. In 1978 and 1979 Brown was a fellow of the American Research Center in Egypt. In the mid-1980s, he led a project to microfilm more than 1,500 ancient Christian manuscripts in Cairo and Jerusalem. From 1993 to 1996 he was director of the BYU

Jerusalem Center. The author of many articles and several books, Brown was a managing editor for *The Coptic Encyclopedia* and an editor for the *Encyclopedia of Mormonism.* He is director of the **Foundation for Ancient Research and Mormon Studies (FARMS)** and editor of the *Journal of* Book of Mormon *Studies.* His Church **callings** include serving as **bishop** twice and **stake president.** He and his wife, Gayle, have five children.

BURTON, H. DAVID (1938–). Businessman, presiding **bishop.** Born on 26 April 1938 in Salt Lake City, Utah, Burton graduated with a bachelor's degree in economics from the University of Utah and then earned a master's degree in business administration from the University of Michigan. He became a **high councilor, stake president,** and for 14 years secretary to the **presiding bishopric.** In 1992 he became first **counselor** in the Presiding Bishopric and in 1996 was sustained as presiding bishop. He and his wife, Barbara, are parents of five children.

BYBEE, ARIEL (1943–). Mezzo-soprano. Born 9 January 1943 in Reno, Nevada, Bybee is a graduate of **BYU** and also studied at the University of Southern California. At the Metropolitan Opera in New York City, she performed in a variety of operatic roles.

– C –

CALLING. The basis of service in the Church, a lay organization relying on volunteers for its functioning. **General authority, stake president, bishop, Relief Society** president, **ward** librarian, home teacher, **missionary,** scoutmaster, teacher of 10-year-olds in **Primary**—all of these are callings. **Active** Church **members** fill many callings during the course of their lives. Although time-consuming, callings are to be performed conscientiously and willingly. Many attest to the value of experiences that without accepting callings they would not have had.

Two characteristics of callings deserve explanation. First, they come from the top down. It is the bishop who must staff the many positions in his ward by issuing calls to ward members. **Presidents** of stakes, general authorities, and **area** authorities similarly staff positions in the areas of their assigned jurisdiction. The expectation is that loyal Church members will respond affirmatively when asked to fulfill a specific responsibility. One does not apply. Second, callings are temporary. With the exception of the 15 general authorities who make up the **First Presidency** and the **Quorum** of the **Twelve Apostles**, callings are for a limited period of time. Full-time missionaries serve for 18 months, two years, or, in the case of mission presidents, three years. Other positions are more flexible in their duration.

The conception of the calling occasions some adjustment for those who are accustomed to the upward mobility of business and government. In the Church, empire building is not welcomed. One who has been a bishop or stake president can suddenly find that his calling is that of a choir director or **Sunday School** teacher. Those who have seen Mormon missionaries in different locations may not be aware that missions, too, are callings. One may indicate a willingness to serve and must pass standards of **worthiness**, but the call itself comes from Church headquarters, at which time one discovers where the missionary service will be. *See also* MISSIONARY PROGRAM.

CANADA. *See* NORTH AMERICA.

CANNON, ELAINE A. (1922–2003). Journalist, author, **Young Women** leader. Born in Salt Lake City, Utah, on 9 April 1922, Cannon grew up and attended school there. Starting as a teenager, she wrote a daily column for the *Deseret News* and edited the women's section. In 1942 she married D. James Cannon and became the mother of six children. She became a radio artist for both NBC and CBS while locally hosting a TV talk show. She wrote for national magazines like *Better Homes and Gardens* and *Seventeen*. From 1950 to 1954 she served on the president's White House Committee on Children and Youth. For the Church magazine *The Improvement Era* she coedited with **Marion D. Hanks** a section addressed to youth. In 1960 she was named to the general board of Young Women and from 1978 to 1984 served as general president. In the 1980s she was vice-president of the National Council of Women. She wrote many self-help and inspirational books as well as one on Mormon artist Minerva Teichert.

CANNON, FRANK JENNE (1859–1933). Newspaperman, politician, territorial delegate, U.S. senator. A son of George Q. Cannon and Martha Jenne Cannon, Cannon grew up in Salt Lake City, Utah. He served as a reporter for the *San Francisco Chronicle* in 1880. In 1882 he was appointed deputy clerk and recorder for the city of Ogden, Utah. He moved to Washington, D.C., in 1883, and during 1883 and 1884 he served as private secretary for territorial delegate John T. Caine. Returning to Ogden, Cannon was elected county recorder for Weber County in 1882. From 1887 to 1893 he served as editor of the *Ogden Herald*, a Mormon-affiliated newspaper. In 1886 he wrote *Life of Joseph Smith the Prophet*, but because of a controversy concerning his personal life, the authorship was attributed to his father, George Q. Cannon. After the 1891 division of the Mormon people into the two national political parties, Cannon served as delegate to the Republican National Convention in 1892. In 1894 he was elected as Utah's territorial delegate to Congress, and he served from 1895 until Utah's admission as a state in 1896. In 1896 the legislature elected Cannon as one of Utah's first senators, and under the system then in force, he served four years from 1896 to 1900. In 1896 he bolted the Republican Party to support the Silver Republican Ticket in opposition to the Gold Standard and William McKinley's election. He remained in the Republican Party during his senatorial term, but in 1900 he joined the Democrats and served as chair of the Utah state Democratic Party convention in 1900. In 1902 he was elected chair of the Utah state Democratic Party, and in 1903 he served as editor of a Democratic Party organ, the *Utah State Journal*. He served as delegate to the national Democratic Party convention in 1904.

In 1905 Cannon broke with the **LDS** Church and became editor of the *Salt Lake Tribune*, which was then owned by Thomas Kearns and a virulently anti-Mormon journal. This led to his **excommunication** from the LDS Church. He moved to Denver, Colorado, in 1909 to serve as editor of the *Rocky Mountain News*. In 1911 he and Harvey J. O'Higgins published an attack on church **president** Joseph F. Smith in *Under the Prophet in Utah*, which he followed up in 1913 with *Brigham Young and His Mormon Empire*. In 1878 Cannon married Martha Brown. He died in Denver in 1933.

CANNON, GEORGE Q. (1827–1901). Journalist, delegate to Congress, **general authority**. Born on 11 January 1827 in Liverpool, England, Cannon was a teenager in 1842 when his family was converted to Mormonism by his uncle **John Taylor**. They emigrated to Nauvoo, Illinois. Left an orphan by the death of his mother during the journey and of his father shortly after their arrival, George was taken in by John Taylor and assisted him in editing the *Times and Seasons*.

After crossing the plains during the Mormon **exodus**, Cannon was sent to mine gold in California in 1849 and the following year was called as a **missionary** to Hawaii. He mastered the Hawaiian language and, with his fellow missionaries, succeeded on converting many natives to the Church. With assistance, he translated the *Book of Mormon* into the Hawaiian language.

Returning to the mainland, Cannon married Elizabeth Hoagland, published the *Book of Mormon* in Hawaiian at San Francisco, and edited the Mormon newspaper *Western Standard*. In 1858 he was named editor of the *Deseret News*. He was assigned to provide information to newspaper editors and preside over Latter-day Saints in the eastern states. In 1860, he was ordained a member of the **Quorum** of the **Twelve Apostles** and sent to England to preside over the European Mission, returning in 1864. In 1872 he was elected delegate to Congress from Utah Territory.

A **polygamist**, Cannon was expelled from Congress in 1882 for violating the new Edmunds Act. In 1888 he was imprisoned for unlawful cohabitation; like other Mormons in the same situation, he saw himself "a prisoner for conscience' sake." He owned a publishing company and was a director of several businesses. He was a **counselor** to Presidents **Brigham Young**, John Taylor, **Wilford Woodruff**, and **Lorenzo Snow**.

CANNON, MARTHA HUGHES (1857–1932). Physician, politician. Martha Hughes Cannon was the second daughter of Peter Hughes and Elizabeth Evans. Shortly after Cannon's birth in Wales her family joined the Church of Jesus Christ of Latter-day Saints and emigrated to the United States in 1858. After a two-year stay in New

York City, due to the poor health of her father, the family then emigrated to Utah. Her sister, Annie, died during the overland journey while her father died three days after reaching the Salt Lake Valley. Her mother remarried James P. Paul, a widower with four children of his own.

At a very young age, Cannon displayed unusual intelligence and strong individuality. She always dreamed of becoming a doctor and constantly worked toward this goal. At 14, with apparently little education, Cannon began teaching school. Unfortunately, she experienced difficulty in maintaining discipline with some of the bigger students. The following year she found a job as a typesetter for the *Deseret News* and the *Woman's Exponent*. Cannon saved almost all of her money and applied it to her medical school fund. Eventually, she enrolled in the University of Deseret (University of Utah) in preparation for medical school. In 1878, she entered the medical school at the University of Michigan. She received her M.D. in 1880 and continued her education at the University of Pennsylvania and the National School of Elocution and Oratory. Cannon returned to Salt Lake City, Utah, and opened a private medical practice. She also worked as a resident doctor at the Deseret Hospital. While at the hospital, she met her future husband, Angus Cannon, a member of the board of directors and **president** of the Salt Lake Stake. In 1884, she married Cannon, becoming his fourth wife. Cannon lived abroad during each of her pregnancies to prevent her husband from going to jail. She lived in England between 1886 and 1887 and used the services of many facilities in France, England, and Switzerland.

Cannon worked in the political sphere as well. She constantly championed women's voting rights for various suffrage organizations. In one of the most dramatic state senator races, Martha, one of five Democratic candidates, vied for one of five senatorial seats. Her husband ran for the same seats on the Republican ticket. The Cannons did not directly run against each other, and each could possibly have gained a seat in the state senate. Only Martha garnered this prize. While in the position, she introduced many important and progressive acts of legislation that included a bill establishing the State Board of Health, the Pure Food Law, and the State School for the Deaf, Dumb, and Blind. She also served as a member of the State Board of Health, the board of directors of the State Deaf and Dumb

Institute, and vice president of the American Congress of Tuberculosis. In 1915 her husband of thirty-one years died in Salt Lake City. The last twelve years of her life, Cannon worked at the Graves' Clinic in Los Angeles. She died in Los Angeles on 10 July 1932.

CANNON, SYLVESTER Q. (1877–1943). Businessman, engineer, **general authority.** A son of **George Q. Cannon,** Sylvester was born on 10 June 1877 in Salt Lake City, Utah. His graduation from the University of Utah was followed by completion of an engineering degree at MIT. From 1899 to 1902 he served as a **missionary** in the Netherlands and Belgium. In 1904 he married Winifred Saville.

After directing a land and irrigation survey of Weber River in Utah, Cannon returned to Holland as mission **president** for two years. From 1912 to 1925 he was engineer for Salt Lake City. Among the projects he supervised was a major reservoir and control of air pollution. He was **counselor** in a **stake** presidency and in 1917 became president of the Pioneer Stake. In 1925 he was named **presiding bishop,** thus a key figure in the administration of **Heber J. Grant.** Among many other construction projects Cannon supervised plans for the construction of the Idaho Falls Temple. In 1939 he joined the ranks of the **Quorum** of the **Twelve Apostles.**

CARD, ORSON SCOTT (1951–). Writer. Born in Richland, Washington, Card served as a **missionary** in Brazil. He earned degrees at **BYU** and the University of Utah. Best known for his science fiction, Card received the Hugo and Nebula awards for best novel in 1986 and 1987. A series of American fantasy, the Alvin Maker series, is set in a magical version of the American frontier and contains many parallels and echoes of the **prophet Joseph Smith.** His Homecoming Saga recasts Mormon **scripture** as science fiction. A novelized historical biography *Saints* touches upon many events of early Mormon history. *A Storyteller in Zion* presents the challenges of being a writer in the Mormon culture setting. Several contemporary novels emphasize character and moral dilemmas. Card's works have been translated into Catalan, Danish, Dutch, Finnish, French, Polish, Japanese, and other languages. He and his wife, Kristine, live in Greensboro, North Carolina. They have five children.

CARMACK, JOHN K. (1931–). Lawyer, businessman, **general authority**. Born on 10 May 1931 in Winslow, Arizona, Carmack was a **missionary** in the West Central States Mission and served in the U.S. Army during the Korean War. He received a B.A. degree from **BYU** and a law degree from UCLA. Carmack was a legislative assistant in the California legislature, president of a Los Angeles law firm, and president of the Westwood Bar Association. In West Los Angeles he was chairman of the board of the Chamber of Commerce and member of the executive council for Los Angeles council of Boy Scouts of America.

In the Church, Carmack was a **bishop's counselor, high councilor, stake** president, **regional representative**, and **president** of the Idaho Boise Mission. In 1984 he became a member of the First **Quorum** of the **Seventy**. Named an emeritus general authority in 2001, Carmack was named director of the Perpetual Education Fund.

CATHOLICISM. Although neither group accepts the ultimate authority claims of the other, Mormons and Catholics are similar in their insistence on the need for legal authority in the church; on the importance of **sacraments**, or **ordinances**; and on basic social values. Despite examples of cooperation and sometimes even mutual admiration, however, opinions of one another have not always been positive. The Mormon perception of Catholicism has sometimes been very critical because most converts to Mormonism come from **Protestant** backgrounds with a traditional anti-Catholic animus. At the same time, until the breakthroughs in Central and South America, predominantly Catholic countries proved especially unreceptive to the Mormon message. These two details explain both the make-up of the Mormon population and the frustrations encountered by Mormon proselytizing. It is not entirely surprising, then, to find references in some early Mormon sermons and writings to the tyranny of the pope and the superstition of Catholics. Biblical expressions such as "whore of Babylon," which Protestants had long put to polemical purposes against the Catholic Church, were repeated by some Mormons, along with counterparts in the Mormon scriptures such as "the great and abominable church." Some Mormon accounts of the Great **Apostasy** were in effect indictments of historical Catholicism.

Since the latter part of the 20th century the attitude toward Catholics has considerably softened. In 1958 a reference by a Mormon **general authority** to the Catholic Church as "most abominable above all other churches" was removed in a revised edition of the book. Articles in Mormon magazines more carefully described the apostasy as occurring in the first and second centuries, exculpating later Catholics, who were victims, not villains. Some publications even began emphasizing the many basic points on which Mormons and Catholics agreed or at least shared similar positions. Contributing to the more amicable attitude are the proselytizing successes in largely Catholic countries; an awareness that Mormons and Catholics can make common cause against an overwhelmingly secular world; and more sophisticated historical and theological scholarship that discourages the demonizing of such a large part of Christianity.

Catholic views of Mormons remain negative. Rome sees Mormons as one of the "sects," or "**cults**," which a more neutral usage has labeled "new religious movements." Catholic works on Mormons are few and range from the irresponsible and inaccurate to a few works containing fairly reliable history and sociology.

CELIBACY. Mormons do not consider celibacy a requirement for the **priesthood**. Indeed, the married state is considered to be on a higher level and essential to the highest degree of salvation. On the other hand, in the sense of abstinence from sexual intercourse as long as one is unmarried, celibacy is in fact an expectation. *See also* MARRIAGE.

CENTRAL AMERICA AND MEXICO. In 1875 the first Mormon **missionaries** entered Mexico and arranged for the publication of a pamphlet in Spanish. A few converts were made, but most of them were unsteady. The next phase occurred with the colonization of northern Mexico by Anglo Mormons. Many of these settlers were driven out during the Mexican Revolution, but some of them returned. A few hundred native Mexicans rallied to the Mormon religion as well.

After World War II the Church grew rapidly. Many young Mexicans were instructed in Church-owned schools and served as **missionaries**. **Stakes** and **wards** were organized. A **temple** was built in

Mexico City in 1983. At the end of 2005 there were 1,043,718 **members** in 206 stakes and 1,408 wards with 12 temples. Not until 1947 did missionaries enter Guatemala. By the end of 2005 there were 200,537 members in 40 stakes and 236 wards, and a temple was constructed in 1984. Other Central American countries also saw rather dramatic increases. At the end of 2005 membership totals were as follows:

Country	Members	Stakes
Costa Rica	33,036	5
El Salvador	94,296	16
Honduras	116,416	20
Nicaragua	52,184	7
Panama	40,897	7

CENTRO ESCOLAR BENEMERITO DE LAS AMERICAS. Church-owned preparatory school on the northern outskirts of Mexico City founded in 1963. Starting with 15 teachers and 125 students, the school had 120 teachers and 2,100 students in 1999. Housing is provided for 1,065 students. **Seminary** classes are taken by all students. The library contains 90,000 volumes. In addition to college preparatory courses, many students participate in sports or artistic pursuits. Sponsored performing groups include the Banda de Guerra, Porristas, the Rondalla, the Symphony Orchestra, the Choir, and Ballet Folklorico. In 1994 the Agricultural Institute was established, a one-year program in horticulture. About 80 percent of the students continue their education on the university level.

CHAPLAINS. During World War I, **B. H. Roberts** was a chaplain in the Utah National Guard and later one of three chaplains with the American troops in France. During World War II, 46 Mormon chaplains served. Mormon chaplains have continued to serve with the U.S. military, holding general worship services, counseling with military personnel, and performing duties for Latter-day Saint military personnel. In 1995 Kay Schwendiman, former chaplain for the 96th Army Reserve Command, became chairman of the United States National Conference on Ministry to the Armed Forces, representing 250 faith groups in providing assistance to chaplains. In part because of the requirement that chaplains have a degree in religious education, the number of Mormon chaplains in the armed services does not equal the percentage of Mormons serving.

CHASTITY. A term little understood in the late 20th century, chastity refers to abstaining from sexual relations outside of **marriage**. The increased chance of unwanted pregnancy, sexually transmitted diseases, and emotional scars that linger are among the practical reasons for rejecting promiscuity and choosing a chaste pattern of behavior. Ultimately, chastity is one of the commandments of God. Although violations inevitably occur, they are to be deplored, not shrugged off. The appropriate response for violation is **repentance**.

"CHOOSE THE RIGHT." Title of a popular Mormon hymn, with words by Joseph L. Townsend and music by a Salt Lake City, Utah, candy maker named Henry A. Tuckett, first printed in a song book of 1909. In the final generation of the 20th century the three words assumed greater prominence when used in awards given to children in **Primary** and, even more, when the letters CTR were widely used as a logogram on pins, rings, and other examples of Mormon kitsch.

CHRISTENSEN, CLAYTON M. (1952–). Scholar, **area authority seventy.** Born on 6 April 1952 in Salt Lake City, Utah, Christensen served as a missionary in Korea from 1971 to 1973. After earning a bachelor's degree in economics at **BYU** in 1975, he attended Oxford University as a Rhodes Scholar, earning an M.Phil. in applied econometrics in 1977. He then earned an MBA degree at Harvard Business School in 1979. Later, in 1992, he was awarded a doctorate in business administration by Harvard and then became a faculty member at the Harvard Business School.

Christensen founded three successful companies. He was named a White House fellow in 1982, serving as an assistant to the secretary of transportation. He served as an advisor to the Brigham and Women's Hospital in Boston and was a member and chairman of the board of directors of the Massachusetts Affiliate of the American Diabetes Association. He was elected a member of the Town Meeting in Belmont, Massachusetts. For the Boy Scouts of America, Christensen was scoutmaster, den leader, and chairman of the troop committee. His **callings** in the Church included that of **bishop** and **counselor** in the presidency of the Massachusetts Boston Mission. In April 2002 he became an area authority seventy. His statement "Why I Believe," found on his website, emphasizes the opportunities to serve afforded by the Church. He and his wife, Christine, have five children.

CHRISTENSEN, JOE J. (1929–). Educator, **general authority**. Christensen was born on 21 July 1929 in Banida, a farming community in southeastern Idaho. As a young man, he served as a **missionary** in Mexico and Costa Rica. His college training was at Utah State University and **BYU**. After a tour of duty in the U.S. Air Force and completion of his university degrees, he was employed as a **seminary** and **institute** teacher.

With his wife and six children, Christensen went to Mexico in 1970 to preside over the Mexico City Mission. Called as associate Church commissioner of education, he spent the next several years establishing seminary and institute programs in many countries. For four years he was **president** of the **Missionary Training Center** in Provo, Utah. In 1985, he was appointed president of **Ricks College**. In 1989, he became a general authority as a member of the First **Quorum** of the **Seventy** and in 1993 was sustained a member of its presidency. He became an emeritus general authority in 1999.

CHRISTIANITY. Mormons have an inclusive definition of Christianity, including within its boundaries **Catholics**, **Protestants**, Orthodox, and, of course, themselves. This does not mean they consider all forms equally valid or all ideas right. The term is not therefore a declaration of total agreement but a simple way of designating those who accept **Jesus Christ** as the Savior. On the other hand, some of their opponents deny that Mormons are Christians on the grounds that they do not accept the creeds of historic Christianity starting in the fourth century. By such a definition, some Mormons have responded, the original Christians of Bible times would be excluded. Whatever others may say, Mormons declare their faith in Jesus Christ as Creator, Redeemer, Lord, and Master, now physically resurrected, one of the three persons in the Godhead. Some whose claim to Christian identity has not been challenged believe far less about Christ.

CHRISTOFFERSON, D. TODD (1945–). Attorney, **general authority.** Born on 24 January 1945 in American Fork, Utah, Christofferson majored in English and international relations at **BYU.** After serving as a **missionary** in Argentina from 1964 to 1966, he earned a juris doctorate from Duke University. A law clerk for U.S. District Court Judge John J. Sirica during the Watergate hearings, he then joined a Washington law firm, specializing in legal work for financial institutions. Christofferson lived in Tennessee, Virginia, and North Carolina. He participated in interfaith organizations, received the Silver Beaver Award of the **Boy Scouts** of America, and served as chairman of the Middle Tennessee Literacy Coalition and chairman of Affordable Housing of Nashville.

In the Church, Christofferson's **callings** have included **seminary** teacher, **high councilor, bishop, stake president,** and **regional representative.** In 1993 he was called to the First **Quorum** of the **Seventy** and in 1998 became a member of its presidency. He and his wife, Kathy, have five children.

THE CHURCH OF JESUS CHRIST OF LATTER-DAY SAINTS. Official name of the Church popularly known as the Mormon Church with its headquarters in Salt Lake City, Utah. It is a world Church with members in all inhabited continents. When formed in 1830, the organization was known as the Church of Christ and for a brief period by some as the Church of the Latter-day Saints, but in 1838 the present name was given by revelation (***Doctrine and Covenants*** 115:4): "For thus shall my church be called, even The Church of Jesus Christ of Latter-day Saints."

Although long, the name admirably conveys important ideas. The definite article "the," capitalized and included as part of the name, is significantly not the indefinite article "a." Mormons see theirs as God's church on earth, uniquely authorized and recognized by Him. Although such exclusivity appears arrogant and does not encourage ecumenism, Mormons answer that the designation is not their own but God's and that they fully acknowledge sincerity, goodness, and truth wherever found.

The term *church* conveys the importance and value of organization. Mormons believe that **Jesus Christ** deliberately founded an organization—both at the time of his earthly ministry in Palestine and at the time of the **restoration** in 1830. The desire of some to "go it alone" without institutional religion is incompatible with the human need for instruction, support, and especially the **sacrament** of the Lord's Supper and other **ordinances** of salvation, for all of which the Church is vital.

"Of Jesus Christ"—these words indicate the "ownership" of the Church, whose it is, the source of its authority. It is not the prerogative of human beings on their own to organize the Lord's church. They can go through the motions, of course, even for the crass motive of obtaining a tax-exempt status, but without divine authorization a church is not his. Careless librarians and others who classify works on Mormonism as non-Christian, perhaps because of a surface similarity between "Mormon" and "Muslim," have probably paid little attention to the official name.

"Of Latter-day Saints" refers to the members of the Church. For many people, the word *saints* designates those from Mary and the original apostles to the person most recently elevated through the Catholic Church's canonization procedures. As used in the New Testament, the word referred simply to members of the church, as when Paul wrote to the saints at Corinth or Ephesus. To differentiate themselves from such original, or early-day, saints, Mormons call themselves Latter-day Saints. While the Church derives its authority from above, it is here pronounced also to be "*of* the Latter-day Saints." It belongs to them as well as to God. As a lay organization each **ward** or **stake** requires the services of many unpaid laborers. Those named to positions, from the **president** of the Church on down, receive the approval of the members by a **sustaining** vote. See also FIRST VISION; MISSION OF THE CHURCH.

CLARK, J(OSHUA) REUBEN (1871–1961). International lawyer, ambassador, and **general authority**. Born in Grantsville, Utah, on 1 September 1871, J. Reuben Clark grew up in a small town environment. He attended Latter-day Saints' College in Salt Lake City, Utah, and came under the influence of its president, **James E. Talmage**. In 1898 he graduated as valedictorian from the University of Utah.

Clark moved east to attend Columbia Law School. An appointment as assistant solicitor in the U.S. State Department and then as solicitor in 1910 led him to work on problems with Mexico. Although he left the State Department with the election of Woodrow Wilson, Clark continued to accept such government appointments as general counsel for the American-British Claims Commission, special assistant to the attorney general, executive officer to the judge advocate general, and special counsel for the U.S. negotiators at the Washington Arms Conference of 1921–1922. After returning to Utah for a period, J. Reuben Clark was again called into government service. From counsel to the U.S. commission pressing claims against Mexico he went on to become undersecretary of state and then special advisor to Dwight W. Morrow, U.S. ambassador to Mexico. From 1930 to 1933 Clark was U.S. ambassador to Mexico.

In 1933, even though he had never held any high Church office, Clark was named a **counselor** in the **First Presidency**. For 28 years he served in sequence as counselor to Presidents **Heber J. Grant**, **George Albert Smith**, and **David O. McKay**. Because of his extensive experience and strong will, he made a significant contribution to all of these **presidents**. When, from 1951 to 1959, Clark became second instead of first counselor, his memorable statement was, "In the service of the Lord, it is not where you serve but how" (*Conference Reports*, April 1951, 154).

Clark was intimately involved with the introduction of the **welfare program**, the evacuation of **missionaries** from **Europe** in 1939, the reopening of the missions after World War II, and the building of many chapels. A student of the scriptures, he produced his own harmonization of the gospels and a series of radio lectures on the Great **Apostasy**. After studying the implications of modern translations of the **Bible**, he spoke in favor of the Church's continued use of the King James Version. As the Church's educational system of **seminaries** and **institutes of religion** expanded, Clark insisted that all teachers must adhere to belief in the atonement of **Jesus Christ**, the divine calling of **Joseph Smith** as **prophet**, and the continued legitimate leadership of the successive Church presidents.

A conservative Republican, Clark was less than enthusiastic about U.S. participation in World War II, deplored the use of the atomic bomb, warned against the power of the military-industrial elite, made some comments construed as anti-Semitic, and lamented "our dwindling sovereignty." At the same time, he acknowledged that these were personal opinions, not official Church positions.

CLARK, KIM B. (1949–). Educator. Born on 20 March 1949 in Salt Lake City, Utah, Clark grew up in Spokane, Washington, and then served a two-year **mission** in Germany. In 1974 he earned a B.A. degree at Harvard University, followed by an M.A. in 1977 and the Ph.D. in 1978. He became George F. Baker professor of business administration, and, in 1995, dean of the Harvard Business School. He was inaugurated as president of **BYU–Idaho** on 12 October 2005. He and his wife, Sue, have seven children.

CLAYTON, WILLIAM (1814–1879). Clerk, musician. Born 17 July 1814, in Preston, Lancashire, England, Clayton joined the **LDS** Church in 1837, as part of the first group converted in England. The following year **Elders** Heber C. Kimball and **Orson Hyde**, who had led the missionary effort, returned to Kirtland, Ohio, and they ordained Clayton as second **counselor** in the English mission presidency. He served in this **calling** until emigrating to Nauvoo, Illinois, in 1840. In Nauvoo, Clayton served as private secretary to **Joseph Smith** and clerk for the **Nauvoo Temple**. In addition to recording Joseph Smith's revelation on celestial marriage, Clayton performed the ceremonies for four of Smith's plural marriages. Clayton also held several civic positions, including Nauvoo city treasurer, recorder for the Nauvoo city council, and member of the Nauvoo Legion band. At a camp in Iowa after Mormons were driven from Nauvoo, Clayton wrote *Come, Come, Ye Saints*, which has become a favorite LDS hymn. While a member of the 1847 pioneer company, Clayton invented a "roadmeter," which measured the distance traveled by a wagon wheel. In Utah, Clayton acted as the auditor of public accounts for the Provisional State of Deseret. When Congress organized Utah as a territory, Clayton also served as territorial auditor of public accounts and territorial recorder of marks and brands. Besides his civic duties, Clayton also served as secretary for Zion's Cooperative Mercantile Institution for a number of years. On 4 December 1879, Clayton died in his Salt Lake City, Utah, home.

CLERGY. In the usual sense, the Church has no clergy, except possibly **general authorities**. It is a lay organization. With no divinity schools and no paid ministry, the **LDS** Church does not follow the practice of other churches. No young Mormon looks forward to becoming a full-time clergyman in the Church; the concept does not exist. With the expansion of **membership**, of course, there are those who are employed by the Church. These include teachers in the **seminaries** and **institutes of religion**, editors of magazines, librarians, and professionals and secretaries in many different departments. These full-time positions are regarded as employment, not **callings**.

On the level of the congregation, or **ward**, interaction is between fellow members, all amateurs or laity, although some occupy positions of responsibility. Visitors are sometimes surprised to find that the person conducting a meeting is actually a barber or a grocer. In the Church, however, he may be the **bishop**. **Missionaries** serve full-time during their 18-month or two-year calling, but they are not paid for this. Their sustenance-level stipend comes from their own savings, support of their families, or, in some cases, funds donated to the missionary program. Never do these young men and women think of themselves as professional clergymen in the sense of having chosen a life's career.

COLONIZATION. If colonization refers to the establishment of new settlements, Mormons have been in the forefront of colonization. Looking at the different phases of Mormon history, we discover the beginnings of such conscious establishment of settlements in Missouri. The same process was repeated in Illinois with the build-up at Nauvoo and the establishment of several settlements in the region.

But it was in the west that Mormon colonization moved into high gear. The initial establishment of Salt Lake City, Utah, in the Great Salt Lake Valley (1847) was followed by the deliberate peopling of the region as pioneers were sent out to establish communities in designated locations. Dots appeared on the map, as it were, as new settlements were founded north and south of Salt Lake City. Ambitious plans for a far-flung empire led to Mormon communities as far away as the Salmon River in Idaho and San Bernardino, California, but the political and military pressures of the mid-1850s led to a pull-back from these most distant outposts.

Partially because of the population pressure caused by a high birth rate and a steady flow of new immigrants, the settlement expansion continued. By the death of **Brigham Young** in 1877, more than 300 settlements had been founded. (These are listed in Milton R. Hunter,

Brigham Young the Colonizer.) By the end of the 19th century, more than 500 had been founded. If the Mormon colonization was any different from that taking place all across the American landscape, it was in its organization and advance planning. Sites were selected on the basis of preliminary reconnaissance that assured a supply of water and soil that was cultivable. A leader was named and people were called to join the new settlement on the basis of needed skills. Madcap individualism was suppressed in favor of the community interest, as lots were assigned and work assignments handed out.

Of course there was the initial phase of confronting an environment devoid of amenities or even minimal shelter. Living in tents or wagon boxes was followed by putting up simple shacks or cabins. If necessary, a wall to provide protection against Indians was built. Planting, irrigating, cultivating, and the initial harvest were always an arduous, suspenseful drama. The extreme hardship of the initial phase often led to premature deaths, sometimes to defections. As time went on, however, homes were improved, the community became larger and more adequate in providing basic needs, and civic pride manifested itself in parades and celebrations.

Although the completion of the transcontinental railroad in 1869 ended Utah's isolation in some respects, it did not mean the end of colonization. And those who left the more settled areas to strike out in their wagons for a new site several hundred miles away were pioneers as much as were those who first came to the Salt Lake Valley in 1847. Each place had its heroic leaders, its founding fathers and mothers. Some of the settlements and their dates follow: Little Colorado River in Arizona (1876); Bunkerville, Nevada (1877); Star Valley, Wyoming (1879); St. Johns, Arizona (1879); Rexburg, Idaho (1882); Colonia Juarez, Mexico (1885); Cardston, Alberta, Canada (1887). *See also* ILLINOIS PERIOD; MISSOURI PERIOD.

COMMANDMENTS. Mormons are often urged to "keep the commandments." This is meant to include not only the Ten Commandments (but not the detailed dietary proscriptions of the Mosaic law) and such commands from Jesus as to preach the gospel unto all the world, but also instructions from the Lord in modern revelation. The **Word of Wisdom** has been construed as a commandment. The specific covenants of **baptism** and the **temple**—generally to live a life of Christian service and unselfishness—also become obligations one should keep. To those who might see such an emphasis as legalism, a failure to understand the liberty with which Christ made humans free, Mormons would reply that **Jesus Christ** said, "If ye love me, keep my commandments" (John 14:15), and that his yoke is easy and his burden light (Matt. 11:30). They fully recognize that without the grace of God their efforts would be meaningless.

COMMUNITY OF CHRIST. Current name of the organization formerly named the **Reorganized Church of Jesus Christ of Latter Day Saints (RLDS)**. Because of having constantly to explain that they were not Mormons, not members of the **Church of Jesus Christ of Latter-day Saints** (the primary focus of this dictionary), members of the RLDS Church assembled at world conference in April 2000 decided by a vote of 1,979 to 561 to adopt a new name, **Community of Christ**. Membership is close to 250,000 in about 50 countries and has remained relatively static for the past several decades. The history of this church up to 2001 is treated under its official name to that point, Reorganized Church of Jesus Christ of Latter Day Saints.

To give an accurate current picture that differentiates the Community of Christ from the Church of Jesus Christ of Latter-day Saints, several points deserve mention. Both groups reject the practice of **polygamy**, but the Church of Jesus Christ of Latter-day Saints, starting with **Joseph Smith** no later than 1841, allowed it until the **Manifesto** of 1890. Administratively, at the top of the Community of Christ are a presidency of three and a quorum of twelve apostles. The president of the Community of Christ is no longer required to be a descendant of Joseph Smith. Starting in 1984, women can be ordained to the **priesthood**. Several women are apostles. The Community of Christ has a paid ministry, including not only general officers but pastors in its congregations and missionaries. Tithing, the major source of income for sustaining church operations, is defined as 10 percent of income after taxes and after "what is needed for basic living needs." The Community of Christ accepts as scripture the **Bible**, ***Book of Mormon***, and ***Doctrine and Covenants*** (its own version) but not the ***Pearl of Great Price.*** Revelation is not confined to these works. According to the Community of Christ, "God is revealed to us through scripture, the faith community, prayer, nature, and in human history."

The Community of Christ owns two **temples**: (1) one at Kirtland, Ohio, which is viewed as a historic site and is open to tourists who wish to view its interior as well as exterior; and (2) one at Independence, Missouri, dedicated in 1994. The ceremonies and **ordinances** associated with Latter-day Saint temples, including endowments and **baptism for the dead**, are not administered by the Community of Christ. The Independence temple, striking architecturally, is a center of education, meditation, and peace.

On 14 June 2006 the Community of Christ announced a downsizing within the organization. Through "early retirements, voluntary separations and involuntary separations," about 80 people would be let go. More than 400 people, including ministers at churches and workers at headquarters in Independence, Missouri, remained on the payroll. *See also* MCMURRAY, W. GRANT; SCHISMS; SUCCESSION; VEAZEY, STEPHEN M.

COMMUNITY SERVICE. Church members are encouraged to participate in their communities, volunteering when possible to assist deserving programs. **Wards** and **stakes** often organize themselves to assist in community projects. The full-time **missionaries** throughout the world also assist the communities to which they are assigned on a regular basis. *See also* HUMANITARIAN AID; WELFARE PROGRAM.

CONFERENCE CENTER. Large assembly hall in Salt Lake City, Utah, completed in April 2000. The fan-shaped auditorium has a capacity of 21,000 and is used for **conference** sessions, pageants, and other public events. In addition to the auditorium, the building has over 60 translation booths, a theater with 900 upholstered seats, and underground parking for 1,300 vehicles. The roof is landscaped with fountains, trees, and flowers. The center was constructed to meet the highest seismic standards.

CONFERENCES, GENERAL. Gatherings in April and October of each year at the **Conference Center** (after a century and a quarter of meeting in the **Tabernacle**) in Salt Lake City, Utah, where members and officers listen to addresses from the **general authorities** and women leaders of **auxiliaries**. A report by **auditors** is presented and the names of current general authorities are presented for the **sustaining** vote of the congregation. Through some 2,600 satellite dishes, radio and television broadcasts of conference proceedings reach a world-wide audience. In addition, the conference meetings can be accessed by personal computers. The proceedings are published in the *Ensign* each May and November and also in a series entitled *Conference Reports*.

CONFERENCES, STAKE. Gatherings of members in a **stake** that until 1979 occurred every three months. Then they were reduced to two per year. During a two-day period several meetings, or sessions, are held. **General authorities** and stake authorities are sustained by vote, and instructional and inspirational addresses are given. Visiting general authorities address the stake every other year. *See also* SUSTAINING.

CONFIRMATION. A sacred **ordinance** following **baptism**. Seated in a chair, the recipient has hands laid on his or her head by one or more individuals who hold the **Melchizedek Priesthood** authority. By the authority of that **priesthood** and in the name of **Jesus Christ**, the officiator confirms the recipient a member of the **Church of Jesus Christ of Latter-day Saints**, bestows the Holy Ghost, and adds additional words of blessing and counsel.

CONSTITUTION OF THE UNITED STATES. This foundational document is commonly referred to as "inspired." "And for this purpose have I established the Constitution of this land, by the hands of wise men whom I raised up unto this very purpose, and redeemed the land by the shedding of blood" (*Doctrine and Covenants* 101:80). The primary concern in the 19th century was protection in the free exercise of religion. From the public announcement of **polygamy** in 1852 through the next generation, Mormons claimed protection of the practice as part of their religion, but this claim was struck down by the Reynolds decision (1879), in which the Supreme Court made a distinction between protected belief and not-necessarily-protected action. An 1839 statement by **Joseph Smith** that the Constitution would be imperiled, hanging as it were by a thread, but would be saved by the elders of the Church, is at least partially explained by his frustration at the unwillingness or inability of the federal government to protect the persecuted Latter-day Saints. Individuals and groups within the Church have cited the statement at different points in time in explanation of their political views.

COOK, QUENTIN L. (1940–). Attorney, **seventy, general authority.** Born in Logan, Utah, to J. Vernon and Bernice Kimball Cook, he served as a missionary in England from 1960 to 1962. After returning to Logan, Cook married Mary Gaddie. They are the parents of three children. He earned a bachelor's degree in political science in 1963 from Utah State University and a J.D. from Stanford Law School in 1966. Living in Hillsborough, California, he worked for 27 years as a corporate attorney, serving as managing partner of Carr, McClellan, Ingersoll, Thompson, and Horn. He served as president and CEO of the California Healthcare System and for a time as vice chairman of Sutter Health System.

In the Church, Cook served as a member of the presidency and as **president** of the San Francisco Stake, a **regional representative**, and an **area authority seventy**. He served as a member of the Second **Quorum** of the Seventy and was called to the First Quorum of the Seventy on 5 April 1998 and to the Presidency of the Seventy on August 1, 2007. On the call of Henry B. Eyring to the **First Presidency**, Cook was called to the Quorum of the **Twelve Apostles** on October 6, 2007.

CORRELATION. In 1960, building on earlier efforts, the **First Presidency** started a review of Church programs. Three coordinating committees were created, one each for children, youth, and adults. A permanent Correlation Department was established in 1972. The purposes of correlation have been to assure that **auxiliaries** and other Church programs function to support the **family** rather than displace it; to maintain order among the different auxiliaries and programs; to assure that lesson materials and other publications of the Church are doctrinally sound; to simplify Church programs; and to bring all Church-sponsored activities under the direction of the **priesthood**.

The entire curriculum of the Church was reviewed, reorganized, and rewritten so that the **gospel** would be taught at the three stages of life—childhood, youth, and adulthood—in a coherent way, at the appropriate level, and with proper reinforcement and review. Care was exercised to avoid overemphasizing some points and leaving out others. This revised, systematic curriculum has been translated into many languages. Also shaped by correlation have been Church magazines and the weekly **family home evening**. Scheduled Church meetings were consolidated so that only one trip to church on Sunday would be required. In short, the ongoing correlation program attempts to assure that the Church will function with maximum efficiency in achieving its purposes. *See also* MISSION OF THE CHURCH.

COSTA, CLAUDIO ROBERTO MENDES (1949–). General authority. Born on 25 March 1949 in Santos, Brazil, Costa and his family lived in poverty. To supplement the family's meager income, he shined shoes on the street. When he was 12 years old, he met Mormon **missionaries** and took them home to meet his family. Most of the family joined the Church, but Claudio held out.

By age 17, he was manager of a shoe store. Then he left home to complete his military obligation, after which he moved to Sao Paulo. He worked in the mail room of a bank and rose to become manager. Accumulating a record of successful leadership, Costa successively became manager of five different companies.

At age 27, he was baptized a **member** of the Church. After studying at the Paulista Institute for Gems and Precious Metals, he became manager of a jewelry store. Three years later, at a significant reduction in pay, Costa accepted full-time employment with the Church as associate area manager over **seminaries** and **institutes**. From 1990 to 1993 he was **president** of the Brazil Manaus Mission. In April 1994, he was called to be a member of the Second **Quorum** of the **Seventy.** In 2001, he became a member of the First Quorum of the Seventy. He and his wife, Margareth, have four children.

COUNCIL OF FIFTY. *See* FIFTY, COUNCIL OF.

COUNCIL OF TWELVE APOSTLES. *See* TWELVE APOSTLES, QUORUM OF THE.

COUNSELOR. An important, easily overlooked position, or **calling**, in the functioning of the Church at all levels. Soon after the organization of the Church in 1830, **Joseph Smith** became **president** and had two **counselors**, the three making up the **First Presidency**. In time, the same kind of three-person executive body appeared throughout the Church organization. The **presiding bishop** has two counselors. Presidents of the general **Relief Society**, **Sunday School**, **Young Men**, **Young Women**, and **Primary** each have their two counselors. **Area** presidencies, **stake** presidencies, and **ward** bishoprics are similarly constituted, as are the presidencies of **priesthood quorums** and stake and ward **auxiliary** organizations. Over each of the 344-plus **missions** a president is assisted by two counselors, and the same is true of each **temple**.

At meetings of these three-person groups decisions are made. Although the counselors give advice, their role is not thus limited. The counselors function as sounding boards and sources of information. They also lighten the load of the president or bishop by taking on specific responsibilities assigned to them. Counselors accumulate training and experience. Many who are called to the position of bishop or president, including women in Primary, Young Women, and Relief Society, served previously as counselors.

COVEY, STEPHEN R. (1932–). Popular lecturer, author, business consultant. Born on 24 October 1932 in Salt Lake City, Utah, Covey earned a B.S. in business administration from the University of Utah, a master's degree in business administration from Harvard, and a doctor's degree from **BYU**. From teaching business management and organizational behavior, Covey expanded his scope through lectures, training programs, and consulting for private businesses. In 1997 he organized the Franklin-Covey Company, a worldwide management consulting firm. He is the author of several best-selling books, including *Seven Habits of Highly Effective People* and *First Things First*.

An active member of the Church, Covey has served as **bishop, mission president**, and **regional representative**. He wrote *Spiritual Roots of Human Relations* and *The Divine Center*. In 1994 he received the International Entrepreneur of the Year award. *Time Magazine* named him one of 25 most influential Americans. In 2003 he received the National Fatherhood Award. He is on the board of directors of the Points of Light Foundation, which mobilizes volunteers in many communities. He and his wife, Sandra, have nine children.

COWDERY, OLIVER (1806–1850). Attorney, **general authority,** one of the **witnesses of the** *Book of Mormon*. Born at Wells, Vermont, on 3 October 1806, Cowdery remained there and received basic education. In 1826 he moved to New York to join his older brothers. He took a job as a schoolteacher in 1829. Boarding with the parents of **Joseph Smith,** Cowdery found out about the translation of metal plates and, after receiving a **revelation,** worked as scribe and copyist in 1829–1830. Cowdery testified of several miraculous experiences: the appearance of John the Baptist to restore the **Aaronic Priesthood;** the appearance of Peter, James, and John to restore the **Melchizedek Priesthood;** and being one of the witnesses of the *Book of Mormon*. His testimony is printed in all editions of the book. At the Church's organization in 1830, Cowdery was called as "second **elder."** When a presidency was organized, he became an associate **president.** He also had the title of Church recorder in 1830–1831 and 1835–1837. He assisted in preparing some of the early revelations for printing and wrote a series of letters that remain a basic primary source.

In 1838 Cowdery joined others in disputing some of the Church's organizational, economic, and political policies. He was **excommunicated** along with some other dissidents. For 10 years he was out of the Church, practicing law in Kirtland, Ohio, before moving to Tiffin, Ohio, in 1840. In 1847 he moved to Wisconsin. Despite a good reputation in the community, he was defeated in a bid for the state legislature. In 1848 he rejoined the Church at Council Bluffs, Iowa, reaffirming his earlier testimonies. Failing in health and short of funds, he was unable to proceed directly to Utah but remained near relatives in Richmond, Missouri. There he died on 3 March 1850 at age 43.

COWLEY, MATTHEW (1897–1953). General authority, missionary to the **Polynesians.** Born 2 August 1897 at Preston, Idaho, the son of Apostle Matthias Cowley, who soon moved his family to Salt Lake City, Utah, Matthew left on a mission to the New Zealand

Maoris at age 17. During his five years there he learned the language, preached, translated **scriptures**, and developed a great love for the people.

After graduating from the University of Utah, Cowley attended law school at George Washington University. He married Elva Taylor in 1922 and worked in the office of Utah senator **Reed Smoot**. He practiced law in Salt Lake City, serving twice as county attorney.

In 1938 he was called to be mission **president** in New Zealand. Beloved by the Maori people as *Tumuaki*, Cowley knew them by name and often stayed in their homes. When the other American missionaries returned to the United States because of World War II, he remained in order to look after the Church members in New Zealand. In all, this mission lasted nearly eight years.

In 1945 Cowley was called to the **Quorum** of the **Twelve Apostles**. The next year he was made president of the Church's Pacific missions. Traveling by air, he visited not only New Zealand but also Samoa, Tonga, the Cook Islands, and Hawaii. In 1949 he also visited Japan and China, holding conferences and helping establish the Church there. A down-to-earth man who related easily to people, Cowley was a favorite speaker wherever he went. He died on 13 December 1953.

CREATION. In the general sense that they believe the world is not a product of chance but of deliberate creation by God, Mormons are creationists. But they do not insist on a limited time frame for the process, regarding the "days" spoken of in Genesis as creative periods of indefinite length. Nor do they consider creation to be ex nihilo, the bringing of the world into existence from nothing. Rather, reasoned **Joseph Smith** on the basis of the Hebrew verb, creation could mean causing the world to come into existence by assembling or organizing existing material elements into a new combination. The creation of humans could likewise mean the combining of physical bodies with an immortal spirit; the individual spirit was not created on earth but had existed in a pre-mortal state. As far as earth and the mortal phase of existence are concerned, the emphasis is not on the imperfectly understood process but on the fact of God's intentionality and divine purpose. *See also* PLAN OF SALVATION.

CROSS. The symbol found throughout the Christian world is not used in Mormon worship or architecture. President **Gordon B. Hinckley** explained that "the cross is the symbol of the dying Christ, while our message is a declaration of the living Christ." Absence of the cross among Mormons by no means signifies denial of the atoning sacrifice of Jesus Christ through the suffering that began in Gethsemane and was completed on Golgotha.

CULT. Term used by some sociologists of religion to describe churches not part of "historical" or "orthodox" **Catholicism** or **Protestantism** or that reject all or some of the historic Christian creeds. Although used dispassionately by Max Weber and others, the term is often used as a term of disparagement, even contempt, by those who see themselves as superior to upstart religions. Recognizing the unfortunate polemical uses of the term, some recent scholars have preferred the term *new religious movements* to describe groups of relatively recent origin. Objecting to being defamed by avowed enemies or to being excluded from **Christianity**, some Mormon defenders have pointed out inconsistencies in usage of the term and have argued that primitive **Christianity** itself possessed all the supposed criteria of a cult.

– D –

DAHLQUIST, CHARLES W., II (1947–). Attorney, Church leader. Born on 5 August 1947, he grew up in Boise, Idaho, earned a bachelor's degree from **BYU** in 1971, and received a juris doctorate from the University of Utah in 1974. He served as scoutmaster, **ward Young Men** president, branch **president**, **high councilman**, **stake** president, and president of the Germany Hamburg Mission. Winner of the Silver Beaver Award, he served on the executive board of the **Boy Scouts** of America. In 2004 he became general president of Young Men. He and his wife, Zella, have five daughters.

DANCE. Unlike some religions of a Puritan or Pietist tradition, Mormons have welcomed dancing as a legitimate form of recreation, even worship. Crossing the plains during the **exodus** from Illinois, they would often rejuvenate themselves around the campfire in the evening by getting out the fiddles and kicking up their heels in reels and schottisches. In the West every community found that dances provided necessary recreational relief.

As new dance fashions were introduced, they were often perceived as suggestive or improper. Thus at social events sponsored by the Church, leaders did not welcome the new dance styles, starting with the waltz in the late 19th century and continuing through the foxtrot and, after the middle of the 20th century, the jitterbug, swing, the twist, and various styles associated with rock and roll. At first the new dance step was forbidden. Then it was often gradually accepted as long as certain guidelines were followed. Adult leaders supervising social events did not wish to encourage behavior that seemed tasteless or sexually provocative. At the same time they realized that a strict exclusion of current dance steps would render their sponsored activities unpopular among young people.

Throughout the Mormon communities of the West and in **ward** and **stake** recreational activities, social dances—square, country, and ballroom dancing—have continued in the 20th century. For many years the **Young Men** and **Young Women** sponsored dance instruction and put on a giant dance festival in the University of Utah stadium. The church has also sponsored dance festivals in various regions.

DANITES. (1) A controversial paramilitary organization among the Mormons in 1838–1839 during the **Missouri Period**. Some Danites engaged in illegal activities against some Missourians, no doubt rationalized in their own minds as self-defense, a justified reaction to the persecution they were experiencing. To determine the extent of this violence requires sifting through contradictory accounts by participants in the events. On balance, however, it seems clear that Mormons suffered far more than they inflicted. It is unclear whether the group was initially sponsored by **Joseph Smith** or whether it was an unauthorized group started privately by Church member Sampson Avard. The evidence is mixed. Joseph Smith and others of the **First Presidency** knew of the organization and much of its activity. In the 1980s the discovery of early diaries and letters from the Missouri Period indicated the existence of a public Danite organization that assumed responsibility not only for the defense of the community but also for the construction of homes and providing supplies.

(2) In the **Illinois Period**, during the **exodus**, and during the subsequent **Utah Period**, the Danite organization did not exist, but the legend took on a life of its own in 50 or more novels portraying the Danites as sinister night riders who intimidated and brutalized ordinary people. John D. Lee or his editor, J. H. Beadle, used the term in *Lee's Confessions*, whether accurately or hyperbolically is not known. The various discussions helped produce a highly negative stereotype of Mormonism.

DEACON. At the age of 12, **worthy** male Church **members** are ordained deacons, an office in the **Aaronic Priesthood**. They perform such assignments as passing the emblems of the **sacrament** (called Eucharist in some other churches) to Church members, collecting **fast offering**, and assisting in the maintenance of the building and grounds. Deacons are grouped into **quorums** of 12 or fewer members. A **president**, two **counselors**, and a secretary are called. An adult adviser teaches and trains. This is the first level, or office, of priesthood service. At age 14 comes ordination to the office of a **teacher**.

DEAD SEA SCROLLS. Discovered in 1947, the Dead Sea Scrolls consist of materials produced and copied between 200 BC and 70 AD by the separatist Jewish settlement of Qumran. The community was annihilated by the Romans, but these records had been placed in sealed earthenware jars. Because of their great significance for understanding the Judeo-Christian world of the first century, Mormons have been interested in them. Some popular speakers and writers claimed striking parallels between the scrolls and Mormonism, but serious Mormon scholars, while interested, have been appropriately cautious. In 1996 the Provo International Conference on the Dead Sea Scrolls brought scholars from many different countries to **BYU**. **FARMS** produced a database on CD-ROM that contains a fully integrated and computerized collection of Dead Sea Scrolls texts.

DESERET. (1) A *Book of Mormon* term meaning "honeybee." (2) The first name chosen for the new territory Mormons hoped would become a state in the West. It was rejected in favor of Utah but remained attached to several businesses and activities.

DESERET ALPHABET. A phonetic alphabet promoted by **Brigham Young** and others in the 1850s. Partially modeled on Pitman shorthand by George Watt and Wilford Woodruff, the new alphabet was supposed to be easier to learn by foreigners. A few books were published in the Deseret Alphabet, but because of the prohibitive cost of putting all publications of the territory into this new type, it was abandoned.

DESERET BOOK COMPANY. A book company owned by the Church's Deseret Management Corporation. Its publishing arm publishes many of the writings about and for Mormons. Its retail arm, consisting of stores in several Western states, sells its own publications, works by other publishers, and general trade books. In 1999 it produced a compact disc called GospeLink (since updated), which included conference addresses, Church periodicals, and hundreds of books by **general authorities** and other writers. In 2006, Deseret Book announced separate mergers with Bookcraft and Seagull Books, publishers of books for the Mormon market.

DESERET INDUSTRIES. A thrift store and rehabilitation center. There are 49 such stores in the western United States. Any surplus clothing is shipped to the **Humanitarian Center**, where it is sorted and baled for sending where needed anywhere in the world.

DESERET MORNING NEWS. Daily newspaper owned by the Church and published in Salt Lake City, Utah. Started in 1850 and taking its name from the *Book of Mormon* word meaning "honeybee" that had been proposed as the name of the territory, the *Deseret News* was originally a weekly. Later a semiweekly edition was produced and from 1867 also a daily. Changing from an evening to a morning publication in 2001, the newspaper's name became *Deseret Morning News.* It contains the sections found in other newspapers: news, editorials, comics, and classifieds. It subscribes to national news services. Editorially it has expressed a conservative to moderate position with special attention to moral values. Of special interest is the section entitled *Church News*, published weekly in the Saturday edition, which enables readers to keep abreast of news of the Church worldwide. In 1997, a new nine-story building to house the editorial and production departments was dedicated in Salt Lake City.

DESERET TRUST COMPANY. Established in 1972, it assists donors by providing professional trust services, including administering trusts established for the benefit of the Church and its entities. Deseret Trust Company reports to the **presiding bishopric**.

DEW, SHERI L. (1953–). Editor, publisher, women's leader. Born on 21 November 1953 in Ulysses, Kansas, Dew graduated from **BYU** in 1977. After taking courses on the graduate level and working as an assistant editor with Bookcraft, she became editor and associate publisher of *This People* magazine. Employed by **Deseret Book Company** in 1988, she was associate editor, director of publishing, vice president of publishing, and finally from 2002 president. She wrote biographies of **Ezra Taft Benson** and **Gordon B. Hinckley** and other books. She was a **ward** and **stake Relief Society** president before becoming a member of the Relief Society general board. From 1907 to 2002, she was second **counselor** in the general Relief Society presidency.

DIALOGUE: A JOURNAL OF MORMON THOUGHT. Quarterly periodical started in 1966 by editors **G. Eugene England** and G. Wesley Johnson, then graduate students at Stanford University. *Dialogue* includes historical articles, essays, fiction, poetry, photography, art, book reviews, and letters to the editor. Not sponsored by the Church, *Dialogue* has served as an outlet for a range of opinion and scholarship about Mormonism.

DIDIER, CHARLES (1935–). General authority. Born on 5 October 1935 in Ixelles, Belgium, Didier became fluent in French, Flemish, English, Spanish, and German. After earning a bachelor's degree in economics at the University of Liege, he became an officer in the Belgian Air Force Reserve. A convert, he was baptized in 1957. Didier served as **president** of the France Switzerland Mission, **regional representative,** and **Sunday School** general president. In 1975 he became a member of the First **Quorum** of the **Seventy**, serving in its presidency from 1992 to 1995 and again from 2001 to the present. He and his wife, Lucie, have two children.

DISPENSATION. Mormons have a view of salvation history that includes a series of dispensations, efforts by God to reach humankind through the divine saving gospel. Each of these efforts, represented by such figures as Adam, Noah, Abraham, and Moses, was followed by a declension, or **apostasy**. This dispensational pattern includes certain corollaries. For instance, the gospel of **Jesus Christ** did not originate in first century Palestine but instead goes back to the creation. Indeed, it had been spelled out and agreed to in the pre-mortal existence. The mission of Jesus Christ on earth included the unique, infinite atonement for the sins of all humans, but the Church he then founded carried no guarantees of permanence. The warnings of a "falling away" were part of the teaching of both Jesus and the original apostles (2 Thess. 2:3). The Great Apostasy merely repeated a process that had occurred repeatedly before.

The restoration of the gospel by **Joseph Smith** marked the beginning of the final dispensation. The time had come in the divine economy for the final act, the dispensation of the fullness of times. By contrast, the Christian church of the first and second centuries represented the dispensation of the meridian of time. If the geographical sweep of Mormonism included all the world, at least in the intention to carry the message to all people, the temporal sweep is equally extensive. In a sense, therefore, it is incorrect to see Mormonism as a new religion less than two centuries old. In the view of its adherents, it is the "eternal gospel" restored to earth in the culminating phase of human history. *See also* PLAN OF SALVATION.

DISSENT. The Church has not insisted on the kind of uniformity that denies human nature, the natural process of growing in knowledge, or legitimate differences of opinion. Those who become **inactive** are not the objects of persecution. In due course many such individuals resume full participation. **Excommunication** is more often for behavior than belief.

But belief is not a matter of indifference, especially if one is teaching or influencing others. **J. Reuben Clark** declared that those who teach in Church classes must accept three things: the divinity of **Jesus Christ**; the divine calling of **Joseph Smith** as a **prophet**; and the legitimacy of the present head of the Church as the holder of **priesthood** keys. A teacher in the Church setting who rejects any of these fundamentals would be transgressing the limits of dissent. How, Clark asked, could a person presume to teach as a representative of the Church while undermining its basic position?

Anyone who wishes to pursue interests outside the curricula of the Church may of course do so in individual conversation, study groups, meetings of professional associations, or private reading and research. But members are cautioned to avoid acrimony, to maintain perspective, and to be patient. The meetings of the Church are intended to accomplish certain goals. They are not to be disrupted or turned into free-for-all discussions, with impassioned statements of private views on controversial historical and theological issues. "He that hath the spirit of contention is not of me, but is of the devil, who is the father of contention" (*Book of Mormon*, 3 Nephi 11:29). The unity sought within the Church derives from sustaining the **general authorities**, a feeling of love and mutual respect among members, a shared vision of life and its purposes, fidelity to covenants, and the access of all to the inspiration of the Holy Spirit. *See also* ACTIVITY; POLITICS; SCHISMS; SUCCESSION.

DISTRIBUTION CENTERS. Church-owned stores throughout the world that sell authorized literature, **temple** clothing, and curricular materials in many languages. Included are **scriptures**, lesson manuals, handbooks, forms, audiovisual materials, hymn books, and video and cassette types. Using order forms printed in the *Ensign*, people may order such material by mail. **Garments** may also be purchased at these centers.

DIVORCE. Although regarded as an evil, divorce is permitted by the Church. The rate of divorce among U.S. Mormons is slightly lower than in the general population. Those who marry in the **temple**, because of a shared religious commitment, have far fewer divorces. When temple marriages fail, the parties may, after a civil divorce, request from Church authorities a "cancellation of **sealing**," which has the effect of rescinding the relationship after death. *See also* MAR-RIAGE.

DOCTRINE AND COVENANTS. One of the four standard works or **scriptures** of the Church. Mostly made up of **revelations** issued by **Joseph Smith**, the work also contains prayers, letters, and official declarations by other **prophets**. Although the subject matter has to do with specific problems that arose in the early years, the principles are broadly applicable. The work is divided into 138 sections, equivalent to chapters, which in turn are subdivided into verses. Examples of the subject matter include: the atonement of **Jesus Christ** (section 19), **baptism** (section 22), **sabbath** day (section 59), the three levels or glories that await humans after death (section 76), **priesthood** (sections 84, 107, 121), the code of health known as the **Word of Wisdom** (section 89), the **manifesto** officially ending **polygamy** in 1890 (official declaration 1), and the granting in 1978 of the priesthood to all **worthy** males of whatever race (official declaration 2).

The revelations issued by Joseph Smith were first circulated in handwritten copies or printed in Church newspapers. As early as 1833 an effort was made to compile them into a work entitled ***Book of Commandments***, but its printing was stopped by mob action in Missouri and very few copies were salvaged. In 1835 the first edition of *Doctrine and Covenants* included the revelations from the ill-fated earlier work and others received since. The most important later editions, edited and expanded, appeared in 1844, 1876, 1921, and 1981. Twenty or more editions in translation have appeared.

DRUGS. In the period before the medical breakthroughs at the end of the 19th century, Mormons were not different from other people in seeking relief from suffering by means of patent medicines. Various home remedies were also used. With the improvements in medicine starting at the end of the 19th century and extending to the present, Mormons were glad to experience the benefits. This meant taking advantage of improved anesthetics and using prescription drugs according to the recommendation of their doctor. The substantial increase in medicines made available by drug companies and the willingness of doctors to prescribe these, including anti-inflammatory and mood-altering pills, affected the entire population. The **Word of Wisdom** bars the use of alcohol, tobacco, tea, and coffee. By extension, it would also preclude drug dependency. The "recreational" use of marijuana, LSD, rave, meth, and other "hard" drugs is considered foolish, self-destructive, and a callous mistreatment of one's physical body. To assist individuals in breaking such addictions, and those to alcohol and tobacco, **LDS Family Services** offers a 12-step program of recovery.

– E –

ECCLES, MARRINER STODDARD (1890–1977). Businessman, Federal Reserve official, treasury official. Marriner Eccles was the oldest child of David Eccles and his plural wife, Ellen Stoddard. Ellen and her children spent time in both Baker, Oregon, and Logan, Utah, because of her husband's business interests in both areas. Eccles briefly attended Brigham Young College; however, he left school in 1909. His father did not encourage his children to attend college for he found it unnecessary for a profitable business career. The following year, Eccles served a **mission** to Scotland. Two years later, he returned home, and his father died shortly thereafter. Not only did Eccles assume responsibility for his mother, brothers, and sister, but served as executor of his mother's share of his father's large estate. Although David Eccles' legal wife, Bertha Eccles, received the widow's share of his property, Marriner and the other children received a child's share. In 1913 Marriner married Maysie Campbell Young. Eccles worked as the president of the Hyrum State Bank and the director of the Thatcher Brothers Bank. In 1916 he organized the Eccles Investment Company, a holding firm, to manage his father's legacy left to the Logan Eccles family. By 1920, Eccles assumed control of various businesses, including Stoddard Lumber, Sego Milk, and Anderson Lumber. He served as president of Ogden First National Bank and of Utah Construction Company. During the Great Depression, Eccles recommended increased federal deficit spending to weather the financial difficulties. Impressed with the young man, President Roosevelt asked Eccles to join his staff as the assistant to Secretary of Treasury Henry Morgenthau Jr. The following year President Roosevelt nominated Eccles as the head of the Federal Reserve System. In this capacity, Eccles orchestrated two important pieces of legislation, the Federal Housing Act of 1934 and the Banking Act of 1935. Eventually, President Truman removed Eccles as the chair of the board of governors of the Federal Reserve System. Marriner spent much of his remaining years writing and speaking about world overpopulation and against the U.S. military intervention in Vietnam.

ECUMENICAL MOVEMENT. A loosely defined movement to bring Christian denominations together, ultimately, according to the hopes of some, to erase distinctions and restore the unity that existed prior to the Protestant Reformation or even prior to the "great schism" between the Eastern and Western church. By their own choice as well as that of the ecumenists, Mormons have not participated in meetings of the ecumenical movement. Similarly, Mormons do not belong to the National Council of Churches or the World Council of Churches. The basis for the **restoration** expressed in the **First Vision**—that the existing churches were wrong, meaning that they lacked authority and taught as doctrine the commandments of men—leaves little room for compromise on basic theological positions. On the other hand, Church leaders have recognized a broad commonality among people of faith, as opposed to secularists. Friendships have been formed across denominational lines, and mutual good wishes have been expressed. In disaster relief and different forms of humanitarian aid the Church has worked effectively with others.

EDUCATION. Although often limited by poverty and practical exigencies, the Church from its beginning advocated the pursuit of knowledge both formally through schooling and informally through personal effort. Literacy is essential for reading the **scriptures**. To be ignorant and uninformed is to be handicapped if not disqualified as a citizen, a parent, and a **missionary**. During the **Illinois Period**, in addition to primary schools operated by individual teachers, Church leaders at Nauvoo planned to establish a university but their efforts were derailed by **persecution** and the **exodus**.

In the Great Basin, the schooling of children began almost immediately and expanded through public and private primary schools. Thousands of students learned the rudiments, the three Rs, and other subjects as well. The **Sunday School** mainly taught religion, including basic morality and the scriptures, but through its periodical, *The Juvenile Instructor*, also expanded awareness of the natural world, geography, and literary and historical figures. Compulsory education was not yet standard in America, and most students stopped attending school after a few years. To provide opportunity for a high school education, the Church began establishing "academies" in the 1870s. Eventually there were academies throughout the Mountain West and in the colonies in Canada and Mexico. With the advent of compulsory public schooling, the Church-sponsored academies were closed, turned over to the state, or developed into institutions of higher learning.

In the 20th century, Church schools, essentially high schools, were established in New Zealand, Tonga, Samoa, Mexico, and several South American countries. As **membership** continued to increase, these were scaled back or closed. Young people were encouraged to obtain an education through public schools. To provide basic skills and open doors of opportunity, the **Relief Society** sponsored a literacy program.

On the level of higher education the Church operates **BYU, BYU–Idaho, BYU–Hawaii**, and **LDS Business College**. Students from throughout the United States and from many other countries attend these institutions. However, these institutions cannot accommodate all Latter-day Saint college students and cannot accept all those who apply for admission. To supplement public schools and universities the Church provides **seminaries** and **institutes of religion** where feasible.

EDUCATION WEEK. Each year in August thousands of people gather at **BYU** for a week of educational and religious lectures by prominent speakers, including some **general authorities**. Classes are offered in self-improvement, **family** relations, religious education, history, science, youth interests, health, and literature. Originally called Leadership Week, the first annual meeting, intended for those holding leadership positions in the Church, took place in the winter of 1922 with 2,046 in attendance. Education Week was soon opened up to all interested members 14 years of age and older. Except for when it was canceled during and immediately after World War II, attendance has steadily increased each year. The 1999 Education Week hosted 29,775 registrants. Selected lectures were telecast over the Church satellite system. In 1998, **Ricks College** began sponsoring its own Education Week, starting with 300 classes offered by 45 instructors to about 2,000 people.

EIGHT WITNESSES. *See* WITNESSES OF THE *BOOK OF MORMON.*

ELDER. (1) An office in the **Melchizedek Priesthood**. Male Church members who pass standards of **worthiness** are ordained elders at the age of 18. Adult male converts are ordained as soon as possible after their **baptism**. **Elders** possess authority to perform all the functions of the lesser **Aaronic Priesthood**, including baptism and administering the **sacrament**. In addition, they have the necessary authority to confer the gift of the Holy Ghost in the **ordinance** of **confirmation**. Elders are organized into **quorums** of as many as 96 people with a **president**, two **counselors**, and a secretary. They meet weekly for instruction and the planning and reporting of service projects.

(2) A form of address for male missionaries and for **general authorities** except members of the **First Presidency** and **Presiding Bishopric**.

EMERITUS. Status of **general authorities**, specifically the First **Quorum** of the **Seventy**, who have been honorably released at the age of 70. Members of the Second Quorum of the Seventy serve for a five-year term and are then released, but are not considered to have emeritus status. Members of the **First Presidency** and Quorum of the **Twelve Apostles** have lifetime tenure.

EMPLOYMENT RESOURCE CENTERS. Devoted to assisting the unemployed, underemployed, self-employed, and unskilled, local centers help patrons to set goals, obtain practical training, prepare résumés, and master interview skills. Computer and Internet connections assist in pursuing job leads. For the self-employed, workshops are provided. The centers work in close cooperation with the Perpetual Education Fund in countries where it is established. In 2006, 286 centers operated in more than 50 countries. The previous year the centers helped more than 222,000 people.

ENDOWMENT. *See* TEMPLES.

ENGLAND, G. EUGENE, JR. (1933–2001). Essayist, poet, founder of private Mormon organizations and periodicals. Born in Logan, Utah, on 22 July 1933, Eugene England received the usual primary and secondary education. He married Charlotte Hawkins, and the two of them served as **missionaries** in Samoa from 1954 to 1956. They went on to have six children.

After graduating from the University of Utah in 1958, England attended MIT for one year and then entered the graduate program in English at Stanford University, receiving his M.A. in 1969 and a Ph.D. in 1974. His professional career has taken him to St. Olaf College in Minnesota and, in 1977, to **BYU**, where he won several coveted teaching awards. After retirement, he continued teaching at Utah Valley State College.

Along with G. Wesley Johnson, England was founding editor of *Dialogue: A Journal of Mormon Thought* in 1965. He promoted Mormon creative writing through his own poetry and essays, critical reviews and anthologies, and the **AML**, which he cofounded in 1977. He served as **counselor** in four bishoprics, and as branch **president**, **bishop**, and **high councilor**.

ENSIGN. Official magazine of the Church, published monthly beginning in January 1971. The *Ensign* includes editorials, nonfiction articles in history and doctrine, fiction, poetry, news of events in the Church, and even some humor. Especially important are the May and November issues, which publish the proceedings of the April and October **general conference**.

ESPECIALLY FOR YOUTH. A summer program, started in 1976 at the **BYU** campus, where 172 young people ages 14 to 18 gather. Directed by 15 counselors, they participate in recreational, cultural, and devotional activities. In 2004 1,400 participants met. The program has expanded to 34 states, Canada, the United Kingdom, and Ireland. Selected speakers from these sessions tour other **stakes** by request.

EUROPE. The first preaching of Mormonism in Europe began with the mission to Great Britain in 1837. The *Millennial Star*, which started publication in 1840, was filled with the details of conversion and emigration, first to Nauvoo, Illinois, then to the Great Basin in the West. By the middle of the 19th century, **missionaries** were proselytizing in various parts of the continent. Except for scattered individual conversions, the area of success on the continent was limited to Scandinavia. By 1900, close to 100,000 European Mormons had emigrated.

In the 20th century, proselytizing was extended to France, the Netherlands, and Germany. A preliminary effort leading to a few converts was made in Czechoslovakia. However, all European missionary efforts were interrupted by World War II. When missionaries returned to Europe after the war, they looked up the scattered surviving **members** and added to their number by conversions. Success increased in the 1960s and after. Where numbers were sufficient, **wards** and **stakes** were established, local members were called to positions of responsibility, and **temples** were constructed. It was a generation of growth and maturation. Long kept out of Eastern Europe by the conditions of the cold war, Mormon missionaries began to gain access during the 1980s. Missions have been established in the Czech Republic, Poland, states of the former Yugoslavia, Bulgaria, Romania, Greece, the Ukraine, Armenia, and Russia. At the end of 2005 membership for the different European countries stood as follows:

Country	Members	Stakes	Wards	Temples
Armenia	2,083			
Austria	4,138	2	13	
Belgium	6,267	2	11	
Bulgaria	2,084			
Czech Republic	1,981			
Finland	4,500	2	15	1
France	33,200	9	60	
Germany	37,149	14	91	2
Greece	631			
Hungary	4,147			
Iceland	225			
Italy	21,791	4	26	

Netherlands	8,286	3	19	1
Norway	4,134	1	7	
Poland	1,531			
Portugal	37,812	6	35	
Romania	2,483			
Russia	18,785			
Spain	39,784	9	56	1
Sweden	8,862	4	24	1
Switzerland	7,699	4	23	1
UK	181,872	46	284	2
Ukraine	9,951			

Although the percentage growth in Europe was not so rapid as in **South America** or **Asia**, it has been steady. Second- and third-generation Mormon families in Europe have demonstrated tenacity. Many young members study in **seminary** and **institute of religion** classes, after which they serve full-time missions. In 2003 the church began the establishment of outreach centers at institutes of religion in Western Europe to assist in reactivation and fellowshipping young single adults. Experienced leadership has been built up. **General authorities** of European origin have included F. Enzio Busche, Dieter F. Uchtdorf, and Erich W. Kopischke (Germany); Charles A. Didier (Belgium); Derek A. Cuthbert (England); Jacob de Jager (Netherlands); and Hans B. Ringger (Switzerland).

EVANS, RICHARD LOUIS (1906–1971). Radio announcer, civic leader, **general authority**. Born on 23 March 1906 in Salt Lake City, Utah, Evans served as a **missionary** to England as a young man and gained experience as an assistant editor of the *Millennial Star*. In 1928 he became an announcer for KSL radio in Salt Lake City and the following year began announcing for the weekly broadcast of the **Mormon Tabernacle Choir**. "Once more we welcome you within these walls, with music and the spoken word, from the Crossroads of the West"; "May peace be with you, this day and always"—such expressions became readily recognized throughout the country. Evans's short talks, or "sermonettes," were widely appreciated. Many of them were published in books, including *This Day and Always*. He also wrote a newspaper column for King Features Syndicate.

In 1937 Evans began a long career as managing editor and later senior editor of the *Improvement Era*. The next year, only 32 years old, he became a **general authority** as one of the **presidents** of the First Council of **Seventy**. In 1947 he was appointed director of **Temple Square**. In 1953, at age 47, he became one of the **twelve apostles**. He was president of the Utah Alumni Association, president of the Knife and Fork Club, and, in 1949, president of the Salt Lake Rotary Club. He later became president of Rotary International. Evans died in 1971 at the age of 65.

EXCOMMUNICATION. A formal action that deprives a person of Church membership. Careful procedures are described in the *General Handbook of Instructions*. Grounds for such an action vary from flagrant moral infractions to the deliberate teaching of false doctrine or belonging to **apostate** groups. Exercising considerable latitude in addressing such problems, **bishops** also have the option of imposing lesser penalties of disfellowshipment or a temporary suspension of some privileges. Previously called church courts, such procedures are currently called disciplinary councils. **Melchizedek Priesthood** holders may be excommunicated only by a disciplinary council convened by a **stake president**. When excommunication proceedings are instituted, the person charged is allowed the opportunity for a hearing, records are kept, and appeals are allowed. These proceedings are regarded as confidential. While attempting to maintain the integrity of the Church and its purposes, bishops are urged to be solicitous and kind in order, where possible, to bring the offender back into fully participating membership. *See also* DISSENT.

EXODUS. After the **prophet Joseph Smith** was assassinated in June 1844, most Mormons accepted the leadership of **Brigham Young** and the **Quorum** of the **Twelve Apostles** in August. The attempt to remain in Nauvoo, Illinois, signaled by continued in-migration and construction on the **temple**, had to be given up under the insistent and increasingly violent pressure of the **anti-Mormons**. In February 1846 the wagons started moving out from the city, across the Mississippi River, and to the plains of Iowa. By fall, only a few inhabitants remained in Nauvoo.

Under Brigham Young's direction, leaders organized these 10,000 or so refugees into companies; provided protection and nourishment during whatever period of time they would be en route; determined a place of ultimate settlement; got the people to that destination in good order; and established them there in such a way that an ugly competition for property claims would be avoided. Of some help was the recruitment of 500 males into the **Mormon Battalion**, which, although it seemed oppressive to many at the time, did get one group to the West under government direction and provided a payroll to aid the others.

By the late fall of 1846 and early winter of 1847, Mormons were strung out in various encampments throughout Iowa. Along the banks of the Missouri River near present-day Omaha, Nebraska, and Council Bluffs, Iowa, they built temporary settlements for the winter, which remained inhabited for several years as a mustering and jumping-off place for the westward migrants. On 14 January 1847 Brigham Young issued a set of instructions called "The Word and Will of the Lord" (*Doctrine and Covenants*, section 136). Organized into companies, the people were to cooperate in helping one another, raising crops, building houses, and sending a company of **pioneers** westward to locate a place of settlement and put in crops.

The pioneer company of 143 men, 3 women, and 2 children set out in mid-April. In their number were Young and seven other apostles. A detailed account of the journey was kept by diarists William Clayton and Thomas Bullock, carefully recording the distance traveled each day, as calculated by a mechanical odometer constructed for the purpose and attached to a wagon wheel. Their destination was already known, Young and his colleagues having studied various accounts and maps made by mountain men and explorers, including John C. Frémont. They regarded this exodus as the fulfillment of earlier plans and prophecies of Joseph Smith. One effort to dissuade them was reportedly made by Jim Bridger. Another was made by **Samuel Brannan**, who came from California in a vain effort to persuade Young to settle there.

On 21 July advance scouts entered the Salt Lake Valley, and the party began plowing and planting on 23 July. Brigham Young entered with the remainder of the company on 24 July. He pronounced it as indeed the right place. For the next few weeks members of the advance company explored, surveyed, established simple shelters, coaxed water from the stream onto the dry soil, and planted crops. Then many returned eastward to get their families. This original exodus consisted of more than just one small exploring company. Joining the advance company in a kind of convergence were Mississippi converts, one contingent that had been detached from the Mormon Battalion because of poor health, and soon from California other discharged soldiers from the battalion. Behind the advance company other groups had been moving westward and over several weeks, company after company entered the Valley. By December 1847 something close to 2,000 were trying to establish themselves in their promised land.

By the 1850 census 11,380 people inhabited Great Salt Lake City, Utah, and the small settlements in the immediate vicinity. Others making their way westward, or temporarily halted in Missouri, were still experiencing their own "exodus." The comparison with the children of Israel led by Moses from Egypt to their promised land could not be avoided. In January 1847 Brigham Young had a revelation and proclaimed, "I [God] am he who led the children of Israel out of the land of Egypt; and my arm is stretched out in the last days, to save my people Israel" (*Doctrine and Covenants* 136:22.) Although pioneering and **colonization** did not stop with the original westward thrust, the initial exodus had saved the destitute Mormons and established them in their land of refuge. *See also* ILLINOIS PERIOD; SUCCESSION; "THIS IS THE PLACE" MONUMENT.

EYRING, HENRY (1901–1981). Scientist. Born on 20 February 1901 of Mormon parents in Colonia Juarez, Mexico, Henry moved with his family to Arizona. Along with the usual rough and tumble of boyhood in rural America, Henry did well in his schooling, graduating from Gila Academy in Thatcher, Arizona. When he went off to attend the University of Arizona at Tucson on scholarship, as Eyring often recounted in later years, his father told him that his religion did not require him to believe anything untrue. Graduating with a bachelor's degree and completing a master's degree the following year, Eyring pursued his doctorate at the University of California at Berkeley, receiving a Ph.D. in 1927.

After a year as an instructor at the University of Wisconsin, a year in **Europe** working with Michael Polanyi and others, and a one-year lectureship at Berkeley, Eyring accepted an appointment at Princeton University. He advanced to the rank of full professor and became director of the Textile Research Institute. In 1946, he became professor of chemistry and dean of the graduate school at the University of Utah, his professional home for the remainder of his life. A prolific scholar, Eyring produced more than 350 publications, including four books. Professional associations included the American Chemical Society, of which he served as president, the National Science Board, and the American Association for the Advancement of Science. Recipient of the National Medal of Science, the Joseph Priestley Celebration Award, the Berzelins Gold Medal from the Swedish Academy of Science, and the Wolf Prize in Chemistry from the Wolf Foundation in Israel, Eyring also received honorary degrees from 15 different universities. One colleague listed the following as scientific disciplines to which Eyring was a significant contributor: mining engineering, metallurgy, ceramics, fuels, explosives, geology, plastics, fibers, lubricants, organic chemistry, molecular biology, analytical chemistry, radiation chemistry, electrolytic chemistry, quantum chemistry, and statistical mechanics. Perhaps his most basic discovery was the absolute rate theory of treating chemical reaction kinetics and other rate processes.

Always a devout member of the Church, Eyring served on the general board of the **Sunday School** for many years. In addition to articles in Church magazines, he wrote *The Faith of a Scientist* (1967). He and his wife, Mildred Bennion Eyring, had three sons: Edward M., Henry B., and Harden. Mildred died in 1969, and in 1971 Eyring married Winifred Brennan. Until nearly the end of his life he participated in an annual 50-yard dash with his graduate students.

EYRING, HENRY B. (1933–). General authority, second **counselor** in the **First Presidency**. Second son of the eminent scientist **Henry Eyring**, Henry B. Eyring was born on 31 May 1933 in Princeton, New Jersey. He received a bachelor's degree in physics from the University of Utah. After serving as an officer in the U.S. Air Force, he attended the Harvard Graduate School of Business, receiving his MBA and a doctorate in business administration. He married Kathleen Johnson. Accepting a position at the Stanford Graduate School of Business, he taught but also entered the business world as founder and director of a computer manufacturing company. In 1971, he was named president of **Ricks College**.

In the Church, Eyring served as **bishop**, **regional representative**, member of the **Sunday School** general board, and commissioner of the Church Educational System. In 1985, he became a general authority as first counselor in the **Presiding Bishopric**. In 1992 he became a member of the First **Quorum** of the **Seventy** and in 1995 a member of the Quorum of the **Twelve Apostles**. In October 2007 he was called as second counselor in the First Presidency. On 4 February 2007 he was called as first counselor to President Thomas S. Monson of the First Presidency.

– F –

FAMILY. In an age of family breakdown, Mormons are among those fighting to preserve the nuclear family as the best assurance of safety and fulfillment for individuals and the best protection against social disintegration. Not sealed off from the larger society, Mormons have their share of dysfunctional families, divorce, and other signs of tension. To combat these problems, principles are taught in all of the **auxiliary** organizations as well as **seminaries** and **institutes of religion.** Members are encouraged to participate in a weekly **family home evening.** Each **ward** provides support through **home teaching** and **visiting teaching.** In addition to whatever community assistance might be available, the resources of the **welfare program** and **LDS Family Services** assist the Church in strengthening its families.

As part of their belief in the **ordinances** of the **temple**, Mormons have faith that righteous families will endure beyond the grave. "Families can be together forever"—these words begin the chorus of one of their hymns. Such an eternal union of husband and wife, parents and children, is dependent on receiving the **sealing** ordinances of the temples either in this life or, if one has not had the opportunity, vicariously after death, and living in faithful obedience to the **commandments.**

Considering that strong families are a benefit to all of society, the Church sponsors public service announcements that have been widely used by radio and television stations. Nondenominational in application, these announcements stress principles such as spending time with children. On 23 September 1995 the **First Presidency** issued the proclamation on the family, reaffirming traditional values (see appendix 2). *See also* MARRIAGE.

FAMILY AND CHURCH HISTORY DEPARTMENT. In 2000 the Historical Department of the Church merged with the Family History Department of the Church to form the Family and Church History Department, in order to better serve the expanding membership of the Church.

Head of the Family and Church History Department is the Church historian and recorder. As has been true throughout most of the history of the Church, this individual is a **general authority**. His role is not that of a working research historian or genealogist but of administering and coordinating history-related activities.

Family History creates online products and seeks to deliver indexes and images to personal home computers or family history centers. Both the Family History Library and a division called Worldwide Support assist researchers directly and train local family history consultants. The Family History Library, in Salt Lake City, Utah, is one of the premier research libraries for genealogical research, with books and records and especially microfilm rolls of primary sources from all over the world.

Church History adopted a horizontal reorganization of its staff, resulting in the department-wide functions of collections development, preservation, and public programs being integrated across the traditional institutional boundaries of archives, library, and museum. A new 250,000-square-foot facility called the Church History Library will be completed in 2009 to provide state-of-the-art storage, preservation, and public research services for the ever-expanding historical collections of the Church.

A long-range project of Church History is the publication in approximately 30 volumes of the papers of **Joseph Smith**, edited and annotated according to professional standards. In addition to collecting diaries, oral histories, and local records from throughout the

Church, the department makes them available to researchers through organizing and cataloging; selective printed publication; compact discs of certain collections, including census and immigration records; and selective digitalized online publications. *See also* GENEALOGY.

FAMILY HISTORY. *See* GENEALOGY.

FAMILY HOME EVENING. A regularly scheduled time once a week in which families enjoy recreation and some form of instruction or spiritual enhancement. To some extent such activities occur naturally within families, but the urbanization and intensified pace of life in the 20th century has combined with evidence of **family** breakdown to increase concern among Church leaders. Building on earlier programs going back to the 1910s, the program as it now exists was instituted in 1965. Manuals were issued containing lessons and suggested activities. To assure time for holding family home evening, no Church meetings were scheduled on Monday. Responding to interest from others, the Church has publicized the family home evening program broadly and has readily shared its resource materials.

FAMILYSEARCH. Provider of **family** history and **genealogy** resources, FamilySearch.org, launched on 24 May 1999, allows free access to the Church's searchable database of 81 million names. More than 100,000 hits a day attest to the fact that people throughout the world utilize this resource. The long-range goal is to make images and indexes as widely available as possible.

FARNSWORTH, PHILO (1906–1971). Father of television. Born near Beaver, Utah, Farnsworth early showed an aptitude for mathematics and technology. As early as age 13, he won a national contest with an invention related to automobiles. Living in Idaho at the time, interested in electricity and radio, he drew an "image dissector" for his teacher, Justin Tolman. Tolman copied the drawings in his notebook, which later turned out to be crucial evidence in a battle over the television patent.

In 1921, the Farnsworths moved to Provo, Utah, where Philo attended **BYU**, married Elma "Pem" Gardner, and aroused the enthusiasm of a few collaborators for his television scheme. In 1926, he moved to San Francisco to work on the project. Overcoming obstacles one at a time, Farnsworth and his friends finally produced an electronically transmitted image. "In 1927 when I first saw a television image transmitted without any moving parts," he said, "I believe I felt the greatest thrill of my lifetime before or since, and I have had quite a lot of them."

When a Russian scientist, Vladimir Zworykin, showed up at the laboratory and claimed to represent Westinghouse, Farnsworth showed him everything. Later Zworykin, who actually worked for RCA, fought Farnsworth for the patent rights. Examining the evidence, including Tolman's earlier notebooks, the U.S. Patent Office upheld Farnsworth's claims. Farnsworth died on 11 March 1971. About 20 years later, his statue was placed in the rotunda of the nation's capitol, joining **Brigham Young**'s to represent the state of Utah.

FASTING. Abstaining from food and drink. Combined with **prayer**, fasting contributes to feeling close to God. Often people requesting special blessings or inspiration in making personal decisions will fast. In addition, **members** are urged to fast from two meals on the first Sunday of each month and to pay a generous **fast offering.** On this day a meeting is devoted to the expression of personal **testimony**.

FAST OFFERING. A donation to the Church on the first Sunday of each month, the equivalent of the meals one has abstained from. These funds are specifically designated for helping the poor and needy. Increased poverty and the expansion of the Church into areas of the world where many people live close to the subsistence level have increased the need for assistance. Church **president Spencer W. Kimball** urged members to donate not merely the cost of two meals but substantially more when possible. Unlike many relief programs, the fast offering program results in 100 percent of the donation going to the assistance of the needy.

FAUST, JAMES E. (1920–2007). Attorney, legislator, **general authority**. Born on 31 July 1920 in Delta, Utah, James E. Faust attended school in Salt Lake City, Utah. He served as a **missionary** in Brazil and afterwards entered the U.S. Air Force, reaching the rank of first lieutenant. After World War II, Faust entered law school at the University of Utah and received the J.D. degree in 1948. As a lawyer, he was president of the Utah Bar Association in 1962–1963. He was elected to the state legislature as a Democrat from 1949 to 1951. President John F. Kennedy appointed him to the Lawyers Committee for Civil Rights and Racial Unrest.

In the Church he served as **bishop**, **high councilor**, **stake** president, and **regional representative**. In 1972 he became an **assistant to the twelve** and **area** supervisor in **South America**. In 1976 he was named one of the presidency of the First **Quorum** of the **Seventy**, and in 1978 became a member of the Quorum of the **Twelve Apostles**. As **president** of the International Mission, with responsibility for members and **investigators** in parts of the world without organized missions, he traveled widely, displaying an ability to relate to people of all races and nationalities. In 1995 he became second **counselor** in the **First Presidency**. He and his wife, Ruth, had five children.

FEMINISM. As the term was understood in the 19th century, Mormons were feminists. Mormon women were among the first to vote and participated in the national movement for female suffrage. Basic spiritual equality between women and men has always been assumed: both men and women may achieve salvation in the fullest sense of the word. In the **Relief Society** and other **auxiliary** organizations women exercised leadership roles from nearly the beginning of the Church.

The current women's liberation movement has led to some complications. Some militant feminists have disparaged the role of wife and mother, some going so far as to advocate abolition or restructuring of the **family**. While a few Mormon women were caught up in the rhetoric of national and world feminism in its extreme form, other Mormon feminists, less extreme, have expressed concern about such issues as education and employment, child care, and male abuse of power. Church leaders, including the women leaders in the Relief Society, try to show sensitivity to legitimate concerns. That female education and professional accomplishment are valued is evident from the women selected to serve in leadership positions. Several thousand young women serve as full-time **missionaries.** At the same time, Church leaders have insisted on the importance of the family. Rather than putting males and females into opposition, they pursue a partnership on the general Church level, in the **stakes** and **wards** and in the family. *See also* WOMEN, ROLES OF.

FIFTY, COUNCIL OF. A council formed by **Joseph Smith** in the spring of 1844. At its origin, this body appeared to be intended as the basis for establishing the political Kingdom of God on earth as part of the onset of the **millennium.** Three nonmembers of the Church were included. In practical terms the fifty (whose membership overlapped in part with the **Quorum** of the **Twelve Apostles**) helped organize Joseph Smith's presidential campaign in 1844, supervised the migration to the West, and in territorial Utah met at infrequent intervals. Since it was not an essential body of government in church or state, it lapsed.

FIRESIDE SERVICE. A Church-sponsored meeting outside the regular scheduled meetings of the Church, sometimes held in private homes, more often in a **ward** meetinghouse or **stake** center. Typically, all the youth of a stake are invited to hear a musical presentation or a talk that will be of special interest to them. There is greater latitude in choice of subject matter than in a **sacrament** meeting.

FIRST PRESIDENCY. The **president** of the Church and his two **counselors.** Upon the death of the president, the First Presidency is dissolved, the two counselors resuming their place in the **Quorum** of the **Twelve Apostles.** Historically, the First Presidency was organized in 1832 with **Joseph Smith** as president. Although on different occasions additional counselors, or assistants, were added to the First Presidency, the standard pattern was that of three individuals: the president and two counselors. Counselors who have been especially influential in the First Presidency, not including those who became president of the Church, are **Sidney Rigdon, Hyrum Smith, George Q. Cannon, J. Reuben Clark, Hugh B. Brown, N. Eldon Tanner, Thomas S. Monson,** and **James E. Faust.** As with all bishoprics and presidencies, the First Presidency functions as a unit, and the counselors, besides acting as advisers, perform many of the necessary functions.

FIRST PRINCIPLES. Faith in **Jesus Christ**, **repentance**, **baptism**, and laying on of hands for the gift of the Holy Ghost. Based on Acts 2:37–38, with the assumption of faith on the part of those addressed, these are the basics taught throughout the Mormon **scriptures**. Although faith is given priority, this is not a salvation-by-faith-alone doctrine. Nor is it an approach to salvation that disparages organized religion, for the **ordinances** of baptism and **confirmation** require the authority of **priesthood.** Although not usually listed as one of the first principles, enduring to the end is implicitly the fifth principle. Without continued faithfulness, the whole process is frustrated. The first principles and ordinances are not the whole of the **gospel.** To them are added other covenants and ordinances, such as those of the **temples.** But the first principles are foundational. They are never superseded. One's entire life is to be one of faith, repentance, and enduring. The commitments made at baptism and confirmation are renewed by regularly partaking of the **sacrament** throughout life.

FIRST VISION. The first **revelation** received by **Joseph Smith**. The setting was upper New York State, where competition between the different Christian denominations was intense. Some members of the Smith family, living just outside Palmyra, became Presbyterians. Young Joseph, not yet 15, was attracted to the Methodists but was confused by the "war of words and tumult of opinions" (*Pearl of Great Price*, Joseph Smith History 1:10). A reading of James 1:5 prompted him to take his dilemma directly to God in prayer, which he did in the spring of 1820. After an evil power tried to stop his effort, a great vision came: a pillar of light and two divine beings, one of them referring to the other as his son. Joseph was told that his sins were forgiven, that he should join none of the existing churches, and that in the future, if faithful, he might be the means of bringing back the true Christian faith. Local ministers reacted to Joseph's experience with ridicule and **persecution.** Such things may have happened in the days of the **Bible,** they said, but not now.

In the 20th century, some historians claimed there was no evidence of any religious revivals in Palmyra, New York, in the year 1820, but historians Milton Backman and D. Michael Quinn have discovered several examples of such activity in the immediate area, as Joseph said. For Mormons the First Vision is God's declaration, unequivocally and utterly authoritative, of the results of the Great **Apostasy** and the need for a **restoration**. Joseph Smith was only 14 years of age at the time. Not for another 10 years, in 1830, would the time be ripe to establish the Church.

FOLKLORE. Like all peoples, Mormons convey stories orally. Many of the stories told and passed on from generation to generation have to do with miracles of healing or dreams. The modernization associated with the 20th century has perhaps modified Mormon popular storytelling, but it still occurs in the form of "urban folklore." One recurring tale in the Mormon oral tradition recounts appearances of "the Three Nephites," characters from the *Book of Mormon* who were promised that they could remain on earth and not taste of death. Prominent in the study of Mormon folklore have been folklorists Hector Lee, Austin and Alta Fife, Thomas E. Cheney, and **William A. Wilson**. Others, such as Jan Harold Brunvaand, have supervised collecting and published articles on Mormon folklore.

FORMS OF ADDRESS. In any culture, one of the usages that has to be learned is the proper forms of address. For example, do you address the monarch as "King" or "Your Majesty"? Is the local parish priest properly addressed as "Reverend" or "Father"? Mormons are no exception, having their own standard usage. The following is descriptive—not an attempt to lay down rules, in other words, but to describe how Mormons do it.

The most widely used titles are "Brother" and "Sister," used for adult Church members of the male and female gender, respectively. Children are not addressed in this way, nor are nonmembers. Although occasionally heard in isolation, these words usually accompany the last name, as "Brother Smith" or "Sister Martinez."

A **bishop** and two **counselors** preside over a **ward**. The bishop is referred to as "Bishop Jones," for example, or often simply "Bishop," while the counselors are "Brother Taylor" or "Brother Gonzales." Among the **general authorities** there is a **presiding bishop**. He is known as "Bishop Burton." His counselors are also addressed as "Bishop."

The term *president* applies most importantly to the president of the Church, who is properly addressed or referred to as President **Gordon B. Hinckley** or President Hinckley. His two counselors have the same title, being addressed as President Monson or President Faust. Note that the term *bishop* is not attached to the counselors in a **ward** bishopric, but the term *president* is used for counselors in **stake** presidencies and the counselors in the First Presidency.

There are many presidents in the Church. On the stake level the presiding triumvirate is a stake presidency, all three of whom are addressed and referred to as "President." There are also presidents of general, stake, and ward **auxiliary** organizations, and of the many **priesthood quorums** throughout the Church. While it is not improper to address all of these by the title of president, it is common usage to employ the terms *Brother* or *Sister*.

Another term often used is **elder**. All worthy male members are ordained to the office of elder in the **Melchizedek Priesthood** at the age of 18 or 19. Yet all such elders are not usually addressed by this title. Those properly so addressed are all general authorities, with the exception of those in the **First Presidency** and **Presiding Bishopric,** and all male **missionaries** during their two-year missions. Female missionaries are "Sister," as in Sister Lambson.

Examples of well-meant but awkward and improper usage include the following: Prophet Hinckley (although sustained as "prophet, seer, revelator" and referred to in the third person as "the prophet," the term is not used as a form of address); Apostle Oaks (although those in the **Quorum** of the **Twelve Apostles** are apostles, the term is not used as a form of address); and Mr. Hinckley (which comes across as lacking in respect). First names are used by Mormons like everyone else, but in formal settings, as **conferences** or other Church meetings, even individuals who are close friends use the appropriate titles.

FOUNDATION FOR ANCIENT RESEARCH AND MORMON STUDIES (FARMS). An independent research and service organization established in 1979 as a nonprofit, tax-exempt, educational corporation. Dedicated to scholarly research having to do with the history, culture, language, geography, politics, and law of the ***Book of Mormon*** and other ancient **scriptures**, FARMS published a widely circulated newsletter, *FARMS Review of Books*, a semiannual *Journal of* Book of Mormon *Studies*, and other books and research papers. In 1999 FARMS established the Center for the Preservation of Ancient Texts (CPAT), which sponsored an electronic **Dead Sea Scrolls** database and a series of Islamic texts. In 2006, FARMS was brought under the umbrella of the **Neal A. Maxwell Institute for Religious Scholarship**.

THE FRIEND. A monthly magazine published for the children of the Church since 1971. In addition to stories and puzzles, *The Friend* publishes accounts of children's activities and achievements from throughout the Church. Instruction about leaders, history, and religious teachings is pitched at a simple level. Its predecessor magazine for children was entitled *The Children's Friend*.

FUNDAMENTALISTS. (1) In general, those who are seeking to return to the "fundamentals" of something, as with the **Protestant** fundamentalists of the early 20th century. Martin Marty and other scholars have applied the term more widely as they study "fundamentalisms" not only in **Christianity** but also in Islam and other world religions. Just how Mormonism fits into this broad terminology is not simply stated, for in their own conception Mormons have returned to the basics of primitive Christianity, while in the eyes of their detractors they have deviated from the norms of historic Christianity.

(2) Within the context of Mormon history, fundamentalists, according to current usage, are those who still cling to the practice of **polygamy**, and in some cases, versions of the **United Order**. They are **excommunicated** from the Church when discovered. Some have never been members of the Church. The use of the term *Mormon* to refer to these groups is frequently misleading because the uninformed often confuse them with members of the Church of Jesus Christ of Latter-day Saints. The Church office of public affairs, attempting to convey to the reality of what the Church teaches and practices, deplores the use of the term *Mormon fundamentalists*, as it so readily leads to misunderstanding.

Several fundamentalist groups exist more or less clandestinely. Estimates of their number living in the West vary from 20,000 to 30,000, but, according to scholar Brian C. Hales, this number may be too high. Prosecutions of the illegal activity of polygamy are few, partly because of the practical problem of providing for the children if parents are imprisoned or deprived of income, and partly because of a changed climate of opinion that tolerates many kinds of behavior by consenting adults. In recent years, however, extensive prosecutions have occurred for child abuse and underage marriages. *See also* MANIFESTO.

– G –

GARMENTS. White underwear worn by adult Mormons after receiving their endowments in the **temples**. This conservative underclothing has simple, unobtrusive markings symbolic of **gospel** ideals. Garments are not available in the general retail market but are purchased through Church **distribution centers**.

GATES, SUSA YOUNG (1856–1933). Suffragist, women's leader. The second daughter of Lucy Bigelow and **Brigham Young**, Susa Young Gates attended the University of Deseret (University of Utah) where she completed courses in stenography and telegraphy. In 1870, Gates, her mother, and her sister, Eudora, moved to St. George, Utah. There, she arranged various activities that involved organizing the Union Club, a social group for the local young men and women, and worked in the St. George temple as a recorder. Shortly thereafter, she married Alma Dunford, a local dentist. However, marriage responsibilities and her husband's alcoholism quickly overwhelmed the 16-year-old Gates. She divorced her husband in 1877. Three years later, much better prepared for marriage, she married Jacob Gates. In 1885, she accompanied her husband on his **mission** to Hawaii. The family remained there for the next five years. She also served on the general board of the Young Ladies Mutual Improvement Association (YLMIA) and the general board of the **Relief Society**, and she edited several Mormon publications for women. Gates continually participated in political, educational, and social causes. She continually championed the causes specific to women, which consisted of women's suffrage, genealogy, history, and education. She annually attended the National Council for Women on behalf of the YLMIA and served as the Press Committee chair for three years, and on two occasions, she represented the National Council of Women at its international conference. In educational matters, Gates organized the Brigham Young Academy's (now BYU) Music Department and Domestic Science Department. Utah's governor John C. Cutler appointed Gates to a six-year term on the board of directors of the Agricultural College of Utah (now Utah State University). While serving in this capacity, she initiated the Domestic Science Department here also. Gates created the Utah chapter of the Daughters of the American Revolution. While serving as president of the Daughters of the Utah Pioneers, she established the Hall of Relics. Finally, she worked as the head librarian of the Genealogical Society of Utah. She died in 1933 after suffering from cancer.

GATHERING. The "gathering of Israel" (**Articles of Faith**, no. 10) included not only the return of the Jews to the Holy Land but the concentration of Church members in a location in the Western Hemisphere where they would build a temple to God.

Early gathering places in Ohio, Missouri, and Illinois attracted converts. As they joined the Church in other parts of the United States, **members** would, where possible, migrate to the current gathering place, often called the Latter-day **Zion.** After the **exodus** to the West, it was the Salt Lake Valley in Utah that drew members in by the thousands, many of them converts from **Europe**, year after year through the second half of the 19th century.

Due to population pressures, limited job opportunities, and a desire to build up the Church in many parts of the world, the gathering in Utah slowed down in the 20th century. Church leaders urged members to remain where they were. But longing for the opportunities that drew other immigrants to America, many Mormons continued to move to the Salt Lake Valley if possible. Wishing to live in the midst of fellow believers, they continued to move to Utah and other mountain states, although at a slower rate. It was a time of transition.

After World War II, especially since the 1960s, the pattern of growth through **missionary** proselytizing greatly increased Mormon members and **wards, stakes,** and **temples** in all of the 50 states and in **Europe, Central America and Mexico, South America, Asia,** and **Africa.** On 1 December 1999, the **First Presidency** repeated "the long-standing counsel to remain in their homelands rather than immigrate to the United States." Individuals are considered gathered into the Church and Kingdom of God when they are baptized.

GENEALOGY. The discipline or activity of searching ancestry, including the preparation of pedigree charts and **family** reconstitution, or family group, sheets. Motivated by the doctrine of **baptism for the dead,** Mormons have been diligent genealogists since the 1840s. The vicarious **ordinance** work performed in the **temples** was based upon the genealogical research that allowed members to perform proxy service for their deceased ancestors.

In 1894 a genealogical society was organized. As an official designation, the name was changed to Family History Department in 1987, although the previous term was still used for some of the activities. From the 1930s, and especially after World War II, an ambitious microfilming project was launched. In many countries of the world, wherever permission could be obtained, ecclesiastical records and vital statistics were filmed.

The Family History Library in Salt Lake City, Utah, houses a vast collection of volumes and, most importantly, microfilm and microfiche records from many countries of the world. Through 4,500 branch libraries these materials are available to researchers in more than 40 countries. The Family History Library is just one part of the **Family and Church History Department** that is in the process of creating new products that will assist people in doing genealogical research and will contribute substantially to the delivery of genealogical information anywhere it is desired. In 2005, digital cameras began to be used and a massive program launched to digitize the 2.4 million rolls of microfilm. The long-range goal is to make all this material available through the Internet. *See also* FAMILYSEARCH.

GENERAL AUTHORITIES. Leaders of the Church on the general, as opposed to the local, level. When the Church was organized in 1830, the organization was simple: **Joseph Smith** was first **elder** and **Oliver Cowdery** was second elder. Soon Smith became **president;**

he and his two **counselors** constituted the **First Presidency**. In 1835 the **Quorum** of the **Twelve Apostles** was organized. When a quorum of the **seventy** was created, its seven leaders were known as the First Council of the **Seventy**. A **presiding bishop** was appointed very early, and, finally, a **patriarch** to the entire Church was designated. From the 1830s to the recent past these have been the Mormon general authorities.

During the past generation this basic structure has been adjusted according to needs. In 1941, in order to visit the increasing number of **stakes, assistants to the twelve** were appointed. In 1967 **regional representatives** were established—not considered general authorities—as a kind of intermediate supervisory level. In 1976 the First Council of the Seventy and the assistants to the twelve were released and called to the new First Quorum of the Seventy. In 1989 a Second Quorum of the Seventy was established, appointments to which were for a five-year term. These seventies are all general authorities and, among other responsibilities, are typically assigned to the presidencies of specific geographical **areas**. On the grounds that his functions were now adequately performed by stake patriarchs, the general Church patriarch was declared emeritus in 1979 and the position left unfilled.

The total number of general authorities thus has enlarged, consisting of the First Presidency (3), Quorum of the Twelve Apostles (12), presidency of the seventy (7), First Quorum of Seventy (52), Second Quorum of Seventy (28), and Presiding Bishopric (3).

GENERAL HANDBOOK OF INSTRUCTIONS. Official guide containing instructions for local leaders such as **stake presidents** and **bishops**. Given the lay nature of the Church organization, such guidance is helpful in answering questions ranging from the keeping of records to the care of buildings. Although local leaders must exercise judgment according to the varying circumstances that arise, the handbook helps assure a minimum uniformity. Not available in bookstores, the handbook is distributed to the Church officials it is intended to assist.

GENESIS GROUP. In 1970, three **African American** Latter-day Saint men met together to discuss common needs and issues. Assigned to meet with them were three of the **twelve apostles: Gordon B. Hinckley, Thomas S. Monson**, and **Boyd K. Packer.** As a result of those meetings, the **First Presidency** and the twelve apostles decided that an organization should be established as a support group for African American Latter-day Saints in and around Salt Lake City, Utah. The outcome of that decision was a dependent branch, organized in October 1971. The name *Genesis*, meaning beginning, was chosen by the African American members. President was Ruffin Bridgeforth; first **counselor**, Darius Gray; and second counselor, Eugene Orr. After the death of Bridgeforth in 1997, Darius Gray became president. Membership is approximately 60 percent nonwhite—African Americans, Africans, African Carribean, Latinos, Polynesians—and 40 percent white, including parents of adopted African American children and several biracial couples. Members of the Genesis Group maintain membership in their home **wards**. Meetings are held monthly and do not conflict with regularly scheduled church meetings. *See also* BLACKS.

GENTILE. (1) Generally, in Jewish usage, a non-Jew. (2) In informal Mormon usage uncommon now, but frequently used in the 19th century for a non-Mormon. In the 19th century both Mormons and non-Mormons generally used the term. More recently, its use is generally confined to humor and anecdotes. It has been humorously remarked that Salt Lake City is the only place where a Jew is a Gentile.

GODHEAD. God the Eternal Father, his son **Jesus Christ**, and the Holy Ghost. Mormons prefer the term Godhead to Trinity because of the creedal terminology associated with the latter. Mormons consider the three divine beings as separate individuals whose unity is one of purpose and intent. When Jesus was baptized by John the Baptist, the Father's voice was heard from heaven, and the Holy Ghost descended like a dove (Matt. 3:16). When Jesus was in Gethsemane, he prayed to his Father, not to himself. When **Joseph Smith** received the **First Vision** in answer to prayer, two beings appeared to him, God the Father and God the Son. Jesus Christ, the Son, has a glorified, resurrected body of flesh and bones, as does the Father, while the Holy Ghost is a personage of spirit (***Doctrine and Covenants***, section 130).

GOSPEL. The good news of **Jesus Christ** and the atonement wrought by him that brings immortality and, on condition of **repentance**, saves humans from their sins. As Mormons use this word, it refers to the *restored* gospel, or the *fullness* of the gospel, as taught in the **scriptures** and by the modern **prophets** from **Joseph Smith** to the present. A more complete view of the "good news" is embodied in the **plan of salvation**, which explains life and its meaning, including the blessings that are in store for those who love God and keep his **commandments**. Basic essentials are the **First Principles** of faith in the Lord Jesus Christ, repentance, **baptism,** and the gift of the Holy Ghost, which along with **resurrection** and judgment are sometimes collectively defined in the scriptures as the gospel. Indispensable to achieving the fullness of salvation, according to the gospel plan, is the **priesthood**, the power to administer the saving **ordinances.**

GRACELAND UNIVERSITY. Founded in 1895 as Graceland College at Lamoni, Iowa, Graceland is sponsored by the **Community of Christ**. Its current enrollment is close to 2,400 students. An urban campus in Independence, Missouri, houses a school of nursing, programs in education, and a seminary. Offering 60 degree programs, it is accredited by the North Central Association of Colleges and Schools.

GRANT, HEBER J. (1856–1945). Businessman, **general authority**, **president** of the Church. Born on 22 November 1856, the son of Jedediah Grant, a **counselor** in the **First Presidency** who died when the boy was still an infant, Heber was raised by his mother, Rachel Ivins Grant. His upbringing included a good basic education and activity in the Young Men's Mutual Improvement Association (YM-MIA). Tall and lanky, he learned to throw a baseball by persistent practice against a barn door and later went on to play on a team that won the territorial championship. Grant's life was a story ideal for author Horatio Alger Jr. Grant learned to write a beautiful Spencerian hand, sold insurance, worked as a bank cashier, saved his money, and bought the Ogden Vinegar Works. The future seemed auspicious.

But he also faced difficulties. After he married Lucy Stringham, she developed serious health problems, which led to her death 12 years later. When Grant became a **stake** president at the young age of

23, the travel and worry so sapped his strength that he suffered from extreme depression and recurrent insomnia. The decline of his business income and the loss of his Ogden factory to a fire added to his burdens.

Called to the **Quorum** of the **Twelve Apostles** in 1882, Grant was assigned to work with the **Sunday School** and the YMMIA. Like other apostles, he traveled, especially to Arizona and Mexico, where he labored among the Yaqui Indians. He remained active in business as owner of a bank, an insurance company, a newspaper, a livery stable, and retail companies. He was also one of the owners of the Salt Lake Theater and the Utah Sugar Company. A crisis came in 1893 with the national depression that led to the loss of his business empire. Still, Grant was able to negotiate loans and assist the Church to survive its financial plight.

He married two additional wives, both of whom had been schoolteachers. Twelve children came from these marriages. Despite his frequent absences, surviving letters give every indication of tender, supportive, and respectful relationships.

Since he had become an apostle at the relatively young age of 26, it was not entirely surprising that he outlived his colleagues to become president of the twelve apostles and, in 1918, president of the Church. Grant's presidency, from 1918 to 1945, included the post–World War I years, the Great Depression, and World War II. Serving on the board of directors of national corporations, he promoted good will for the Church. He was influential in promoting two Hollywood movie productions, *Union Pacific* and *Brigham Young*. Not given to heavy theological discourse, Grant advocated faithfulness and obedience to the **commandments**. He was especially emphatic in urging adherence to the **Word of Wisdom**. He sprinkled his sermons with quotations from popular poet Edgar A. Guest and the essayist and university president David Starr Jordan.

The Church was challenged by the moral laxity of the 1920s and by the economic crisis of the '30s (which for many Mormon farmers was just a further burden added to the agricultural depression they had been experiencing ever since the war). Responding to the former, Grant stressed the old-time virtues, which he exemplified. Although a Democrat, he was extremely critical of the New Deal. The widespread unemployment following the crash of 1929 prompted Grant to introduce the **welfare program** and call a young **stake** president, **Harold B. Lee**, to administer it.

The Church grew steadily. Hundreds of chapels were constructed. Temples were built in Hawaii, Canada, and Arizona. An imposing chapel, still standing although no longer owned by the Church, went up in Washington, D.C. **Missionary** work continued. In 1937 Grant traveled to England to attend meetings commemorating the first missionaries' arrival there one century earlier. World War II necessitated a reduction of the missionary force everywhere and, in **Europe**, a closing down of missions.

As always with presidencies, Grant's counselors shared the responsibility. Anthon H. Lund, Charles W. Penrose, and Anthony W. Ivins played this role through the '20s, and Ivins into the early 1930s. For the remainder of Grant's presidency his counselors were **J. Reuben Clark** and **David O. McKay**. During World War II, with many young Mormons in military service, a committee was organized to supervise the calling of **chaplains** and to prepare a miniature newspaper and special editions of Mormon books for servicemen. Not bellicose, President Grant expressed reservations about the war and recognized that Church members in other countries would rightfully serve in their armed forces.

GREAT APOSTASY. *See* APOSTASY.

– H –

HALES, ROBERT D. (1932–). Businessman, **general authority**. Born in New York City, Robert D. Hales earned a bachelor's degree from the University of Utah and a master's of business administration degree from Harvard University. He was a jet fighter pilot in the U.S. Air Force. Then he became an executive with four major national companies. He served as **counselor** in the **stake** presidency, **regional representative**, president of the England London Mission, first **counselor** in the general presidency of the **Sunday School**, **assistant to the twelve**, member of the First **Quorum** of the **Seventy**, and **presiding bishop**. Hales was ordained one of the **twelve apostles** in April 1994. He and his wife, Mary, have two sons.

HANDCART PIONEERS. Mormon immigrants who crossed the plains not in the standard covered wagons but by walking, carrying their belongings in small two-wheeled carts that were either pushed or pulled. Nearly 3,000 made the journey in 10 companies between 1856 and 1860.

Of the 250 deaths, most were in two companies led by James G. Willie and Edward Martin in 1856. A combination of late departure from England and from Florence, Nebraska, and an unusually early winter led to tragedy. In Wyoming, both of these companies were caught in bitter weather, including icy winds and blizzards. Running out of food, they huddled in camps while waiting for help. Fortunately **Brigham Young** learned of their plight and sent relief from Salt Lake City, Utah. Crossing hundreds of miles in heavy snow, horseback riders and wagon trains found the destitute immigrants, brought food and warm clothing and bedding, and helped carry the survivors on the final lap of the journey.

The mistaken judgment behind the late departure in 1856 was obvious. But it was the courage and heroism of the handcart pioneers and their rescuers that came to be emphasized. On **Temple Square** in Salt Lake City a statue by Torlief Knaphus commemorates "The Handcart Family." In December 2006 a documentary entitled *Sweetwater Rescue* aired on public broadcasting stations in the United States. A visitors center at Martin's Cove in Wyoming offers informative exhibits about the handcart experience. *See also* PIONEERS.

HANKS, MARION DUFF (1921–). Educator, community leader, **general authority**. Born on 13 October 1921 in Salt Lake City, Utah, Hanks was raised and educated there. From 1942 to 1944 he was a **missionary** in the Northern States Mission and then enlisted in the U.S. Navy, serving aboard a submarine chaser. He married Maxine Christensen, and they have five children.

Hanks taught in the **seminary** and **institute** system. In 1953 he became a member of the First Council of **Seventy**. From 1962 to 1964 he was president of the British Mission.

A member of the national executive board of the **Boy Scouts** of America, he earned the Silver Beaver, Silver Antelope, and Silver Buffalo awards. With **Elaine Cannon** he edited a section entitled "Era of Youth" for the *Improvement Era*. For five years he was managing director of the **Latter-day Saints Students Association (LDSSA)** for college students.

He served on the President's Council on Physical Fitness and Sports. Other public service included president of the Salt Lake City Rotary Club and in 1977–1978 district governor; first chairman of the Utah Committee on Children and Youth; chairman of the Salt Lake Cancer Society; chairman of the Mental Health Board; and president of the Community Service Board. He has been on the governing boards of **BYU**, Weber State University, Southern Utah University, and Snow College.

After presiding over the British Mission from 1962 to 1964, he was **area** supervisor for Southeast Asia/Hawaii. From 1980 to 1982 he was executive administrator of the Southeast Asia/Philippines area, living in Hong Kong. He initiated a pioneering effort working with refugees. He chaired the board of the Ouelessebougou Mali–Utah Alliance, which since 1985 assisted with sanitation, agriculture, and literacy in a consortium of 22 villages in Mali.

From 1982 to 1985 Marion D. Hanks was president of the Salt Lake Temple. Then, after serving as executive director of the Priesthood Department of the Church, he was given emeritus status in October 1992.

HARRIS, FRANKLIN STEWART (1884–1960). Agronomist, educator, university president. Born in Benjamin, Utah, on 29 August 1884, Harris moved with his parents and siblings to Juarez, Mexico, in 1889. There, in a rural setting, he grew up. He graduated from Juarez **Stake** Academy in 1903. During his first year at **BYU** his family moved from Mexico to Cardston, Alberta, Canada. Franklin continued pursuing his studies, working as a teaching assistant to **John A. Widtsoe** in soil chemistry, and in 1907 graduated with a B.S. degree. He married Estella Spilsbury in 1908.

After earning a Ph.D. at Cornell University, Harris became a professor of agronomy at Utah Agricultural College (now Utah State University) in 1912, director of the School of Agricultural Engineering and Mechanical Arts, and in 1916 director of the experiment station. He published *The Principles of Agronomy* (1915), *Sugar Beets in America* (1918), and *Soil Alkali* (1920). In 1921 he became president of BYU. At the time the BYU faculty consisted of 78 people, only 10 of whom had doctorates. His was the guiding hand that helped raise the institution to a higher level by building a program, attracting qualified faculty, and in general maintaining high standards.

During the '20s and '30s, Harris was appointed U.S. representative to the Pan Pacific Science Congress in Tokyo in 1926; chairman of a commission to check on conditions among Jews in the Soviet Union in 1929; chairman of the agriculture section of a scientific congress in Mexico City in 1935; and member of an agricultural mission to Iran in 1939 (where later he helped set up the Point Four program). In 1945 he resigned as president of BYU to become president of Utah State University. He retired in 1950 and died in 1960.

HARRIS, MARTIN (1783–1875). One of the three **witnesses of the Book of Mormon**. Born in 1783 in Easton, New York, he married Lucy Harris (a distant cousin) and the couple had at least six children. A veteran of the War of 1812, he purchased a 320-acre farm near Palmyra, New York. For seven years he was elected road overseer. Religiously he was unaffiliated but looked for a restoration of original Christianity.

Sometime after 1824 Harris heard of **Joseph Smith** and the metal plates. Believing what he heard, Harris helped Smith move to Harmony, Pennsylvania, for safety. In 1828 Harris took a transcription of characters from the plates to two scholars, Charles Anthon and Samuel L. Mitchill, for verification. Whatever took place in the interviews, Harris came away convinced that a prophecy in Isaiah 29 had been fulfilled. For a short period Harris assisted Smith as scribe, but when he borrowed and then lost the first 116 pages of the handwritten manuscript, he was removed from that position. He pled for forgiveness and continued to support the project. His testimony of seeing the plates and an angel, signed along with **Oliver Cowdery** and **David Whitmer**, appeared in the front of the **Book of Mormon** when it was published in early 1830. Harris mortgaged part of his farm as security for the printing of the book and later sold part of it to pay the bill.

Harris was baptized the day the Church was organized, 6 April 1830. A year later he moved to Kirtland, Ohio; traveled with Smith to Missouri; and preached Mormonism as a **missionary**. He was a member of the first **high council** at Kirtland. After traveling again to Missouri as a member of **Zion's Camp**, Harris returned to Ohio and, with his two fellow *Book of Mormon* witnesses, selected the first **Quorum** of the **Twelve Apostles**. His first marriage having failed, he married a niece of **Brigham Young**.

From 1837 on Harris became more or less disaffected from the Church. Except for one missionary trip to England, he lived in Kirtland, Ohio. His wife and children moved to Utah in 1856. Harris himself moved there and rejoined the Church in 1870. Many times he bore his testimony of the *Book of Mormon*, reaffirming the testimony he had written for the original 1830 publication. He died in Clarkston, Utah, on 10 July 1875.

HIGH COUNCIL. A body of 12 high priests in the **Melchizedek Priesthood** who assist a **stake president**. Holding regular meetings, a stake high council advises the stake president on matters he presents to it, including the selection of individuals for specific **callings** in the stake. In serious disciplinary actions, the high council discusses and evaluates the evidence along with the stake presidency and ratifies the decision of the stake president (*Doctrine and Covenants*, section 102). Individual high councilmen are given different supervisory and training assignments. They represent the stake presidency by speaking in **ward sacrament meetings** and in other assignments. *See also* EXCOMMUNICATION.

HIGH PRIEST. An office in the **Melchizedek Priesthood**. Those called to serve in **bishoprics**, **stake** presidencies, **high councils**, or as **general authorities** are, if they are not already such, ordained to the office of high priest. **Elders** who have served faithfully in other **callings** are often advanced to the high priest office for reasons of age compatibility. All the high priests in a stake constitute the stake high priest **quorum**. Those in a **ward** are called a high priest group and meet each Sunday for instruction and for planning compassionate service and other activities. The **president** of the Church is the presiding high priest in the Church; the stake president, the presiding high priest in the stake; the bishop, the presiding high priest in the ward.

HILLAM, HAROLD G. (1934–). Orthodontist, **general authority**. Born on 1 September 1934 in Sugar City, Idaho, Hillam served as a **missionary** in Brazil, graduated from **BYU**, and attended dental school at Northwestern University, where he later returned for an advanced degree in orthodontics. He practiced his profession in Idaho Falls, Idaho, and was president of the Rocky Mountain Society of Orthodontists.

In the Church, Hillam was a **bishop**'s **counselor, high councilor, stake president**, and **regional representative**. Then he served as mission president in Portugal. In 1990 he became a member of the Second **Quorum** of the **Seventy**, in 1991 a member of the First Quorum of the Seventy, and in 1995 a member of its presidency. He served as general president of the **Sunday School**. He was named to emeritus status in 2005. He and his wife, Carol, have seven children.

HILL CUMORAH. Near Palmyra, New York, a hill (drumlin) where Mormons believe an ancient prophet buried the inscribed plates later translated and published as the *Book of Mormon*. The precise spot where the plates were buried is unknown. In 1928, the Church purchased the hill and erected a large monument. Since 1937 the hill has been the site of the annual Hill Cumorah Pageant.

HINCKLEY, GORDON BITNER (1910–2008). General authority, Church **president**. Born on 23 June 1910 in Salt Lake City, Utah, Hinckley graduated from the University of Utah in 1932. He was a **missionary** in Great Britain for two years. Employed by the Church as executive secretary of its Radio, Publicity, and Mission Literature Committee, he became executive secretary of the General Missionary Committee in 1951, managing the entire missionary program. He was president of the East Mill Creek **Stake**.

In 1958 he was called as an **assistant to the twelve** and three years later became a member of the **Quorum** of the **Twelve Apostles**. His assignments included serving on or chairing committees on missionaries, **temples, correlation**, and **welfare**. He served on the Church Board of Education and the Board of Trustees of **BYU** and **Ricks College**. Since 1981 he served in the **First Presidency**, as second counselor to President **Spencer W. Kimball**, and from 1985 as first counselor to President **Ezra Taft Benson**. Hinckley traveled in **Asia** after World War II and played a key role in establishing the Church in the Philippines, Taiwan, Hong Kong, Japan, and Korea. With the beginning of a major program of constructing temples in many different countries, it was he more than anyone else who traveled to the different locations and dedicated the new sacred edifices.

In 1995 he became president of the Church. Experienced in dealing with the media, Hinckley launched initiatives to improve the image of the Church, encouraged **community service**, and with good humor responded to the questions of Mike Wallace, Larry King, and other interviewers. In 1998 he announced a goal of 100 temples, which was made realizable by scaling back on their size. He and his wife, Marjorie Pay Hinckley (1911–2004), had five children. Hinckley died in his home in Salt Lake City on 27 January 2008.

HISTORICAL DEPARTMENT OF THE CHURCH. In 1972, as part of a broad administrative reorganization, the Church Historian's Office was renamed the Historical Department of the Church. Originally subdivided into Library, Archives, and Historian's Divisions, it was later reorganized into Library-Archives, Arts and Sites, and History Divisions, and still later into Library, Archives, and Museum. The stated mission of the Historical Department of the Church was to acquire, organize, preserve, and oversee the use of records, publications, photographs, artifacts, and other materials having to do with the history of the Church.

The History Division, under the direction of **Leonard J. Arrington**, was a group of about a dozen professional historians who from 1972 prepared bibliographies, established an oral history program, and produced many books and articles on Church history. In 1982 this group was transferred to **BYU** and designated the **Joseph Fielding Smith Institute for Church History.** In 2006 it was disbanded. Most of its historians were hired by the **Family and Church History Department**, current title of what had been the Historical Department of the Church.

HISTORIC SITES. The following historic sites and visitors' centers are staffed by **missionaries**, senior couples whose assignment is to welcome guests and provide basic information: Beehive House, Salt Lake City, Utah; **Book of Mormon** Historic Publication Site, Palmyra, New York; Brigham Young winter home, St. George, Utah; Carthage Jail, Carthage, Illinois; Cove Fort, Utah; Hill Cumorah, Manchester Township, New York; Independence Visitors' Center, Independence, Missouri; Jacob Hamblin home, Santa Clara, Utah; John Johnson farmhouse, Hiram, Ohio; Joseph Smith Memorial, Sharon, Vermont; Joseph Smith Sr. farm, Manchester Township, New York; Liberty Jail, Liberty, Missouri; **Mormon Battalion** Visitors' Center, San Diego, California; Mormon Handcart Visitors' Center, Alcova, Wyoming; Mormon Trail Center at Historic Winter Quarters, Omaha, Nebraska; Nauvoo Historic District and Visitors' Center, Nauvoo, Illinois; Newel K. Whitney store and home, Kirtland, Ohio; Peter Whitmer farm, Fayette Township, New York; St. George Tabernacle, St. George, Utah; Temple Square, Salt Lake City, Utah. In addition, visitors' centers are located at **temples** in Mesa, Arizona; Laie, Hawaii; Idaho Falls, Idaho; Los Angeles and Oakland, California; St. George, Utah; Washington, D.C.; Mexico City, Mexico; Hamilton, New Zealand; and others.

HISTORY OF THE CHURCH. Articles in the present volume treating Mormon history include **New York Period, Ohio Period, Missouri Period, Illinois Period, Exodus**, and **Utah Period**. Also historical are such topics as **Colonization, Polygamy**, the **Mountain Meadows Massacre**, and **Gathering**. Biographical articles relate to different periods of Church history. One recommendation would be to read in sequence the sketches of the presidents of the Church from the beginning to the present: **Joseph Smith, Brigham Young, John Taylor, Wilford Woodruff, Lorenzo Snow, Joseph F. Smith, Heber J. Grant, George Albert Smith, David O. McKay, Joseph Fielding Smith, Harold B. Lee, Spencer W. Kimball, Ezra Taft Benson, Howard W. Hunter**, and **Gordon B. Hinckley**. Articles treating different geographical **areas** also provide a historical overview.

HOLLAND, JEFFREY R. (1940–). Educator, president of **BYU**, **general authority**. Named president of BYU in 1980, he presided during a decade of expansion and increased visibility of BYU in scholarship and athletics. In 1989 he became a member of the First **Quorum** of the **Seventy**. In 1994, at age 53, he was sustained to the Quorum of the **Twelve Apostles**.

HOME TEACHING. Church members are called upon each month by a team of two **priesthood** holders. The home teachers are urged to become acquainted with the needs of each **family** or individual and prayerfully seek to be of assistance. They are also encouraged to help the family with temporal needs such as home repairs and caring for the sick. A message of inspiration and instruction is delivered, special needs are ascertained, and friendships are formed. The Church is brought into the lives of the people on the ground level, as it were. The original impetus goes back to the instruction (*Doctrine and Covenants*, section 20) that teachers are to "visit the house of each member and exhort them to pray vocally and in secret and attend to all family duties." *See also* VISITING TEACHING.

HOMOSEXUALITY. Same-gender attraction leading to sexual relations has challenged secular governments and churches up to the present. Until 1973 it was labeled a disorder by the American Psychiatric Association. That year, by a 58 percent vote, homosexuality was removed from the list of disorders. The extent to which the condition is genetic and inborn or the result of social conditioning, or some combination of the two, continues to divide researchers. The extent to which society should accept homosexuality in the form of same-sex marriage, view it as a disqualification for such influential adult positions as **priest** or scoutmaster, or devise some compromise is likewise controversial.

Church leaders do not condone cruelty. "Our doctrines obviously condemn those who engage in so-called 'gay bashing'—physical or verbal attacks on people thought to be involved in homosexual or lesbian behavior," said **Dallin H. Oaks**. Those "struggling with the burden of same-sex attraction are in special need of the love and encouragement that is a clear responsibility of Church members." The Church neither endorses nor condemns treatment programs that attempt to lessen same-sex attraction.

HUMANITARIAN AID. To assist those in need or victims of disasters, a variety of channels are used by Mormons. They volunteer or donate to relief programs of their choice. By the payment of a monthly **fast offering** and specific contributions for humanitarian aid, Mormons create a fund that can be drawn upon by **bishops** and the general Church to meet needs. From the 1990s, Church-service **missionaries** were assigned to low-income areas of the central city to give career counseling, budgeting advice, and other forms of assistance. The Church has established employment centers in cities throughout the globe. A large Humanitarian Center in Salt Lake City, Utah, assembles packets of material to be sent to areas of the world in need of assistance. The center draws upon surplus clothing from **Deseret Industries**; donations from companies and institutions of medical equipment, computers, and school supplies; donations from individuals, including handmade baby clothes and quilts; and humanitarian funds. Donations to the Church's humanitarian fund all go for humanitarian aid, with none of them used for administrative expenses.

In the 20 years following 1985, often teaming with other service and relief organizations, the Church assisted 183 countries, distributing more than 51,000 tons of food; 7,600 tons of medical equipment; 68,000 tons of surplus clothing; and 5,700 tons of educational supplies. In addition teams of Latter-day Saint volunteers labored to assist sufferers following natural disasters. *See also* LDS PHILANTHROPIES.

HUNTER, HOWARD WILLIAM (1907–1995). Lawyer, businessman, **general authority**, Church **president**. Born in Boise, Idaho, on 14 November 1907, Hunter received his early education there and became an Eagle Scout. In 1928 he moved to California, married Clara May Jeffs, and earned a juris doctor degree, graduating cum laude from Southwestern University Law School. Admitted to the California State Bar, he became a leading corporate attorney. He served as **bishop**, **stake high councilor**, and president of the Pasadena Stake. While stake president he also served as chairman of the Southern California Welfare Region and Los Angeles Welfare Region. He was on the **temple** committee during the construction of the Los Angeles Temple.

In 1959, at age 51, he became a member of the **Quorum** of the **Twelve Apostles**. He served on the board of directors of several corporations, including First Security Corporation and the New World Archaeological Foundation. He has been president of the **Polynesian Cultural Center**, the Genealogical Society, and the West European Mission. In 1985 he became acting president and in 1988 president of the Quorum of the Twelve Apostles. Clara, his wife of many years, died in 1983. In 1990 he married Inis Bernice Egan. He became president of the Church in June 1994 at age 86 but died in March 1995. *See also* GENEALOGY.

HUNTSMAN, JON (1937–). Businessman, billionaire, philanthropist. Born on 21 May 1937 in Blackfoot, Idaho, Jon Meade Huntsman Sr. grew up in poverty and worked after-school jobs to help support his family. After earning an undergraduate degree at the Wharton School of Business at the University of Pennsylvania, Huntsman earned an MBA degree from the University of Southern California. He became president of the Huntsman Corporation, the largest privately held chemical company in the nation. He served as special assistant to the president under Richard Nixon and vice president of the U.S. Chamber of Commerce. Huntsman gave $40 million to his alma mater, the Wharton School, and pledged $100 million to create the Huntsman Cancer Institute at the University of Utah. He has also sponsored programs for the homeless and shelters for abused women. He has served as a **stake president** and an **area authority seventy**. He and his wife, Karen, are the parents of nine children.

HYDE, ORSON (1805–1878). Missionary, pioneer, apostle. Hyde was born on 8 January 1805 in Oxford, Connecticut. Left an orphan at age 12, he was raised by neighbors. They moved to Kirtland, Ohio, in 1819. There he worked as a clerk in the Gilbert-Whitney store. He joined the Methodists in 1827, but when he heard the preaching of **Sidney Rigdon**, Hyde joined his congregation. When the first Mormon **missionaries** arrived in the fall of 1830, Rigdon accepted the new religion and Hyde soon followed in early 1831.

Immediately Hyde began preaching Mormonism in Ohio, Missouri, Pennsylvania, New York, Canada, and Indiana. In 1834 he married Marinda Nancy Johnson. After returning from the strenuous expedition of **Zion's Camp**, he became a member of the original **Quorum** of the **Twelve Apostles** in 1835. He was one of the original bearers of the message of Mormonism to England in 1837.

In Missouri during the height of the persecutions there, Hyde briefly defected and was **excommunicated**. When he expressed his strong desire to return six months later, he was reinstated as a member and as an apostle. He had no sooner moved to Nauvoo, Illinois, and established his family there than he was called on a special mission to Palestine. Taking months to make the long journey, he arrived in Jerusalem on 24 October 1841 and dedicated the land for the future return of the Jews.

Back in Nauvoo during the final year of the **Illinois Period**, he was introduced to **polygamy** and, after soul-searching, took two plural wives. Three other wives would be added later, and a total of 32 children were born. In the spring of 1844, Hyde became a member of the **Council of Fifty**. During 1846, the year the **exodus** began, he was sent on another mission to England.

Upon his return, Hyde settled in Utah. As a loyal follower and **pioneer**, he led a group to colonize Fort Supply in Wyoming. In 1855 he led a group to settle Carson Valley, Nevada, serving as a probate judge there. In 1858 Hyde was called to lead the Mormon settlements in south-central Utah. He built a home in Spring City, Utah, and for the final 20 years of his life was the Church leader in the area. Hyde also served on the territorial supreme court and in the legislature. *See also* MISSOURI PERIOD.

– I –

ILLINOIS PERIOD. Western Illinois was the main center of Mormonism from 1839 to 1846. Fleeing from Missouri after the extermination order issued by Governor Lilburn W. Boggs, Mormon refugees were received and cared for in Quincy and other Illinois towns. Jailed in Liberty, Missouri, **Joseph Smith** sent out encouraging and inspiring instructions (***Doctrine and Covenants***, sections 121–123). By spring of 1839, Smith having rejoined his family and people, a site for settlement was selected at Commerce, Illinois, on the east side of a bend in the Mississippi River a few miles north of

Quincy. Rechristened Nauvoo (based on a Hebrew word for "beauti-ful"), this became the new **gathering** place and the Mormon center. Nauvoo grew rapidly, eventually reaching a population of some 12,000. (Estimates vary, depending on the year and whether or not the surrounding area is included.) A charter granting the city powers of self-government similar to other Illinois city chargers was granted by the legislature. The Nauvoo Legion, a unit of the state militia, was organized for defense. Two newspapers began publication, a Masonic lodge was formed, even a university was started, although it was one in little more than name.

In a bold stroke, when the Church and its people seemed to be in the depths of persecution and despair, Joseph Smith sent most of the **twelve apostles** to England, where they arrived in 1840. A prelim-inary proselytizing mission there in 1837 had already started mak-ing converts. Nearly 5,000 of these English converts emigrated to Nauvoo, joining other converts from the United States. Even with some loss by attrition, the future of Mormonism in Illinois seemed assured.

Some of the houses erected in the new city were impressive two-story brick structures. Joseph Smith moved his family into a new "mansion house." Funds were raised and construction started on a hotel, the Nauvoo House. A Masonic building served as a cultural hall. Although it is easy to exaggerate the "refinement" of a com-munity still close to its original poverty, this was a town on the rise. The people tried to raise their sights as best they could. Included in the entertainment were dinner parties and balls, circuses, parades, and theater.

In addition to retailing food and clothing, much of the economic life of Nauvoo revolved around the construction of roads, houses, and public buildings. Naturally there was trade with the surrounding area. Located on the banks of the Mississippi, Nauvoo seemed a natural port for whatever trade the river could generate. A manufacturing and agriculture society was established. Plans were put forth for industry and a dam in the river that would greatly enhance its navigability. What was needed to undergird such development was capital, always in short supply.

The Mormon religion experienced important development during this period. Concepts such as eternal progression, the potential deification of humans, and the eternal duration of **family** relationships were enunciated. **Baptism for the dead** was introduced. **Polygamy**, which had been adumbrated earlier, was announced to the inner circle of leaders by a **revelation** in 1843 and began to be practiced by a few of the leading families. The **temple** announced for Independence, Missouri, had been thwarted by persecution and expulsion. Now a new temple, a sacred place for the **ordinance** of endowment and eternal **marriage**, began to rise in Nauvoo, an imposing white edifice on the highest elevation of the city.

Organizationally, **wards** were established as the congregational unit. In 1842 the **Relief Society** was founded as the organization for women. A Council of **Fifty** with ambitious plans for **colonization** and government was initiated. Most importantly, perhaps, the **Quorum** of the **Twelve Apostles**, seasoned after directing the migration from Missouri and by their missionary labors in England, came to occupy the most important administrative role next to the **First Presidency**.

Repeating the pattern of the **Ohio Period**, this doctrinal and institutional creativity aroused opposition. Nearby communities felt threatened by economic, religious, and political competition. As Mormons became numerous, they were a political force, a swing vote if not the dominant vote in the county. Illinois Masons were alarmed by the sudden emergence of a large lodge among the Mormons. Rumors of imperialistic designs and of the new marriage practices began to circulate, sometimes with a kernel of accuracy but often exaggerated and distorted. For a variety of reasons some Mormons defected. Persecution raised its head once again as **anti-Mormons** formed vigilante groups.

Aware of opponents within and fierce enemies without, Joseph Smith did several things simultaneously. He pushed for the continued growth of Nauvoo, especially the completion of the Nauvoo House and the temple—this in the face of the threatened revocation of the city's charter. He initiated an exploring expedition to find an alternative place of settlement in the West. The actual departure of this party was deferred until after the election of 1844. He assigned an apostle, **Lyman Wight**, to lead a company to find a place of settlement in Texas. He gave increased responsibility to the twelve apostles, declaring that they now had all the authority he had. He ran as an independent for president of the United States, sending out the apostles and others to campaign for him.

By late spring of 1844 the opposition mounted in a deafening crescendo. Anti-Mormon newspapers called for the use of violence. Mobs burned Mormon farms and outlying settlements, sending their frightened inhabitants fleeing into Nauvoo for safety. The state of Missouri demanded that Joseph Smith return for trial because of the attempt on former governor Lillburn Boggs's life. Then an opposition newspaper, the *Nauvoo Expositor*, appeared in Nauvoo itself, denouncing Smith and his policies in intemperate terms. The city council declared the newspaper a public nuisance and ordered the destruction of its press, an action that simply fanned the flames. Promised protection by Governor Thomas Ford, Joseph Smith and his brother **Hyrum Smith** were jailed in Carthage, Illinois, where they were assassinated on 27 June 1844. The era of Mormonism's first **prophet** had come to an end, the Church just 14 years old.

The big question now was survival of the Church. Some newspapers expressed confidence that, deprived of their charismatic leader, the Mormons would quickly disperse. **Sidney Rigdon**, who, along with Joseph and Hyrum Smith, had been a member of the First Presidency, put in a bid for the leadership. But at a large gathering of the members at Nauvoo on 8 August 1844 the vote was decisively in favor of the twelve apostles assuming the leadership, with **Brigham Young** as president.

For another year and a half Nauvoo survived. Young and his colleagues provided leadership, continuing the doctrines and policies of Joseph Smith. Construction of houses continued. The temple was finally completed at the beginning of 1846. Although conversion and disaffection continued simultaneously, the balance seemed in favor of continued growth, especially with dramatic successes in England. During 1845, however, anti-Mormon violence in the area combined with demands that the Mormons leave Illinois, which Young and the other leaders agreed to do, hoping first to sell their properties and to have adequate time for preparing wagons and supplies.

By winter of 1845–1846 the writing was on the wall. The capstone of the temple having been laid, more than 6,000 Mormons received their temple ordinances in January and February. With the hoof beats of marauding mobsters raising panic and forcing people from the surrounding settlements to seek protection in the city, and with violence on both sides, the Mormon leaders agreed to depart. Starting in February 1846 refugees moved from the city and across the river—generally by barge, but for a short time on ice—and continued westward into Iowa. Those who required more time continued to be harassed. By the fall of 1846 the Mormons who recognized the leadership of Brigham Young had practically all departed.

Schism and **apostasy** had occurred as early as the 1830s when some refused to follow revelations and policies of Joseph Smith that had not been part of the religion at its beginning, but such dissidents had always been relatively few. Now a larger group, although still a minority, refused or were unable to embark on the arduous journey to the distant Great Basin. Eventually some of these rallied to form the **RLDS** Church.

As a result of renewed proselytizing and growth mostly after the middle of the 20th century, there were 53,047 Church **members** in Illinois at the end of 2005, divided into 12 **stakes** and 90 wards. A temple in a suburb of Chicago was completed and dedicated in 1985. The Nauvoo Temple, closely modeled on the original structure, was rebuilt and dedicated in 2002. In 2004 the Illinois House of Representatives formally expressed regret for the forced expulsion of Mormons from the state in 1846. *See also* EXODUS; MISSOURI PERIOD; NAUVOO RESTORATION, INC.

IMPROVEMENT ERA. Magazine published monthly from 1897 to 1970. At first the official organ of the YMMIA, it enlarged its scope and was effectively the magazine for adults in the Church.

Contents included editorials, doctrine, exhortation, recipes, historical articles, short stories, poetry, and advertisements. Instructions for **priesthood** leaders and messages to be delivered by **ward** teachers, now called **home teachers**, were included. The "Spoken Word" of **Richard L. Evans** was a regular feature. For many years **John A. Widtsoe** published answers to questions under the column title "Evidences and Reconciliations." Addresses by **general authorities** at **general conferences** were printed, selectively for many years and completely from 1942 on. A special section entitled "The Era of Youth," edited by **Elaine Cannon** and **Marion D. Hanks**, appeared from 1960 on. When the final issue of the *Improvement Era* appeared in

December 1970, its circulation was 275,000. Its successor, the *Ensign*, started publication in January 1971.

INACTIVITY. Inactive Mormons are those, sometimes called "nonpracticing" in other traditions, who do not attend Church services. Other indications of this status include failure to observe the **Word of Wisdom** and failure to pay **tithing**. Obviously there are degrees of inactivity, ranging from the person who still has a **testimony** but for a variety of reasons fails to attend the regular meetings to the **apostate** who resents the Church and wants nothing more to do with it. Many from the first group and even some from the second group sooner or later return to full participation. To recognize this variety and to avoid stereotyping, Church leaders now prefer the designation "less active."

INDIANS. *See* NATIVE AMERICANS.

INSTITUTES OF RELIGION. Programs of study in religion for college students. The first of these institutes was established in 1926 at the University of Idaho. When there are sufficient Mormon students, an institute building is usually constructed near a university campus. Courses are offered on the **scriptures**, Church history, world religions, and **marriage** and **family**. Recreational activities, social functions, and worship meetings provide opportunities for Mormon students to interact. Most institute instructors hold the doctorate or a master's degree.

With the expanding Church population and the limited enrollment capacity of **BYU**, institutes have become increasingly important. In 1993, the institute program was made available not only to college and university students but to all young adults between 18 and 30. In 2005, enrollment was 367,034.

INTERNATIONAL MAGAZINES. The *Liahona* is the official international magazine of the Church. The Church publishes the *Liahona* in 50 different languages from monthly to semi-annually, depending on the language. Until 1970, the Church titled international magazines differently in each language, for example, *l'Etoile*, *Der Stern*, *Millennial Star*, *la Stella*, and *Tambuli*. Many articles in the *Liahona* are translated and printed from English-language publications, but other articles are produced by people from the different nations or areas. Eight pages of each issue are filled with news from the country or area served. The *Liahona* is designed "to strengthen the faith of members; to promulgate the truths of the restored gospel; to keep members informed of current and vital Church policies, programs, and events; and to entertain and enrich the lives of Church members" (*Ensign*, September 1986).

INTERNET. The rapid rise of the Internet as a means of communication and a source of information has brought a variety of sites about Mormonism. The official Church website is lds.org. *See also* GENEALOGY.

INVESTIGATOR. Someone who is seriously studying the Mormon religion with a view to possible conversion and **baptism**. When individuals or families indicate a willingness to learn, **missionaries** teach them the restored **gospel** and its requirements in a series of lessons. *See also* REFERRAL.

IVINS, ANTHONY WOODWARD (1852–1934). Businessman, politician, **general authority**. The year following Ivins's birth in Toms River, New Jersey, his family emigrated to the Salt Lake Valley, and they eventually settled in St. George, Utah. At age 23, he participated in an expedition to Arizona and New Mexico to locate sites for possible **colonization**. Later returning as a proselyting **missionary**, he preached the gospel to the Indian and Mexican peoples. In 1882, Ivins presided over the Mexico City mission, learning to speak Spanish fluently. In 1878, Ivins married Elizabeth Ashby Snow, and he engaged in the cattle business as manager of the Mojave Land and Cattle Company and partner in the Kaibab Cattle Company. Politically, he worked as St. George's constable; served as prosecuting attorney for Washington County, Utah; and represented southern Utah counties in the Utah Territorial Legislature. In 1888 he led out in organizing a nascent Democratic Party as the "Sagebrush Democrats." At the same time, he served as St. George **Stake** YMMIA president and as a member of the stake **high council**. In 1888 he became first **counselor** in the stake presidency. As a leader in the Democratic

Party, he served as mayor of St. George and as a member of the Utah state constitutional convention.

For over a decade, Ivins served as the presiding authority in the Mexican colonies. Eight Mormon settlements, located in Sonora and Chihuahua, provided refuge for saints in danger of violating anti-polygamy legislation. The **First Presidency** authorized Ivins to perform plural marriages, illegal in both Mexico and the United States, when proper documentation was presented. He seems to have continued to do so until President **Joseph F. Smith** issued the "second manifesto" in 1904. Ivins returned to Utah when the First Presidency called him as a member of the **Quorum** of the **Twelve Apostles** in 1907. He served in this position until President **Heber J. Grant** called him as second counselor in the First Presidency in 1921. He was called as first counselor in 1925 and remained in that position until his death in 1934.

– J –

JACK, ELAINE LOW (1928–). Leader of **Young Women, Relief Society** general president. After growing up in Cardston, Alberta, Canada, Elaine attended the University of Utah for two years. Marrying medical student Joseph E. Jack in 1948, she moved with him to New York City. His medical training and practice as a surgeon took them to Boston, Alaska, and finally Salt Lake City, Utah. The Jacks have four sons.

Elaine performed community service work for the American Cancer Society and served in medical and auxiliary positions. She served as **ward** Relief Society president, ward Young Women president, **stake** Relief Society president's **counselor**, Relief Society general board member, and counselor to **Ardeth Kapp** in the Young Women general presidency. From 1990 to 1997 she served as general president of the Relief Society.

JACK-MORMON. Colloquial term for someone who is a member of the Church in name only or who never, or hardly ever, attends meetings. (The original usage of the term in the 1840s referred to non-Mormons who were friendly to the Church, but that meaning has lost its currency.) Heard only infrequently now, "Jack-Mormon" has been replaced for most purposes by "inactive" or "less active." *See also* ACTIVITY; INACTIVITY.

JACOBSEN, FLORENCE SMITH (1913–). Youth leader, art curator, historic preservationist. Born on 7 April 1913, Florence Smith was raised in Salt Lake City, Utah. She earned a bachelor's degree in interior design at the University of Utah and in 1935 married Theodore C. Jacobsen. They have three sons.

On the **ward** and **stake** level she worked with the **Primary**, **Boy Scouts**, and **Young Women**. In 1955 the Jacobsens moved to New York City to preside over the Eastern States Mission. Upon their return in 1959, Florence was named to the general board of the Young Women. Two years later she became general president of the organization, serving from 1961 to 1972.

In 1969 Jacobsen directed an ambitious centennial celebration, which included an original movie, *Pioneers and Petticoats*. She played a central role in the production of the musical stage play *Promised Valley* and, growing out of its orchestra and chorus, the establishment of the **Mormon Youth Symphony and Chorus**. Her training in design and historic costume was also called upon when she was assigned to supervise the restoration of the **Joseph Smith** home in Palmyra, New York, and **Brigham Young**'s Lion House in Salt Lake City. She was a member of the National Council of Women and the International Council of Women. She served as a vice president of the National Council of Women.

In 1973 she was appointed Church curator. With a reorganization of the **Historical Department of the Church**, Jacobsen became director of Historic Arts and Sites with responsibility over the many historic sites throughout the United States, serving until 1986. Under her direction, artifacts and works of art that had been poorly displayed or stored in closets and attics were catalogued and restored. Most importantly, the **Museum of Church History and Art** was constructed in order to provide a suitable facility for exhibiting examples of the Church's artistic heritage.

JAMES, JANE ELIZABETH MANNING (1818–1908). African American member. Jane Elizabeth Manning was born to Isaac Manning, a free black, and Phyllis Abbott in Wilton, Connecticut. Isaac Manning died about 1825, and in 1826 Jane was sent to live and work in the household of Joseph Fitch, a wealthy Wilton farmer. She worked here as a servant and was taught some Christian principles, but was given little, if any, educational instruction. She learned to read in her adult years, although she could never write; she signed her name using a mark and "wrote" letters and business items by dictating to friends.

Mormonism was first introduced into southwestern Connecticut during the winter of 1841. Jane heard the message of these **missionaries** in 1842 and was baptized on 14 October 1842. Upon her baptism, she experienced the gifts of speaking in tongues and of healing the sick. In early October 1843, Jane Elizabeth, her son Sylvester (an illegitimate child), her mother Phyllis, two brothers, two sisters, a brother-in-law, and a sister-in-law left Wilton and emigrated to Nauvoo, Illinois. Upon arrival in Nauvoo, she and her family stayed at the Nauvoo House where the **prophet Joseph Smith** provided temporary shelter. Jane Elizabeth remained a member of Smith's household and worked in the Nauvoo House until June 1844.

In 1845 Jane Elizabeth met and married Isaac James, a free black who had been converted in 1839. The two left Nauvoo and moved west across the Mississippi River into Iowa. While traveling through Iowa, Jane Elizabeth gave birth to their first child, Silas F. James on 10 June 1846. Jane Elizabeth and her husband and sons departed their Winter Quarter's encampment on 22 June 1847, and reached the Salt Lake Valley on 22 September 1847.

The James family settled on a farm outside of Salt Lake City, Utah, and raised sheep. Through a community effort, the surrounding farmers, the James family included, slowly prospered and made a decent living. Around 1869, Isaac left his family and divorced Jane Manning James. In 1874, she married Frank Perkins, but this union only lasted two years. She then moved to Salt Lake City and despite a life of poverty she managed her home and raised children and grandchildren. She also remained very active in the **Relief Society** and still found means to donate money for the St. George, Manti, and Logan **temples**. She also contributed to an old folks excursion to Liberty park, to the Lamanite mission, and to the Deseret Hospital.

The biggest trials James faced in life included overcoming racial conflict and the death of her children, as she outlived all of her children and many of her grandchildren. She lived in a society plagued by racial bigotry and was a member of a church whose practices at the time caused her some grief. Because she lived before 1978, she was unable to participate in temple ceremonies, in spite of repeated efforts to do so.

JENSEN, MARLIN K. (1942–). Attorney, **general authority**. Born on 18 May 1842 in Ogden, Utah, Jensen served as a **missionary** in Germany, graduated with a degree in German at **BYU**, and earned the juris doctorate from the University of Utah. Specializing in estate planning with an Ogden law firm, he was also a partner in the Jensen Family Middle Fork Ranch, a 600-head beef operation.

After serving as **bishop, stake president**, mission president, and **regional representative**, Jensen was named to the First **Quorum** of the **Seventy** in 1989. He served as Central European area president. In 2004 he was called as executive director of the **Family and Church History Department** of the Church and as Church historian and recorder. He and his wife, Kathleen, are parents of eight children.

JERUSALEM CENTER. BYU's Jerusalem Center for Near Eastern Studies, on Mount Scopus in northeast Jerusalem, was dedicated in 1989. Public protests by ultra orthodox Jews had attempted to stop construction, but an official ruling that all legal requirements had been met allowed the structure to be completed.

Its seven levels and 120,000 square feet include classrooms, a library, a multipurpose room, a cafeteria and dining rooms, two auditoriums, and dormitory rooms. It was designed by Franklin T. Ferguson, a Salt Lake City architect, in cooperation with David Reznik, a Jerusalem architect.

Selected from a pool of applicants, 169 university students study the **Bible**, the history and culture of Islam, Palestine, post-biblical Judaism, and languages. Weekly field trips take students to sites of historical and cultural significance.

The 320-seat auditorium serves as a concert hall for performances on a 3,000-pipe organ and for groups and individual artists from the community. With increasing violence in Israel, concern for the safety of students led to closing the center's academic programs from 2003 to 2007.

JESSOP, CRAIG D. (1949–). Musician, director of **Mormon Tabernacle Choir**. Born in Millville, Utah, Jessop received a bachelor's degree in music from Utah State University, an M.A. degree from **BYU**, and a doctorate of musical arts from Stanford University. A lieutenant colonel in the U.S. Air Force, he was director of the Singing Sergeants, 1980–1987; conductor of the Band of the United States Air Forces in Europe, 1987–1991; and conductor of the Air Combat Command Heartland of America Band, 1991–1995. He also served as musical director of the Maryland Choral Society, the Rhineland-Pfalz International Choir of Germany, and the Omaha Symphonic Chorus. A baritone vocalist, Jessop performed in the Merola Opera Training Program of the San Francisco Opera. He was a member of the Robert Shaw Festival Singers. In 1995, he became associate director of the Mormon Tabernacle Choir. Named music director in 1999, he served until 2008. He and his wife, RaNae, have four children.

JESUS CHRIST. The Savior and Redeemer of the world. Born in Bethlehem, Jesus performed miracles; called apostles; founded a Church; was betrayed, crucified, and resurrected. The second member of the Godhead (**Articles of Faith**, no. 1), by commission the Creator of the earth (John 1:3), Jesus Christ is the "author and finisher of our salvation" (Heb. 12:2; Moroni 6:4) The Church is named after him; baptized Mormons take upon themselves his name; his sacrifice is memorialized weekly in **sacrament** meetings. Mormons accept the virgin birth; that is, the infant was miraculously conceived by Mary. Of a divine Father and a human mother, Jesus had both divine and human attributes. Literally, he is the only begotten Son of God.

To suggest that Mormons do not believe in Christ or that someone other than Jesus of Nazareth is their Savior is not a harmless misunderstanding but a blatant lie. One among many passages in the *Book of Mormon* states, "We talk of Christ, we rejoice in Christ, we preach of Christ, we prophesy of Christ, and we write according to our prophecies, that our children may know to what source they may look for a remission of their sins" (2 Nephi 25:26). *See also* CHRISTIANITY.

JEWS, JUDAISM. The relationship between Mormons and Jews is ambiguous. Usually the two groups had little or nothing to do with each other, each facing its own trials.

On the level of ideology, Mormons anticipate that prior to the second coming of Jesus Christ many Jews will recognize Him as messiah. In 1841, long before the rise of organized Zionism, the land of Palestine was dedicated for the return of the Jews by Apostle **Orson Hyde**. For a time, on a small scale, proselytizing was specifically tailored for Jewish **investigators**. With relatively small results, the targeted proselytizing was abandoned.

Down to the present, conversions of Jews to Mormonism have taken place on an individual basis, motivated by family connections, dissatisfaction with their previous religion or secularism, and, as Mormons believe, the Holy Spirit. No record is kept of ethnicity and previous religious affiliation, and therefore it is impossible to state the numbers.

Church leaders have consistently expressed friendship for the state of Israel. A flare-up of hostility to Mormons occurred there with the announcement of the construction of the **Jerusalem Center**, but the demonstrations were by a small minority of orthodox Jews and were overcome by the support of well-wishers, including Jerusalem mayor Teddy Kollek, and the agreement that in Israel the Church would not engage in organized proselytizing.

As part of its efforts in **genealogy**, the Church gathered records of Jews, including victims of the holocaust. These have been freely made available, and Jewish families have expressed appreciation. Upon the discovery that **baptism for the dead** was performed for some of the individual Jews on these records, a few protested that they did not want their ancestors turned into Mormons. The Church's position, as with all such vicarious work, is that acceptance of it is entirely voluntary by the individual in the spirit world, that no harm has been done, and that it should make no difference to those who regard such vicarious work as meaningless. But in consideration for the sensitivity of the protestors, Church representatives agreed that the vicarious work for holocaust victims would be ended unless initiated by direct descendants.

Parallels between the Jewish and Mormon experience include the self-image by Mormon **pioneers** during the **exodus** from Illinois that they were the modern equivalent of the children of Israel fleeing Egypt under Moses. Mormons traversed their wilderness and established their **Zion** in a western region where there was a sea of salt, a fresh-water lake about forty miles away, and a river connecting the two, which to this day is called the Jordan River. An examination of visual images of Mormons and Jews in periodicals of the 19th century reveals that both groups were viciously stereotyped along with other unpopular minorities like Chinese immigrants and American Indians.

Mormons consider themselves to be of the House of Israel either by direct lineage or by adoption. Each individual's connection is declared by a **patriarchal blessing** and is usually through the line of Ephraim, grandson of Jacob/Israel.

JOHN WHITMER HISTORICAL ASSOCIATION (JWHA). Officially organized in 1973, by historians and others from the **RLDS** Church, the JWHA has always included people from different religious and secular backgrounds. It proclaims its area of interest as "the study of early Mormonism, the history of the Reorganized Church of Jesus Christ of Latter Day Saints, and **LDS** factions located in the Midwestern United States." JWHA distributes a newsletter, sponsors an annual meeting, cosponsors (with Graceland College) a spring lecture series, and publishes an annual journal. *See also* MORMON HISTORY ASSOCIATION.

JOSEPH FIELDING SMITH INSTITUTE FOR LATTER-DAY SAINT HISTORY. A group of historians at **BYU** whose primary assignment was the research and writing of Church history. Established in 1982 by the transfer and renaming of the group previously attached to the **Historical Department of the Church**, the Institute edited and published primary sources, and worked on a variety of individual projects, as well as sponsoring grants, fellowships, lectures, and scholarly seminars.

In 2005 the Institute was formally disbanded. Jill Mulvay Derr, director of the Institute, issued this statement: "Many of the Institute's former faculty, senior fellows, and staff are currently forwarding their work in Mormon history under the auspices of the Family and Church History Department in Salt Lake City, Utah, or the History Department at Brigham Young University. Scholarship on Mormon women promoted by the Institute's Women's History Initiative continues under the auspices of the Women's Research Institute at Brigham Young University."

JOSEPH SMITH MEMORIAL BUILDING. A building in downtown Salt Lake City, Utah, known as the Hotel Utah since its completion in 1911. After major restoration and renovation, the building was dedicated in 1993 and renamed. Open to the public are a magnificent lobby, a family history area with computers and assistants, a 500-seat theater, and two top-floor scenic outlooks and restaurants. Office buildings of different Church departments occupy eight floors. On the mezzanine level are a chapel and teaching and leadership rooms. In the basement are found a distribution center and an outlet for the purchase of **temple** clothing.

JOURNAL OF DISCOURSES. A 26-volume work published in Liverpool, England, between 1854 and 1884. Based on the shorthand reporting of George D. Watt and others, the *Journal of Discourses* includes many sermons by Mormon leaders of the latter 19th century. Since these sermons were not canonized, they are not official statements of Mormon doctrine. Nevertheless, they touch on many topics and constitute a valuable primary source for historians. A five-volume addendum made up of sermons delivered by Mormon leaders from 1886 to 1898 has been published by Brian H. Stuy under the title *Collected Discourses* (1987–1992).

– K –

KAPP, ARDETH GREENE (1931–). Leader of **Young Women**. Born on 19 March 1931 in Glenwood, Alberta, Canada, Ardeth Greene had a small-town upbringing. While attending **BYU**, she met Heber Kapp, whom she married in 1950.

Living in Utah and California, the Kapps built a series of seven homes. Ardeth worked for the telephone company for 10 years. Later she earned a bachelor's degree in elementary education at the University of Utah, followed by an M.S. in curriculum development from **BYU**. In addition to teaching school and supervising student teachers, Ardeth Kapp worked as a writer and consultant. She authored several books, articles, and instructional manuals.

In the Church she had experiences ranging from **Primary** and **Sunday School** teacher to board member of the **Relief Society.** Having served as **Young Women** president in three **wards**, she was called to the Church's youth **correlation** committee and then the curriculum development committee. In 1972 she became a **counselor** in the general presidency of the Young Women, and from 1984 to 1992 served as general president of the Young Women. The theme repeated in Young Women under her direction included this affirmation: "We will stand as witnesses of God at all times and in all things, and in all places" (from ***Book of Mormon***, Mosiah 18:9).

Her community service includes membership on a citizens planning commission, the board of trustees for the National Coalition against Pornography, and the executive board of the Mental Health Resource Foundation. She accompanied her husband when he was called as president of the Canada Vancouver Mission. She continued to lecture and publish for the Latter-day Saint audience.

KENNEDY, DAVID M. (1905–1996). Banker, political leader, Church leader. Born in Randolph, Utah, on 21 July 1905, David Kennedy lived in this small rural town and performed all the chores common to ranches. Later the family moved to Ogden, Utah. He attended high school at Weber Academy (later Weber State University). At age 20 he married Lenora Bingham. Within two months, he was on his way to Great Britain to serve a Church **mission**.

Returning to Utah in 1928, Kennedy completed studies at Weber College. Then the couple went east to Washington, D.C. David found employment as a clerk with the Federal Reserve Board. He graduated from the George Washington University Law School in 1935 and continued working for the Federal Reserve. Among their Church associates were **J. Willard Mariott**, Senator **Reed Smoot**, and **Ezra Taft Benson**. In 1942 David became a **counselor** in a **ward** bishopric and in 1944 was made **bishop**.

Still employed by the Federal Reserve Board, Kennedy completed a degree at Rutgers University Graduate School of Banking. In 1946 he accepted a position with the Continental Illinois National Bank and Trust Company of Chicago. He ascended to become president and then chairman. For 22 years the Kennedys were contributors to the Chicago community. In the Church he served for 15 years as a counselor in the **stake** presidency.

While at Chicago he served on the board of **Nauvoo Restoration, Inc. (NRI)**. He was chairman of the mayor's committee for economic development, head of the Citizen's Bond Committee, on the board of trustees for the University of Chicago, and on the board of trustees for the Brookings Institution. He chaired a commission that made recommendations on improving the organization of the federal budget.

In early 1969 Kennedy became U.S. Secretary of the Treasury. In less than two years he resigned but remained ambassador at large, traveling to many countries and negotiating on economic matters. He also became U.S. ambassador to NATO. In 1973 he resigned from government. Kennedy then received another **call** from the Church when he was asked to be an ambassador to the world. Traveling to different countries, meeting with high government officials, he was remarkably successful obtaining unofficial or official recognition of the Church. He thus played a key role in the worldwide expansion of Mormonism in the generation following 1973.

KERR, W. ROLFE (1935–). Educator, **general authority**. Born on 29 June 1935 in Tremonton, Utah, Kerr attended Utah State University receiving a bachelor's degree in agriculture. He also earned a master's degree at Utah State University and a doctorate at the University of Utah.

Kerr served as **counselor** in bishoprics, **stake** president, on the **Sunday School** general board, and as **president** of the Texas Dallas Mission. In 1996 he was called to the Second **Quorum** of the **Seventy** and the following year to the First Quorum of the Seventy. Kerr's experience in educational administration included positions at Utah State University, Weber State College, and the University of Utah. He was president of Dixie State College and commissioner of the Utah System of Higher Education. As commissioner of education for the Church from 2005 through 2008, Kerr directed operations of **BYU, BYU–Idaho, BYU–Hawaii**, LDS Business College, and **seminaries** and **institutes of religion** throughout the world.

KIKUCHI, YOSHIHIKO (1941–). General authority. Born on 25 July 1941 in Hokkaido, Japan, Kikuchi graduated from Asia University of Tokyo and became sales manager and then president of businesses. Converted to the Church in 1955, he served as a **missionary** and later as **stake** president in Tokyo. He served as **president** of the Hawaii Honolulu Mission and president of the **temple** in Tokyo before his call to the First **Quorum** of the **Seventy** in 1977. He and his wife, Toshiko, have four children.

KIMBALL, JONATHAN GOLDEN (1853–1938). General authority, beloved preacher known for his humor. Born in Salt Lake City, Utah, on 26 June 1853, J. Golden Kimball was the son of prominent leader Heber C. Kimball, **counselor** in the **First Presidency** of the Church. Only 15 when his father died, Golden became a mule driver. In addition to making some money and acquiring a skill, he acquired the habit of swearing. "You can't drive mules if you can't swear," he said (Cheney, *The Golden Legacy*, 18). At the time he did not participate in Church activities.

In the 1870s Golden and his mother joined other family members as **pioneers** of the Bear Lake, Utah, area. In 1881, at the age of 28, Golden moved to Provo with his brother to attend Brigham Young Academy (now **BYU**). Inspired by **Karl G. Maeser**, he raised his sights. Two years later he accepted a call to serve a **mission** in the southern states, where his down-to-earth way of expression enabled him to communicate with ordinary people.

After his mission, he married Jennie Knowlton. Kimball was sent back to the southern states as mission **president**. In 1892, he was named as one of the First Council of the **Seventy**. For the nearly half century of his life that remained, he associated with other Church leaders, traveled throughout the **stakes** and **wards**, and spoke at the **general conference**.

Tall and lanky, J. Golden Kimball spoke with a high-pitched voice. He never totally abandoned the swearing habit, using words, he said, that were left over "from a much larger vocabulary" (Cheney, *The Golden* Legacy, 37). He was a distinctive personality, an original.

"A lot of people in the Church believe that men are called to leadership in the Church by revelation and some do not," he said. "But I'll tell you, when the Lord calls an old mule skinner like me to be a General Authority, there's got to be revelation" (Cheney, *The Golden Legacy*, 100).

As stories by and about J. Golden Kimball were passed from person to person, they assumed a life of their own. Some were embellished, others invented. He had become a subject of Mormon **folklore**. He died in a car accident in 1938.

KIMBALL, SPENCER W. (1895–1985). Arizona businessman, civic leader, **general authority**, **president** of the Church. Born in Salt Lake City, Utah, on 28 March 1895, Spencer Kimball moved with his family to southeastern Arizona at the age of three. Raised in Thatcher, where his father was **stake** president, he went through the local schools and from 1914 to 1916 preached Mormonism as a **missionary** in the Central States Mission. After one semester of study at the University of Arizona, Kimball was inducted into the army. He married Camilla Eyring and, when his army service was deferred, took a job at a bank. In 1927 he started his own insurance agency in Safford, Arizona. He was prominent in local politics and community service. In 1936 he became president of the Arizona Rotary Club.

From 1924 he was a **counselor** in the **stake** presidency, and in 1938 he became president of the Mount Graham Stake. In 1943 he was called to the **Quorum** of the **Twelve Apostles** and moved to Salt Lake City. In addition to the usual travels to **stake conferences** throughout the Church, Kimball was given special responsibilities over missionary work and assisting **Native Americans**. Under his direction the Indian Placement Program developed as a means of providing educational opportunity for children. He repeatedly preached against racial prejudice. Kimball suffered from health problems, some serious. After throat cancer he could speak only with a hoarse whisper. But he persisted and the people loved him for it.

It was a surprise when at age 78 he succeeded to the presidency of the Church. At the most, people assumed he would preside very briefly. To the contrary, however, his administration from 1973 to 1985 became the most animated in the history of the Church to that time. He greatly expanded the number of missionaries. Countries hitherto unexposed to Mormonism were opened up to proselytizing. **Temples** were erected in many parts of the world, increasing from 15 to 31. **Area** conferences were held, enabling members in Chile and Finland, Korea and Tonga, and many other places, to see President Kimball personally along with other general authorities and in exciting Saturday programs demonstrate costumes, songs, and dances of their own culture. Administrative changes, notably the organization of the First **Quorum of the Seventy**, were made to cope with the rapid growth of **membership**. A great sense of vigor infused the Church under Kimball's leadership. "Lengthen your stride," he urged the members (*Ensign*, November 1974, 117). His own motto was "Do it." In 1978 a longstanding policy of not ordaining **blacks** to the **priesthood** (although some had been baptized as members) was reversed. The announcement, presented as the will of the Lord, was quickly followed by proselytizing in Nigeria, Ghana, and other parts of **Africa**.

Following cerebral hemorrhage, a third round of brain surgery in 1981 left him so weak that for the last three or four years of his life most of the routine business of administration was carried on by his two **counselors**. His wife, Camilla Eyring Kimball, sister of **Henry Eyring**, was a vivacious woman of high intelligence. They had four children. *See also* PROPHET.

KNIGHT, GLADYS (1944–). Celebrated performing artist. Born in Georgia, Gladys sang as a soloist with the local church choir. At age eight, she won the Ted Mack Original Amateur Hour contest. With her cousins, she formed The Pips, producing such hits as "I Heard It through the Grapevine" and "Midnight Train to Georgia." She won Grammy awards, platinum and gold records, a Clio, a CableACE Award, American Music Awards, and a place in the Rock 'n' Roll Hall of Fame and the Rhythm and Blues Hall of Fame.

When her daughter, Kenya, and her son, Jimmy, joined the **Church of Jesus Christ of Latter-day Saints**, Gladys did not immediately show a personal interest. Eventually she agreed to take the **missionary** lessons and was baptized in 1997. In 1999 she addressed the annual Women's Conference. That same year, her son, Jimmy, died at age 36.

Knight continued to accumulate awards, including Grammy for Best Traditional R&B Vocal Performance in 2002 and Grammy for Best Gospel Performance in 2005. She organized and directed Saints Unified Voices, winning the Grammy Award for Best Gospel Choir in 2006.

KOPISCHKE, ERICH W. (1956–). Businessman, educator, **general authority**. Born 20 October 1956 in Elmshorn, Germany, Kopischke earned a degree in business. After service as a **missionary** and in the military, he worked as an executive in the insurance industry. In 1996 he joined the Church Educational System, and in 2000 he was appointed Europe Central area director. In 2003 he was called to serve as president of the Berlin, Germany, mission. He served as a **bishop's counselor, stake high councilor**, district **president**, and stake president. He served as second and first counselor in the Europe Central area presidency. In 2007 he was called to the First **Quorum** of the **Seventy** and assigned to the presidency of the Europe Central Area. He is married to Christiane Glück, and they have seven children.

–L –

LAMANITE. One of the large groupings in the *Book of Mormon* account, named after Laman, a member of the original colony that left Jerusalem. A superficial reading sometimes leaves the impression of a long struggle between "good guys" and Lamanite "bad guys," but the history was much more complex than this, as intermingling occurred and both groups showed the ability at different points to achieve a high level of Christian living or descend to an abysmal depravity.

Since the Lamanites were the survivors at the end of the *Book of Mormon* narrative, they were considered to be among the ancestors of the **Native Americans**, sometimes called Lamanites—a usage sometimes extended to include **Polynesians**. A student performing group from **BYU** called the Lamanite Generation put on a lively show of song and dance that drew from both Native American and Polynesian cultures.

Those employing the term with reference to modern peoples intend to emphasize the promised "flowering," the glorious future, of the scriptural references. But non-Mormon Native Americans do not understand or accept the designation, and some Mormon Native Americans deplore its negative connotations. Some scholars follow John

Sorenson in arguing that the designation should belong only to those from a small area in **Central America**.

LANT, CHERYL C. (1944–). Educator; leader of women, children, and youth. Born 30 January 1944, and raised in Utah, Lant attended **BYU**, where she studied human development and family relations. She developed a phonic-based beginning reading program and with her husband became cofounder and co-owner of a private school for children. Her Church service included **ward Relief Society** president, ward **Young Women** president, and member of the **Primary** general board. In 2005 Lant became general president of the Primary. She and her husband, John, are the parents of nine children.

LATTER-DAY SAINT STUDENTS ASSOCIATION (LDSSA). Organization for Mormon college students. At colleges and universities where there are sufficient numbers of Mormons, the LDSSA sponsors social activities and represents the interests of its student members on campus. Its officers are students, but it has a faculty adviser, usually an instructor from the **institute of religion**.

LDS. Latter-day Saint or Saints. In English-speaking settings, Church members often use LDS instead of Mormon.

LDS FAMILY SERVICES. Professional counseling available to assist members dealing with problems ranging from marital conflict to addiction, depression, and same-gender attraction. Members may approach the agency directly. Often they are referred by their bishop. Adoption services assist in bringing together families who desire to adopt and mothers who voluntarily decide that such would be better for their child. In addition to 55 offices located throughout the United States, the agency has nine international offices. Like other such agencies, LDS Family Services charges a fee.

LDS PHILANTHROPIES. Previously known as LDS Foundation, LDS Philanthropies coordinates voluntary contributions to the Church and its different entities and humanitarian projects. Accepting contributions from nonmembers as well as members of the Church,

LDS Philanthropies applies the funds as needed or according to the specific desires of the donor. The contribution goes entirely to the specified recipient program, with zero deducted for overhead (*LDS Church News*, 17 September 2005).

LEADERSHIP TRAINING. In a lay church with a constantly repeating rotation of people in different positions of responsibility, the challenge of training leaders is immense. The *Handbook of Instructions* explains procedures and lines of responsibility. One of the functions of **ward** and **stake** conferences is to give instruction and answer questions. Throughout the Church each stake has **auditors** who periodically go over the **membership** and financial records and supervise the clerks who keep the records. Visiting **general authorities** and resident **area authority seventies** provided leadership training sessions. Starting on 11 January 2003 periodic leadership meetings were transmitted via satellite in 56 languages to priesthood leaders all over the world. Presidencies of **areas,** stakes, and wards concern themselves with the training and supervision of leaders in their respective jurisdictions.

In 2005, the Church began using e-learning technology for training record keepers, **Primary** teachers, and **Young Women** leaders. In downloadable slide show format, lessons were posted on the website lds.org. German and Spanish translations of some lessons were available, and the lessons were to be translated into Cantonese, Dutch, French, Italian, Japanese, Korean, Mandarin, Portuguese, Russian, Samoan, Swedish, and Tongan.

In addition to such specific training efforts, it should not be overlooked that the Church itself functions as a giant training machine. Young **missionaries**, having necessarily assumed responsibility in decision making and oversight, are well prepared for other **callings**. Serving in positions lower in the hierarchical scale prepares people for moving up. Especially the huge numbers of **counselors**, having participated in discussions and shared responsibility in bishoprics and presidencies, are ready to assume greater responsibility should the occasion arise.

LEE, HAROLD BINGHAM (1899–1973). Civic leader, **general authority**, **president** of the Church. Born in Clifton, Idaho, on 28

March 1899, Lee had a boyhood of farm work, schooling, and the usual Church activity. Precocious, he attended the state normal school and became a school principal at age 17. At age 21, he served a **mission** in Denver, Colorado, preaching, baptizing, and gaining administrative experience. After his mission he became principal of a school in Salt Lake City, Utah, and married Fern Lucinda Tanner. They had two daughters.

After a series of responsibilities on the **ward** and **stake** level, Harold became president of the Pioneer Stake in 1930. He was also first appointed and then elected to the city commission. To help his stake members face the hardships of the Depression, Lee began welfare and work projects. In 1935, he was appointed full-time organizer and administrator for a Church-wide **welfare program**. Named to the **Quorum** of the **Twelve Apostles** in 1941, Lee took on broader administrative responsibilities. Especially important was his effort in the 1960s to promote **correlation**, a simplification of programs.

The death of his wife and his daughter Maureen in 1962 was a personal tragedy for him. The next year he married Freda Joan Jensen, who often accompanied him on his assignments. In 1970 he became a **counselor** in the **First Presidency**. Thus he was thoroughly prepared when in 1972 he became president of the Church. It was a surprise when he suddenly died of heart failure on 26 December 1973.

LEE, JOHN D. (1812–1877). Colonizer, murderer. After serving in 1828 and afterward as a mail carrier in his home city of Kaskaskia, Illinois, 1828, Lee enlisted in the Illinois Mounted Volunteers during the Black Hawk War of 1832. Afterward, he worked as a clerk in Galena, Illinois. In 1833 he married Aggatha Ann Woolsey, and the two of them joined the **LDS** Church in 1838. They lived in Missouri where Lee became a member of the Danites, a semi-secret militia, in 1838. The same year he served a **mission** to southern Illinois, and in 1841 after the saints had moved to Illinois, he served a mission to Tennessee. He served as a city policeman in Nauvoo in 1843, and in 1844 he left Nauvoo to campaign for Joseph Smith, a candidate for president of the United States. He became one of the original members of the Council of **Fifty** in 1845.

In addition to Aggatha Ann Woolsey, Lee married plural wives Nancy Bean, 1845; Louisa Free, 1845; Sarah Caroline Williams, 1845; Sarah C. Williams, 1845; Abigail Sheffer, 1845; Rachel Woolsey, 1845; Polly Ann Workman, 1845; Deletha Moss, circa 1845; Nancy Ann Vance, 1845; Emeline Vaughn Woolsey, 1846; Nancy Gibbons Armstrong, 1847; Mary Vance Young, 1847; Lavina Young, 1847, Mary Leah Groves, 1853, Mary Ann Williams, 1856; Emma Batchelor, 1858; Teresa Morse Chamberlain, 1859; and Ann Gordge, 1865. He settled in Salt Lake City, Utah, in 1848 and remained there until he was called to settle as part of the Iron Mission in Iron County, Utah, in 1850. In September 1857 he was one of the leaders of a body of Iron County militia and a few Paiute Indians in massacring a party of Arkansas emigrants at Mountain Meadows. He was excommunicated from the **Church of Jesus Christ of Latter-day Saints** for his role in the massacre in October 1870. In 1874 he was arrested for his role in the massacre, convicted in 1876, and executed in 1877. He was reinstated in the LDS Church posthumously in 1961.

LEE, REX E. (1935–1996). Attorney, educator, university president. Born and raised in St. Johns, Arizona, Rex Lee started as a student at **BYU** in 1953, served as a **missionary** in Mexico, and returned to graduate with a bachelor's degree. In 1959 he married Janet Griffin. After graduating from BYU and completing law school at the University of Chicago in 1963, Lee became a law clerk for U.S. Supreme Court justice Byron R. White. Then for eight years he practiced with a law firm in Phoenix, Arizona.

In 1972 he became founding dean of the new J. Reuben Clark Law School at BYU. His job of building a reputable professional school was interrupted by government service in 1975 when he became assistant U.S. attorney general and in 1981 when he became U.S. solicitor general. Representing the government, he argued many cases before the Supreme Court.

In 1989 he was appointed president of BYU. Although fighting a battle with cancer, diagnosed in 1987, he functioned with energy, effectiveness, and good humor until 1995, when he resigned because of failing health. Lee was a **bishop, stake president**, and member of the **Young Men** general board. He and his wife, Janet, had seven children.

LITERATURE. Most writing produced by Mormons from the beginning to the death of **Brigham Young** in 1877 is lacking in the literary qualities that would give it lasting interest. This does not mean a total lack of literary production. At the outset the *Book of Mormon*, a work of over 500 pages, signaled a religion for people who were literate, as did the other **scriptures** and early periodicals. But it was not for their literary qualities that believers valued these writings or the pamphlets written in defense of the new religion.

The hymnal compiled by **Emma Smith** in 1835 included borrowed, adapted, and original hymns appropriate for the new faith; it was revised and expanded in later editions throughout the century. Some poetry, mostly doggerel, appeared in the early periodicals, but poets of greater than average ability, like **Eliza R. Snow** and **John Lyon**, were also expressing themselves. Two professors of English, Richard Cracroft and Neal Lambert, later compiled an anthology, *A Believing People*, in which they show examples of the early poetry but also demonstrate that the literary forte, if there was one for the early Mormons, was probably such personal writings as letters and, more importantly, diaries and autobiographies. A memorable example is *Autobiography of Parley P. Pratt*.

During the final quarter of the 19th century, the existence of the **Young Men** and **Young Women** auxiliary organizations (then known as Mutual Improvement Associations) and the establishment of a periodical, *The Juvenile Instructor*, for the **Sunday School** provided outlets for stories and poems. A poet of ambition, Orson F. Whitney, produced an epic entitled *Elias*. The fiction, highly didactic and moralistic, included a serialized novel based on the *Book of Mormon*, *Corianton*, by **B. H. Roberts**; stories and novels by Susa Young Gates; and Nephi Anderson's *Added Upon* (1898), which traces the life of its characters from the pre-mortal existence through this life and on into their continued interaction after death.

In the early 20th century Anderson and others continued to write fiction in the genre known as "home literature." Similar moralism characterized the fiction in Church magazines. The *Relief Society Magazine* did much to stimulate literary interests through courses in literary history and appreciation and by publishing many stories and poems.

Around midcentury, several works by expatriate Mormons appeared. Vardis Fisher published his Harper Prize novel *Children of God: An American Epic* (1939). Maureen Whipple's *Giant Joshua* (1941) is still considered by some the most distinctively Mormon novel. **Virginia Sorenson** was publishing her Mormon novels, *A Little Lower Than the Angels* and *The Evening and the Morning*. Samuel W. Taylor struck a humorous chord in *Heaven Knows Why* (1948).

Since the 1960s, various circumstances have combined to create a renaissance of Mormon literature. The enlarged **membership** means a larger audience. Church magazines like *Ensign*, the *New Era*, and the *Friend* have actively sought authors and published them. Independent periodicals, especially *Dialogue* and *Sunstone,* have provided additional outlets for poetry, essays, and stories as well as reviews making judgments of quality. **Deseret Book Company** has enlarged its publication scope to include fiction, and other publishers have proved receptive to Mormon subjects. The **AML** has provided a forum for discussion and the presentation of new work and has made annual awards. Not least important, **BYU** has become an academic home for several literary historians as well as poets and novelists.

So fertile has been Mormon literature in the present generation— in novels and short stories, drama, poetry, essays, and even religious and devotional pieces—that a listing quickly becomes a bibliography. A few examples must suffice. Productive poets include May Swenson, Clinton F. Larson, Carol Lynn Pearson, Arthur Henry King, Emma Lou Thayne, and Susan Howe. Edward Geary, Mary Bradford, **Eugene England,** and Louise Plummer are notable essayists. Among the many writing Mormon fiction are Levi Peterson (*Canyons of Grace, The Backslider*), Neal Chandler (*Benediction*), Donald R. Marshall (*The Rummage Sale*, *Frost in the Orchard*), Douglas H. Thayer (*Under the Cottonwoods*), Donald S. Smurthwaite (*Fine Old High Priests, A Wise, Blue Autumn*), **Orson Scott Card**, and Tracy Hickman, the last two writers of science fiction.

Some Mormon writers have achieved considerable success outside the field of Mormon literature. Among them are Orson Scott Card and Anne Perry, whose mystery novels set in Victorian England have garnered a wide following.

Persistent tensions in Mormon literature include realism versus idealism, faithfulness versus rebellion, moralism versus open-ended description, seriousness versus humor. In publication there is also tension between sponsored and unsponsored work. Pieces published by Deseret Book or appearing in Church magazines understandably must meet certain standards of the faith. Independent journals and publishers have greater latitude. Significant literature has emanated from both directions.

Largely unrealized is the literary potential of the international Church. Considering the richness of different traditions, one might anticipate Mormon poetry and novels, hymns and essays, biographies and autobiographies from Peru, France, Tonga, Ghana, and Russia, to mention only a few of the possibilities. *See also* MEMBERSHIP; PLAN OF SALVATION; UTAH PERIOD.

LUDLOW, DANIEL HANSEN (1924–). Educator, administrator, writer. Born in Benjamin, Utah, on 17 March 1924, Ludlow was raised and attended school in Spanish Fork, Utah. He graduated from Utah State University in 1946, received an M.A. from Indiana University in 1953, and earned a Ph.D. from Columbia University in 1955. He then accepted a faculty appointment in religious instruction at **BYU.**

In addition to teaching classes, Ludlow served as dean of his college. In 1972 he was called to be the Church's director of **correlation**, continuing until 1988 except for a two-year **mission** presidency in Perth, Australia, from 1981 to 1983.

A gifted teacher, Ludlow became known far beyond his college classrooms. He participated regularly as a lecturer in the extension series "Know Your Religion." He directed semester-abroad programs in Israel and led many tour groups there. He also conducted tours to Mexico and Central America. Author of at least 10 books in addition to many articles and manuals, Ludlow was editor-in-chief of the five-volume *Encyclopedia of Mormonism* published in 1992.

LUND, GERALD N. (1939–). Author, teacher, **general authority**. Lund was born on 12 September 1939 in Fountain Green, Utah. He earned bachelor's and master's degrees in sociology at **BYU** and did postgraduate work in theology and Hebrew at Pepperdine University.

From 1965 he taught **seminary** and **institute** and served as a curriculum writer for the Church Educational System (CES).

He wrote *The Work and the Glory*, a popular multivolume historical novel that follows a fictional family through its experiences in the opening decades of Church history. Transferred to the screen, it achieved some note. Lund also wrote a number of other books, including a series of fictional books on the life and ministry of Christ. He served as branch **president, stake missionary, counselor** in bishopric, **bishop**, stake president. In 2002 he was called to the Second **Quorum** of the **Seventy**. He and his wife, Retta, have seven children.

LYON, JOHN (1803–1889). Poet, missionary, drama critic. Born on 4 March 1803 in Glasgow, Scotland, John Lyon was raised by his mother after his father's death in 1811. He left home to become a weaver's apprentice and then a spinner's apprentice, but lost both positions when economic conditions became tight. Anxious for self-improvement, he took classes in the local charity schools.

At 21, John moved to Kilmarnock, Scotland, and found work as a weaver. He married Janet Thomson. Twelve children were born, eight surviving to adulthood. He joined a local literary society and worked hard to master basic writing skills. To supplement his primary income, Lyon worked as a correspondent for several newspapers of the region, publishing sketches, news items, and poems.

In 1843 he heard a Mormon preacher. After reading the *Book of Mormon* and various tracts, Lyon was baptized in March 1844. Soon after, his wife and older children also joined the new religion. During the next five years he became presiding **elder** of the Mormon congregation in Kilmarnock. He wrote poetry on Mormon themes and published in the *Millennial Star*.

From 1849 he served as a **missionary** in Worcester, England, baptizing at least 360 people. At the end of 1851 he moved to Glasgow as **president** of the missionary district. Along with preaching, baptizing, and traveling, Lyon also found time to write poetry and collect poems previously written. In early 1853 his collected poems were published as *Harp of Zion*, with all proceeds earmarked for the assistance of Mormon immigrants.

Emigrating with his family to Utah in 1853, the 50-year-old Lyon plunged into Church activity. Entering **polygamy**, he took a second wife in 1856. He was appointed president of the Endowment House, where **ordinances** of the **temples** were provided while awaiting the completion of the Salt Lake Temple, and for 30 years he officiated there regularly. Lyon also became official territorial librarian. In addition to publishing many poems in the newspapers, he wrote others that remained unpublished. As drama critic for the *Deseret News* he attended opening nights at the Salt Lake Theatre and gave his evaluations.

A biography by great-grandson T. Edgar Lyon Jr. acknowledges that much of the creative work of the self-taught John Lyon was undistinguished. Yet he often successfully communicated the values and aspirations of his fellow believers, and he was among those who sought to raise the standards of Mormon literary expression.

LYON, T. EDGAR (1903–1978). Educator, **missionary**, historian. Born in Salt Lake City, Utah, in 1903, T. Edgar Lyon was the son of David and Mary Cairns Lyon and a grandson of poet **John Lyon**. He attended the University of Utah for two years and then was called as a missionary to the Netherlands. After his return, he married Hermana Forsberg; they went on to have six sons.

After graduating Lyon taught high school in Rigby, Idaho, and then became a **seminary** teacher. When summer seminars at **BYU** from **Sidney B. Sperry** piqued his interest, Lyon arranged a leave of absence and attended the University of Chicago, where he studied with Edgar Goodspeed and William W. Sweet and earned a master's degree.

Lyon was called at age 30 to be **president** of the Netherlands Mission, serving from 1933 to 1937. He concentrated on training local leadership, which turned out to be timely since World War II forced the evacuation of American missionaries.

Returning to Utah, Lyon was assigned to the new **institute of religion** at the University of Utah. For more than 30 years he taught classes in the **Bible**, *Book of Mormon*, *Doctrine and Covenants*, and Mormon history. His close associate was fellow teacher **Lowell L. Bennion**. Lyon entered the graduate program in history at the University of Utah and in 1962 was awarded the Ph.D. A prolific writer, he authored many articles and manuals.

In the 1960s, Lyon was named official historian for **NRI,** exerting his influence to encourage authenticity in the project and compiling extensive files on the **Illinois Period.** He became an early member of the **MHA** and in 1967 served as its president. He launched a major new one-volume history of Nauvoo and made methodical progress through its early stages. With Lyon's death, this project was inherited by historian Glen M. Leonard, who in 2002 published *Nauvoo: A Place of Peace, a People of Promise.*

– M –

MAESER, KARL G. (1828–1901). Educator, moralist. Born in Vorbrucke, Meissen, Germany, Maeser enjoyed a good education. Private tutoring instructed him in French, Italian, and Latin. He also learned the piano and organ and conducted choirs. Maeser studied at the Krenz Schule and graduated from the Friederichstadt Schullehrerseminar. He became a teacher for a while in Dresden, Germany, and then took employment as a private tutor in Bohemia. In 1854 he married Anna Meith.

In 1855 Maeser came in contact with Mormonism. An agnostic, he was impressed by the sincere **testimony** of the Mormon **missionaries.** After being baptized he was named **president** of the Dresden branch, leading this small group to America the next year. Out of money, he stopped in the eastern United States and worked as a music teacher until he could go on to Utah.

From 1860 on, except for a three-year mission back to Germany, Maeser was an educator. He headed the Union Academy and tutored **Brigham Young**'s children. In 1876 he was named principal of the new Brigham Young Academy in Provo. Young's instructions included, "I want you to remember that you ought not to teach even the alphabet or the multiplication tables without the Spirit of God" (Wilkinson and Skousen, *Brigham Young University: School of Destiny*, 67). His students long remembered him for his aphorisms and moral lessons.

Appointed general superintendent of Church schools, he was released from the Brigham Young Academy so that he could travel and supervise scattered academies. In 1894 he became a member of the superintendency of the **Sunday School**. Crusty but tender of heart, Maeser spoke with a slight accent. He expressed his philosophy of education in *School and Fireside* (1898). He died on 14 February 1901. *See also* BRIGHAM YOUNG UNIVERSITY.

MANIFESTO. Document issued by Church president **Wilford Woodruff** in 1890 that is often regarded as a dividing point in Mormon history in that it marked the end of **polygamy**. Actually, the facts are a little more complex.

The manifesto itself (*Doctrine and Covenants*, official declaration 1) falls short of an absolute prohibition. "My advice to the Latter-day Saints," said Woodruff, "is to refrain from contracting any marriage forbidden by the law of the land." Moreover, there was a distinction between the contracting of a new marriage and the continuation of an existing relationship. Even those willing to discontinue the former would find it difficult to end the latter.

Following the 1890 Manifesto, Mormon polygamy went into a sharp decline. Relatively few new plural marriages—compared to all marriages and to pre-1890 marriages—were performed, mostly outside of the United States. Meanwhile, those who had become polygamists prior to 1890 were steadily dying off. In 1904 a second manifesto was issued and much more rigidly enforced.

The 1890 Manifesto was an official statement of intent. Signaling the beginning of the end of polygamy, it prepared the way for Utah's admission to the union as a state. None of the **general authorities**, none of the **stake presidents**, none of the **bishops** or branch presidents is now a polygamist. The Church does not now advocate polygamy. Anyone found guilty of teaching or practicing it is subject to **excommunication**. *See also* FUNDAMENTALISTS.

MARRIAGE. Marriage is held in high esteem by Mormons. In fact, it is considered a vital part of progress toward eternal life. Although **polygamy** was urged upon the faithful for some 40 years, far more fundamental is marriage itself, the joining together of a man and a woman in the bonds of matrimony. Premarital and extramarital sex are condemned. Marriage provides the necessary structure of love and adult modeling for children. It also enhances the happiness and fulfillment of husband and wife. "Faithfulness to the marriage covenant," said Church **president Ezra Taft Benson**, "brings the fullest joy here and glorious rewards hereafter."

The highest form of marriage is eternal marriage as performed in the **temples**. By **priesthood** authority the officiator pronounces the partners sealed together "for time and all eternity." Because the two partners share the same religious faith and have made the same solemn commitments, temple marriages have a significantly lower **divorce** rate than other marriages.

In terms of actual behavior, of course, Mormon marriage practice falls short of the ideal. Through choice or circumstance, a number of adults remain single. Many marriages are not performed in the temple, although some of these are later sealed as eternal relationships. Despite the greater durability of temple marriages, many marriages end in divorce.

A **First Presidency** statement of 19 October 2004 favored defining marriage as a union between a man and a woman. In June 2006, **Russell M. Nelson**, representing the Church, met with 55 rabbis, archbishops, evangelical leaders, priests of the Greek Orthodox Church, and others to sign a letter and hold a press conference in support of a defense of marriage amendment to the U.S. Constitution. The amendment failed in the U.S. Senate, but proponents, fearful that activist judges would redefine the institution of marriage, promised they would return. The ideal of a stable marriage is repeatedly taught. Probably no other religion emphasizes the importance and eternal significance of marriage to the same degree. *See also* FAMILY; SEALING.

MARRIOTT, J. WILLARD (1900–1985). Businessman, Church leader. Born in Ogden, Utah, on 17 September 1900, J. Willard (or Bill) Marriott had the experience of working on farms, herding sheep and cattle. For two years, from 1919 to 1921, he was a **missionary** in New England. Paying his way with summer jobs, he graduated from Weber College and in 1927 from the University of Utah.

He opened a root beer stand in Washington, D.C., and returned to Utah to marry Alice Sheets. Another root beer stand was followed by a restaurant, the Hot Shoppe. Other restaurants followed: Hot Shoppe Number One, Number Two, and so on. Marriott weathered the Great Depression and expanded his chain of restaurants, as well as moving into airline catering and hotels. After the war he became president of the National Restaurant Association.

Marriott became a **counselor** in the **stake** presidency in 1946 and two years later stake **president** in Washington, D.C. His accomplishments include seeing the completion of the first Mormon chapel there, supervising the expansion of **membership** from one little branch to several stakes, and finally acquiring property and watching the completion of the Washington, D.C., Temple in 1976.

Active Republicans, both Marriott and his wife participated in party politics and supported the arts. He chaired the inauguration committees in 1969 and 1973. For several years he chaired the American Historical and Cultural Society, which sponsored Honor America concerts at the Kennedy Center.

Marriott was awarded an honorary degree by the University of Utah. In return for a substantial gift to the University of Utah, the J. Willard Marriott Library was named after him. A generous donation to **BYU** resulted in the Marriott Activities Center, which houses major athletic events.

MASON, JAMES O. (1930–). Physician, public health administrator, **general authority**. Born on 19 June 1930 in Salt Lake City, Utah, Mason served a full-time **mission** in Denmark. He received a bachelor's degree and then a medical degree from the University of Utah. From Harvard University he received a master's degree and doctorate of public health. He interned at the Johns Hopkins University Hospital in Baltimore, Maryland. He served in the military branch of the U.S. Public Health Service and became an epidemiologist.

Mason was director of the infectious diseases division at a Salt Lake City hospital before being named Church commissioner of health services. In 1978 he returned to the University of Utah School of Medicine as chairman of the Division of Community Medicine. Then he served for four years as executive director of the Utah Department of Health. In 1983 he was named director of the national Center for Disease Control and Prevention in Atlanta, Georgia, and in 1989 became assistant secretary for health and head of the U.S. Public Health Service.

In the Church, Mason served as **bishop, stake president**, and **regional representative**. In 1994 he was called to the Second **Quorum** of the **Seventy**. In 1996 he became president of the **Africa area** and in 1998 president of the Africa West area. In October 2000, he was honorably released from his **calling** as a general authority. He and his wife, Marie, are the parents of seven children.

MAXWELL, NEAL A. (1926–2004). Educator, political scientist, **general authority**. Born on 6 July 1926 in Salt Lake City, Utah, Maxwell graduated from the University of Utah with a degree in political science. For two years he was a **missionary** in eastern Canada. After serving as a legislative assistant to U.S. Senator Wallace F. Bennett, Maxwell accepted teaching and administrative positions at the University of Utah. In 1970 he became executive vice president of the university. He was commissioner of education for the Church Educational System from 1970 to 1976.

In the Church, Maxwell served as **bishop**, general board member for **Young Men**, member of the Adult **Correlation** Committee, and **regional representative**. In 1974, he was named an **assistant to the twelve**. Two years later he was one of the presidency of the First **Quorum** of the **Seventy**. In 1981, at the age of 55, Maxwell became a member of the Quorum of the **Twelve Apostles**.

Known for his eloquent preaching, Maxwell authored more than 30 books. In 1998, the Neal A. Maxwell Presidential Endowed Chair in political theory, public policy, and public service was established by private donors at the University of Utah. In 2006 the Neal A. Maxwell Institute for Religious Scholarship was established at **BYU**.

MCCONKIE, BRUCE REDD (1915–1985). Attorney, **missionary**, **general authority**. Born on 29 July 1915 in Ann Arbor, Michigan, McConkie was raised in Utah. After serving a mission in the Eastern States Mission from 1934 to 1936, he attended the University of Utah Law School, receiving his law degree in 1939. In 1937, while still a student, he married Amelia Smith, daughter of **Joseph Fielding Smith**. McConkie was assistant Salt Lake City attorney and city prosecutor until entering the U.S. Army as an intelligence officer in 1941. At the end of the war he was a lieutenant colonel.

At the relatively young age of 31, McConkie was called as one of the First Council of the **Seventy**. From 1946 he traveled to **stake conferences**, addressed **general conferences**, and for three years served as **president** of the Southern Australia Mission. In 1972 he became a member of the **Quorum** of the **Twelve Apostles**.

A diligent student of the **scriptures**, McConkie came to be acknowledged as a doctrinal authority. As a young man he started the systematic scriptural study that provided the basis for his later exposition. The publication of *Mormon Doctrine* (1958) made his name a household word throughout the Church. Also important was a three-volume commentary on the New Testament. McConkie's personal commitment to **Jesus Christ**, the subject of many of his sermons, led to a six-volume work on the life and mission of the Savior, a hymn entitled "I Believe in Christ," and a moving **testimony** in his final conference address in April 1985. Less than two weeks later he died of cancer.

MCKAY, DAVID O. (1873–1970). Educator, apostle, Church **president**. Born on 8 September 1873 in Huntsville, Utah, McKay lived his early life in a rural environment. He played football and was president of his student body in college. After graduating from the University of Utah in 1897, he was a **missionary** in Scotland. Upon his return he married Emma Ray Riggs and took a teaching job at Weber Academy in Ogden, Utah. He became its principal from 1902 to 1908.

In 1906 he was called to be a member of the **Quorum** of the **Twelve Apostles**. In addition, he became a leader in the general **Sunday School** organization and Church commissioner of education. In 1922–1924 he was president of the European Mission.

Tall and handsome with a head of wavy white hair, McKay was striking. Exuding confidence and good will, he was popular among his people. His sermons were often illustrated with quotations from Shakespeare or his favorite poet, Robert Burns. The McKay family seemed a model with seven children and obvious affection and respect between the parents. When he could find time, McKay returned to his rural Huntsville, where he could ride horses and breathe fresh air.

In 1934 he was called as a **counselor** to Church president **Heber J. Grant**. During the 1930s and '40s he and his colleagues shepherded the Church through the Great Depression and World War II. In 1951 David O. McKay became ninth president of the Church.

Membership had passed the million mark. In addition to continuing emphasis on the **family**, he highlighted missionary work. "Every member a missionary" was an oft-repeated saying of his. From 1951 to 1971, the number of missionaries rose from 2,000 to 13,000, the number of **stakes** from 184 to 500. McKay had an international outlook. During his administration, **temples** were constructed at Los Angeles and Oakland and also in Switzerland, New Zealand, and England.

MCMURRAY, W. GRANT (1947–). Historian, **RLDS** Church authority. Born on 12 June 1947 in Toronto, Canada, McMurray was raised in the RLDS Church. He received a B.A. in religious instruction from Graceland College in 1969 and in 1975 the master of divinity degree from St. Paul School of Theology in Kansas City, Missouri. Starting in 1971, he was employed by the RLDS Church, serving as assistant to the director of the Division of Program Planning (1971–1972), historical research assistant (1972–1973), church archivist (1973–1976), assistant commissioner of history (1976–1982), world Church secretary and executive assistant to the **First Presidency** (1982–1992), and member of the **Quorum** of the First Presidency (1992–1996).

Ordained **president** of the RLDS Church on 15 April 1996, he was the first president of that church not a direct descendant of **Joseph Smith**. For personal reasons, he resigned from his presidential office on 29 November 2004. "I have made some inappropriate choices," he said, "and the circumstances of my life are now such that I cannot continue to effectively lead the church." On 12 October 2005 he was named executive director of Missouri Impact. *See also* VEAZEY, STEPHEN M.

MELCHIZEDEK PRIESTHOOD. The higher **priesthood**, to which every **worthy** adult male in the Church is eligible. It is conferred by the laying on of hands by those who are in authority (**Articles of Faith**, no. 5). Offices within the Melchizedek Priesthood include **elder**, **high priest**, **patriarch**, **seventy**, and apostle. As an indispensable part of the **restoration** of the **gospel**, **Joseph Smith** and **Oliver Cowdery** received the Melchizedek Priesthood in 1829 or early 1830 when the ancient apostles Peter, James, and John appeared and conferred it upon them. At the same time they were ordained apostles and received the keys of the **dispensation** of the fullness of times.

Mormons understand priesthood to be eternal, going back to the pre-mortal existence. Defined as the authority to act in God's name, it has been held by various individuals during the history of the world. The **patriarch** Abraham received it from Melchizedek, a priest and king of Salem, after whom it is named in order to avoid the frequent use of God's name.

Although it is a lay organization with no professional **clergy**, priesthhod is regarded as anything but unimportant; to the contrary, priesthood authority is a prerequisite to the authorized preaching of the **gospel** and validly administering the **ordinances** of salvation. *See also* AARONIC PRIESTHOOD; PRIESTHOOD.

MEMBERSHIP. Technically one becomes a member of the Church upon **baptism** and **confirmation**. Since age eight, the "age of accountability," is the minimum age for baptism, younger children of Mormon families are considered "children of record." The membership figures here will include these.

Starting with the original six members on 6 April 1830, Church membership grew to 26,000 members by 1844, the year of **Joseph Smith**'s death. In 1877, the year of **Brigham Young**'s death, the total reached 115,000. At the turn of the century there were over 283,000 Mormons. In 1919 membership passed 500,000. In 1947, it was 1 million; in 1963, 2 million; in 1979, 4 million; and in 1991, 8 million. At the end of 2005, membership was officially reported as 12,560,869, and in June 2007, the Church reported that it had passed the 13-million member mark.

The growth has not been uniform geographically. In February 1996 a corner was turned, with more than half of members living outside the United States. At the end of 2005, **Central America and Mexico** accounted for more than 1.5 million members, **South America** more than 2.9 million, **Asia** and the South Pacific 1.3 million. The time when Mormonism was exclusively an American church (never completely the case, of course, except at the very beginning) was obviously over. Predictably, differing rates of growth in the different continents will produce a less Anglo-Saxon mix in the future.

To cope with the demands of a skyrocketing membership, Church leaders have sought simplification and coordination through the **correlation** program, divided administrative responsibilities into different world **areas**, and increased the number of **general authorities.**

MENTAL HEALTH RESOURCE FOUNDATION. A nonprofit support organization that follows Church principles to provide resources to assist individuals, health care professionals, social workers, **bishops**, **stake presidents**, or anyone else faced with mental and emotional illness. Books and pamphlets deal with such topics as addictions, aging, bipolar disorders, codependency, depression, eating disorders, and pornography. Sources utilized include the National Institute of Mental Health, Alcoholics Anonymous, and Church articles. An online library can be accessed at MentalHealthLibrary.info.

MERRILL, JOSEPH FRANCIS (1868–1952). Educator, **general authority.** Born to Marriner W. Merrill and Mariah Loenza Kingsbury in Richmond, Utah, Merrill attended local public schools and the University of Utah Normal School. He earned a bachelor of science at the University of Michigan in 1893 and studied at Cornell University and the University of Chicago before earning a Ph.D. at the Johns Hopkins University in physics and electrical engineering in 1899. He had received an appointment as assistant professor of chemistry at the University of Utah in 1893, and he returned to that position after completing the Ph.D. At the University of Utah he served as the director of the Utah state School of Mines and Engineering.

For the next 28 years Merrill's career was focused on Utah. In 1911, while a member of the Granite Stake presidency, he was instrumental in establishing the **LDS** Church's first **seminary** courses for high school students near Granite High School. Through his work, the Utah legislature passed bills that established the University of Utah's School of Mines, Utah Engineering Experiment Station, and the Department of Mining and Metallurgical Research.

In 1898 he married Annie Laura Hyde. She died in February 1917, and he married Emily L. Traub in 1918. In 1928, after 35 years of service to the University of Utah, Merrill left to become the LDS Church's commissioner of education. He brought with him extensive experience in the educational field. In 1931, he was called to be a member of the Council of **Twelve Apostles**. He served in this position until his death in 1952.

MERRILL, MARRINER WOOD (1832–1906). Businessman, **general authority**. Merrill was the son of Nathan Merrill and Sarah Ann Reynolds, the 10th of 13 children. He grew up in New Brunswick, Canada. His mother converted to the **LDS** Church in 1836, but Merrill did not learn of her conversion until he was converted in September 1852. In the spring of 1853, Merrill left his family and all relatives in New Brunswick and traveled to the Salt Lake Valley. Though poorly educated, he was committed to education and made arrangements for his children to receive good educations. In 1857 he freighted supplies during the Utah War.

During the winter of 1859–1860, while residing in Bountiful, Utah, Merrill was called to move to northern Utah and settle in Cache Valley where land was more plentiful and the prospects of financial stability were greater. Along with others he traveled north of Logan, Utah, to help found the settlement at Richmond. He was involved in building and establishing businesses such as railroads, irrigation canals, flour mills, and mercantile stores. In 1861 he was ordained **bishop** of the Richmond **ward** serving for 18 years. In 1879 he was called a **counselor** in the Cache **Stake** presidency where he served for 10 years. In 1884 he was called to serve as the first **president** of the Logan Temple where he served until his death in 1906. In 1889, Merrill was ordained an apostle. Instead of moving to Salt Lake City, he continued living in Richmond and traveled to Salt Lake City to meet with the other general authorities. Ten years later, while still serving in the **Quorum** of the **Twelve Apostles**, he was given the added responsibility of presiding over the Cache Stake, serving two years. Upon his release, the stake was divided into three stakes.

A committed **polygamist**, Merrill married Sarah Ann Atkinson, 10 November 1853; Cyrene Standly, 1856; Anna Sophia Angum, 1857; Jennie Jacobson, 1857; Martha Mary Cardon, 1878; and Eliza Lucina Shepherd, 1880. He entered his last marriage to Hulda Maria Erickson in 1901, one of a number of Mormons to marry after the **Manifesto** of 1890.

MEXICO. *See* CENTRAL AMERICA AND MEXICO.

MILLENNIAL STAR. Official publication of the British Mission from its founding in 1840 to its termination in 1970. The complete title was the *Latter-day Saints Millennial Star.* Its contents include editorials, poetry, sermons, **baptisms**, names of **missionaries** and their activities, immigration organization and departures, and letters from various locations in Great Britain as well as the distant **Zion** of Utah. Starting publication when **Joseph Smith** was still alive, it included some of the earliest documents and historical writings of the Church. Especially for the 19th century, it is a valuable primary source.

MILLENNIUM. Like some other Christians, Mormons believe in a future era of a thousand years when the earth will be renewed (**Articles of Faith**, no. 10). In a strict and narrow sense of the word, they are pre-millennialists, believing that the millennial reign will be ushered in by the Second Coming of **Jesus Christ**. However, the obligation to work for improvement in the present is an integral part of the belief. Moreover, during the Millennium life will not be one of simply basking in the sun. Among other activities carried on will be **missionary** work and service in the **temples**.

Many early Mormons thought the Second Coming and the Millennium were very near. As time has gone on, the expectation has faded but not disappeared. The term *latter-day* in the title of the Church designates the present age as the final **dispensation**. The official belief in a winding-up scene and Millennium is still intact. The standard works, or **scriptures**, all have passages pointing forward to such a final act in the drama of human existence. But Mormon leaders are not among the millennialists who count the days or sell off property in order to await the great event. They insist that no one knows the exact timetable. It is simply "near"—a relative term. Members are urged to be ready—that is, have their "house in order" by following the **commandments**.

MISSION, MISSIONARY, MISSIONARY PROGRAM. From its beginning the Church has been a missionary organization. **Members** were anxious to invite friends and relatives to share the joy they had found in the restored **gospel**. On their own or as called by their leaders, Mormon men departed on missionary preaching tours. Some degree of organization, with mission areas and missionaries organized into conferences, or districts, began to take shape.

By the last generation of the 19th century, the basic outline was established: formal call to missionary service from the first presidency, correspondence through the mail from the mission president or mission office, missionaries going two by two and being assigned to specific locations by their president, missionaries being periodically reassigned, and missionaries being formally released at the end of the mission. In the 20th century the following developments took place:

- Young women were called as missionaries.
- Training programs for newly called missionaries were developed.
- Systematic programs for presenting the gospel to **investigators** were developed to assure adequate instruction.
- The number of missions was increased as opportunity allowed.
- Married couples were called as missionaries, both as full-time missionaries and as "Church service" missionaries to assist in a variety of activities, including assisting patrons at **family history** libraries and serving as guides at **visitors centers**.

Those willing to serve as missionaries are interviewed by their **bishop**. **Worthiness** is ascertained and financial arrangements are discussed. People are not paid to go on missions. With the exception of mission presidents, missionaries support themselves from savings, donations from family, **ward** mission fund, a general mission fund, or some combination of these. When the official letter comes from Church headquarters calling one to be a missionary, the specific mission is indicated. The place of service is determined by need of the Church, although the desire of the prospective missionary may be considered.

In 2004, previous missionary plans were replaced by *"Preach My Gospel": A Guide to Missionary Service*. A series of lessons instructs the investigator on the message of the **restoration, plan of salvation, commandments**, laws and **ordinances** of the **gospel**. While passages of **scripture** are used in teaching, flexibility is allowed as the missionary recognizes individual needs and follows the inspiration of the Spirit.

Although young men are encouraged to prepare themselves for mission calls, less than a third of males between ages 19 and 21 actually serve missions. They must desire to serve, pass a test of **worthiness**, and be mentally and physically sound. Young women who express a desire to serve and similarly qualify may be called at age 21.

In December 2006, 53,164 full-time missionaries were serving. In June 2007, the church had 341 missions. In addition, more than 12,000 church service missionaries served from 8 to 32 hours a week as office assistants, hosts at visitors centers, medical doctors, and many other positions that assisted in fulfilling the **mission of the Church**.

MISSION OF THE CHURCH. Building upon scriptural passages and earlier statements by previous Church leaders, Presidents **Spencer W. Kimball** and **Ezra Taft Benson** brought the mission of the Church into sharp focus. It is to "invite all to come unto Christ and be perfected in him" (*Doctrine and Covenants* 20:50; *Book of Mormon*, Moroni 10:32).

This mission has three dimensions: (1) proclaim the **gospel** to every nation, kindred, tongue, and people; (2) perfect the **saints** by preparing them to receive the **ordinances** of the gospel and by caring for the poor and needy; and (3) redeem the dead by performing vicarious ordinances for them in the **temple**.

In other words, through the **missionary**, nonmembers were to be addressed; through the various programs of the Church, members were to receive the saving ordinances and experience development and opportunities for service; and through **genealogy** and temples, those who are dead would receive the blessings of the gospel.

MISSIONARY TRAINING CENTERS. From the 1830s, missionaries were advised to study the **scriptures** and prepare themselves to be effective representatives of the Church (*Doctrine and Covenants*, sections 14–19, 88). To assist them a school operated briefly at Kirtland, Ohio. During the **Utah Period**, at the end of the 19th century, several academies, including the one that became **BYU**, offered brief missionary training classes. For several decades in the early to mid-20th century a "mission home" in Salt Lake City, Utah, provided lodging for newly called **missionaries** as they followed a series of classes that lasted about one week before departing for different fields of labor. A more comprehensive program of instruction came in 1961 with the establishment of the Missionary Language Institute at Provo, Utah, renamed the Language Training Mission in 1963. After 1978, it was called the Missionary Training Center and all missionaries, even those not learning a foreign language, were required to attend.

Following a rigorous program, outgoing missionaries receive instruction in the **scriptures**, missionary techniques, and, where applicable, language. Intensive language instruction follows the "total immersion" approach earlier pioneered by the U.S. military. Some introduction to culture and customs is also included. The typical term for those learning a foreign language is eight weeks. To accommodate the expanding missionary force, missionary training centers have also been established in **South America**, **Europe**, **Asia**, and the **Pacific**. On 22 May 2002 in Ghana, the Church opened its 16th missionary training center throughout the world.

MISSOURI PERIOD. The first Mormons in Missouri were the **missionaries**—Oliver Cowdery, **Parley P. Pratt**, Peter Whitmer Jr., and Ziba Peterson—sent in mid-1830 by **Joseph Smith** on an assignment to preach to the Indians. After unusual success in Ohio these missionaries proceeded westward, reaching Missouri in January 1831, completing a journey from western New York of 1,500 miles. Preaching to the Indians was thwarted by the agent, but a foothold was established. Western Missouri was declared the site of the New Jerusalem (*Doctrine and Covenants*, section 28) with Independence to be "the center place" and site for a **temple** (*Doctrine and Covenants*, section 57). The Mormons from Colesville, New York, moved there. The **gathering** to Missouri had begun.

By 1832 several hundred Mormons had come to Missouri. A printing press was established, two newspapers began publication, and schools were started. The next year saw the publication—interrupted by violence but partially successful—of the ***Book of Commandments***, a compilation of Joseph Smith's **revelations**. Mormons were settling not only in Independence but also in nearby Kaw Township and three other small settlements.

Contrary to instructions, some of the new arrivals came with no visible means of support. Some Mormons made themselves obnoxious by boasting that they were going to take over Jackson County. But the problem of internal discipline might well have been solved had it not been for the outside opposition that finally burst forth into mob violence in 1833. Mobs destroyed the printing press and tarred and feathered two of the Mormon leaders. Several were killed. By November the Mormons were fleeing across the Missouri River northward to Clay County. In an effort to restore his people to their lawful property Joseph Smith came from Ohio at the head of a military force of untrained volunteers, but, recognizing the reality of the situation, disbanded them before any actual battle.

Still looking for a place in Missouri where they might live peaceably, the Mormons moved northward into Caldwell County, newly created in 1836. A center was established at Far West, to which Smith moved his headquarters in 1838. Another center was begun in Daviess County. With the collapse of Kirtland, hundreds came from there to the new Missouri settlements. Those who owned land and property in Jackson County hoped that through legal processes they might return.

But friction seemed unavoidable. The Mormons were not faultless. **Sidney Rigdon** spoke out against dissenters, threatening them with violence, and declared that if mobs attacked again there would be a war of extermination. A paramilitary group, the **Danites**, resorted to violence against Church enemies, justified as self-defense. The Mormons did not limit their settlements to Caldwell County, as many in the Missouri legislature had thought they would, but insisted on their right to settle anywhere.

There was an abundance of guilt on the other side as well. Rabid **anti-Mormons** were eager to drive their enemies out and seize their property. A riot occurred when Mormons tried to exercise their right to vote. Seventeen were killed in a massacre at Haun's Mill. Militias armed on both sides. In this setting Missouri's Governor Lilburn W. Boggs issued his "extermination order": Mormons must leave the state or suffer extermination. When Far West was besieged and tensions were high, Joseph Smith and a few of his colleagues attempted to meet with the other side and negotiate. Instead, they were seized and thrown into prison.

The stage was set for the exodus of the Mormons from Missouri, accomplished in late 1838 and early 1839 under the direction of leaders left at large including **Brigham Young**, Heber C. Kimball, and Edward Partridge. In the cold season of the year, carrying such few belongings as they could salvage, some 12,000 Mormons straggled— in companies, as families, even individually—eastward to seek refuge in Illinois. The **RLDS** Church (now **Community of Christ**) later made its headquarters in Independence.

On 25 June 1976 Governor Christopher S. Bond rescinded the infamous 1838 extermination order. In 1997 a temple was completed and dedicated in St. Louis. At the end of 2005, 59,377 Mormons lived in Missouri, divided into 14 **stakes** and 98 **wards**. *See also* ILLINOIS PERIOD; OHIO PERIOD; ZION'S CAMP.

MONSON, THOMAS SPENCER (1927–). Businessman, **general authority**, **counselor** in the **First Presidency**, Church **president**. Born on 21 August 1927 in Salt Lake City, Utah, Monson received his primary and secondary education there. He served in the U.S. Navy during World War II and subsequently graduated from the University of Utah with a degree in business management.

Monson became a **bishop** at the age of 22. He was employed by the Newspaper Agency Corporation as executive in the advertising division. For Deseret News Press he took the position of sales manager, later becoming general manager. He was president of Printing Industry of Utah and a member of the board of directors of Printing Industry of America. He became a counselor in the **stake** presidency. In 1959 he was called to be president of the Canadian Mission and lived at its headquarters in Toronto for three years.

At age 36, he was called to be a member of the **Quorum** of the **Twelve Apostles**. Chairman of the board of the Deseret News Publishing Company and a member of the board of Newspaper Agency Corporation, he also served on the National Executive Board of **Boy Scouts** of America, receiving both the Silver Beaver and Silver Buffalo awards. He belonged to the Utah Association of Sales Executives, the Salt Lake Advertising Club, and the Salt Lake Exchange Club. For many years he was a member of the State Board of Regents. In 1985, Monson became second counselor in the First Presidency, and in 1995 first counselor to President **Gordon B. Hinckley**. On 4 February 2008 he was called as president of the Church.

MORMON. (1) The proper name of a great *Book of Mormon* prophet who lived at the end of the fourth century. In addition to leading his people militarily, Mormon abridged previous records into the plates later used by **Joseph Smith** in translating the *Book of Mormon*. The book is thus named after a person.

(2) Nickname for members of the **Church of Jesus Christ of Latter-day Saints**. Because it suggests a primary loyalty to an individual prophet and leaves out the central figure of **Jesus Christ**, the term has long been discouraged or carefully placed within quotation marks. But because of the length of the official title of the Church the shorter nickname has proved irresistible. Even Church writers and journalists use it. Properly used, the term applies strictly to the Church of Jesus Christ of Latter-day Saints, not **fundamentalism** and not the **Community of Christ**.

MORMON BATTALION. A battalion of the U.S. Army during the Mexican War (1846–1847) recruited from the Mormon refugees encamped in Iowa after their forced departure from Nauvoo, Illinois.

The point of view of the U.S. government is revealed in an entry dated 2 July 1846 in the diary of President James K. Polk: "Col. Kearny was also authorized to receive into service as volunteers a few hundred of the Mormons who are now on their way to California, with a view to conciliate them, attach them to our country, & prevent them from taking part against us" (Polk, *The Diary of a President*). The Mormon leaders, on the other hand, saw this as a chance to gain help in their migration. Not only were the battalion members fed and clothed during their westward march, but also the pay they earned as soldiers was made available to help their families. Approximately 500 men signed up. Accompanying them were about 80 women, some working as laundresses, and a few children. Recruiter Captain James Allen (promoted to colonel) first led the battalion. When he died en route, after an interim arrangement, Colonel Philip St. George Cooke became commander.

The battalion proceeded overland to Santa Fe. One group of sick, including nearly all the women and children, after wintering at Pueblo, Colorado, went on to the Salt Lake Valley, where they arrived on 28 July 1847, just four days after **Brigham Young**. The rest of the battalion left Santa Fe, marched in a southwestward direction through New Mexico, across southern Arizona and Southern California, and arrived at San Diego in January 1847. Most of them were discharged at Los Angeles in July 1847.

During a pivotal year in the colonization of the West, the Mormon Battalion found itself involved in important events: the settling of San Diego, the gold discovery at Sutter's Mill that precipitated the great California gold rush, and the colonizing of the Salt Lake Valley. *See also* ILLINOIS PERIOD.

MORMON HISTORIC SITES FOUNDATION. An independent foundation dedicated to preserving and restoring sites important in Church history. Formed in 1992 as the Ensign Peak Foundation, the group subsequently adopted a name reflective of its many interests. It has assisted in many projects. The most ambitious of these was the restoration of historic Kirtland, Ohio. Its journal, *Mormon Historical Studies*, is published semiannually.

MORMON HISTORY ASSOCIATION (MHA). An organization formed in December 1965 to further the research and publication of Mormon history. Since its first meeting in 1966, the MHA has held annual meetings, organized adjunct sessions in connection with other professional associations, given awards, and published a newsletter and the *Journal of Mormon History*. *See also* JOHN WHITMER HISTORICAL ASSOCIATION.

MORMON TABERNACLE CHOIR. A celebrated singing group started in the 1860s. For many years its leader was **Evan Stephens**, who increased its size to more than 300 voices. The choir became more widely known with the beginning of weekly live radio broadcasts in 1929, later extended to television, which included also a brief "sermonette," the "spoken word," by **Richard L. Evans**. Its members, amateur in the sense that they are unpaid, are trained musicians, selected by audition, who rehearse every Thursday evening. From

1975 to 1999 its director was **Jerold D. Ottley**. He was succeeded by **Craig D. Jessop**. In 2008 Mac Wilberg, internationally famed choral arranger, succeeded Jessop.

The Mormon Tabernacle Choir has made recordings for CBS Masterworks Records, London-Decca, Argo, and Bonneville Records. It has performed major choral works with the Philadelphia Symphony, Utah Symphony, and Jerusalem Symphony Orchestras. Tours within the United States started under director Evan Stephens. In recent years the choir performed concerts in Japan, Korea, Brazil, Western Europe, Russia, and Israel.

In 2003 the choir was awarded the National Medal of Arts. In 2006 the choir won the Laureate of the Mother Teresa Award for edifying the world through inspirational choral performances and recordings.

MORMON YOUTH SYMPHONY AND CHORUS (MYSC). Two groups of musicians between ages 18 and 33 established in 1969. Like the **Mormon Tabernacle Choir,** MYSC was sponsored by the Church. Musicians with experience in other orchestras and choruses were selected by audition. In addition to performing at **general conferences**, the groups made commercial recordings. The conductor since 1974 was Robert C. Bowden, who also composed and arranged some of MYSC's music. He retired after 25 years of service.

On 1 June 1999 this organization was disbanded. The chorus, renamed the Temple Square Chorale, became a training choir for the Mormon Tabernacle Choir. The orchestra was renamed the Orchestra at **Temple Square**, with no age requirement for membership.

MORONI. Pronounced in English with the accent on the second syllable and a long final vowel: more-own-eye. (1) A prominent leader at the close of the *Book of Mormon*. (2) A resurrected being, who appeared to **Joseph Smith** several times. (3) The statue on the top spire of many **temples**, mistakenly thought by many to be the angel Gabriel. Moroni is sometimes identified as fulfilling Revelation 14:6.

MORRISON, ALEXANDER (1930–). Pharmacist, public official, **general authority**. Born on 22 December 1930 in Edmonton, Alberta, Canada, Morrison joined the Church as a college student. He earned a Ph.D. from Cornell University in 1956 and nine years later a master's degree in pharmacology. He obtained a faculty appointment in public health at the University of Guelph and rose to become department chairman. With the Health Protection Branch of the Canadian government, Morrison promoted laws and regulations to control contaminants. For many years he worked with the World Health Organization, chairing the Scientific and Technical Advisory Committee to the Special Program for Research and Training in Tropical Diseases. In this capacity he made many trips to different nations of **Africa**.

In the Church, Morrison served as branch **president**, **bishop**, and **regional representative**. In 1987, he became a general authority as a member of the First **Quorum** of the **Seventy**, then as a member of the Second Quorum of the Seventy, and again as a member of the First Quorum of the Seventy. In October 2000, he was awarded emeritus status. He and his wife, Shirley, have eight children.

MOUNTAIN MEADOWS MASSACRE. Tragic incident in September 1857 in which virtually an entire wagon company, at least 120 people, was killed by Mormon militiamen and a few Paiute Indians as they were passing through southern Utah on their way to California. The incident must be explained by identifying specific factors that converged at Mountain Meadows in 1857, including war conditions, poor communications, and perhaps provocation.

The summer of 1857 brought the announcement that U.S. troops were on their way to install a new governor in Utah Territory. Some of the soldiers bragged that they intended to kill Mormons, especially Mormon leaders. On the grounds that he had not been notified of his replacement, **Brigham Young** announced that the U.S. troops would be treated as a hostile force. During the latter part of 1857 and early 1858 the Mormon militia was mobilized, preparations were made to evacuate Salt Lake City, Utah, and the supply trains of the advancing army were harassed and burned. Mormons hoped for assistance from Indian allies, who had no love for Americans in general.

The Baker-Fancher wagon train company was from Arkansas. As they moved southward through Utah, they required supplies. Since the Mormons were preparing for war, they generally refused to sell to the company. Rumors of conflicts appeared, but the precipitating events seem to have occurred in Cedar City, Utah, with the harassment of Barbara Morris (the wife of a member of the bishopric and the mother of a member of the **stake** presidency) and, in particular, a conflict over the charges for milling some grain. War hysteria intensified what otherwise might have been solvable conflicts. Stake **president** and militia major Isaac Haight sent militia major John D. Lee and others to Mountain Meadows, where the company had camped to recuperate. They initiated an attack on the company, and when their assault failed, Haight mobilized the militia to assist them in massacring the emigrants. Some Paiutes were involved in the attacks, but local militiamen committed most of the murders.

In initiating the attacks, Haight acted against the consensus of the stake presidency and **high council**, who voted to send a messenger, James Haslam, on horseback to Salt Lake City to obtain instructions from Brigham Young. Young sent a letter with Haslam telling Haight that the settlers "must not meddle with them [the emigrants]." Haslam reached Cedar City two days after the massacre.

The attacks occurred between September 7 and 10 and the massacre took place on September 11. The settlers took most of the emigrants' property. Seventeen children survived the massacre and were returned to Arkansas in 1859.

Although some violence had occurred elsewhere, with the conclusion of hostilities in 1858, investigation into the massacre began. In 1859, Brigham Young, then a private citizen but leader of the Mormon people, offered assistance in bringing the perpetrators to justice, but the federal judges and U.S. marshal refused to accept his offer. In 1876–1877 John D. Lee, Mormon Indian farmer and one of the participants in the massacre, was tried, convicted, and executed by firing squad. None of the other participants was ever tried, either because they turned states evidence, because the U.S. Attorney was unable to accumulate sufficient evidence to try them, or because they escaped U.S. marshals sent to apprehend them.

Juanita Brooks, who wrote the most thorough study of the subject to date, saw the massacre as being the result of a collective hysteria. She did not hold Brigham Young responsible but described the subsequent execution of Lee as an act of scapegoating in the sense that others on the local level had also been involved in the unfortunate decision. At the beginning of the 21st century, histories of the massacre—especially those by Will Bagley and Sally Denton—(and even novels and motion pictures) sought, without any direct evidence, to fasten responsibility on Brigham Young. In response, a number of prominent historians have challenged these allegations. As of this writing, Ronald Walker, Richard Turley Jr., and Glen Leonard have a manuscript in press with Oxford University Press that should correct the record.

Since the massacre, Mormon leaders have denounced the act. They do not consider it justified by the fact of their own **persecution**. **Anti-Mormons** have repeatedly used this incident as an excuse for Mormon bashing, although the general Church **membership** and the **general authorities** bear no responsibility, which must rest with members of the Iron County, Utah, militia, and especially Haight, who led in organizing the affair.

On 11 September 1999, the dedication of a monument at the site was attended by descendants of those in the wagon train and the Mormons who participated. Seeking emotional closure to a painful chapter of history, President **Gordon B. Hinckley** said, "I come as a peacemaker. This is not a time of recrimination or the assignment of blame. . . . It is time to leave the entire matter in the hands of God who deals justly in all things. His is a wisdom far beyond our own." Speaking for the descendants of the victims, the Reverend Stanton Cram of Springdale, Arkansas, said, "We are finding out that we are good people on both sides, decent people—people who want to do the right thing. . . . No one in this world today has any blame for that, and we don't have any right to hold this evil against the Mormon Church or the people here." In 2007, **Elder Henry B. Eyring**, then a member of the **Quorum** of the **Twelve Apostles**, offered an apology for the massacre, placing the blame squarely on the Iron County militia. *See also* JUANITA BROOKS.

MOVIES. As a form of public entertainment, movies became popular in the 20th century. Like other people, Mormons attend movies. The Church counsels its members to avoid NC-17- and R-rated movies.

In the early 20th century, when Mormons appeared in movies as subjects, which was not often, Church members were stereotyped as sinister and manipulative or as quaint and simple-minded. For example, *Trapped by the Mormons*, a silent film, shows a missionary in England who mesmerizes a fair damsel in order to abduct her and take her to a fate worse than death in Utah. An exception is *Brigham Young*, made with the Church's cooperation for the 1947 centennial of the **exodus**, which portrays a heroic leader.

At the beginning of the 21st century, a flurry of movies appeared made by Mormon producers, directors, and often actors. Richard Dutcher produced *God's Army*, *Brigham City*, and *States of Grace*. *Best Two Years* showed the difficulty of proselytizing in the Netherlands and the humanness of the young **missionaries**. *The Work and the Glory*, a successful historical novel in several volumes, was recreated on film by director Sterling Van Wagenen. *The Other Side of Heaven*, based on the missionary experiences of John A. Groberg in Tonga, was directed by Mitch Davis. Several comedies spoofed Mormon behaviors: *Singles Ward, Home Teachers*, *R.M.*, and *Mormons and Mobsters*. *Saints and Soldiers*, a well-reviewed movie about the adventures of a unit of soldiers behind enemy lines in World War II, includes one Mormon character, but his religious identity is never explicit.

The realities of the market have discouraged some. Accustomed to the raucous and irreverent, many moviegoers are not drawn to films that take religion seriously. Christians who long for the spiritual component in entertainment are often prejudiced against anything Mormon. With such predictable audience reaction, investors are reluctant to fund Mormon movies. Richard Dutcher's ambitious recreation of **Joseph Smith** languishes.

Yet the mere existence of competent young Mormons, trained in film schools and experienced from work on other projects, assures that Mormon movies will continue to appear. *See also* EXODUS.

MOYLE, HENRY D. (1889–1963). Attorney, **general authority**. Born on 22 April 1889 in Salt Lake City, Utah, he was the son of James H. Moyle, a prominent Utah Democrat. Henry enrolled at the University of Utah in 1905, receiving his B.S. degree in mining engineering. From 1909 to 1911, he served a full-time mission in the Swiss-German Mission and remained in **Europe** for one year to study at Freiberg University. Returning to the United States, he pursued a law degree at the University of Chicago and earned the J.D. degree in 1915.

Enlisting in the U.S. Army, Moyle became an officer but remained in the United States during World War I. After the war, he began his own law practice. Moyle invested in several businesses, including the Deseret Livestock Company, the Wasatch Oil Company, and a silver mining company. A lifelong Democrat, he served as Utah's Democratic Party chairman and unsuccessfully ran for governor in 1940.

After serving in **ward** and **stake** positions, he was called to the **Quorum** of the **Twelve Apostles** in 1947. Active in organizing and promoting the **welfare program**, he assisted the Church in legal and business affairs. In June 1959, he became second **counselor** in the **First Presidency** under President **David O. McKay**.

MUSEUM OF CHURCH HISTORY AND ART. Following a series of earlier museums that housed artifacts, the present building in Salt Lake City, Utah, adjacent to **Temple Square** was dedicated and opened in 1984. Staffed by curators, historians, and art historians, the museum's basic purpose is to preserve and exhibit significant material remains, crafts, and art from the Mormon past as well as work being produced at the present. A voluntary staff of docents assists in greeting, providing tours and explanations, and visiting schools.

An especially interesting part of the permanent exhibit consists of works by Mormon artists of the 19th century who studied in France and brought back the style of the French impressionists. A handsome volume entitled *Harvesting the Light* prepared by art historian Linda Gibbs was published by the museum. Portraits of Church leaders from the beginning are numerous. For each of the Church presidents a collection of artifacts has been assembled. Temporary exhibits are changed every few months. Periodic Church-wide competitions result in submissions in different artistic media from many countries. *See also* ART.

MUSIC. From the beginning of the Church, music has been part of Mormon worship. Although Mormon musicians have achieved success as composers or performers in the larger arena, here we shall consider music in the Church setting.

In 1830 **Emma Smith** received instructions (*Doctrine and Covenants*, section 25) to compile a hymnal, which she did, publishing her collection in 1835. Hymns from the **Protestant** tradition were included, adapted where necessary, as well as new works by Mormons. As opportunity allowed, this hymnal was revised and expanded in a series of later editions, with music being added to the text by the 1870s. The present official edition was published in 1985. Editions in Spanish, French, German, and other languages have versions of 100 or more of the English hymns but also add others from their respective traditions.

Congregational singing was supplemented by choirs, as for the dedication of the Kirtland Temple in 1836. During the **Illinois Period** singing instructors and the arrival of trained musicians among converts from England led to some ambitious public performances. During the **Utah Period** bands and orchestras were popular. Concerts featured local performers and touring instrumental and vocal virtuosi. An examination of the concert offerings in Salt Lake City, Utah, during the last quarter of the 19th century shows a provincial capital with about as much urbanity and refinement as other cities of the same size. The great Adelina Patti and Jenny Lind thrilled Utah audiences. Gilbert and Sullivan operettas were heard and enjoyed. Helping to raise the standards of music among Mormons were several immigrant converts, including C. J. Thomas, John Tullidge, and George Careless, who gave lessons, wrote criticism, and directed groups.

Many **wards** had choirs, their quality depending on the available voices and the talent of the director. The choir with the greatest prestige was the one that came to be known as the **Mormon Tabernacle Choir**. When **Evan Stephens** took over its direction, the choir's fame expanded through many tours in Utah and eventually outside as well. In 1893 it performed at the Chicago Columbian Exposition and won second prize. In the 20th century and up to the present, the Mormon Tabernacle Choir has continued to be the most public expression of Mormon musicianship, especially as it began its network radio broadcasts in 1929 (later extended to television).

Also in the **Tabernacle** was a great pipe organ. Constructed originally by Australian convert Joseph Ridges, the organ has been improved periodically. The most recent upgrading, completed in 1988, was described by organ historian Barbara Owen in *The Mormon Tabernacle Organ: An American Classic* (1990). Frank W. Asper and **Alexander Schreiner** were the two famed organists for many years. Tabernacle organists Robert Cundick, John Longhurst, and Clay Christiansen, along with assistant organists Bonnie Goodliffe, Linda Margetts, and Richard Elliott, have occupied the great console both as accompanists for the choir and in solo performances. Universities have contributed significantly in teaching composition and training instrumental and vocal performers. **BYU, BYU–Idaho,** and **BYU–Hawaii** sponsor choir and instrumental performances and train successive cohorts of musicians.

Mormon musical composition goes back to the 19th century. Evan Stephens was a prolific composer of hymns and anthems. In the 20th century B. Cecil Gates wrote many single numbers, cantatas, and oratorios. **Leroy Robertson,** a highly accomplished professor of composition, completed *Oratorio from the **Book of Mormon***. Crawford Gates, Robert Cundick, and Merrill Bradshaw are among those who have composed serious choral or operatic works. Tabernacle Choir director Mac Wilberg has achieved international acclaim for his choral arrangements. On a more popular level, the 1947 musical drama *Promised Valley*, composed by Crawford Gates, continued to be produced for many years. Lex d'Azevedo's *Saturday's Warrior*, a dramatic presentation of the **plan of salvation**, employed popular rhythms.

Choirs organized by **seminaries** and **institutes** have performed to large audiences. Especially important in furthering music have been the programs at BYU, BYU–Hawaii, and BYU–Idaho. They not only train music majors but also provide experience for many other students in different choral and instrumental performing groups. As young people with such training return to their home **wards** and **stakes**, they raise musical standards throughout the Church.

With the expansion into parts of the world outside the United States and Western Europe, two principles are in tension. Creativity and a rich diversity are consistent with the scriptural injunction to "prove all things; hold fast to that which is good" (1 Thess. 5:21). Mormonism does not insist on transforming everyone into a single mold. On the other hand, in the interest of unity, the Church desires to have some practices, including worship services, that are the same for its members everywhere. Allowing centrifugal forces to operate without restriction could create chaos.

Up to the present it is the unifying principle that has predominated, as when African Mormons were told that drums were not appropriate to **sacrament** meetings. Yet they have been allowed as part of weekday Church activities, and cultural evenings featuring national and indigenous music and dance have been a popular activity in different parts of the world. In whatever form their music takes, Mormons are still fond of the revealed declaration to Emma Smith in 1830: "The song of the righteous is a prayer unto me" (*Doctrine and Covenants*, section 25). *See also* MEMBERSHIP.

MYSTICISM. Belief in and practice of direct contact, or union, with God, found in both **Christian** and non-Christian traditions. In its classic formulation, as represented by Plotinus and St. John of the Cross, Mormons are not mystics. Their concepts of God and man are simply not conducive to the kind of absorption described by Plotinus as "the flight of the alone to the alone." According to a looser definition, emphasizing direct communication from God to humans, Mormons might qualify, although they do not use the term *mysticism*, preferring **revelation**, inspiration, Holy Ghost, and other terms.

The return to the presence of God that awaits the righteous after death is not a reabsorption into the ground of being. Individual identity is retained, although it operates in perfect harmony with God. For the faithful, such unity begins in this mortal life. Jesus prayed in Gethsemane that "they may be one, even as we are one" (John 17:22). *See also* PLAN OF SALVATION.

– N –

NATIVE AMERICANS. American Indians, or Amerindians. The relationship between white Mormons and Indians has been one of unusual interest. On the one hand, early Mormons, practically all of whom were of white American or European ethnicity, experienced the same conflicts with the native population as other westward-moving Americans. On the other hand, Indians were regarded as descendants of the **Lamanites** described in the *Book of Mormon*. A glorious future was promised for them. Because of the large number of Indians and mestizos in Central and South America, the growth of the Church in those regions is also seen as fulfillment of the scriptural promise.

NAUVOO RESTORATION, INC. (NRI). A Church-founded non-profit corporation that supervises the partial restoration of historic Nauvoo, Illinois, which was occupied by Mormons from 1839 to 1846. Called to assist at NRI were young **missionaries** and older couples, who could play the roles of such period figures as blacksmiths and act as guides for visitors. Restored Nauvoo has become a major attraction not only for tourists but also for school children on field trips. *See also* ILLINOIS PERIOD.

NEAL A. MAXWELL INSTITUTE FOR RELIGIOUS SCHOLARSHIP. Located at **BYU**, this institute serves as the umbrella organization for the Middle Eastern Text Initiative (METI), Center for the Preservation of Ancient Religious Texts (CPART), and the FARMS. The Maxwell Institute publishes the *Journal of* Book of Mormon *Studies* and the *FARMS Review.* Rather than let uninformed or agenda-driven writing about Mormons to go unchallenged, the *FARMS Review* solicits specific reviews and rebuttals, often lengthy. Whether agreeing with the critic of the Church or the apologist (defender), or perhaps accepting some assertions from both, interested readers have a good means of keeping up with ongoing research. Also affiliated with the Maxwell Institute since 2006 is *Brigham Young University Studies*.

NELSON, RUSSELL M. (1924–). Physician, **general authority**. Born on 9 September 1924, Nelson grew up in Salt Lake City, Utah, and graduated from the University of Utah in 1945. His medical studies, also at the University of Utah, led to the M.D. degree in 1947. After a residency at Massachusetts General Hospital in Boston, he transferred to the University of Minnesota, earning a Ph.D. in 1954.

Nelson has been director of the Thoracic Surgery Residency at the University of Utah and chairman of the Thoracic Surgery division at **LDS** Hospital. Among other professional positions he has been president of the Society for Vascular Surgery, a director of the American Board of Thoracic Surgery, chairman of the Council on Cardiovascular Surgery for the American Heart Association, and president of the Utah State Medical Association.

Nelson has served extensively in the Church. After serving as a **stake president** for seven years, he became general president of the

Sunday School in 1971. Later he was a **regional representative**. In 1984 he became a member of the **Quorum** of the **Twelve Apostles**. Nelson has been especially effective in gaining recognition in **Europe** and **Asia**, thus promoting the international growth of the Church. He and his wife, Dantzel, are parents of 10 children. On 12 February 2005, Dantzel died of cancer. In 2006 he married Wendy Watson.

THE NEW ERA. Monthly magazine for youth, which began publication in January 1971. It contains photographic essays, features on youth activities in different parts of the world, and inspirational articles and stories.

NEW YORK PERIOD. Initial period of the Church, from April to December 1830. Organized on 6 April 1830, the Church had its first home in western New York. The family of **Joseph Smith** lived just outside Palmyra. It was there that the **First Vision** occurred in 1820 and there that Smith gained his first followers during the translation of the *Book of Mormon*, published there in the spring of 1830.

Some early sources identify the place of the meeting that formally organized the Church as Manchester, while others say Fayette. After comparing their memories, Mormon leaders determined that Fayette was where it happened, although it is not improbable that an important meeting took place in Manchester at about the same time. To satisfy legal requirements, six men—Joseph Smith, **Oliver Cowdery**, and four others—were listed as charter members. A group of perhaps 50 people, filling and overflowing the house, were in attendance. Immediately, of course, the Church grew larger with the addition of those already **baptized** and other converts.

The New York phase of the Church as an organization lasted from April through December 1830. Three centers were the foci of the fledgling organization: Fayette (the Whitmers), Manchester (the Smiths), and Colesville (the Knights). Conferences were held at Fayette in June and September.

During these months not all of the activity was confined to New York. **Missionaries** embarked on preaching journeys, including the important mission of Oliver Cowdery, **Parley P. Pratt**, Peter Whitmer Jr., and Ziba Peterson to Missouri via Ohio. As he had done the previous year, Joseph Smith sometimes stayed at the home of his wife's parents in Harmony, Pennsylvania, more than a hundred miles from Palmyra and just across the state boundary.

To judge how much of Mormonism was introduced during this initial phase, one must look at the *Book of Mormon*, which became the chief missionary tool and gave the new religion its nickname. Joseph Smith began work on his "inspired revision" of the **Bible**. Approximately the first 40 **revelations**, now published as sections of the *Doctrine and Covenants*, emanate from the New York Period. Among the topics introduced were: **priesthood** authority, the obligation of missionary work, the **sacrament** prayers, the assignment of preparing a hymnal, description of the duties of different offices, and the **gathering**. Although the **twelve apostles** were not yet called, this future development was predicted. The proclamation of the **gospel** to the Indians was begun, and the place where **Zion** was to be built (Missouri) was specified. Apocalyptic and millennial, Mormonism already showed some of the characteristics it would retain throughout its history.

It also began to experience **persecution**. Ridicule had been the lot of Joseph Smith from the time of his First Vision. Twice he was taken before a local court and charged with being a disorderly person. The early Mormons were harassed, as on the occasion when a mob broke up the temporary dam placed in a stream in order to allow **baptisms**.

In December 1830 the New York Mormons were instructed to move to Ohio (*Doctrine and Covenants*, section 37), which most of them did in the first two or three months of 1831.

In the 20th century the Church developed monuments and historic sites in the vicinity of Palmyra, New York. Conversions produced a build-up of the Church in the state. At the end of 2005 New York State had 69,882 Mormons, including 15 **stakes**. **Temples** were dedicated in Palmyra (2000) and New York City (2005). *See also* MISSOURI PERIOD; NATIVE AMERICANS; OHIO PERIOD.

NEW ZEALAND. *See* PACIFIC; COWLEY, MATTHEW.

NIBLEY, HUGH W. (1910–2005). Professor of ancient history, linguist, scholarly defender of Mormonism. Born on 27 March 1910 in Portland, Oregon, Nibley early showed signs of precociousness in his avid reading. He served as a Swiss-German missionary. Upon his return he attended UCLA, graduating summa cum laude in 1934. His Berkeley doctorate of 1938 was awarded after completing a dissertation in ancient history titled "The Roman Games as the Survival of an Archaic Year-Cult."

During World War II Nibley was a noncommissioned intelligence officer, first in England and then in the battle of Normandy and on the continent. After the war he took a post at **BYU**, where for some 40 years he offered courses on ancient history, Greek literature, patristics, and the Mormon **scriptures**. Nibley read voraciously in Greek, Latin, Hebrew, Arabic, and numerous modern languages. He studied Egyptian at the Oriental Institute in Chicago and Coptic at Berkeley. He has poured out a stream of writings, some of them published in the learned journals, many of them in Church magazines. In 1990 a two-volume festschrift, *By Study and Also by Faith*, was published in his honor, containing contributions by former students and colleagues, both in and out of the Church.

His massive work on the ***Book of Mormon*** gives example after example of its congruity with the ancient world. His erudition enabled him to show striking parallels between the Book of Abraham and ancient Egypt, between Mormonism and early Christianity. To critics who say that such parallels fall short of proof, Nibley responded with the challenge to explain how, short of **revelation**, a relatively uneducated **Joseph Smith** could come up with such details. His voluminous writings—including such titles as *Lehi in the Desert*, *The World and the Prophets*, *The Ancient State*, and *Temple and Cosmos*—are published in *Collected Works of Hugh Nibley*. See also PEARL OF GREAT PRICE.

NORTH AMERICA. Organized in New York State in 1830, the Church has always had its main center in the United States. But its message was preached to "all the world" as opportunity allowed. It has always been a misunderstanding, at least partially, to describe it as "an American church," just as it would not be accurate to describe the Catholic Church as "an Italian church."

Nevertheless, throughout the 19th century 90 percent or more of its members lived in the United States. As converts joined, they responded to the doctrine of **gathering** and moved to headquarters.

Only gradually was that practice reversed, starting with recommendations to remain where they were around the turn of the 20th century, becoming much more emphatic after World War II.

At the end of 2005 **membership** remained strong in Utah (1,752,467), California (756,807), Idaho (385,131), Arizona (344,473), Washington (245,665), Nevada (167,822), Oregon (142,545), and Colorado (128,723). The 20th century, especially since World War II, witnessed a dispersion of membership into other parts of the United States. Every state now has Mormon **stakes** and **wards**. **Temples** have been constructed in California, Washington, Oregon, Idaho, Nevada, Colorado, Georgia, Texas, Illinois, Missouri, and other states. (See appendix 3.)

Early preaching expeditions into eastern Canada in the 1830s led to some conversions, but gathering and the successive **persecutions** and moves of the Church left no permanent membership there. At the end of the 19th century, as part of a continuing program of **colonization**, Mormons moved into Alberta, Canada, and established settlements at Cardston and elsewhere. A **stake** was organized there in 1895.

At the end of 2006 there were 71,205 members in Alberta, divided into 22 stakes and 170 wards. Just as there had been an outward, centrifugal tendency in the United States, so membership in Canada spread. As a result of births, proselytizing, and movement of people from other areas, Mormons could be found in all parts of the country: Ontario (44,330), British Columbia (28,492), Quebec (9,681), Saskatchewan (5,280), Nova Scotia (4,661), Manitoba (4,285), New Brunswick (3,046), Newfoundland (675), Prince Edward Island (353),Yukon Territory (278), and Northwest Territories (147). In addition to the Cardston Temple, constructed in 1923, temples were completed at Brampton, Ontario, in 1990; in 1999 at Halifax, Nova Scotia, and Regina, Saskatchewan; and in 2000 at Longieil, Quebec. *See also* CENTRAL AMERICA AND MEXICO.

– O –

OAKS, DALLIN H. (1932–). Lawyer, educator, **general authority**. Born in Provo, Utah, on 12 August 1932, Dallin Oaks was raised in Provo by Stella Harris Oaks, his accomplished, widowed mother. He attended **BYU**, from which he received a B.A. degree in accounting in 1954. After three years at the University of Chicago Law School, serving as editor of the law review his senior year, Oaks graduated with a J.D. degree in 1957.

After serving as a law clerk to Chief Justice Earl Warren of the U.S. Supreme Court, Oaks moved back to Chicago, where he specialized in corporate litigation for a law firm before accepting a faculty position at the University of Chicago. In addition to serving as associate dean of the law school, he became executive director of the American Bar Foundation. He authored many articles on legal and historical subjects. From 1971 to 1980 Oaks was president of BYU. From 1975 to 1978 he was president of the American Association of Presidents of Independent Colleges and Universities. In 1980 he left his university presidency and became a Utah Supreme Court justice for three and a half years. From 1980 to 1985 he was chairman of the board of directors of the Public Broadcasting Service (PBS).

His Church positions include serving as **stake** mission **president** in Chicago, member of the presidency of the Chicago South Stake, and **regional representative**. In 1984 he was called to be a member of the **Quorum** of the **Twelve Apostles**. Dallin Oaks and his wife, June (who died of cancer in 1998), are the parents of six children. In 2000 he married Kristen McMain.

OAKS, ROBERT C. (1936–). Military officer, **general authority**. Born on 14 February 1936 in Los Angeles, California, Oaks earned a bachelor's degree in military science from the Air Force Academy, received a master's degree in business administration at Ohio State University, and attended the Naval War College. He became senior vice president of operations at U.S. Airway. He retired from the U.S. Air Force as a four-star general. Oaks served as **bishop's counselor**, **high councilor**, district **president's counselor**, **mission** president's **counselor**, and **stake** president. In 2000 he became a member of the Second **Quorum** of the **Seventy** and a member of the presidency of the seventy in 2004. He and his wife, Gloria, have six children.

OHIO PERIOD. From early 1831 to 1838. During the same years, western Missouri was the second center of Mormon activity. A mission to the Indians of western Missouri by **Parley P. Pratt** and others stopped in the vicinity of Kirtland, Ohio, a suburb of modern Cleveland. Finding seekers, or restorationists there, the **missionaries** succeeded in converting more than a hundred of them, which immediately gave Ohio about as many members as lived in New York. Among these early Ohio converts was **Sidney Rigdon**, a preacher known for his eloquence and leadership ability.

Not long after **Joseph Smith** heard of these developments, Rigdon having traveled to New York, instructions were given that the New York Mormons should move to Ohio (*Doctrine and Covenants*, sections 37, 38). Smith moved to Kirtland in February with his family. Not long after, in the summer of 1831, he traveled to Missouri and designated Independence as a **gathering** place. For the next few years, Mormon converts flowed into either Ohio or Missouri, with Smith living for most of the time in or near Kirtland, Ohio.

An examination of the *Doctrine and Covenants* shows Ohio to be the scene of many important developments during the 1830s. It was there that the Church organization made important advances from its simple beginnings. The office of **bishop** was created and a **high council** was established. In 1835 the **Quorum** of the **Twelve Apostles** was formed along with the Quorum of the **Seventy**. A School of the Prophets provided instruction for missionaries and Church officers. Periodicals were published, providing an outlet for **revelations** received by Smith as well as other instructions. In 1835 many of these revelations, which had earlier circulated in handwritten form or appeared in the periodicals, were published as the *Doctrine and Covenants*.

Kirtland became a nerve center of missionary activity, with proselytizers traveling outward through Ohio and wider regions and then returning. As new converts arrived in the Kirtland vicinity, a boom town atmosphere was created. Many houses were constructed. In 1836 the Kirtland **Temple** was finished and dedicated. An impressive structure for a religion that had been in existence just six years and whose members were mostly poor, the temple was the scene of visions to Joseph Smith and Pentecostal experiences for many others.

Although even in the brief **New York Period** several basic characteristics of Mormonism took form, the few years in Ohio saw important developments not only in organization but in doctrine. The health code known as the **Word of Wisdom** was issued. The gradations of eternal salvation were described (*Doctrine and Covenants*, section 76). An economic program of consecration and stewardship was introduced (*Doctrine and Covenants*, section 42). Joseph Smith continued work on his inspired revision of the **Bible** and produced the Book of Abraham after acquiring Egyptian papyri.

The creativity of the Ohio Period both organizationally and doctrinally took place against a backdrop of obstacles and opposition. Simply providing for the incoming Mormons was an enormous economic challenge. Not surprisingly, the influx, which meant Mormon domination, led to opposition and **persecution** by others in the region. To provide capital for construction, a Mormon bank was established. In an era of largely unregulated banking, the failure of wildcat banks was not unusual, but when the Kirtland Anti-banking Society (renamed to circumvent a statute) collapsed, all who suffered losses were bitter, including not only outside investors but, more importantly, some of the Mormon leaders. Historian Milton Backman has estimated that as many as 10 to 15 percent of the membership withdrew from the Church. It was the tumult over these matters, with opposition from within and without, that led to the flight of Joseph Smith and the great majority of Mormons in 1838.

Kirtland rapidly waned as a Mormon center. A few members lingered there for the next several years, and some much longer, but for practical purposes it was abandoned in 1838 as a church settlement. The Kirtland Temple, later acquired by the **RLDS** Church, still stands. In the second half of the 20th century Mormonism enjoyed a resurgence in Ohio as some Church members from the West moved there and as convert **baptisms** increased their number. At the end of 2005 there were 55,128 members in the state, with 12 **stakes** and 86 **wards**. *See also* MISSOURI PERIOD; *PEARL OF GREAT PRICE*.

ORDINANCE. A ceremony or procedure by which special blessings of God are mediated to the recipient, roughly equivalent to the term *sacrament* as used in the general Christian tradition. While the form and words are important, an ordinance, to be valid, must be performed by authority of the **priesthood**. Essential to salvation are **baptism** and **confirmation**, although these may be performed vicariously for the deceased in the **temples**. Priesthood ordination and certain temple rites are considered prerequisites for salvation in the highest degree. Other ordinances include the naming of children and administering to the sick.

OSMOND, DONNY (1957–). Singer, actor. Born on 9 December 1957 in Ogden, Utah, Donny Osmond is the son of George and Olive Davis Osmond. At age five, he launched his career in music when he sang with his siblings on the Andy Williams Show. He became famous for his solo song "Puppy Love." By his early 20s, he had released 23 top-40 songs. In 1976, Donny and his sister Marie began their own television show on the ABC network, which lasted four seasons. During the 1990s he performed in Andrew Lloyd Weber's *Joseph and the Amazing Technicolor Dreamcoat*—more than 2,000 performances in five years. He hosted a TV game show from 2002 to 2004. Donny Osmond and his wife, Debra Glen, are the parents of five sons. His website donny.com gives his answers to questions about his Mormon religion.

OSMOND, MARIE (1959–). Singer, actress. Born 13 October 1959 in Ogden, Utah, Marie performed as a child with her siblings, the children of George and Olive Davis Osmond. By the time she was a teenager, Marie had appeared on the Andy Williams Show, recorded the hit record "Paper Roses," and performed with her brothers before a sold-out crowd at New York's Madison Square Garden. With her brother Donny she hosted a variety TV show in 1976–1979 and from 1998 to 2000 a daytime talk show. Marie has written several books, developed the Marie Osmond Fine Porcelain Collection dolls, and raised money for charitable foundations. After the birth of her third child she suffered from severe postpartum depression, later writing a book on her experience to increase public awareness of the condition. With her brother Donny she hosted the Miss America Pageant at Atlantic City in 1999. After a lapse of 20 years, Marie returned to public performance in 2006 with a 15-city Christmas tour. She and her husband, Brian Blosil, have raised eight children. In March 2007 it was announced that she and her husband were divorcing.

OTTLEY, JEROLD (1934–). Musician, director of **Mormon Tabernacle Choir**. Born in Salt Lake City, Utah, on 7 April 1934, Jerold Ottley received his primary and secondary education there. In 1951 he moved to New Zealand and served as a **missionary** there from 1953 to 1955. Returning from his mission, he married JoAnn South in 1956. They have two children. Ottley graduated from the University of Utah in 1961. His master's degree in music was awarded by **BYU**; the doctorate, the D.M.A., by the University of Oregon in 1972. He also studied at the Academy of Music in Cologne, Germany.

Named director of the Mormon Tabernacle Choir in 1975, Ottley raised the level of its performance to new heights by a scrupulous selection of voices through auditions and intensive rehearsal. His wife, JoAnn Ottley, a highly accomplished soprano, assisted the choir as vocal coach. Jerold Ottley was an adjunct professor of music at the University of Utah and from 2005 a visiting professor at **BYU–Hawaii.** *See also* MUSIC.

– P –

PACIFIC. In addition to the Philippines, other Pacific islands have experienced steady expansion of Church **membership** from the 19th century. The following membership figures are for the end of 2005:

Country	Members	Stakes	Temples
American Samoa	14,252	4	
Cook Islands	1,807		
Fiji	14,120	4	1
Guam	1,669		
Marshall Islands	4,296		
Micronesia	3,504		
Niue	230		
North Mariana Islands	811		
Papua New Guinea	14,850	1	
Tahiti	21,567	6	1
Tonga	52,421	16	1
Western Samoa	63,640	16	1

The state of Hawaii has 65,447 members in 15 **stakes.** A **temple** at Laie was the first constructed outside the continental United States. A temple at Kona was completed in 2000.

Somewhat different because of size are Australia and New Zealand, which administratively are in the Pacific area. The first preaching of Mormonism in Australia started as early as 1840, but it was in 1851 that a mission was established. In the 19th century progress was slow. Anti-Mormon speeches and newspaper articles discouraged converts, and the **gathering** policy led many of the strong members to emigrate. In 1904, the first meetinghouse in Australia was constructed at Wooloongabba. As elsewhere, the latter half of the 20th century saw greater progress. At the end of 2005, 111,098 Australian members were divided into 32 stakes and 190 **wards**. A temple was dedicated at Sydney in 1984; four other temples followed.

In New Zealand the trajectory was similar. **Missionaries** arriving in the 1850s were able to convert only a few. By 1880 there were only 133 members. Then the missionaries began preaching to the Maoris and enjoyed much greater success. One of the great missionaries to the Maoris was **Matthew Cowley**. Expansion also occurred among New Zealanders of European ancestry. In 1958 two institutions were completed and dedicated: the Church College of New Zealand and the New Zealand Temple, both at Hamilton, south of Auckland. By the end of 2005, 96,027 members were divided into 25 **stakes** and 148 **wards**. *See also* ASIA; BRIGHAM YOUNG UNIVERSITY–HAWAII; POLYNESIAN CULTURAL CENTER; POLYNESIANS.

PACKER, BOYD KENNETH (1924–). Educator, **general authority**. Born on 10 September 1924 in Brigham City, Utah, Packer also grew up there. He enlisted and became a bomber pilot during World War II, serving in the Pacific Theater. Upon his return he studied at Weber College and Utah State University, from which he received B.S. and M.S. degrees. Subsequently he earned a doctor of education degree at **BYU**.

After accepting a position with the Church Educational System, Packer became supervisor of **seminaries** and **institutes of religion**. Active in community affairs, he served as a city councilman. He was then called to serve as **president** of the New England Mission.

In 1961 Packer became one of the **assistants to the twelve** and in 1970, at the age of 45, a member of the **Quorum** of the **Twelve Apostles**. He traveled throughout the world, gave countless sermons, officiated in the formation of **stakes**, and published several books. Special areas of responsibility have included **correlation** and education. He has served on the Church Board of Education and the Board of Trustees of BYU. He married Donna Edith Smith in 1947. They have 10 children.

PAGEANTS. Dramatic presentations of historic or scriptural events, usually in an outdoor setting. Pageants have become a popular means of commemoration. Usually produced locally, they vary in quality. Large casts assure a theatrical experience for many who would not have it otherwise. Scheduled in the summer, they attract not only the local population but also tourists as audiences. The largest of the pageants is the Cumorah Pageant at Palmyra, New York. Another, in Cache Valley, Utah, portrays the life of **Martin Harris**.

PARKIN, BONNIE D. (1940–). After earning a bachelor's degree from Utah State University, Parkin taught elementary school, was a docent for the Utah Symphony, and served as a page for the Utah Senate. She was **ward Primary** president, ward **Relief Society** president, **stake Young Women** president, and a member of the Relief Society general board. She served with her husband when he was **mission** president in England. She became a **counselor** in the general presidency of Young Women and in 2002 general president of the Relief Society. She was released from her position in April 2007. She and her husband are parents of four sons.

PATRIARCH. A **priesthood** holder ordained to give **patriarchal blessings** to Church members. Until 1979 a general Church patriarch, a descendant of the Joseph Smith Sr. family, was counted among the **general authorities**. On the grounds that **stake** patriarchs performed the function adequately, the patriarch to the Church, Eldred G. Smith, was retired in 1979. In principle, there is at least one patriarch in each **stake**.

PATRIARCHAL BLESSINGS. After receiving a **recommend** from a **bishop**, a member of the Church may receive an individual blessing from a **patriarch**. By the laying on of hands, the patriarch pronounces the person's lineage, whether by blood or adoption, leading back to

Abraham. By inspiration, the patriarch gives additional promises and counsel for guidance in life. Blessings are recorded and transcribed. One copy is preserved in the Church archives. Another copy is retained by the individual receiving the blessing. Mormons look upon their patriarchal blessing as a source of comfort, inspiration, and guidance.

PATRIOTISM. Mormons have expressed their loyalty to governments in general from the beginning. Frustrated at the failure of state and federal government to protect them in Missouri and Illinois, Mormons insisted on their devotion to the country. They argued that although the Constitution of the United States was divinely inspired (*Doctrine and Covenants*, section 101), corrupt individuals were responsible for the problems. Despite being forced to flee to the West, Mormons enlisted in the **Mormon Battalion** during the Mexican War and some fought in the Civil War. During the anti-**polygamy** prosecutions of the 1870s and 1880s, enthusiasm for the country may have cooled, but this did not prevent a vigorous effort to obtain statehood for Utah, which was accomplished in 1896. During the Spanish-American War and subsequent military conflicts, Mormons have served in the military service. Those living in countries other than the United States were expected to be loyal to their rulers. Wherever they live, Mormons proclaim loyalty to their country. *See also* ARTICLES OF FAITH, no. 12; POLITICS.

PEARL OF GREAT PRICE. One of the four standard works of **scripture** along with the **Bible,** *Book of Mormon,* and *Doctrine and Covenants*. First published in 1851 by Apostle Franklin D. Richards, the book is a compilation of five writings previously published in Church periodicals: (1) portions of the first eight chapters of the Genesis text that restored by **revelation** the writings of Moses; (2) the Book of Abraham, a translation from Egyptian papyri brought to **Joseph Smith** in 1835; (3) Matthew 24, a selection from **Joseph Smith**'s inspired revision of the Bible; (4) an autobiographical account of Joseph Smith's early life and visions, including the **First Vision**, as written in 1838; (5) and the **Articles of Faith**.

In 1967 eleven fragments of the papyri once in the possession of **Joseph Smith** were discovered. They turned out to be from an Egyptian religious work called *The Book of Breathings*, and the Book of Abraham is clearly not a direct translation of these papyri. Mormon defenders, especially **Hugh Nibley**, raised questions as to whether those particular fragments were the ones underlying the Book of Abraham, stated that we do not know what Smith meant by "translation," and pointed out many parallels between the Book of Abraham and ancient writings. Some other items once included in the *Pearl of Great Price* are no longer there; the most important of these are now placed in the *Doctrine and Covenants*. The *Pearl of Great Price* was accepted as a standard work of scripture by a vote of approval in **general conference** on 10 October 1880.

PERRY, L. TOM (1922–). Business administrator, **general authority**. Born in Logan, Utah, on 5 August 1922, L. Tom Perry served as a **missionary** in the northern states, after which he joined the U.S. Marines and served for two years in the Pacific.

After the war he married Virginia Lee (they had three children) and attended Utah State University, receiving a B.S. degree in finance in 1949 and doing some graduate work. He was employed as treasurer and vice president of retail business companies, living in Idaho, California, New York, and Massachusetts. He served in two bishoprics, on a **high council**, and in two **stake** presidencies. He was **president** of the Boston Stake.

Called to be an **assistant to the twelve** in 1972, Perry became a member of the **Quorum** of the **Twelve Apostles** in 1974. He served as a member of the Church Board of Education and the General Welfare Services Committee. In 2004–2005 he served as president of the Europe Central area. He headed the Church's participation in the bicentennial of the United States celebration. His wife Virginia died in 1974. Two years later he married Barbara Dayton.

PERSECUTION. Opposition or harassment, especially when motivated by religious or ethnic prejudice. Mormons were opposed from the beginning. The activities against them have included verbal denunciation, misrepresentation, ridicule, vexatious lawsuits, imprisonment, mob attacks, and murders. Violence against them included tarring and feathering, burning homes and barns, driving off cattle, raping, and killing. Opposition on the level of the anti-**polygamy** statutes led to fines, prison terms, denial of the right to vote, and finally confiscation of Church property. Even if legal, all such harassment was experienced by Mormons as persecution. **Joseph Smith** described the reaction to his account of the **First Vision** as persecution. In their own self-image, Mormons believed the label identifed them with the New Testament **saints**, who were told by the Lord, "Blessed are ye when men shall revile you, and persecute you, and shall say all manner of evil against you falsely, for my sake" (Matt. 5:11).

From the point of view of their opponents, of course, the activity was perfectly justified. When mobs or individuals struck out against the Mormons, this was self-defense, consistent with the history of vigilantism in the 19th century. When it was the government that promoted the activity, as in the campaign against polygamy, they were not persecuting people for religious belief but prosecuting stubborn lawbreakers. Point of view was all important.

Contrary to popular impression, motivation for the opposition to Mormonism was not primarily because of disgust with polygamy. That stick was used to beat them with, especially from the end of the Civil War to the 1890 **Manifesto**. But denunciation and harassment started much earlier and continued to flare up after the abandonment of polygamy. Antagonism due to religious differences was exacerbated by fears of the Mormons as a political or economic power. *See also* EXODUS; ILLINOIS PERIOD; MISSOURI PERIOD; NEW YORK PERIOD; OHIO PERIOD; UTAH PERIOD.

PETERSON, LEVI S. (1933–). Fiction writer, biographer. Born in Snowflake, Arizona, he received a bachelor's and master's degree at **BYU** and a Ph.D. at the University of Utah in 1965. He taught English at Weber State University in Ogden, Utah, where he was director of the honors program. Peterson's short stories and novels almost always have Mormon characters, and a strong comic streak is present, most notably in *The Backslider*. The incongruities of the religious life in a secular world also produce tragic scenes. Two collections of short stories and a second novel, *Aspen Marooney*, have been well received. In 1988 Peterson published a biography of **Juanita Brooks**, which won the Evans Biography Award. He became editor of *Dialogue: A Journal of Mormon Thought*.

PIONEER(S). (1) Anyone who clears the way or the original settlers of an area. (2) The specific company, known as "the pioneer company," led by **Brigham Young** to go ahead of the others and establish the place of settlement in 1847. (3) All early settlers in the West. Needing to have a cutoff date for membership qualification, the Daughters of Utah Pioneers and Sons of Utah Pioneers specified 1869, when the railroad reached Utah, as the year before which the settlers were "pioneers." (4) Those who went out in a process of continuing **colonization** to establish settlements in adjacent states, Mexico, and Canada in the last two or three decades of the 19th century. (5) People first converted to Mormonism in any state or country, who establish the foundation for Church growth there. In this sense there are 20th-century and 21st-century pioneers in different American states; in the Philippines, Korea, and Thailand; and in France, Russia, and Nigeria. *See also* EXODUS.

PIONEER DAY. July 24. It was on this date in 1847 that **Brigham Young** emerged from the mountains, beheld the Salt Lake Valley, and proclaimed it "the right place" for settlement. As early as 1849, Church members began celebrating the date as Pioneer Day. Like other commemorations celebrating past events, Pioneer Day has always included a parade as well as speeches, picnics, and various kinds of recreation. Since it is a state holiday in Utah, the long parade has been expanded to include many high school bands, civic groups, politicians, U.S. military units, and different denominations. A strong Mormon tone remains in that many floats are sponsored by **wards**, and the historical themes they commemorate have to do with Mormon history.

PLAN OF SALVATION. An explanation of the purpose of human life drawn from the standard works, especially the modern **scriptures**. All humans naturally confront the questions "Where do I come from? Why am I here? Where am I going?" Mormons answer these questions in the plan of salvation.

Essentially it consists of three acts, or phases, of existence, each of which can be subdivided. First, the preexistence, or pre-mortal, stage during which all humans existed as spirit children of God. In a great council in heaven the Heavenly Father put forth a plan by which the spirits would come to earth. His firstborn son, **Jesus Christ**, volunteered to come to earth to atone for the sins of the world and to be the first fruit of the **resurrection**. All human beings born on earth accepted this plan in their pre-mortal state.

Born on earth, a veil of forgetfulness preventing any recollection of the prior existence, human beings enter a state in which two purposes are achieved. First, they gain a physical body. It is this physical body that will be recovered at the time of resurrection; without it the spirit could never obtain a "fulness of joy." Earth life is also a time of probation, a time in which to demonstrate one's real character, ability to withstand temptation, and willingness to repent. In this setting we show the kind of person we really are.

At death one enters the post-mortal phase of existence. Death is in essence the separation of the spirit from the body. The physical body, a mere shell, is placed in the grave and deteriorates. The spirit never ceases to exist. It enters the spirit world, still conscious and aware of its self-identity. This is a time during which instruction, even **missionary** proselytizing, is provided for those who, through no fault of their own, never had the opportunity to hear the **gospel** during earth life. Then come the resurrection and final judgment. Resurrection is the reuniting of the physical body (or the reassembled component elements of that body) and the spirit. By the atonement of Jesus Christ it comes to all, regardless of goodness or badness of one's actions.

The judgment determines the ultimate reward or punishment. Rather than a simple division into heaven or hell, there are three kingdoms, or degrees, of glory, each with an unknown number of subdivisions (*Doctrine and Covenants*, sections 76, 88). The lowest was the telestial kingdom, followed by the terrestrial and celestial kingdoms. It is in the highest level of the celestial kingdom that the righteous regain the presence of God.

Eternal salvation is characterized by continued progression. Ultimately, in the eons to come, those who qualify at the highest level become co-heirs with Christ and, joining God the Father in a heavenly aristocracy of character, even have the capacity to create worlds. Such is the plan that explains the meaning of life, its trials and tribulations, and where it is all headed. The *Book of Mormon* calls it "the merciful plan of the great Creator."

PLURAL MARRIAGE. *See* POLYGAMY.

POLITICS. Mormons proclaim loyalty to nation and currently acknowledge the inappropriateness of direct Church involvement in political matters. This basic stance is emphasized when the Church seeks permission for its **missionaries** to proselytize in a country. It is a good-faith statement and not a subterfuge. Still, historically, there have been counter-tendencies.

During the **Illinois Period** and later in territorial Utah where Mormons were the great majority of the population, they often voted as a block to elect their own people to office. This led to charges of "theocracy." A standard answer at the time was that people who chose to be represented by individuals of their own faith were only exercising their rights. During Utah's territorial period, voters divided into the Liberal party and the People's party. The latter, representing the majority of the population, the Mormons, won most elections, but the Liberals promoted their own ticket and even won some local elections. The federal government appointed the governor, territorial secretary, district attorney, U.S. marshal, and federal judges. From 1857 until Charles S. Richards's appointment in 1893, the federal government appointed no Mormons to territory-wide office in Utah.

In the 1890s, the introduction of the national political parties, with Mormons and non-Mormons in both parties, reduced fear of ecclesiastical domination, and Utah became a state in 1896. A leading Church authority, polygamist B. H. Roberts, a Democrat, was elected to the House of Representatives in 1898. Committee hearings were held, and he was not allowed to take his seat. When monogamist Reed Smoot, an apostle, was elected U.S. senator in 1903, the Senate Committee on Privileges and Elections held another round of committee hearings that lasted until 1907. A vote in the Senate allowed him to retain his seat. For about 30 years Smoot served as a respected and influential senator. Other Mormons holding influential office have included James H. Moyle, assistant secretary of the treasury;

Edgar Brossard, member of the U.S. Tariff Commission; Elbert D. Thomas, U.S. senator; **Ezra Taft Benson**, secretary of agriculture; **David Kennedy**, secretary of the treasury; Stewart L. Udall, secretary of the interior; and Michael Leavitt, secretary of health and human services. In addition to Utah's senators and representatives, Mormons have also been elected to office in other states, as Governor George Romney of Michigan, Governor Mitt Romney of Massachusetts, U.S. Senators Gordon Smith of Oregon and Harry Reed of Nevada, and senators and members of Congress from several states. In 2007, Harry Reed became senate majority leader.

Candidates for public office who ridicule religion, the **family**, or traditional morality would probably not garner support from Mormon voters. But there is no edict from the Church dictating how one must vote. When Church **president Heber J. Grant** came out in opposition to repealing the Prohibition amendment, the majority of Church members voted for repeal. It is sometimes assumed that Mormons are Republicans, but, like other Americans, the majority of them voted for Democrat Franklin D. Roosevelt. If they seem to stand in the Republican camp at present, this is because Republicans have in some instances successfully tarred Democratic candidates as opponents of traditional values, especially in the "red" states in the South, Midwest, and Rocky Mountains. There is no signal from the Church president dictating how votes must be cast. Party alignment is always subject to change. Both Republicans and Democrats, not to speak of Libertarians and others, continue to enlist Mormons to their ranks.

In other countries as well as the United States, Church members are encouraged to participate in the public process. Some have served on local councils and even national legislatures. Such participation, along with different kinds of community service, is expected to continue.

Although as late as the 1960 election, the Church president publicly expressed his support for one of the candidates, the Church as such has not openly endorsed a presidential candidate since 1936. In official statements, the **First Presidency** has asserted its neutrality in political matters. In January 2007 the following official statement was issued: "Elected officials who are Latter-day Saints make their own decisions and may not necessarily be in agreement with one another or even with a publicly stated Church position. While the

Church may communicate its views to them, as it may to any other elected official, it recognizes that these officials still must make their own choices based on their best judgment and with consideration of the constituencies whom they were elected to represent."

Church leaders have, however, taken positions on issues that they consider moral, and as late as 1954 on issues that might be considered political, such as returning Weber State College to the Church and legislative apportionment. Moral questions on which the leadership has taken stands in recent years include liquor by the drink, Sunday closing, and pari-mutuel betting. The Church leadership also opposed the proposed Equal Rights Amendment, arguing that it would undermine traditional family values and legal protections for women.

POLYGAMY. The practice, known technically as polygyny, by which an individual husband takes more than one wife. Publicly announced in 1852, Mormon plural marriage was officially terminated when a **manifesto** was issued by Church **president Wilford Woodruff** in 1890. An average of perhaps 25 percent of the families lived in polygamy in the late 19th century, even when it was publicly advocated and defended. Considering the Church's spectacular growth in the late 20th century, it is clear that only a very small percentage of all the Mormons who have ever lived practiced polygamy. Yet the media and critics continue to associate polygamy with the Church, and many uninformed people continue to associate the practice with Mormonism. The work of scholars allows us to consider the subject in somewhat greater detail with respect to its origins, its extent, its success or failure, and its termination.

Origins. As the Church was organized in 1830, polygamy was not part of its practice. The **revelation** authorizing it is dated 12 July 1843, the year prior to **Joseph Smith**'s death (*Doctrine and Covenants*, section 132). There is some evidence that Smith considered the possibility as early as 1830–1831, and it is probable that he married Fanny Alger as a second wife in 1833 or 1835. Nevertheless, it was in Nauvoo, Illinois, after 1842 that polygamy was privately introduced to some people along with the new **temple ordinances**.

The original reaction was usually shock and rejection. But after personal struggle and prayer—on the part of **Joseph Smith** and his wife **Emma Smith; Hyrum Smith**, the **twelve apostles**, and their wives; and the women who became plural wives—a small number of Church leaders became polygamists. Since the practice was not publicly acknowledged, exact numbers are difficult to come by. As an educated guess, less than 100 began practicing polygamy before the departure of the Mormons from Nauvoo in early 1846.

Motives are difficult to determine with any confidence. Not surprisingly, critics of the practice assumed that lust was behind it. Clearly, however, Mormons saw it in a religious context. It was defended as a biblical practice that by specific divine authorization could again be allowed. It was part of "the restoration of all things."

Extent. How many Mormons were polygamous in the 19th century? As already indicated, practically none until 1843, after which a relatively small group of leaders were inducted into it. The practice was officially admitted and defended from 1852. Its formal termination, with the Manifesto of 1890, came 38 years later. At the end of the century, a figure sometimes heard was 2 percent of the population, but this estimate was disingenuous, for it included only polygamist males in the numerator, while the entire Church membership was included in the denominator.

Estimates for the late 19th century have varied between 25 and 35 percent of the families. The higher figure refers to certain settlements, or **wards**, and includes in the numerator all children whose mothers are married, or have been married, to a polygamist male. Changing the definition obviously changes the percentage, and critics, defenders, and historians of the practice have not always clearly spelled out their criteria for inclusion or exclusion. It cannot be far off to say that roughly 25 percent of the entire Church population during the **Utah Period** lived in polygamous households, with variations from place to place and from decade to decade.

Even if 30 percent of Mormons were in polygamy in some way, that is still a minority of the **membership**. Yet virtually all of the leadership—**general authorities, stake presidents, bishops**—were polygamists, and the practice loomed very large in the public perception of Mormons.

Success or failure. Contemporary charges of miserable failure, portraying plural wives as chattels and the children as neglected waifs, are inaccurate. Likewise, glowing descriptions by some defenders of polygamy are unreliable. The several hundred divorces granted to plural wives, and approved by **Brigham Young**, are sufficient evidence of some marital malfunction. The fact seems to be that the success of these marriages depended on the people involved. Anecdotal evidence and diary accounts indicate that there could be cooperation and mutual support between the wives. Allegations to the contrary notwithstanding, children of plural marriages tended to be healthy and intelligent. On the other hand, there is no evading the inherent limitations of time and financial resources; a polygamist father could not give the same time and attention to individual wives and children as could a monogamist. However, a simple examination of divorce ratios is sufficient to prove that monogamy as well as polygamy varies greatly across a spectrum ranging from beautiful harmony to disastrous breakdown, with most coming somewhere in between.

Termination. Succumbing to a prolonged, increasingly intensive anti-polygamy campaign, Church president **Wilford Woodruff** issued a manifesto in the fall of 1890. Often cited as the end of Mormon polygamy, the document itself did not claim so much. Its concluding words are "And I now publicly declare that my advice to the Latter-day Saints is to refrain from contracting any marriage forbidden by the law of the land." It was not possible to make a clean break that would suddenly cause the system to vanish. The following points seem worthy of consideration.

1. Many husbands continued to support, live with, and have children by plural wives married before the manifesto. While agreeing not to enter any new plural marriages, they could not abandon those they already had even if a strict reading of the law seemed to require it. By a gentleman's agreement these were not prosecuted. Continuing to support wives and families seemed fair, and in time, if there were no new plural marriages, the system would die out.

2. Some new plural marriages, perhaps 1 to 300, were secretly performed with the approval of some **general authorities** between 1890 and 1904. Some of these were performed outside the boundaries of the United States, even on the high seas, where it was reasoned no law of the land made them illegal. Others used different forms of casuistry to justify their action: the manifesto

had only "recommended"; promises made under coercion need not be observed; the manifesto was addressed "to whom it may concern" and it does not concern me. When the clandestine plural marriages following 1890 were uncovered during the hearings for the seating of Senator **Reed Smoot**, a second manifesto was issued by Church president **Joseph F. Smith** in 1904 with a greater determination to enforce it.

3. After 1904, only **fundamentalists** have continued to perform plural marriages. They are **excommunicated** when discovered and are not properly called Latter-day Saints, or Mormons.

The practice of polygamy continues by people who are not Church members, both in the United States and Canada as well as in other countries. Numbers are very hard to come by. Several groups, even while rejected and excommunicated by the Church, claim that they represent true Mormonism. In addition to breaking the laws of the state against being married to more than one person at the same time, polygamists in the present generation have been associated with welfare fraud and child abuse.

Not relishing the association of these activities with the Church in the public mind, the general authorities and their spokesmen repeatedly insist that it is a misnomer to call polygamists *Mormon* polygamists. To say that the Church teaches or advocates polygamy today is false. *See also* UTAH PERIOD.

POLYNESIAN CULTURAL CENTER. A theme park located in Laie, Hawaii, on the north shore of the island of Oahu. A nonprofit corporation that provides employment to hundreds of Polynesian students at the campus of **BYU–Hawaii**, the center preserves and displays different Polynesian cultural traditions through song, dance, and crafts. In April 2003 the Polynesian Cultural Center welcomed its 30 millionth visitor.

POLYNESIANS. Missionary proselytizing began as early as 1843 among some of the Polynesians and was resumed later in the century. Each of the Polynesian groups has its own history of **pioneer** conversions, **persecution**, and continuity. Although not clearly stated in the **scriptures**, the idea is often expressed that Polynesians are heirs of the Abrahamic covenant by their descent from *Book of Mormon* peoples. In addition to substantial numbers of Mormon Polynesians in New Zealand, Hawaii, Samoa, Tonga, Tahiti, and other islands, many have emigrated to other locations, such as Australia or the United States. At **BYU–Hawaii** approximately one third of the students are from the different island countries of the **Pacific**.

PRATT, ORSON (1811–1881). Mathematician, **missionary**, **general authority**. Born in Hartford, New York, on 19 September 1811, Pratt had little formal schooling but avidly pursued different subjects on his own. In 1830 his older brother **Parley P. Pratt** taught him the new religion of Mormonism and **baptized** him. As was common at the time, Orson immediately went on a preaching mission. He participated in many of the experiences at Kirtland, Ohio, was a member of **Zion's Camp**, and in 1835 at the age of 24 became one of the original members of the **Quorum** of the **Twelve Apostles**. In 1836 he married Sarah Marinda Bates.

Pratt was one of the legendary missionaries of early Mormonism, traveling through the eastern states, Canada, Scotland, and England. Returning from England in 1841, he found a crisis. His wife had been introduced to **polygamy** in his absence. During much of 1842 Pratt was in turmoil, refusing to support **Joseph Smith** and the other apostles on some matters. He and his wife were excommunicated in August. Before the year had ended they were rebaptized and Orson Pratt was again one of the twelve apostles.

After the Mormons were forced out of Nauvoo, Illinois, during the great **exodus** to the West, Pratt was in the **pioneer** company that led the way. One of a small group of advance scouts, he entered the Salt Lake Valley on 21 July 1847, three days before **Brigham Young**. He invented an odometer to measure the mileage during the trip and supervised the surveying of the new location after their arrival.

Somewhat of a philosopher and mathematician, Pratt did not work within the context of the major universities of the Victorian era. But audiences on the Mormon frontier were interested in his lectures on such subjects as light and causation. Sometimes his teachings were too abstruse for Brigham Young, who occasionally reprimanded him. In 1875 President Young declared that Pratt's position of seniority in the twelve apostles was determined not by his original ordination but his readmission in 1842—which had the practical effect of putting Orson behind **John Taylor** in seniority. Yet Young recognized Pratt's deep commitment to Mormonism and did not want to lose his services.

In addition to Sarah, Pratt married four other wives before the move to the West. Two others were added later. Eventually he was the father of 45 children. Such personal involvement in plural marriage made Pratt the ideal choice as its defender. When the practice of polygamy was publicly announced in 1852, Pratt preached the main sermon and immediately began publishing *The Seer*, a periodical in Washington, D.C., dedicated to defending the practice. In 1870, when the prominent minister John P. Newman attacked polygamy, Pratt faced him in a public debate, the text of which was published in newspapers and as a pamphlet. The topic was not whether polygamy was good or bad but whether the **Bible** sanctioned it. The Mormons thought Pratt was the clear winner. *See also* OHIO PERIOD.

PRATT, PARLEY PARKER (1807–1857). Poet, **missionary**, **general authority**. Born 12 April 1807 in Burlington, New York, Parley Pratt married Thankful Halsey in 1827 and moved to Ohio. Having been a Baptist, he became a follower of **Sidney Rigdon**'s brand of the Campbellites. In 1830 he sold out and with his wife traveled to New York. Leaving her on a canal boat to continue their intended journey, he suddenly left her, explaining that he felt strongly that there was some special work for him in that part of the country. There he first saw the ***Book of Mormon***. After reading it with enthusiasm, he traveled to the Palmyra, New York, area; met **Hyrum Smith**; and was soon baptized.

With **Oliver Cowdery** he was called on a mission to the Indians in Missouri (***Doctrine and Covenants***, section 32). During the journey, they stopped at Kirtland, Ohio, and introduced Mormonism to Sidney Rigdon and his congregation. The conversion of Rigdon and most of his congregation paved the way for the establishment of a new center for the Church. Continuing on to Missouri, Pratt and his travel companions made contact with the Indians and, more important historically, provided the information leading to the declaration of Missouri as the new **Zion**. During the remainder of the 1830s Parley Pratt and his family participated in the exciting and trying events of early

Mormon history. They were driven from Jackson County, Missouri, in 1833. In 1834 he served in **Zion's Camp**. In 1835 he was named one of the original members of the **Quorum** of the **Twelve Apostles**. Pratt served on many missions, including one to Canada and in 1840 to England. There he edited the *Millennial Star*. His literary skills were also employed in the writing of pamphlets like *Voice of Warning* (1837). Pratt's hymns were among the most popular in Mormon worship, including "An Angel from on High," "Jesus, Once of Humble Birth," and "The Morning Breaks, The Shadows Flee."

After the Mormons moved west to Utah, Pratt assisted in drafting a constitution. He served in the territorial legislature. Much of his time was taken in settling and providing for his families. His wife Thankful died in 1837, after which he married Mary Ann Frost. Starting in 1843 he took plural wives and eventually became the father of 30 children.

The last of his wives, Eleanor McComb McLean, had not been legally divorced from her husband, an alcoholic in San Francisco. McLean, the father, kept the children and took them to Arkansas. A nasty custody suit followed. Pratt was attempting to recover Eleanor's children when he was charged with alienation of affection and acquitted. He tried to return to Utah by joining an immigration company when McLean overtook him, stabbed him twice, and shot him in the neck. Pratt was unarmed.

Although just 50 years old at the time of his death in 1857, Parley P. Pratt made important contributions during Mormonism's first generation. His autobiography, assembled from his unpublished manuscripts, is considered a classic. *See also* OHIO PERIOD.

PRAYER. A faithful Mormon approaches God in prayer evening and morning as well as any other time there is a special need or desire. **Family** prayers are held daily. A prayer of blessing and thanks is uttered at mealtime. All Church meetings are started and ended with prayers, known respectively as invocations and benedictions. Except for the **ordinances** of **sacrament** and **baptism**, fixed or written prayers are not used. Standard usage includes addressing God at the beginning of the prayer and concluding "in the name of Jesus Christ." The prayer should otherwise come from the heart and be appropriate for the occasion.

PRESIDENT. A common title in the Church organization, referring to the person who stands at the head. Thus there is a president of a **stake**, of **priesthood quorums**, of such **auxiliary** organizations as **Primary**, **Sunday School**, **Young Men**, and **Young Women** on the **ward**, **stake**, and general level. Although the head of the ward is a **bishop**, a congregation not yet large enough to achieve ward status is led by a branch president. Each of the 347 missions is presided over by a mission president.

The president of the Church stands at the head of the whole Church on earth, although the real head is regarded as **Jesus Christ**. In addition to his title of president, the Church president is sustained as "**prophet**, seer, and revelator" and is often referred to as "the prophet." He is the presiding **high priest** of the Church and holds all the keys, or authority, for its functioning on earth. One characteristic of Mormon organization is that each of these presidents is assisted by two **counselors**, the three of them constituting a presidency. Clerks or secretaries as needed also assist. As a **form of address**, the term *president* is regularly used for the president of the Church and presidents of stakes and **missions**. Others holding the title are more commonly addressed as **brother** or **sister**.

PRESIDING BISHOP. One of the **general authorities** of the Church. The presiding bishop and his two **counselors** form the Presiding Bishopric. Unlike other bishoprics, with responsibility for a single **ward**, the Presiding Bishopric oversees the entire Church.

Under the direction of the president of the Church, the presiding bishop and his counselors exercise specific responsibility over receiving **tithing** and other income, helping the poor, planning and erecting buildings, and maintaining **membership** records. In addition the Presiding Bishopric has had responsibility for the **Aaronic Priesthood**, the young men from 12 to 18 years of age, and even for young women of the same age. In 1977 presiding bishops were officially assigned to the presidency of the **Young Men** and **Young Women**. The growth of Church membership led to some decentralization. Under the supervision of **area** presidencies, area directors for temporal affairs were established. The Presiding Bishopric provides training, planning, and technical support.

PRIEST. An office in the **Aaronic Priesthood**. Young men are eligible for ordination as priests at age 16. They acquire authority to perform not only the functions of **deacons** and **teachers**, but in addition, under the direction of their **bishop**, to **baptize**, administer the **sacrament**, and ordain other priests, **teachers**, and **deacons**. This is the highest office of the Aaronic Priesthood. The priests in a **ward** are organized in a **quorum** of 48 or fewer. Their president is the ward bishop, with two priests serving as **counselors**. They meet regularly on Sundays with an adult adviser for study and training. In principle they are preparing for the **Melchizedek Priesthood** and **missionary** service.

PRIESTHOOD. The power or authority of God granted to **worthy** male Church members to act in his holy name for the salvation of human beings. Priesthood must be specifically received by ordination from someone who holds it (**Articles of Faith**, no. 5). It is not, therefore, a right that one arrogates to himself and not the prerogative of every baptized believer.

For the **restoration** of the Church to be efficacious, the authority to act in God's name had to be restored, which **Joseph Smith** described as having occurred by means of heavenly messengers. A church without such authority, or where the founder simply decides to work on his own, is an empty shell. **Baptisms**, or any of the other **ordinances**, if performed without priesthood authority, lack the essential ingredient that makes them valid. Mormons do not connect priesthood with professional preparation in divinity school. It is widely distributed by the ordination of every worthy male 12 years of age and older.

The two major divisions are the **Aaronic Priesthood** and **Melchizedek Priesthood**. In the Aaronic Priesthood are three offices: **deacon**, for which one is eligible at age 12; **teacher**, at age 14; and **priest**, at age 16. Each of these priesthood offices has specific rights and prerogatives; for example, as a deacon one may pass the **sacrament** to the congregation, but not until becoming a priest may one perform baptisms. At age 18 a male is eligible to be ordained an **elder** in the Melchizedek Priesthood. All male **missionaries** are called elder, whatever their priesthood. Later, depending on responsibilities, a man may be ordained a **high priest**. The **seventy** was previously a local office, but now it is reserved for general and **area authorities**. In each **ward** during priesthood meetings there are separate classes for the different offices: deacon, teacher, priest, elder, high priest.

Two important qualifications limit priesthood claims by any individual. First, God will recognize those things done in His name only to the extent that they are done in righteousness. Priesthood must not be used as an excuse for intimidation or unkindness. Second, in practice one exercises priesthood authority under the direction of ecclesiastical superiors, who possess the keys, or authority, of administration. Thus before performing a baptism, one must have approval from one's file leader.

PRIMARY. Organization for children under the age of 12. The Primary Association was founded in 1878 when Aurelia Spencer Rogers received approval from Church leaders. Primary soon spread to other **wards** and settlements. A general presidency of three women began to supervise the different Primaries in the 1890s. In 1902 they began publication of *The Children's Friend*, a magazine containing lessons as well as stories and pictures to interest children. It was superseded by the *Friend* in 1971. A program of sequential classes—with manuals, goals, and badges for achievement—was organized for both boys and girls. In 1980 Primary meetings were moved from weekdays to Sunday. Through classes and discussion, by participation in prayer and singing, children learn principles that prepare them for **baptism** and, in the case of the boys, **priesthood** ordination at age twelve.

PROPHET. One who legitimately transmits the will of God to the human race. A prophet must have been designated by God and be the recipient of divine communications. The biblical prophets are the prototypes. Part of the **restoration** that was Mormonism was the reappearance of prophets.

In a general sense all have access to this heavenly gift, for "the testimony of Jesus is the spirit of prophecy" (Rev. 19:10). More specifically, however, the title is reserved to those who are God's designated spokespersons on earth. In Mormon usage, members of the **First Presidency** and all of the **twelve apostles** are "prophets, seers, and revelators," but it is the **president** of the Church who specifically holds the keys of authority during his administration. It is he who is sometimes called simply "the prophet." The word designates not his administrative role, that of president, but his closeness to God, his capability and responsibility to convey God's message to Church members and all mankind. Not only is he endowed with this authority by being specially set apart by the other apostles, but he is also **sustained** by the uplifted hand of members throughout the Church, who thus testify that they accept him in the prophetic role.

From the prophet **Joseph Smith** to the present, Mormon leaders have worn the prophetic mantle. The title does not imply divinity or sainthood in the traditional sense of the word. Prophets are human beings. They are not worshiped. But faithful Latter-day Saints listen to their counsel with great respect. A common injunction, expressed in a song for children, is "Follow the prophet."

PROTESTANTISM. Some consider Protestants to be all Christian churches that are not Roman **Catholic** or Orthodox. During the Protestant Reformation of the 16th century, mainstream, or magisterial, Protestants included Lutherans, Calvinists, and Anglicans, each with different subgroups. Common principles were said to include salvation by faith, the unique authority of the **Bible**, the priesthood of all believers, and the two sacraments of baptism and the eucharist. But even these main groups could not agree on everything; for example, Zwingli and Luther denounced each other's view of the eucharist.

More radical 16th-century Protestants, including the Anabaptists, were rejected and persecuted by Catholics and mainstream Protestants alike. New groups came into existence later, notably Baptists and Methodists. With new organizations and repeated division and subdivision, by the 20th and 21st century there were hundreds of churches. Mormons are not Protestants. They do not trace their origin to the Protestant Reformation. Sometimes they emphasize their belief in a **restoration** as opposed to a *reformation*, but this ignores the existence of Protestant restorationism. Each of the so-called Protestant principles—salvation by faith alone, the inerrancy and sufficiency of the Bible—would be found unacceptable by Mormons, but of course many Protestants now also find these slogans to be inadequate.

The major premise that all **Christianity** is divided between Catholics and Protestants, followed by the minor premise that Mormons are neither Catholic nor Protestant, leads inevitably to the conclusion that they are not part of Christianity. Mormons see themselves as neither Catholic nor Protestant but decidedly Christian, even uniquely faithful to the purity of original Christianity. Theological distinctions notwithstanding, Mormons have much in common with many Protestants and Catholics in worship, lifestyle, and social agenda. Mormon, Catholic, and Protestant congregations have occasionally been able to cooperate, help one another, and achieve mutual respect.

PUBLIC AFFAIRS. The department responsible for disseminating information about the Church to media. News releases are prepared about programs and events. Radio and television programs are also produced. In addition to the central office at Church headquarters, **area** offices with full-time directors have been established in such major cities as Washington, D.C., Toronto, and London. More than 3,500 local public affairs directors on the level of **stakes** and **missions** are coordinated from the central and regional offices.

PUBLICATIONS. *See DESERET NEWS; ENSIGN; THE FRIEND; IMPROVEMENT ERA;* INTERNATIONAL MAGAZINES; *JOURNAL OF DISCOURSES; MILLENNIAL STAR; THE NEW ERA; RELIEF SOCIETY MAGAZINE; TIMES AND SEASONS. **Dialogue** and **Sunstone** are privately printed. Refer to "Periodicals and Yearbooks" in the bibliography.

– Q –

QUORUM. A unit of the **priesthood** in the Church organization; thus the Quorum of the **First Presidency**, the Quorum of the **Twelve Apostles**, the First Quorum of the **Seventy**. On the level of **wards** and **stakes**, when a male receives the **priesthood**, he enters a quorum for the particular office to which he is ordained: **deacon, teacher, priest, elder,** or **high priest**. Quorum meetings are held regularly.

QUORUM OF THE TWELVE APOSTLES. *See* TWELVE APOS-TLES, QUORUM OF THE; GENERAL AUTHORITIES.

– R –

RASBAND, RONALD A. (1951–). General authority. Born 6 February 1951 in Salt Lake City, Utah, Rasband attended the University of Utah. From 1970 to 1972 he was a **missionary** in the Eastern States Mission. He became president and chief operations officer of the Huntsman Chemical Corporation and then a self-employed businessman. He served as **bishop**, **high councilor**, and from 1996 to 1999 president of the New York New York North Mission. In 2000 he became a member of the First **Quorum** of the **Seventy** and in 2005 entered its presidency. He and his wife, Melanie, are parents of five children.

RECOMMEND. A certificate of **worthiness** necessary for entrance into the **temples**. A searching interview by one's **bishop** determines one's faithfulness to commitments and attitude toward the Church and its leaders. A follow-up interview is conducted by a member of the **stake** presidency. A recommend is valid for two years. Then the interviews are repeated, offering opportunity for self-evaluation and updating. In 2007 because of apparent abuse of the recommend privilege including the reported sale of some recommends on Internet sites, recommends were marked with an electronic code unique to each individual. A determination of worthiness similar to a recommend, although not necessarily resulting in a signed certificate, is made prior to being called as a **missionary** or to fill different positions of responsibility.

REFERRAL. The name of a person who has shown an interest in the Church, which is turned over to the **missionaries**, who then offer to schedule meetings for teaching the **gospel** prior to conversion and **baptism**. Church members are encouraged to explore such a possibility with friends and family. Otherwise missionaries rely on random door knocking, street contacting, or other inefficient methods of finding people willing to investigate Mormonism. Growth of the Church has been most spectacular in areas where members have been diligent in making referrals.

REGION. A grouping of several **stakes**. Smaller than an **area**, the region is an intermediate level.

REGIONAL REPRESENTATIVES. Priesthood leaders called to provide supervision over **regions**. They trained local leaders and visited conferences in the region, but were not considered **general authorities**. In 1995, this position was discontinued and replaced with that of **area authority**.

REID, HARRY M. (1939–). Attorney, attorney general, U. S. senator from Nevada, senate majority leader. Born in Searchlight, Nevada, 2 December 1939, Reid earned an A.S. at Southern Utah University and a B.S. in history and political science in 1961 at Utah State University, where he and his wife converted to Mormonism. He moved to Washington, D.C., where he worked for the police force while earning a J.D. at George Washington University in 1964.

Reid returned to Nevada where he practiced law and entered politics. After serving in the state legislature, he was elected to the state assembly in 1967 and served as lieutenant governor from 1971 through 1974. Active in Democratic politics, in 1974 he unsuccessfully ran for senator against former governor Paul Laxalt. Reid served as Nevada gaming commissioner from 1977 to 1981 and served two terms in the U.S. House of Representatives from 1983 through 1987. Elected to the U.S. Senate in 1986, he won successive elections. After serving as minority whip and minority leader, he was elected majority leader in 2006. During his term as majority leader, Reid actively opposed the administration position on the war in Iraq. He also worked actively for immigration reform. Reid has served as an **elders quorum president, stake high counselor**, and **Sunday School** president. He is married to Landra Gould, and the two have five children.

RELIEF SOCIETY. Women's organization of the Church. Organized in Nauvoo, Illinois, in 1842, with **Emma Smith**, wife of **Joseph**

Smith, as first president, the Female Relief Society, as it was first called, performed charitable service and solicited contributions. Joseph Smith explained that it was essential to the completeness of the Church. By 1844 it had reached a membership of 1,341.

With the death of Joseph Smith in June 1844 and the subsequent turmoil and **exodus**, the Relief Society suspended official operations. Women worked and met together on occasion, but not until 1854 did **Brigham Young** reinitiate the Relief Society on the **ward** level. The organization carried out charitable work, and some of the societies made clothing for Indian women and children. In 1866 the Relief Society was reorganized on a general church level with **Eliza R. Snow** as president.

During the last generation of the 19th century the Relief Society raised silk worms in the effort to establish sericulture. A grain storage program was organized. Nurses, midwives, and female doctors were selected, and money was raised to assist in their training. The organization founded and operated a hospital. Relief Society women were outspoken in defending Mormonism and in agitating for female suffrage. A semimonthly publication, *Woman's Exponent*, provided instruction and inspiration. Two of the organization's prominent leaders were Eliza R. Snow and **Emmeline B. Wells**.

In the 20th century the Relief Society expanded its educational role. Through the *Relief Society Magazine* lesson materials were provided in theological, cultural, and homemaking areas. With some Relief Society leaders professionally trained as teachers, psychologists, and social workers, the organization enlarged its role in child placement, in cooperation with other agencies, and sponsored health clinics. As the **welfare program** got under way during the 1930s, Relief Society presidents throughout the Church worked in close cooperation with ward **bishops**.

For many years Relief Society women studied courses in literature and comparative cultures, but this has been superseded by greater emphasis on spiritual training. Homemaking, considered broadly, continues to be a central part of the society's program. The voluntary membership and dues requirement was replaced in 1971 by automatic membership for all Mormon women. One of the central features of the organization, whose origins go back to Nauvoo, continues to be the **visiting teaching**, with each adult female member of the Church—all of whom are members of the Relief Society—receiving regular visits, support, and compassionate service.

Although promoting the home as a primary area of woman's responsibility, the organization recognizes the diverse life situations and needs of its members. The increasingly complex life patterns of women in the United States combined with the growth of the Church abroad have combined to present major challenges. In 1992, the sesquicentennial year of its organization, the Relief Society announced that each ward unit would undertake a community service or literacy project.

Remembering the number of **stakes** (2,733) and wards (27,087) in the Church, one notes that thousands of women are receiving administrative, teaching, and service experience. Passivity or timidity have not been the characteristics of this dynamic organization. Its motto from the beginning has been "Charity never faileth."

RELIEF SOCIETY MAGAZINE. Monthly magazine published by the **Relief Society** from 1915 to 1970. Intended to reflect and serve the women of the Church, it included reports on activities, recipes, and addresses given at the annual Relief Society conference. Creativity was encouraged by the publication of poetry and short stories. Lessons were published on religion, art, social science, and literature. When it was terminated in 1970, the magazine had 301,000 subscribers.

REORGANIZED CHURCH OF JESUS CHRIST OF LATTER DAY SAINTS (RLDS). A church that came into existence after the middle of the 19th century as an alternative to the **Church of Jesus Christ of Latter-day Saints** then led by **Brigham Young.** In the aftermath of the death of **Joseph Smith** some fragmentation occurred as different groups put forth claims to **succession.** Most remained small and later disappeared. The RLDS Church continues and though small by comparison—circa 260,000 versus 12 million plus—expresses an alternative vision of the **restoration.**

The departure to the West of the main body of the Church after their expulsion from Nauvoo, Illinois, left a minority of scattered Mormons who needed more time to prepare, followed one or another rival claimant, or had not made up their minds what to do. By 1851–1852 Jason W. Briggs and Zenos H. Gurley Sr. were rallying followers in Wisconsin. In addition to rejecting the leadership of the **Quorum** of the **Twelve Apostles** and Brigham Young, Briggs and Gurley looked forward to the time when "young Joseph," the **prophet**'s son, could take the leadership. On 6 April 1860 Joseph Smith III traveled to Amboy, Illinois, and accepted the position of prophet and president of the RLDS Church.

From its beginning the RLDS Church disassociated itself from its larger rival. Not only was the practice of **polygamy** denied but even the fact that Joseph Smith had introduced it (now well established). Other practices characteristic of early Mormonism were abandoned, such as the **gathering**, and the **ordinances** of the **temples** were rejected. For many generations RLDS people looked forward to the construction of a temple in Independence, Missouri, as the founding prophet had foretold, but when a structure was completed in 1993 it became a place of worship and education "dedicated to the pursuit of peace" with no special temple rituals being practiced. In 1881 RLDS headquarters were established at Lamoni, Iowa, where in 1895 **Graceland University** (formerly Graceland College) was founded. When Joseph Smith III died in 1914, three of his sons in a row succeeded to the presidency, followed by a grandson. In 1996, with the presidency of **W. Grant McMurray**, the insistence on lineal family succession was abandoned.

Through most of its existence the RLDS Church tried to draw sharp distinctions between itself and the Church of Jesus Christ of Latter-day Saints, on the one hand, and **Protestantism**, on the other. However, beginning in the 1960s the RLDS Church began to identify itself more with mainstream **Christianity** in its liberal or progressive forms. This tendency required soul-searching and redefinition. A 1970 report entitled *Exploring the Faith* discussed many topics that would be readily subscribed to by other Christians while maintaining some of the original Mormon distinctiveness.

"Inspired declarations" from the RLDS Church president have been issued from time to time. On this basis blacks were ordained to the **priesthood** (1865), polygamists in **Asia** and **Africa** were allowed to join the Church if they would not take on more wives (1972), women were ordained to the priesthood (1984), and the temple at Independence was announced (1984) and subsequently completed. In April 2000, after many years of discussion, the RLDS Church adopted a new official name, **Community of Christ**. *See also* EXODUS.

REPENTANCE. One of the first principles of the **gospel (Articles of Faith**, no. 4). When the apostle Peter was asked by his listeners what they should do, he replied, "Repent, and be baptized every one of you in the name of Jesus Christ for the remission of sins, and ye shall receive the gift of the Holy Ghost" (Acts 2:38). Mormons do not **baptize** infants. For the change of direction in one's life required of faithful Church **members**, there is no prescribed ritual such as penance, but Mormon writers, echoing a centuries-old Christian description, have said that proper repentance includes recognition, remorse, confession to proper Church authorities, and restitution where possible. With most humans the need for repentance continues throughout life.

RESTORATION. The basic idea of bringing back something that was there before; in Christian religious thought, the bringing back of the beliefs and practices of original **Christianity**. Mormons are restorationists. **Joseph Smith** sought to bring back the organization of the primitive Christian church and the true doctrines that had been lost during the Great **Apostasy**. Unlike some other restorationists, Smith also brought back such Old Testament concepts and usages as **Zion**, **polygamy**, and **temples**. Of central importance to the restoration as Smith conceived it was the appearance of heavenly beings and the actual transmission of the keys of authority from previous dispensations to the present. It was not to be a scholarly enterprise but one infused with divine power.

All of Mormonism is not summed up by the idea of restoration. The reestablishment of **prophets**, who would be the recipients of continuing **revelation**, meant that a direct channel of communication existed between God and the human race.

RESURRECTION. The reuniting of the spirit with the physical body. The spirit of individual humans is indestructible. It could live forever, a disembodied presence, but as such it could never obtain a fullness of joy. It was **Jesus Christ** who broke the bonds of death by his own resurrection and then made possible the resurrection of the entire human race. Resurrection comes to all, good and evil, thanks to the atoning sacrifice of **Jesus Christ**. Without pretending to know the exact mechanism by which it is accomplished, Mormons believe in a physical and literal resurrection, first of Jesus, then of others, and ultimately of the entire human race.

REVELATION. Communication from God. While accepting the **Bible** as **scripture** and thus God's word to the human race, Mormons usually use the term *revelation* to describe not the written **scriptures** but additional heavenly manifestations.

The **First Vision** of **Joseph Smith** is an example of such revelation. Angelic messengers from God appeared to Smith on many occasions. Communications have sometimes come in dreams, as in the Bible. The most common form of divine revelation is by means of "the still small voice," the whisperings of the Holy Spirit. Rejecting the idea that such miraculous intervention was limited to biblical times, Mormons are strongly convinced of the importance of "continuing revelation" (**Articles of Faith**, no. 9).

Who is eligible to receive revelation from God? Here two principles must be kept in salutary tension. On the one hand, all may petition God for guidance. Especially after **baptism** and **confirmation**, Church **members**, if **worthy**, may enjoy the constant companionship of the Holy Ghost, which includes spiritual prompting to assist in decisions. Individuals may also receive more dramatic manifestations. Such revelation is available for one's personal needs or responsibility, as parent in a family, **bishop** over a congregation, and the like.

On the other hand, guidance for the entire Church comes through the **president** and other **general authorities**. The **First Presidency** and the **Quorum** of the **Twelve Apostles** are **sustained** by a vote of the membership as "**prophets**, seers, and revelators." The instruction that comes from these leaders, especially the current president, is considered to have the same status as the canonical scriptures. Church members are urged to read the conference addresses as they are published in the *Ensign* twice a year and apply them to their lives. Members are also to seek personal manifestation to confirm that these messages come from God and to show how they may be applied.

What might appear to be anarchic decentralization, with everyone having access to the divine source, is in fact qualified by a subsidiary principle. Divine guidance for the whole Church comes to the president. Guidance for a congregation may come to its bishop, guidance for a family to its mother or father.

RICHARDS, LEGRAND (1886–1983). Businessman, **general authority.** Born on 6 February 1886 in Farmington, Utah, Richards spent much of his early life in Tooele, Utah, where his father, George F. Richards, was **stake** president. George F. went on to become one of the **twelve apostles** in 1906.

Much of LeGrand's early years were spent in farming. He attended business college in Salt Lake City, Utah. In 1905 he departed on a **mission** to the Netherlands. Upon his return in 1908 he met Ina Ashton, whom he married the following year. After about a year of employment in Portland, Oregon, the young family returned to Salt Lake City, where he worked for a lumber company. Then he was called to be **president** of the Netherlands Mission, serving from 1913 to 1916.

Back in Salt Lake City, Richards founded a realty company. He became **bishop** of his Sugar House **Ward** during several years of the 1920s. After a short-term mission in the East, he moved his family to Glendale, California. After serving as bishop of the Glendale Ward he became president of the Hollywood Stake. In 1934 he was **called** to be president of the Southern States Mission.

Returning to Utah in 1937, Richards again established a real estate business, became bishop of the University Ward, and in 1938 was called to be the Church's **Presiding Bishop.** For the remainder of his life he was one of the general authorities of the Church. As presiding bishop he was responsible generally for "temporal affairs" but also for the young men of the **Aaronic Priesthood.** Procedures were modernized, record keeping improved, a major building program launched. In 1954 LeGrand became a member of the **Quorum** of the **Twelve Apostles.** In the many **stake conferences** he visited and twice a year in **general conferences** he addressed the people, urging them to live their religion, bearing testimony to their faith.

Perhaps the accomplishment that touched more people than any other was his book. As president in the Southern States Mission, LeGrand prepared a topical plan to assist his missionaries in teaching the **gospel**. Responding to requests, he expanded on his earlier plan and in 1950 published *A Marvelous Work and a Wonder*, a presentation of Mormonism on the introductory level, buttressed by scriptural passages that he had used from the time he was a young missionary in Holland. The book went through many editions, and its proceeds were consecrated to the missionary program.

RICKS COLLEGE. Formerly a two-year accredited college at Rexburg, Idaho, owned by the Church, now **BYU–Idaho**. Originally the Bannock Academy, one of several **stake** academies at the time, the institution was renamed after stake **president** Thomas E. Ricks in 1903. A relatively small school of less than 200 students, Ricks College expanded to 5,150 by 1971. After a brief experiment with a four-year program it returned to its junior college status.

Ricks College offered liberal arts training and programs in nursing, agriculture, and other technical areas. Many of its students went on to complete bachelor's degrees at four-year institutions. Enrollment continued to climb, pushing past the cap to reach about 9,000 students. In 2000 it was announced that the institution would become a four-year college. The following year Ricks College took the new name of BYU–Idaho.

RIGDON, SIDNEY (1793–1876). General authority. Born on 19 February 1793 near Pittsburgh, Pennsylvania, Sidney experienced a Christian conversion as a young man and became a Baptist preacher. He married Phebe Brooks. His popular preaching style made his First Baptist Church one of the largest in Pittsburgh.

Longing for the purity of early Christianity, Rigdon became connected with the Mahoning Baptist Association, which included among its leaders Alexander Campbell and Walter Scott, who would soon found the Disciples of Christ. Rigdon did not follow them, however, but instead pastored a congregation in Mentor, Ohio. Among his parishioners he formed a communal society called "the Family."

In October 1830 four Mormon missionaries came to Ohio, including **Parley P. Pratt**, whom Rigdon had converted to the Reformed Baptist faith. After hearing their message and reading the *Book of Mormon*, Rigdon accepted **baptism**. About a hundred of his congregation followed him into Mormonism. He traveled to Fayette, New

York; met **Joseph Smith**; and soon was assisting the **prophet** as a scribe.

During the **Ohio Period**, **Missouri Period**, and **Illinois Period** of Mormon history, Rigdon was a prominent figure. He participated with Joseph Smith in the great **revelation** on the graded salvation of souls after death (***Doctrine and Covenants***, section 76). He became a **counselor** in the **First Presidency**. He taught classes in Kirtland, Ohio, and assisted in preparing a lecture series, "Lectures on Faith." In Illinois he served on the Nauvoo City Council and as postmaster. When Joseph Smith declared his candidacy for president of the United States, Rigdon became the vice presidential candidate.

Rigdon was not always stable. In 1832, when along with Smith he was seized by a mob and tarred and feathered, he suffered head injuries and perhaps never fully recovered. Whatever the reason, he could be an unsettling influence. In Missouri he gave two inflammatory sermons that exacerbated the ill will already present. Upon the death of Joseph Smith in June 1844, Rigdon rushed from Pittsburgh and offered himself as "guardian" of the Church. By this time, however, the steadier hand of **Brigham Young** had demonstrated itself, and the Church members voted in favor of Young and the **twelve apostles** over Rigdon.

Rigdon lived for 32 more years, but they were anti-climactic. He established a Church of Christ in Pennsylvania, but it soon fizzled. In 1863, living in Freedom, New York, he founded the Church of Jesus Christ of the Children of Zion, but it too proved short-lived. A common charge was that Rigdon was the real brains behind Mormonism—that he provided the theology and had written or at least transmitted to Joseph Smith the transcript that became the *Book of Mormon*. In fact, he did not meet Smith until after the Church had been organized. Rigdon made important contributions during the first 14 years of Mormonism and then went his separate way.

ROBERTS, BRIGHAM HENRY (1857–1933). Missionary, politician, **general authority**. Born in Warrington, England, on 13 March 1857, Roberts emigrated to Utah as a boy and worked on farms, in mines, and in a blacksmith shop. Possessed of a powerful drive for self-improvement, he read voraciously and graduated from the territorial University of Deseret. At age 21 he married Sarah Louisa Smith, six years later he took a second wife, and six years after that a third. Roberts' employment included working as a journalist. His Church assignments included serving as a missionary in the United States and Great Britain. From 1888 he was a general authority and a member of the First Council of the **Seventy.**

During the 1890s when national parties came to Utah, Roberts became a Democrat. He served in the convention that drafted a constitution for the new state. After losing a close race for the U.S. House of Representatives in 1895, he was elected in 1898, only to become the center of a storm of controversy as a national campaign was organized to oppose seating him. After committee hearings in Washington, D.C., Roberts was denied his seat on the grounds that he was a **polygamist.**

Roberts had a brilliant mind and a forceful prose style. Works of apologetics included defenses of the *Book of Mormon* and of **Brigham Young** as **Joseph Smith**'s lawful successor. As a historian he compiled a massive, multi-volume source collection (*History of the Church of Jesus Christ of Latter-day Saints*) and wrote a magisterial narrative history in six volumes (*Comprehensive History of the Church*) that, even with its flaws, retains its value.

Some notes on a half dozen problems that had been raised by critics about the claims of the *Book of Mormon*, with reflections and reactions by Roberts, were published as B. H. Roberts, *Studies of the* Book of Mormon. Some have seen these notes as proof that he had privately lost his faith in the Mormon **scripture**, about which he had earlier written eloquent defenses. But his continued willingness to accept Church **callings**, including the presidency of the Eastern States Mission, and his later fervent **testimony** of the *Book of Mormon* make it more likely that the unpublished notes were tentative, exploratory, or intended to provoke answers rather than his own definitive faith statement. *See also* POLYGAMY.

ROBERTSON, LEROY JASPER (1896–1971). Musician, composer. Born on 21 December 1896 in Fountain Green, Utah, Robertson grew up on a farm. He showed musical aptitude but had little opportunity for formal training. He was sent to Provo, Utah, to attend Brigham

Young High School, after which he attended the Boston Music Center, graduating in 1923.

In 1925, Robertson became a professor of music at **BYU**. While there he continued his own formal training, receiving his A.B. and M.A. in music. In 1948 he accepted the chairmanship of the music department at the University of Utah. He received the Ph.D. from the University of Southern California in 1954. He retired in 1964.

Robertson was a serious composer. Among his compositions an overture won first prize in a 1923 competition, a quintet for piano and string won first place in 1936, and *Trilogy* won the coveted Reichhold award in 1947. His compositions were performed by many symphony orchestras and chamber groups in both **Europe** and the United States. In 1952 he completed an oratorio based on the *Book of Mormon*; its recording was pronounced by critic Lowell Durham to be the high point in serious music among the Mormons. Robertson also contributed several works to the Church hymnal.

ROCKWELL, ORRIN PORTER (1813–1878). Bodyguard, hotelier, deputy sheriff. A neighbor of the **Joseph Smith** family near Palmyra, New York, Rockwell joined the Church at age 17 or 18. He followed the Mormons to Ohio and Missouri and finally to Nauvoo, Illinois, where in 1840 he became one of Smith's bodyguards. In 1842 Rockwell was caught in Missouri and arrested for the attempted murder of Governor Lilburn Boggs, who had issued an extermination order against the Mormons. Unable to convict Rockwell, the Missouri court released him after eight months. After the murder of Joseph Smith and **Hyrum Smith**, Rockwell participated in the defense of Nauvoo. He shot and killed an **anti-Mormon** leader named Franklin Worrell. During the migration to the West, he was a guide and hunter.

In Utah he became a deputy sheriff. He established a Pony Express station and hotel and raised horses. For several years Rockwell refused to cut his hair, claiming a promise from Joseph Smith that no harm would befall him if he let his hair grow. Just how many men were victims of his weapons is difficult to determine, for he became a popular folk hero; rumors and unconfirmed stories circulated. Sometimes he was called "the Destroying Angel" of Mormonism. In 1877 he was arrested and charged with a murder that had taken place in 1858, but he died before the trial.

ROMNEY, GEORGE (1907–1995). Businessman, civic leader, Church leader. Born on 8 July 1907 in the Mormon colonies in Mexico, Romney was five when his parents moved to Los Angeles, California, in 1912 during the Mexican Revolution. The next year they moved to Oakley, Idaho, where his father began farming. Low prices forced abandonment of the farm, and the family moved to Rexburg, Idaho. In 1921 the family moved to Salt Lake City, Utah. In addition to construction work on his father's house-building projects, George attended high school and played football, baseball, and basketball. He also courted Lenore LaFount.

In 1926 Romney began two years of foreign **missionary** proselytizing in Scotland. Inspired by mission president **John A. Widtsoe**, George was transferred to London and gained administrative experience as a secretary in the mission office. Returning home in 1928, he entered the University of Utah and also took speedwriting classes at a business college. Anxious to be in Washington, D.C., where Lenore had moved and had graduated from George Washington University, George landed a job on the staff of Senator David I. Walsh, Democrat, of Massachusetts. In 1930 he accepted a job with Aluminum Company of America (Alcoa) and moved to California, where Lenore was pursuing a movie career. They finally married in 1931.

Moving back to Washington, D.C., the Romneys participated in different community activities. Then he took a job with the Automobile Manufacturers Association in Detroit. In 1941 he became managing director of the Automotive Council for War Production. After the war he went to work for Nash-Kelvinator. In 1954 he became CEO of American Motors, which enjoyed a rise in production and profits under his direction.

Romney headed a Citizens Advisory Committee on School Needs, became chairman of Citizens for Michigan, and in 1962 was elected governor of Michigan, serving three terms. A front-runner for the Republican presidential nomination in 1968, Romney lost out partly because he claimed, with perfect justification, that he had been "brainwashed" during a tour in Vietnam. He was appointed secretary of housing and urban development. In the Church, Romney served in many capacities, including several years as **stake** president in Detroit. After his retirement he continued to promote volunteerism throughout the country.

ROMNEY, MITT (1947–). Businessman, Massachusetts governor. Born 12 March 1947 in Detroit, Michigan, son of **GEORGE ROMNEY** and Lenore Romney. He attended Cranbrook School, Stanford University, and **BYU**, graduating as valedictorian. He earned an MBA at Harvard and in 1975 the J.D. at Harvard Law School. Romney was vice president of Bain and Company and in 1984 cofounded Bain Capital. In 1999 he was named president and CEO of the Salt Lake City Olympic Games, then facing a serious financial crisis. Through reorganizing, cutting expenses, and increasing revenue, the games ended with a profit.

In 1994 Romney ran as Republican candidate for U.S. Senate from Massachusetts, losing to Senator Ted Kennedy. In 2002 he was elected governor of Massachusetts. He became president of the Republican Governors Association. In 2006 he announced that he would not run for reelection. He was a contender for the Republican nomination as candidate for president of the United States. Both Republican and Democrat opponents often cited his religion as a reason they would not vote for him. He argued that there should be no religious test for public office and that his support of traditional values was what the majority of voters wanted. In 2007 he announced his candidacy for the presidency of the United States. He suspended his campaign on 7 February 2008 after falling behind John McCain in the primaries.

Always **active** in the Church, he served as **missionary** in France, **bishop**, and **stake president**. He and his wife, Ann, have five sons.

– S –

SABBATH DAY. From the beginning Mormons have sought to remember the Sabbath day and keep it holy. Like other Christians, they designated Sunday for this purpose, although in countries where this proves difficult, like Israel, they have readily shifted to the seventh day.

The central activity of the Sabbath is worship. At **sacrament** meeting Mormons pray, sing, listen to sermons, and most importantly partake of the emblems of the sacrament in remembrance of the sacrifice of Christ. Other meetings include **priesthood**, **Relief Society**, and

Sunday School. In 1980 these meetings were consolidated into a single time block, including **Young Women** and **Primary** meetings. For **bishops** and other leaders there is usually an additional preparation meeting.

During the remaining hours of the Sabbath, members are on their own, but they are urged to avoid regular work where possible as well as secular recreation. The hours of this day are to be dedicated to **prayer**, letter writing, visiting the sick and lonely, appropriate family activities, music, and **scripture** study. Somehow this day should be set apart from the rest of the week and provide nourishment for the spiritual side of human nature that is so easily neglected.

In a **revelation** in 1831 (*Doctrine and Covenants*, section 59) **Joseph Smith** announced, "And that thou mayest more fully keep thyself unspotted from the world, thou shalt go to the house of prayer and offer up thy sacraments upon my holy day; for verily this is a day appointed unto you to rest from your labors, and to pay thy devotions unto the Most High."

SACRAMENT. In Mormon usage the sacrament of the Lord's Supper repeated each week in sacrament meeting. Bread and wine (replaced by water after a **revelation** authorized it) are blessed by prayers specified in the *Book of Mormon* and *Doctrine and Covenants*. Regarded as a solemn remembrance and acknowledgment of the sacrifice of **Jesus Christ**, the sacrament includes no claim of transubstantiation or real presence. The regular partaking of the emblems by Church **members** is also considered a renewal of covenants and a recommitment to observe the **commandments**. Sacraments in the broad sense are usually described by Mormons as **ordinances**. *See also* SABBATH.

SACRAMENT MEETING. The main meeting for worship held in **wards** and branches throughout the Church each **Sabbath**. Although somewhat informal when compared to the structured worship of liturgical traditions, sacrament meetings follow a standard format:

1. Hymn by congregation
2. Announcements
3. Opening prayer or invocation
4. Sacramental hymn

5. Blessing and distribution of the sacrament
6. Speakers
7. Musical selection
8. Closing hymn
9. Closing prayer or benediction

Those unfamiliar with Mormon practices sometimes find the sacrament meeting lacking due to the inclusion of small children in the congregation with some inevitable noise and the unprofessional quality of music and sermons. On the other hand, if one recalls that a lay organization, entirely volunteer, is putting on the meeting, it can be recognized that it performs its basic purpose entirely adequately. Certainly the personal growth that goes with participation is abundantly evident. Those who attend these meetings regularly attest to hearing excellent instruction and being inspired to live better lives.

One sacrament meeting each month, normally the first, is designated as a "fast and testimony meeting." Instead of the usual sermons, members of the congregation who wish to do so stand and "bear **testimony**," telling what their religious faith means to them. *See also* FASTING; TESTIMONY.

SACRED GROVE. In the spring of 1820 **Joseph Smith**, desiring to know which church he should join, retired to a grove of trees near his home in Palmyra, New York. The **First Vision** set in motion the events that led to the organization of the **LDS** Church on 6 April 1830. The grove of trees that Smith prayed in, or one that seems to fit the requirements, has been designated the Sacred Grove and is a popular tourist site.

SAINTS. Synonymous with "**members** of the Church." Following the New Testament usage according to which Paul wrote to "the saints" at Ephesus or Corinth or another city where there were Christians, Mormons do not assign any special sanctity to the term, although obviously members are expected to live a life dedicated to God. There is no canonization process. The venerable dead, the heroic figures of the past, are not the subject of any special cult or veneration. Prayers are not addressed to them.

SALVATION. *See* PLAN OF SALVATION.

SAMUELSON, CECIL O. (1941–). Physician, educator, **general authority.** Born on 1 August 1941 in Salt Lake City, Utah, Samuelson received his medical degree from the University of Utah, after which he served his residency at Duke University Medical Center. Returning to the University of Utah, he became successively professor of medicine, dean of the school of medicine, and vice president of health services. He became senior vice president of Intermountain Health Care. His interest in rheumatic and genetic diseases led to the publication of many articles as well as eight books or chapters of books.

Samuelson served as **stake high councilor**, stake **president**, and **regional representative**. In 1994 he became a member of the First **Quorum** of the **Seventy**. In 2003 Samuelson became the 12th president of **BYU**. He and his wife, Sharon, have five children.

SATAN. A spirit personage who leads the forces of evil and tries to defeat God's purposes. In the pre-mortal existence this spirit, a child of God, rebelled and took with him a portion of the host of heaven—that is, other spirits. Since then Satan has tried to frustrate the **plan of salvation.** Knowing human weaknesses, he tempts individuals to the path of destruction. But those who have faith and keep the **commandments** will be safe, for God is more powerful and will ultimately prevail.

SATANISM. Rituals and cultic practices that have included the worship of **Satan.** Found in different time periods and geographical locations, Satanism has appeared even in modern, relatively educated communities. Mormons are warned by their leaders to have nothing to do with such practices.

SCHISMS. Splinter groups that leave the main body on grounds of differing beliefs or rejection of authority. The phenomenon is not limited to Mormonism. With regard to the **LDS** Church, such groups began appearing in the 1830s. At the death of **Joseph Smith** rival claims to the **succession** were put forth. The most successful of these, the **RLDS** Church, became a significant denomination.

With the official end of **polygamy**, new schismatics appeared. The schismatic groups remained small. Many have disappeared.

Because it is impossible to give separate histories of each splinter group, the present reference work concentrates on the mainstream **Church of Jesus Christ of Latter-day Saints**, popularly called Mormons. A group of a few score or a few hundred people that does not claim to be part of the Church, whose members are **excommunicated** if discovered, cannot receive equal space in a work of this kind. Further information on the many different groups claiming a connection with the **restoration** may be found in Steven L. Shields, *The Latter Day Saint Churches: An Annotated Bibliography*, listed below in the bibliography. At the same time, it is recognized that **dissent** and schism occur. *See also* BICKERTONITES; COMMUNITY OF CHRIST; DISSENT; FUNDAMENTALISTS; MANIFESTO; REORGANIZED CHURCH OF JESUS CHRIST OF LATTER DAY SAINTS; RIGDON, SIDNEY; STRANG, JAMES J.; SUCCESSION; WIGHT, LYMAN.

SCHREINER, ALEXANDER (1901–1987). Musician, **Tabernacle** organist. Born in Nuernberg, Germany, on 31 July 1901, Schreiner attended the Melanchthon School. His parents were musical and gave him the opportunity to learn piano. At a very young age he began accompanying at the Mormon branch. In 1912 his family moved to Salt Lake City, Utah. Young Schreiner was placed in school and learned English by the "assimilation" method. He resumed piano study. Then he added organ study and earned money by playing as a theater organist. In 1922–1924 he served as a **missionary** in California.

Returning to Salt Lake City, he became one of the Tabernacle organists. On leave, he studied organ and theory in Paris with Henri Libert, Charles-Marie Widor, and Louis Vierne. He also received an appointment as University Organist at UCLA, where for nine years he taught classes and performed recitals. Anxious to pursue his education, Schreiner earned a B.A. from the University of Utah. Continuing on the graduate level in musical composition under **Leroy J. Robertson**, he earned a Ph.D. in 1954. For over 30 years he was on concert tour yearly. He composed many organ voluntaries as well as *Concerto for Full Orchestra and Organ*. Several Church hymns are set to music by Schreiner, including "God Loved Us, So He Sent His

Son." He was the recipient of several honorary degrees. He retired in 1977. Schreiner and his wife, Margaret, had four children.

SCIENCE. The basic attitude of Mormonism toward science has always been positive. Truth will not contradict truth. Especially in the 20th and 21st centuries many Mormons became scientists. Studies demonstrated that Utah had more scientists per capita than any other state. Examples of Mormon scientists are **Henry Eyring**, prominent chemist; Harvey Fletcher, physicist and inventor; and **Philo Farnsworth**, inventor of television.

Controversy over scientific issues has flared up from time to time, as Mormons with a literal interpretation of **scripture** have condemned those with a more flexible interpretation. In the early 21st century, when critics cited DNA analysis of native populations as evidence against the *Book of Mormon*, several highly trained Mormon scientists responded by pointing out fallacies in the argument. The Mormon scientific community has faith in God's ultimate power while acknowledging that His will may be worked through a variety of means. *See also* CREATION.

SCOTT, RICHARD GORDON (1928–). Nuclear engineer, **general authority**. Born on 7 November 1928 in Pocatello, Idaho, Scott grew up in the Washington, D.C., area, where his father was employed by the Department of Agriculture. He graduated from George Washington University in mechanical engineering and, after serving as a **missionary** in Uruguay, returned to do postgraduate work in nuclear engineering at Oak Ridge, Tennessee. From 1953 to 1965 Scott served on the staff of Admiral Hyman Rickover. He directed research and application of the use of nuclear energy for military purposes and land-based power plants. Later he was a consultant for nuclear power companies.

In 1965 Scott was called to be president of the Argentina North Mission in Cordoba. After his return in 1969 he was a **regional representative** in Uruguay, Paraguay, and the eastern United States. In 1977 he became one of the First **Quorum** of the **Seventy** and in 1988 a member of the Quorum of the **Twelve Apostles**. He and his wife, Jeanene (who died in 1995), are the parents of seven children, five of them living.

SCRIPTURE. (1) The four "standard works": the **Bible**, *Book of Mormon*, *Doctrine and Covenants*, and *Pearl of Great Price*. Proclaiming of the *Book of Mormon* as scripture at the Church's beginning in 1830 signaled a belief in an open, not closed, canon. The acceptance of both the *Doctrine and Covenants* and the *Pearl of Great Price* as standard works was made official by a **sustaining** vote of the members of the Church in **general conference**.

(2) Whatever is spoken by God's representatives when they are divinely inspired (*Doctrine and Covenants*, section 68). Although in common parlance "scripture," or "scriptures," as used among Mormons refers to the four standard works, this broader meaning is a reminder that **revelation** continues, that the living **prophets** express God's will to the current generation, and that God, the ultimate source of truth, is not to be constrained. *See also* PROPHETS; REVELATION.

SEALING. **Ordinance** performed in the **temples** joining husband and wife, parents and children, in a relationship that continues after death as well as during mortality. When a temple **marriage** establishes such a sealing between husband and wife, children born to that union are considered "born in the covenant" and do not have to be sealed in a separate ceremony, for the eternal **family** unit was created by the temple marriage. People who are married outside of the temple may, upon their conversion or a later decision to do so, go to the temple to have their marriage sealed. Any children they have may go with them and participate in the sealing ordinance. Participation in temple ordinances is dependent upon **worthiness**, which is determined by a **bishop**. Ultimate enjoyment of the eternal blessings is always contingent upon faithfulness.

SECT. *See* CULT.

SEMINARIES. Religious instruction for youth of high school age, roughly 14 to 18, provided on a released-time basis for one class period each day in buildings adjacent to or nearby the regular school. The first seminary of this type began in 1912 in Salt Lake City, Utah; the program then expanded through those western states with a sufficient population of Church members. Seminary classes are taught by individuals with the same training and credentials as teachers in the public schools. The four-year curriculum includes Old Testament, New Testament, *Doctrine and Covenants*, and *Book of Mormon*. Where the released-time arrangement has not been allowed, perhaps because of an insufficient population of Church members, seminaries are conducted in the early morning prior to the beginning of the school day. Alternatively, especially for scattered students where other arrangements are not feasible, correspondence or home-study courses are available. *See also* INSTITUTES OF RELIGION.

SENIOR CITIZENS. In the late 19th century, organized outings and celebrations for "old folks" at least gave some recognition to the most advanced age group. At present, their health enhanced by adherence to the **Word of Wisdom**, more and more Mormons, like everyone else, are living many years beyond retirement.

The inherent problems of old age—dependency, loneliness, pain, disorientation—are faced by Mormons like everyone else. The increased incidence of Alzheimer's disease has been a painful challenge for many families. On the other hand, for Mormon senior citizens the "golden years" are alleviated by following a program of **home teaching** and **visiting teaching** that, when it works, sees to it that each person has others assigned to provide friendship, assist when required, and report special needs; provide activity in the **temples**, which occupies many, giving them something to do, people to associate with, and a sense of usefulness; give opportunities for **missions**, with retired couples especially in demand, some of them serving one mission after another; and surround with strong families that continue to accept responsibility for the love and care of aging parents and grandparents. *See also* FAMILY.

SEVENTY. An office in the **priesthood**. First established during the **Ohio Period** in 1835, the seventies had primarily a **missionary** responsibility. They were to work under the direction of the **Quorum** of the **Twelve Apostles**. For most of its history the seventy were simply those holders of the **Melchizedek Priesthood** who were ordained to this office with special orientation toward proselytizing. The seven presidents were called the First Council of the Seventy and were regarded as **general authorities** of the Church.

In 1975, to meet the needs of the expanding membership, the First Quorum of the Seventy was organized. It included those who previously had been called **assistants to the twelve**. Its leadership was a presidency of seven. In 1986 **stake** quorums of seventies were discontinued. In 1989 a Second Quorum of the Seventy was organized, also under the direction of the same seven presidents, the Presidency of the Seventy. Membership in the second quorum was to last about five years.

Under the direction of the **First Presidency** and the Quorum of the Twelve Apostles, members of the First and Second Quorums of the Seventy supervise training of leaders, attend **stake conferences**, and especially serve as presidencies over the **areas** of the Church throughout the world. In 1997 three additional quorums were created—the Third, Fourth, and Fifth Quorums—made up of men called to serve for five or six years on a Church-service basis. That is, they were to continue their present employment and reside in their homes. Of the 134 men first called to this position, 128 had already been serving as area authorities and henceforth would be identified as **area authority seventies**.

SHIPP, ELLIS REYNOLDS (1847–1939). Physician, educator. Born in Iowa to William F. and Anna Hawley Reynolds, Ellis emigrated with her family to Utah shortly after they joined the church. After the death of her mother and until her father remarried a year later, Ellis shouldered the responsibility for her father's house and her four brothers and sisters. She attended school with **Brigham Young**'s children in the Beehive House. In 1866 she married Milford B. Shipp. They were the parents of 10 children, 5 of whom survived infancy.

Shipp attended the University of Deseret and the Woman's Medical College of Pennsylvania, graduating in 1878. She did postgraduate work at the University of Michigan Medical School. After she returned to Utah, she opened a School of Obstetrics and Nursing in Salt Lake City, teaching women physiology, obstetrical procedures, and basic health information. She served on the board of the Deseret Hospital. After World War I's outbreak, Shipp opened extension programs in Mormon communities in Blackfoot, Idaho; Vernal, Utah; and Colonia Juarez, Mexico. She also participated in the Utah

Reaper's Club and the Utah Woman's Press Club. She also published a volume of poetry. Just four years before her death, the Woman's Medical College awarded her an honorary degree and Utah inducted her into the Utah Hall of Fame.

SHUMWAY, ERIC B. (1939–). President, **BYU–Hawaii.** Raised in St. Johns, Arizona, Shumway served as a **missionary** in Tonga before graduating from **BYU** with bachelor's and master's degrees in English, in 1964 and 1966, respectively. His book *Intensive Course in Tongan* was published by the University of Hawaii Press in 1971. In 1973, he received his doctorate in English literature at the University of Virginia.

Shumway accepted a position as instructor of English at **BYU–Hawaii**, then called Church College of Hawaii. In 1975 he was named chair of the Communications and Language Arts Division and in 1980 vice president for academics.

President of the Tongan Mission from 1986 to 1989, Shumway returned to Hawaii as acting president of the **Polynesian Cultural Center.** In 1994 he became president of BYU–Hawaii. In 2007 he was called to be president of the Nuku'alofa (Tonga) Temple. He has served as **bishop, high councilor, stake** president, and **area authority seventy.** He and his wife, Carolyn, have seven children. In 1996–1997 Carolyn was named American National Mother of the Year.

SINGLES. Unmarried adults who are Mormons face the same economic and social challenges as other singles. In addition, they must find their way in a Church that includes **marriage** among the prerequisites for the highest salvation.

A variety of factors have increased the number of single adults: later marriage age, increased **divorce**, and acceptance of the single lifestyle in the larger society. One study showed that **LDS** single adults were divided into three groups: divorced or separated, 23 percent; widowed, 13 percent; never married, 63 percent. Among these singles there is consistently a gender disproportion, with more women than men.

The Church has responded to the needs of singles by providing recreational activities, appointing committees for single adults on the

ward and **stake** level, establishing wards or branches for singles where the demand is sufficient, and including material on singles in manuals and Church periodicals.

SMITH, BARBARA BRADSHAW (1922–). Relief Society president. Born in Salt Lake City, Utah, on 26 January 1922, Barbara Bradshaw attended the local schools. She married Douglas H. Smith, an insurance executive, who later became a **general authority** as a member of the Second **Quorum** of the **Seventy**. They have seven children. In the Relief Society she had experience as a teacher and as **ward** president. (Her mother and sister were presidents of their ward Relief Societies at exactly the same time.) Smith served on the Relief Society **stake** board and then on the general board.

From 1974 to 1984 she was general president of the Relief Society, a decade during which the movement for women's liberation became more assertive and women's issues assumed an unprecedented prominence. Employment, **birth control**, abortion, **divorce**, one-parent families—such issues could not be ignored. In the meantime, economic conditions created welfare needs, and the women leaders of the Relief Society participated on every level of Welfare Services.

An opponent of the Equal Rights Amendment, Barbara Smith found herself under attack from those on the other side. She explained her position: "I stand as a representative of an organization that is in favor of rights for women. However, we may differ with some people on the best way or ways to achieve these rights. In my opinion, the Equal Rights Amendment is not the way" (B. Smith, *A Fruitful Season*, 227). She appeared on Phil Donahue's television show to explain this position.

Attempting to meet the needs of a variety of Mormon women—old and young; different races, ethnic groups, and nationalities; married and single—the Relief Society under President Smith's leadership adapted its teaching materials and introduced new resources. To celebrate the achievements and contributions of women, the Monument to Women was created in Nauvoo, Illinois, and dedicated in June 1978. Upon her release as general president in 1984, Smith accompanied her husband to Hong Kong, where for three years he served in the presidency of the **area**.

SMITH, BATHSHEBA BIGLER (1822–1910). Suffragist, **Relief Society** general president. Born 3 May 1822 in Shinston, West Virginia, Bathsheba grew up in a well-to-do southern family, so she received a good education considering the time and place of her childhood. When she was 15, her family joined the Church and emigrated to Missouri just in time for the final expulsion of Mormons. Her family then moved to Nauvoo, Illinois, where in 1841 she married George A. Smith, then a member of the **Quorum** of the **Twelve Apostles** and later a member of the **First Presidency.** Early in her marriage Smith faced hardships, including the frequent absence of her **missionary** husband. Her husband also entered into plural marriage. As first wife, Smith often had to mediate problems between other wives. She was a charter member of the Relief Society at its organization in 1842 in Nauvoo.

After moving to Utah, Bathsheba taught her children and engaged in charitable work. As her children reached maturity, she traveled with her husband on his Church assignments. Following her husband's death in 1875, Smith worked in the **temple** and from 1888 to 1901 served as a **counselor** to the **LDS** Relief Society's general president, Zina Young. After Young's death, Smith was called as the general president. She served from 1901 until her death in 1910. During her tenure, Smith encouraged women to become self-sufficient by learning how to sew, weave, spin, knit, raise their own food, and better their homes. Smith also campaigned in the women's suffrage movement.

SMITH, EMMA HALE (1804–1879). Relief Society president. Born in Harmony, Pennsylvania, where she met **Joseph Smith,** then working as a laborer in her area. Denied the permission of her parents to marry Joseph, Emma eloped (she was 22) on 18 January 1827, after which the newlyweds moved to Manchester, New York. Joining the new Church in 1830, Emma experienced **persecution** and frequent moves along with her husband. Her first three children, including a set of twins, died soon after birth, as did two other infants and an adopted baby boy. Surviving sons were Joseph III, Frederick, Alexander Hale, and David Hyrum.

She was appointed to select hymns for the new Church (a compilation published in 1835). In Nauvoo, Illinois, Smith became president in 1842 of the new organization for women, the Relief Society. She was among the first women to experience the **ordinance** of endowment even prior to the completion of the Nauvoo Temple in 1846.

When **polygamy** was "unofficially" introduced about 1840, Emma consented to her husband's marriage to plural wives but soon had second thoughts. Torn between aversion to this practice and loyalty to her husband, she suffered great emotional stress. After Joseph's death in June 1844, she refused to accept the leadership of **Brigham Young**, quarreling with him over property claims.

During the remainder of her life, Emma remained in Nauvoo, denying that her late husband had introduced polygamy—a denial psychologically understandable but untrue to historical reality. She married Lewis Bidamon, who assisted in raising her remaining five children. In 1860 her oldest son, Joseph III, became president of the **RLDS** Church, which she joined.

Although tension continued to exist between her and the leaders of the **Church of Jesus Christ of Latter-day Saints** in the West, she treated Mormon visitors kindly. In time they preferred to overlook the closing phase of her life by emphasizing instead the courage, faith, and loyalty of her life up to the death of her husband in 1844. *See also* TEMPLES.

SMITH, GEORGE ALBERT (1870–1951). General authority, Church **president**. Born on 4 April 1870 in Salt Lake City, Utah, George was the son of John Henry Smith and grandson of George A. Smith, both of whom were in the **Quorum** of the **Twelve Apostles** and **counselors** in the **First Presidency**. He studied at Brigham Young Academy and the University of Utah. He married Lucy Emily Woodruff, a granddaughter of **Wilford Woodruff**.

From 1892 to 1894, he was a **missionary** in the Southern States Mission. Work for the Republican Party led to being appointed receiver for the Land Office in 1896 and again in 1902. In 1903, at the age of 33, Smith was called to the Quorum of the Twelve Apostles. He had a special interest in the YMMIA. He served on its general board and, from 1921 to 1935, as its general superintendent. An advocate of the **Boy Scout** organization, he promoted its inclusion in the Church youth program. For years of service in scouting he was awarded the Silver Beaver and the Silver Buffalo.

Although afflicted with poor eyesight and chronic debilitation (from lupus erythematosus), Smith kept busily involved. President of the European Mission from 1919 to 1921, he made a special effort to make friends with government leaders. In 1938 he visited the Church missions in Australia, New Zealand, and several **Pacific** islands.

Smith took a keen interest in Church history sites and trails. He attended the dedication of a monument to **Joseph Smith** at Sharon, Vermont, in 1905. He helped to found the Utah Pioneer Trails and Landmarks Association, which erected many monuments, including the **"This Is the Place" Monument**. By seniority he became **president** of the Quorum of Twelve Apostles in 1943. Upon the death of President **Heber J. Grant** in 1945, Smith became president of the Church. He was 75 years old.

For six years, from 1945 to 1951, Smith led the Church. Among the achievements of these postwar years were the dedication of the new Idaho Falls Temple in 1945, the construction of many meetinghouses, the expansion of a program for microfilming genealogical records, and the rapid growth of missionary activity. Under his direction the Church sent substantial relief supplies to **Europe**.

His personal creed, which he allowed to be published in 1932, was an inspiration to many. Among its 10 goals or ideals were "I would be a friend to the friendless and find joy in ministering to the needs of the poor" and "I would not be an enemy to any living soul" (Pusey, *Builders of the Kingdom*, 255).

SMITH, HYRUM (1800–1844). Patriarch, general authority. Older brother and close associate of **Joseph Smith**, Hyrum was associate president of the Church at the time of his death. Born on 9 February 1800 in Tunbridge, Vermont, where he received some primary schooling, Hyrum moved with family to Manchester, New York, about 1816. For the next several years he worked on the family farm and occasionally hired out. He married Jerusha Barden in 1826.

When his brother Joseph was working on the manuscript of the *Book of Mormon*, Hyrum, a believer from the first, assisted. He was one of the eight **witnesses of the *Book of Mormon*** allowed to see and handle the metal plates. When the Church was organized in 1830, Hyrum was among the six original members. Immediately he began preaching, going on several **missions** in New York and later in Ohio and Missouri. Along with the rest of the Church, Hyrum experienced the **persecutions**, moved to Missouri, served several months in jail, and spent the closing years of his life in Illinois. After bearing six children, his wife Jerusha died. His second wife, Mary Fielding, bore two more children, including **Joseph F. Smith**.

In addition to being the companion and confidant of his brother, Hyrum held important positions in the Church: assistant president from 1834, **counselor** in the **First Presidency** from 1837, presiding patriarch, and associate president. In June 1844 he refused the opportunity to take his family to Cincinnati, instead staying by his brother Joseph during their imprisonment in Carthage Jail. There both of them were killed by a mob on 27 June 1844. Latter-day Saints regard the brothers as martyrs.

SMITH, JOSEPH (1805–1844). Founding **prophet** of the **Church of Jesus Christ of Latter-day Saints**, Church **president;** sometimes known as Joseph Smith Jr. to distinguish him from his father. The external life of Joseph Smith—his places of residence, his travels, his public statements—is easily enough recounted, although even on this level his life was not easily lived, for he had more than his share of pain and trial. The internal life, the religious experiences, the dimension of **revelation** or **prophecy**—these are, of course, understood differently by believers and nonbelievers. He recognized the ultimate ineffability of such matters in a famous statement made at the end of his life: "No man knows my history; I cannot tell it. I shall never undertake it. If I had not experienced what I have, I should not have believed it myself" (J. F. Smith, *Teachings of the Prophet Joseph Smith*, 361.) In the present brief sketch the emphasis will be on the external matters, with the religious experiences and contributions presented in the way Smith told them to others and the way they have been accepted by his followers.

Born in Sharon, Vermont, on 23 December 1805, Joseph was the third living son of Joseph Smith Sr. and Lucy Mack Smith. Poor but hard working, the Smith family—nine children, not counting still-births or infant deaths—moved from farm to farm. In 1816, like other New Englanders, they moved into New York State, settling on a farm near Palmyra. Broadly Christian, reading and believing the **Bible**, the Smiths became unsettled over the question of religion during revivals. In this context, young Joseph, still a teenager, prayed to God, asking what he should do. The result was the **First Vision**, during which the Lord instructed him to join none of the existing churches, for they had all gone astray.

During the 1820s, between the ages of 15 and 25, Joseph Smith grew to adulthood, worked on the family farm, and hired out as a laborer. Reputed to be able to find treasure through a seer stone, he was briefly employed to dig for buried Spanish gold, but the enterprise failed. The most important events of these years, as he later saw them, were the appearances of an angel, who told him where to find buried metal plates. He was not allowed to take them at first, for he coveted them for their monetary value, but in 1827, after four years of discipline and purifying his heart, Joseph was allowed to take possession of them for purposes of translation. The same year he married **Emma Hale Smith**.

During the next two and a half years, Joseph moved to Harmony, Pennsylvania, and with the assistance of scribes worked on translating the hieroglyphics from the plates into English. Although ridiculed by ministers and others, he had the confidence of his parents, his siblings, his wife, and a few friends who provided financial support. Some of these were selected as **witnesses of the *Book of Mormon***.

When the resurrected John the Baptist appeared to Smith and Cowdery and gave them **priesthood** authority, they **baptized** each other and began baptizing others. In the spring of 1830 the *Book of Mormon* was published and on 6 April the Church was organized with six men to satisfy the legal requirement. During the next 14 years, from age 24 to 38, Joseph Smith's life was anything but dull. The head of a church and a movement, he had to answer many specific questions. Revelations on matters ranging from instruction to individuals on their duty to administrative details to lofty theological principles were issued by the prophet one by one. Eventually these were compiled into a volume entitled ***Doctrine and Covenants***.

Smith led the fledgling **LDS** Church, with a hundred or so members, to a new location at Kirtland, Ohio. At the same time he announced that the new **Zion** was to be built in western Missouri. During most of the 1830s, therefore, Mormon converts converged on these two locations. Smith himself lived at Kirtland but led an expedition to assist his persecuted followers in Missouri and in 1837 moved there with his family.

Opposition to the new religion had started early. Harassment in New York, verbal denunciation, burning of houses and barns, tarring and feathering, beating, and lynching—the early Mormons experienced all of this as not only terrorism but as **persecution**, the expected fate of the Lord's disciples. Smith himself had his life threatened and was tarred and feathered in Ohio. In Missouri, where the Mormons were driven from the state, Joseph Smith and several of his associates were imprisoned for several months in a jail at Liberty, Missouri. In the depths of despair, he still managed to maintain the rightness of his position, to provide inspiration to his followers, and to produce some of his most sublime revelations (*Doctrine and Covenants*, sections 121–123).

After escaping his captors, Joseph joined the bedraggled Mormons in western Illinois and there on the banks of the Mississippi River established a new center at Commerce, renamed Nauvoo. Illinois was the setting for the final period of Smith's life. In addition to his position as president of the Church, Smith became mayor of the city and an officer its militia. Missouri officials demanded Smith's extradition. Efforts to obtain protection or relief from the federal government came to naught. In addition to the rising tide of **anti-Mormonism** in surrounding towns, a small number of **apostates** denounced Smith, and to some extent the two groups cooperated.

Matters came to a head with the publication of an opposition newspaper, *The Nauvoo Expositor*, and a decision by the city council, including Smith, to destroy the press. Outraged opponents decried the act as inimical to freedom of the press. Some of these enemies, in speeches and editorials, called for solving the Mormon problem by the violence of "powder and ball." Charged with riot for destroying the press and assured by the state's governor that he would be safe, Smith was arrested and placed in Carthage Jail. Accompanying him were his brother, **Hyrum Smith**, Apostle **John Taylor**, and others.

Whipped up by anti-Mormons, militia members transformed themselves into a lynch mob. On 27 June 1844, with blackened faces, they fired into the jail from the outside and, charging up the stairs, attacked from the inside with guns blazing. In a few moments Hyrum Smith and Joseph Smith were killed. John Taylor was wounded.

It is hard to be neutral about Joseph Smith. His enemies and detractors viewed him as an imposter, a con man who took advantage of a gullible people. Mormons remembered his kindness and humor and charismatic leadership. Mormons do not believe that he was perfect. They do not worship him. For them he was a human being but one chosen by God to be the prophet of the last **dispensation**. He brought back to earth **priesthood** authority; restored the Church; brought forth the *Book of Mormon*, *Doctrine and Covenants*, and *Pearl of Great Price*; led his people through times of perilous persecution and displacement; founded a city; and revealed many important religious truths. When he died, he was 38 years old. *See also* APOSTASY; CHURCH OF JESUS CHRIST OF LATTER-DAY SAINTS; COWDERY, OLIVER; ZION'S CAMP.

SMITH, JOSEPH F. (1838–1918). General authority, Church **president**. Although Fielding is his middle name, he is traditionally known as Joseph F. to distinguish him from his son. Born to **Hyrum Smith** and Mary Fielding Smith in Far West, Missouri, on 13 November 1838, he was carried by his mother to refuge in Illinois. He was only five years old when his father and uncle, the **prophet Joseph Smith**, were killed. As his mother took charge of seven children during the flight from Nauvoo, Illinois, and the trek to the Salt Lake Valley, young Joseph F. drove his mother's wagon. He was nine when they arrived in Salt Lake City.

Joseph F. worked hard in the fields and tending cattle. He was only 13 when his mother died. Two years later, having had only minimal schooling, he was called as a **missionary** to Hawaii, where for the next four years he mastered the language and gained leadership experience. Soon after his return he married Levira Smith. With her permission he married as a plural wife Julina Lambson, who was later followed by four others. He eventually fathered 43 children.

From 1860 to 1863 Joseph F. was a **missionary** in Great Britain. He was elected to the Utah Territory legislature and the Salt Lake City council. In the Church he served on his stake **high council**, worked in the Historian's Office, and officiated in ceremonies in the Endowment House. In 1867 he was ordained a member of the Quorum of **Twelve Apostles**. In 1874–1875 and again in 1877 he was president of the European and British Missions. For a while he was president of the Davis County, Utah, **stake**. In 1880, at the age of 41, he became second **counselor** in the **First Presidency** of the Church.

When **John Taylor** died in 1887, Smith continued as one of the twelve apostles and became a counselor to new Church president **Wilford Woodruff**. With the coming of national political parties to Utah, Joseph F. became a Republican. He participated in the Church policy decisions of the 1890s, continuing as a counselor to **Lorenzo Snow** in 1898. When Snow died in 1901, Joseph F. Smith became **president** of the Church.

As president, he worked to bring Mormonism into the 20th century by emphasizing its American loyalty, first in the Spanish-American War and later during World War I. Although **anti-Mormonism** continued during the hearings for Senator-elect **Reed Smoot** and afterward, President Smith emphasized education, missionary expansion, the construction of needed Church buildings, and the acquisition of historic sites. Known for his sensible discussions of doctrinal matters, he gave many sermons and wrote articles, from which the book *Gospel Doctrine* was compiled in 1918. A **revelation**, "Vision of the Redemption of the Dead," was added to the ***Doctrine and Covenants*** in 1981. *See also* POLYGAMY.

SMITH, JOSEPH FIELDING (1876–1972). Historian, doctrinal authority, **general authority**, Church **president**. Born in Salt Lake City, Utah, on 19 July 1876, Joseph Fielding Smith was the son of **Joseph F. Smith** and Julina Lambson. Since his father was out of the country during much of the 1880s, the boy was supervised by his mother, a midwife. He milked cows and did other farm work. In 1898 at the age of 22 he married Louie Shurtliff and the next year was called as a **missionary** to England.

Returning in 1901, Smith took employment in the Church Historian's Office. When his father became president of the Church that same year, he became a confidant and assistant. In 1905 and again in 1907 he wrote pamphlets defending the Church's practices against critics. Louie gave birth to two daughters, but during her third pregnancy she had complications and died. After several months of loneliness, Joseph married Ethel Reynolds, who became the mother of five sons and four daughters.

In April 1910 he was called to the **Quorum** of the **Twelve Apostles**. **Temple** and genealogical work were themes he often stressed.

He edited the *Utah Genealogical and Historical Magazine*. For 20 years he was in the presidency of the Salt Lake Temple either as a **counselor** or as president. Church history also was a passion. From his initial appointment as assistant Church historian in 1906 Smith went on to become Church historian from 1921 to 1970.

In 1937 his wife Ethel died. The next year, at age 62, he married Jessie Evans, a well-known contralto. A loving companion for the remaining 34 years of his life, she had a keen sense of humor that made her a well-known character in her own right. From 1950 Joseph Fielding was president (or acting president) of the twelve apostles. In 1965 he was **called** to be a counselor to the **First Presidency**. In 1970, at age 94, he became president of the Church. He supervised the reorganization of some departments, the expansion of missionary work, and the dedication of two temples.

SMOOT, REED (1862–1941). U.S. senator from Utah, **general authority**. Although born on 10 January 1862 in Salt Lake City, Utah, Smoot was raised in Provo, Utah, where his father was mayor and **stake president**. Reed studied at the new Brigham Young Academy from 1876. As a young man of 22 he became superintendent of the Provo Woolen Mills and also married Alpha Eldredge. Except for about a year's absence as a **missionary** in England (1890–1891) his base of operations was Provo. Manager of Provo Commercial and Savings Bank, he was also vice president of Grant Central Mining and a director of Los Angeles and Salt Lake Railroad. From 1884 he was appointed a director of the Utah Territory Insane Asylum in Provo. In 1900 he became a member of the **Quorum** of the **Twelve Apostles**.

Elected U.S. senator from Utah in 1903, after clearing his candidacy with the Church presidency, Smoot was immediately challenged. Issues included the alleged continuation of **polygamy** among the Mormons and Smoot's status as a Church **general authority**. For two and a half years the Senate Committee on Privileges held hearings. Accusers testified. Church leaders were summoned and cross-examined. Although the committee voted against Smoot, the Senate itself allowed him to keep his seat. For about 30 years Reed Smoot was an apostle in the Church, a leader of Utah Republicans, and a highly regarded member of the U.S. Senate.

SNOW, ELIZA ROXCY (1804–1887). Poet, author of hymns, **Relief Society** president. Born in Massachusetts but raised in Ohio, Eliza learned of Mormonism and in 1835 with other family members joined the new faith. With other Latter-day Saints the Snows were forced to leave Ohio, then to leave Missouri, and then to seek refuge in Illinois. Eliza published poems defending and encouraging her people and became a school teacher.

In 1842 she participated in the founding of the **Relief Society**, serving as secretary. She also became a plural wife of **Joseph Smith**, following whose death in 1844 she became a plural wife of **Brigham Young**. With the other Mormons who were driven from Nauvoo, Snow made her way westward, arriving in the Salt Lake Valley in the fall of 1847. There she continued to write and publish poetry, participated in a study group known as the Polysophical Society, and after 1866 led the reorganized and revitalized Relief Society. She also helped found organizations for children and young women. Until her death in 1887 was looked upon as leader of the Church's women. She wrote several hymns, including "O My Father," which includes the idea of a pre-mortal existence prior to this life and of a Heavenly Mother.

SNOW, LORENZO (1814–1901). Missionary, general authority, president of the Church. Born on 3 April 1814 and raised on a farm in Ohio, Snow received not only a common school education but, unusual for the time, completed high school and one term at Oberlin College. Becoming acquainted with Mormonism when **Joseph Smith** briefly resided at nearby Hiram, Ohio, the Snow family, including Lorenzo's sister **Eliza R. Snow**, became converts, Lorenzo in 1836. During his 20s he gained experience through a series of missions, presided over congregations in London, and led a party of emigrants from England to Illinois.

Snow arrived in Salt Lake City, Utah, in 1848 and one year later was named to the **Quorum** of the **Twelve Apostles**. Another mission took him to Italy, Switzerland, and Malta. In the 1860s he went to the Hawaiian Islands for a brief time and helped impose discipline on a rebellious leader. When not away on such missions, Snow was a community leader in Utah. For 29 years he served in the territorial legislature. He led the settlement of Brigham City, which became a model of economic cooperation and later impressed the visitor and writer Edward Bellamy.

Snow married four wives before leaving Illinois. In 1886 he served a prison term for violating the Edmunds Act but was released in early 1887 when his conviction was partially overturned by the U.S. Supreme Court. By seniority he became president of the twelve apostles in 1889 and in 1893 president of the newly dedicated Salt Lake Temple. In 1898, although old and weak, Lorenzo Snow became president of the Church. During his three-year administration he extricated the Church from serious financial indebtedness by strongly urging members to pay **tithing** and issuing bonds, extended missionary proselytizing to Japan, and issued with his **counselors** an address to the world. *See also* POLYGAMY.

SOARES, ULISSES (1958–). General authority. Soares was born on 2 October 1958 in Sao Paulo, Brazil. His parents converted to the Church when he was a child, and he was baptized when eight years old. After serving as a full-time **missionary** in the Brazil Rio de Janeiro Mission, he resumed his education, earning a bachelor's degree in economics from Pontificia Catholic University and an MBA from National Institute of Post Graduate Study. Employed by Pirelli Tire Company, he changed course when offered employment by the Church, first as an auditor and then as Director of Temporal Affairs.

Soares's experience in Church **callings** has been extensive. He was **elders** quorum president, **counselor** in the bishopric, **stake** executive secretary, **high councilor,** and stake **president**. Then for three years he was president of the Portugal Porto Mission. In April 2005, he became a general authority as a member of the First **Quorum** of the **Seventy**. He and his wife, Rosana, are the parents of three children.

SORENSEN, DAVID E. (1933–). Businessman, entrepreneur, **general authority**. Born on 29 June 1933 in Aurora, Utah, Sorensen attended **BYU**, Utah State University, and the University of Utah. He was a **missionary** in the Central Atlantic State Mission. After military service in the U.S. Army he had a successful career as president of United Homes, Inc.; chief executive officer of North American Health Care; chairman of Cal-Utah Feeders; and board vice chairman of Nevada Community Bank. He was a **bishop**, **high**

councilor, **stake** president, and **president** of the Canada Halifax Mission. Called to the Second **Quorum** of the **Seventy** in 1992, Sorensen became a member of the First Quorum of the Seventy in 1995. He and his wife, Verla, are the parents of seven children.

SORENSON, JOHN L. (1924–). Anthropologist, expert on the *Book of Mormon*. Born on 8 April 1924 in Smithfield, Utah, Sorenson received his early education there. After service as a first lieutenant in the U.S. military during World War II, being trained as a meteorologist, he served as a **missionary** in New Zealand and the Cook Islands, where he prepared a Raratongan grammar. From **BYU** he received a B.S. and M.A. degree in archaeology, after which he pursued a doctorate in anthropology at UCLA, receiving the Ph.D. in 1961.

Sorenson became director of Social Sciences for General Research Corporation, Santa Barbara, California, from 1964 to 1969. He headed his own research corporation before returning to BYU in 1971. For 15 years he taught courses in anthropology and served as consultant in applied social sciences, chairman of University Studies, and chairman of the Department of Anthropology. His doctoral dissertation explored the effects of Geneva Steel on two Utah communities. Unconventional warfare and insurgency, along with transportation policy, were the focus of his research in the 1960s. A cultural anthropologist in the broad sense, Sorenson has been interested in language, cultural networks, and group personality.

Throughout his adult life Sorenson has also been especially persevering as a student of the *Book of Mormon*, examining its text through the eyes of an anthropologist and exploring its possible Mesoamerican milieu. A participant in the University Archaeology Society and the New World Archaeological Foundation, he prepared reports and published papers on many specific topics. His early *The World of the* Book of Mormon (1955), based on a series of lectures, was followed by studies of such topics as brass plates, wheeled figurines, and the *Book of Mormon* as a Mesoamerican codex.

Sorenson's *An Ancient American Setting for the* Book of Mormon appeared in 1985, an unrivaled work in showing respect for the text and due regard for geographical reality and the present state of knowledge about ancient Mesoamerica. In 1990, with Martin H. Raish, he compiled a two-volume bibliography of pre-Columbian transoceanic contacts with America. In 1998, he published *Images of Ancient America: Visualizing* Book of Mormon *Life*, a massive photographic compilation of suggested parallels, and the same year he began editing *Journal of* Book of Mormon *Studies*.

Among the founders of **FARMS**, Sorenson has been highly effective in organizing team research, facilitating publication of information as it becomes available, and encouraging younger scholars. In addition to his service as a missionary, Sorenson has at different times been a **bishop** and **high councilor**. He retired from his university duties as an emeritus professor in 1986 but has continued his scholarly interests.

SORENSON, VIRGINIA (1912–1991). Novelist. Born on 17 February 1912 in Provo, Utah, Virginia Eggertson also lived in Manti and American Fork, Utah, during her childhood. In the early 1930s she was a student at **BYU**. After marrying Frederick Sorenson, an English professor, she moved to California. Two children were born. Later, after a divorce, she married the novelist Alec Waugh, with whom she lived in Tangier. In 1981 they returned to the United States. She died in North Carolina in 1991.

Sorenson's writings included such children's books as *Miracles on Maple Hill* (1957), for which she won the Newbery Award. Her Mormon people and culture provided the subject matter for most of her fiction, including *A Little Lower Than the Angels* (1942), *On This Star* (1946), *The Neighbors* (1947), *The Evening and the Morning* (1949), *Many Heavens* (1954), and *Kingdom Come* (1960). A series of semi-fictional pieces first appearing in the *New Yorker* was published as *Where Nothing Is Long Ago* (1963).

SOUTH AMERICA. Parley P. Pratt attempted to proselytize in Chile in 1851–1852, but had practically no success. In 1925 the South American continent was dedicated for the preaching of Mormonism. At first conversions were limited to a few German immigrants.

After World War II **missionaries** were sent to most countries of South America. Chapels were constructed. **Scriptures**, lesson materials, and other publications were translated into Spanish and Portuguese. By the 1960s the Church was experiencing spectacular growth. In Brazil the first **stake** was created in 1966, and by the end of 2005 there were 193 stakes; 1,247 **wards**; and 928,926 members. Two **general authorities** have been Brazilians—Helio da Rocha Camargo and Helvecio Martins, the first **black** general authority.

Other South American countries have seen the Church grow from small beginnings, in some cases from zero to impressive heights. At the end of 2005, the Mormon presence in South America stood as follows:

Country	Members	Stakes	Wards	Temples
Argentina	348,396	70	451	1
Bolivia	148,630	22	156	1
Brazil	897,091	187	1,212	4
Colombia	149,973	26	158	1
Ecuador	170,736	32	212	1
Paraguay	61,308	9	56	1
Uruguay	86,943	16	103	1
Venezuela	134,597	24	173	1

Missionary work had also begun in Guyana, Surinam, and French Guiana. South America was divided into six **areas**: South America North, South America South, South America West, Chile, Brazil North, and Brazil South. Much of the success of the Church in South America can be attributed to the build-up of local leadership. As much as one third or even one half of the missionary force in these countries is made up of indigenous young men and women. After completion of their missions, they form a pool of talent and leadership experience.

SPAFFORD, BELLE SMITH (1895–1982). President of the **Relief Society**. Born on 8 October 1895 in Salt Lake City, Utah, Belle was educated through the secondary school level and then spent two years at the University of Utah. Thirsty for education, she later took many additional courses. In 1921 she married Earl Spafford. Named general president of the **Relief Society** in 1945, Belle occupied a prominent leadership role for nearly 30 years. Her accomplishments included raising funds for the construction of a beautiful Relief Society building, encouraging women to do voluntary work in the community, and establishing a health **missionary** program. She also participated in national and international organizations, including the National Council of Women, of which she served as president in 1968–1970.

SPERRY, SIDNEY B. (1895–1977). Educator, linguist. In his honor, since 1971 an annual symposium, the Sidney B. Sperry Lecture Series, brings together at **BYU** scholars who present papers on selected topics from the **scriptures**.

SPORTS. From almost the beginning of the Church, members have participated in sports activities to some degree. We know, for example, that **Joseph Smith** enjoyed wrestling, pitching quoits, and even playing an early form of baseball or one-o-cat. It was really after the Mormons moved west that sports blossomed. Especially after the Civil War, Utah Territory Church members played cricket, baseball, bowling, boxing, wrestling, horse racing, and later football and basketball. Some of these activities took place at the Church academies and **BYU**.

In 1971, with a rapidly expanding **membership**, Church leaders ended the all-Church competitions but encouraged a continuation of sports activity on the local level. Anxious to provide wholesome activities for young people, local leaders of **Young Men** and **Young Women** included sports in their weekday programs. During winter months these often take place in **ward** cultural halls. Intercollegiate and intramural athletics are sponsored by BYU, and **BYU–Hawaii**. **BYU–Idaho** has an extensive program in intramural athletics. *See also* DANCE.

STAKE. A stake is an administrative subdivision of the Church comprising several **wards**. Depending on the number and size of the wards, stake **membership** ranges from 1,500 to 3,000 members. The term is derived from Isaiah 54:2–3.

Year	Stakes
1950	180
1960	319
1970	537

1980	1,218
1990	1,784
2000	2,581

By April 2007 there were 2,745 stakes worldwide.

STANDARD WORKS. *See* SCRIPTURE.

STEPHENS, EVAN (1854–1930). Director, **Mormon Tabernacle Choir**, 1890–1916. In addition to directing the **Mormon Tabernacle Choir**, Evan Stephens had private students and conducted special choruses of children and youth. For a period of time he headed the Stephens Opera Company.

STRANG, JAMES J. (1813–1856). Leader of a schismatic group. Strang's community encountered internal dissension and outside opposition. In 1856 Strang was assassinated. Before he expired, he refused to name a successor. The Strangites on Beaver Island were rounded up, put onto steamships, and taken to Chicago where they disembarked. Many of them gravitated to those who in 1860 would form the **RLDS** Church. Those who clung to their Strangite identity were led for several decades by a disciple of Strang, Wingfield Watson. The Strangites now number less than 100, mainly living in and around Burlington, Wisconsin, and Artesia, New Mexico. *See also* SUCCESSION.

SUCCESSION. When **Joseph Smith** was murdered in 1844, the Church faced a crisis of succession. Who was the lawful successor as **prophet** and **president**? Had this been provided for in the **revelations**? Or must there be a struggle between competing claimants?

At the death of every Church president since, it has been the president of the **twelve apostles** who became the next president. On two occasions, 1877–1880 and 1887–1889, some time lapsed before the new **First Presidency** was organized, the twelve apostles acting as presidency during the interim. During his presidency, **Wilford Woodruff** said that he believed that in the absence of direct revelation to the contrary, the senior member of the **Quorum** of Twelve Apostles should automatically become president and that the change should take place immediately. Since then, the transition has taken place shortly after the president's death. A **sustaining** by the **membership** of the Church in conference expresses acceptance of the new leader, but this is not an election.

SUNDAY SCHOOL. Church **auxiliary** organization founded in 1867, building on a local Sunday School started by **Richard Ballantyne** at Farmington, Utah, in 1849. The first general superintendent was **George Q. Cannon.** A general board was appointed, lesson materials were produced, and a periodical, *The Juvenile Instructor*, was started. Children under 12 attend **Primary**.

SUNSTONE. Independent magazine published by the Sunstone Foundation, a nonprofit corporation. Subtitled *Mormon Experience, Scholarship, Issues, and Art*, *Sunstone* states on its title page that it is interested in "feature- and column-length articles relevant to Mormonism from a variety of perspectives; news stories about Mormons and the **LDS** church, and poetry, psalms, and limericks." Short stories are published and an annual award given for the best fiction. Annually in Salt Lake City, Utah, and at irregular intervals in other cities, the Sunstone Foundation sponsors a symposium, including papers and panel discussions on Mormon-related issues.

SUSTAINING. When individuals receive a **calling** to positions in the Church, those in the same jurisdiction have the opportunity to express their "common consent" by vote. The person conducting the meeting says, "All those willing to sustain X as **bishop** of the **ward** may express it by raising the hand," or words to this effect. With rare exceptions the resulting votes are unanimous. The attitude expressed by the sustaining vote is that of willingness to follow the leadership and do what is in one's power to support and assist those called to specific responsibilities. In a lay organization, good will and support of others provide the necessary atmosphere for growth and service.

– T –

TABERNACLE. (1) Building in Salt Lake City used for **general conferences** and other large assemblies or concerts. Completed in 1867, the Tabernacle is 250 feet long and 150 feet wide. Its dome-shaped roof has the appearance of half an egg shell or, as some have suggested, the back of a turtle. Constructed before the railroad arrived, the structure was made with many wooden dowels and even rawhide was used to reinforce and strengthen the lattice trusses in the attic. (2) The word *tabernacle*, of Old Testament origin, was also used to describe buildings put up in some of the **stakes**, but that usage is now rare.

TALMAGE, JAMES E. (1862–1933). Educator, university president, **general authority**. During the 1920s and early 1930s Talmage was a central figure in attempting to explain the consistency of the Mormon religion with the findings of modern science. His view was that the means of creation were not known, or at least were not part of the Mormon religious understanding, but that the earth and the human race owed their existence to God. *See also* CREATION.

TANNER, NATHAN ELDON (1898–1982). Businessman, politician, **general authority**. Reflecting admiration for his many contributions, the Salt Lake Area Chamber of Commerce named Tanner "Giant in our City" in 1978. In 1980 **BYU** named him Executive of the Year and named the new Management School building after him. "President N. Eldon Tanner will go down in history as one of the greatest **counselors** ever to serve in the **First Presidency** of the Church," said Apostle **Marvin J. Ashton.** "He is a man of few words and much performance."

TANNER, SUSAN W. (1953–). General president of **Young Women** from 2002 to 2008. She and her husband, John, are parents of five children.

TAYLOR, JOHN (1808–1887). Missionary, apostle, Church **president**. His was a holding action. The Edmunds Act (1882) and Edmunds-Tucker Act (1877) brought intense pressure on the Mormons, which by 1890 would eventuate in the **manifesto** formally ending **polygamy**. But during his lifetime Taylor refused to yield. With other Mormon leaders he went into hiding, leading the Church from "the underground." There he died of heart failure on 25 July 1887.

TEACHER. In addition to its general meaning, an office in the **Aaronic Priesthood**. Having already served as a **deacon**, a young man may be advanced to teacher at 14. Then at age 16, assuming **worthiness**, he is advanced to the office of **priest**. Teachers are organized into a **quorum** of 24 or less and, like other holders of the **priesthood**, meet on Sundays for instruction. During weekdays they often have service projects and social activities.

TEMPLE SQUARE. A square block at the center of Salt Lake City, within which stand some of the Church's most sacred and historic buildings and monuments: the Salt Lake Temple, the **Tabernacle**, the Assembly Hall, two **visitors centers**, and several sculptural works, including a replica of Thorvaldsen's renowned *Christus*.

Even in pioneer times Temple Square attracted visitors. Guides were showing people around as early as 1875. For much of the 20th century guided tours were conducted by volunteers. In the 1990s, most tours were conducted by full-time **missionaries**, young women from different countries. Tours were available in French, German, Spanish, Japanese, Chinese, and other languages. During the holiday season each year the trees are illuminated with 750,000 lights. More than 5 million visitors come annually to Temple Square, making it one of the major tourist attractions in the nation. *See also* TEMPLES.

TEMPLE SQUARE CONCERT SERIES. Concerts performed almost every Friday and Saturday evening of the year in the Assembly Hall on **Temple Square**. Admission is free and open to everyone over eight years of age. Orchestras, choirs, ensembles, and instrumental and vocal soloists are included. Performers are selected by a volunteer committee on the basis of tapes submitted. The concerts are sometimes held more often, as, for example, the performances given in connection with the Gina Bachauer International Piano Competition.

TEMPLES. Temples are not for regular worship services but are places in which "worthy" Church **members** participate in sacred ceremonies, or **ordinances.** In a general sense Mormon temples are analogous not to a church meetinghouse or synagogue but to the ancient temples described in the **Bible**.

Faithful Mormons describe the temple experience as a noble, Christ-centered service, a spiritual high point in their lives. To participate in the temples one must be not only a member of the Church but the holder of a signed **recommend**, or certificate of **worthiness**, from one's **bishop** and **stake president**. That curious nonmembers are not allowed into the temples has to do not so much with their secretiveness as their sacredness. Observation by curious, perhaps whispering and finger-pointing tourists would be disruptive to the purpose of the buildings. Temples are scheduled for virtually constant use from early in the morning until late at night. Prior to its dedication, a new temple is open to the general public for viewing during a specified period of time.

TESTIMONY. The conviction or assurance of the truth of the **gospel**, or more specifically of **Jesus Christ** and the modern **prophets**. When this conviction is expressed in words, one "bears testimony." Such certitude, ultimately dependent on the Holy Ghost, is promised to and claimed by readers of the ***Book of Mormon***: "And when ye shall receive these things, I would exhort you that ye would ask God, the Eternal Father, in the name of Christ, if these things are not true; and if ye shall ask with a sincere heart, with real intent, having faith in Christ, he will manifest the truth of it unto you, by the power of the Holy Ghost" (Moroni 10:4–5).

One Sunday each month Mormon congregations have a "fast and testimony meeting," in which individuals who wish can stand and express their feelings, that is, bear their testimony, about the gospel. Testimonies are expressed by Mormons in other meetings as well, often in conjunction with a sermon or **missionary** instruction.

THEOLOGY. Both in the technical sense of a doctrine of God and in the larger sense of religious beliefs about life and its purpose, Mormons have a theology. Indeed, students of Mormonism describe their belief system as rather complex, requiring more than a little study in the **scriptures** and various Church publications to master. But in two related respects Mormonism fits uneasily into usual theological discourse. First, Mormonism proceeds from revealed truth with virtually no effort made to employ standard philosophical terminology. Second, there is no class of professionally trained Mormon theologians.

Although some individual Mormons have had advanced study in philosophy, theology, or religious studies, such training is not considered necessary.

"THIS IS THE PLACE" MONUMENT. Monument on the east bench overlooking the Salt Lake Valley, commemorating the arrival of the original **pioneers** in July 1847. According to later recollections, when **Brigham Young** first beheld the valley on 24 July 1847, he said, "This is the right place. Drive on." Abbreviated to "This is the place," the saying was often repeated as an indication of divine protection and selection. A smaller memorial was replaced in 1947, the centennial year, by an imposing monument designed and sculpted by Mahonri M. Young. *See also* EXODUS.

THREE WITNESSES. *See* WITNESSES OF THE *BOOK OF MORMON*.

TIMES AND SEASONS. (1) Mormon newspaper published in Nauvoo, Illinois, 1839–1846. Motto: "Truth Will Prevail." Editors included Ebeneezer Robinson, Don Carlos Smith, and Robert B. Thompson, as well as **Joseph Smith**, **Wilford Woodruff**, and **John Taylor**. (2) Unofficial website discussing Mormon issues.

TINGEY, EARL C. (1934–). Corporate lawyer, **general authority**. Born in Bountiful, Utah, on 11 June 1934, Tingey served as **missionary** in Australia and then graduated from the University of Utah Law School with a juris doctorate. At New York University he received a master of corporate law degree. For three years he was a captain in the U.S. Army with the Judge Advocate General Corps. Tingey was an attorney on Wall Street. He was **bishop** of the Manhattan **Ward**, **counselor** in the Eastern States Mission presidency, **president** of the Australia Sydney Mission, and **regional representative.** He was called to the First **Quorum** of the **Seventy** in 1990 and in 1996 became a member of its presidency. He and his wife, Joanne, have four children.

TITHING. One tenth of income, paid to the Church on a voluntary and confidential basis. At an individual interview with their **bishop** at the end of the year, **members** verify the amount of their contribution and state whether or not they consider it a full tithing. Tithing is not mandatory. Failure to pay does not result in **excommunication**. Tithing is nevertheless considered a **commandment** and is paid faithfully by fully committed members. Tithing funds are sent by the **bishop** to Church headquarters, where they are accounted for and dispensed for such purposes as building and maintaining meeting-houses and **temples**, support of missions, and church educational activity. *See also* AUDITORS.

TRIPLE COMBINATION. Three of the standard works of scripture—the *Book of Mormon*, *Doctrine and Covenants*, and *Pearl of Great Price*—when published together as a single volume. These works are of course also published separately.

TWELVE APOSTLES, QUORUM OF THE. Group of **general authorities** who have been ordained to this office in the **Melchizedek Priesthood**. When selected, a new apostle is presented in **general conference** for the **sustaining** vote of the Church **membership**. He then receives an ordination by the laying on of the hands of the **First Presidency** and the other members of the **Quorum** of the Twelve Apostles.

Apostles hold their office for life. Special witnesses of **Jesus Christ**, possessing the keys or rights of presidency, as a **quorum** they have taken the helm of leadership at the death of every Church **president**. The president of the apostles, after sustaining by a vote in general conference, has then been ordained the new president of the Church. *See also* SUCCESSION.

– U –

UCHTDORF, DIETER F. (1940–). Airline pilot, **general authority**. Born in Ostrava, Czechoslovakia, on 6 November 1940, Uchtdorf grew up in Frankfurt, Germany, as a member of the Church. After service in the German Air Force he graduated from airline pilot school in Bremen, Germany, attended Business Administration

School in Cologne, Germany, and the International Management Institute in Lausanne, Switzerland. An airline captain, he headed pilot school for Lufthansa and became senior vice president for flight operations. He served as **Young Men** president in his **ward**, **stake high councilor**, and **stake** president. In 1994 he was called as a member of the Second **Quorum** of the **Seventy**. In October 2004 he became a member of the Quorum of the **Twelve Apostles**. In 2008 he was called as second counselor in the First Presidency. He and his wife, Harriet, have two children.

UNITED ORDER. A system of cooperation not currently in operation in which Church **members** would give all their property to the Church, receive back a portion of it as a stewardship, continue to donate surplus production, and generally live in a framework of mutual support and equality. Some of the spirit of consecration and the United Order remains in the tradition of dedicating one's life to God's work on earth, commitments made in the **temples**, financial donations such as **tithing** and **fast offering**, and the ideal of equality that allows lay leaders of different wealth and background to work together as **brother and sister**. In the **welfare program** also these lay leaders have banded together in the spirit of fellowship to provide for those in need.

UTAH PERIOD. Roughly the second half of the 19th century. Following its origins in New York and unsuccessful efforts to establish itself in Ohio, Missouri, and Illinois, the great majority of Church **members** moved westward in a great **exodus** and established themselves in the Great Basin of the Rocky Mountains, with the headquarters in the Salt Lake Valley.

Statehood for Utah was achieved in 1896. During the closing quarter of the century, the Church was already showing signs of being much more than a one-state Church. Outposts had been established in Colorado, Arizona, Nevada, New Mexico, Idaho, Wyoming, and even Canada and Mexico. **Missionaries** were having success in Samoa, Tonga, New Zealand, the southern states, and **Europe**, and many of the convert families were staying put rather than migrating. But for half a century at least, Utah was a place of refuge and consolidation as well as continued adaptation.

– V –

VEAZEY, STEPHEN M. (1957–). President, **Community of Christ.** In 1992 he was named to the Council of Twelve Apostles of the Community of Christ church and in April 2002 became president of the council. In March 2005 he was approved as president of the church by a vote of a special World Conference in Independence, Missouri. On 3 June 2005, Veazey was ordained president of the Community of Christ. He and his wife, Cathleen, have three children. *See also* MCMURRAY, W. GRANT.

VINAS, FRANCISCO J. (1946–). Educator, **general authority.** In 1996 Vinas was called to be a member of the Second **Quorum** of the **Seventy** and in 1998 the First Quorum of the **Seventy.** He and his wife, Cristina, have three children.

VISITING TEACHING. Program of the **Relief Society** by which each member of the organization—now including all adult female **members** of the Church—is visited regularly, at least quarterly with additional telephone contacts. Those assigned as visiting teachers normally go as a team of two. They bring a teaching message, an item of instruction or inspiration. Most importantly, they show a personal interest in the person being visited. Where personal or family problems exist, they render whatever help they can. If the situations are extreme or if financial troubles loom large, the visiting teachers report back to the **ward** Relief Society president, who is able to enlist the help of the ward **bishop** in providing an appropriate response. *See also* HOME TEACHING.

VISITORS CENTERS. Departments or bureaus, usually in separate buldings, at historic sites where visitors can ask questions and obtain literature. Visitors centers are staffed by Church **members,** some of them serving as full-time **missionaries,** others as part-time volunteers. The first such center was established in 1902 at **Temple Square** in Salt Lake City, Utah, following complaints about the misrepresentation being purveyed to tourists by **anti-Mormons** or uninformed cab drivers. Other visitors centers are located near Palmyra, New York; in Nauvoo, Illinois; in Independence, Missouri; and at several of the **temples.** *See also* HISTORIC SITES.

– W –

WARD. The Church's basic ecclesiastical unit, similar to a parish or congregation. Membership is ordinarily somewhere between 300 and 700.

Year	Wards
1951	1,666
1961	3,143
1971	5,135
1981	11,063
1991	15,511
2001	22,249

In April 2007, the official report claimed 27,475 wards and branches worldwide.

WELCH, JOHN W. (1946–). Lawyer, writer, editor, student of **scriptures.** He has been **Sunday School** teacher, **bishop, high councilor,** and **counselor** in the **stake** presidency.

WELFARE PROGRAM. A continuing program instituted by the Church during the 1930s when the Depression had produced high unemployment and hardship. People in need are expected to look first to the resources of their **family.** Any assistance from the Church is regarded as temporary. Moreover, there is an expectation of work; one should not expect a handout. The underlying objective is not a dependency class but self-reliant members.

WELLS, EMMELINE B. (1828–1921). Leader of Mormon women, editor, **Relief Society** president. In 1910 Wells became general president of the Relief Society and thus official leader of Mormon women. In the Utah State Capitol stands a marble bust from the women of Utah in honor of "A Fine Soul Who Served Us."

WHITMER, DAVID (1805–1888). Early follower of **Joseph Smith** and one of the special three witnesses, along with **Oliver Cowdery** and **Martin Harris**, who testified that an angel showed them the metal plates from which the *Book of Mormon* was translated. Whitmer moved to Richmond, Missouri, where for 50 years he ran a livery stable and became a respected citizen. Many thought that his complaints about Joseph Smith would lead him to disavow his testimony. But to the end of his life he consistently held to his sworn statement. *See also* WITNESSES OF THE *BOOK OF MORMON*.

WIDTSOE, JOHN ANDREAS (1872–1952). Scientist, educator, **general authority**. From 1900 he was director of the Utah State Agricultural Experiment Station. Extensive research and travel assisting the farmers of the state led to early publications on dry farming. In 1905 he transferred to **BYU**, where he organized a department of agriculture. Then in 1907 Widtsoe was appointed president of Utah State Agricultural College. He published *Dry Farming: A System of Agriculture for Countries under a Low Rainfall* in 1910 and in 1912 a book on irrigation. In 1916 Widtsoe was selected as president of the University of Utah in Salt Lake City.

While pursuing his professional life, Widtsoe continued to teach classes and serve in different Church assignments. He published *Joseph Smith as Scientist* in 1908 and in 1915 *A Rational Theology*. In 1921, he was called as a member of the **Quorum** of the **Twelve Apostles**. In 1927 he became **president** of the European and British Mission, living in London until 1933. He had direct responsibility for the *Improvement Era*, the official Church magazine, and published a monthly column, "Evidences and Reconciliations," in which he answered many historical and doctrinal questions.

WIDTSOE, LEAH DUNFORD (1874–1955). Home economist, granddaughter of **Brigham Young**. Leah D. Widtsoe was an accomplished instructor, specializing in nutrition. She studied, lectured, and wrote. She was an advocate and model of the educated Mormon woman, serving as president of the Salt Lake Federation of Women's

Clubs and on the board of the Salt Lake Council of Women. With her mother, **Susa Young Gates**, she wrote on Brigham Young. Collaborating with her husband, **John Widtsoe**, she wrote *The Word of Wisdom: A Modern Interpretation*. She had seven children, three of whom reached maturity.

WIGHT, LYMAN (1796–1858). General authority, schismatic. He was among those who looked to "young Joseph," Joseph Smith III, to become leader of the Church, but since Wight was faithful to such practices as **polygamy** and **temple** ceremonies, he would have been a stormy petrel had he lived to participate in the **RLDS** Church. He died in central Texas on 31 March 1858 while attempting to move his followers north to Missouri. The movement, sometimes called the Wightites, quickly dissolved.

WILKINSON, ERNEST L. (1899–1978). Attorney, educator, university president. Wilkinson left the **BYU** presidency to become Republican candidate for the U.S. Senate in 1964, but lost. He returned to the presidency of BYU the year after his loss. He served on the board of directors of many corporations and received many awards, including the George Washington Medal from the Freedom Foundation and the Distinguished Service Award from his alma mater.

WILSON, WILLIAM A. "BERT" (1933–). Folklorist, educator. Born on 23 September 1933 at Tremonton, Utah, Wilson received his B.A. and M.A. degrees from **BYU**. At Indiana University he earned a Ph.D. in folklore. After serving on the faculty of BYU, from 1978 to 1984 he served as director of the Folklore Program at Utah State University.

In 1985 he returned to BYU, serving as chair of the English Department, director of the Charles Redd Center for Western Studies, and director of the BYU Folklore Archives. He published over 35 articles and one book on Mormon folklore. He was named the Karl G. Maeser Distinguished Faculty Lecturer at BYU and received the Grace Arrington Award for Historical Excellence and the Utah Governor's Award in the Arts. Among other Church positions, Wilson has served as **bishop** and **high councilor**. He married Hanele Blomqvist in 1957. They are the parents of four children.

WIRTHLIN, JOSEPH B. (1917–). Businessman, **general authority.** Drawing upon his business and church experience, Wirthlin made significant contributions in many areas of activity. As supervisor or executive administrator he had responsibility for the Southeast United States and Caribbean Islands (1978–1982) and Brazil (1982–1984). He was **president** of the **Europe area** of the Church from 1984 to 1986.

WIRTHLIN, RICHARD B. (1931–). Economist, pollster, **general authority.** Church callings included service as **bishop, high councilor, counselor** in **stake** presidencies, and **regional representative.** He was called to the Second **Quorum** of the **Seventy** in 1996. He and his wife, Jeralie, are the parents of eight children.

WITNESSES OF THE *BOOK OF MORMON*. In each copy of the ***Book of Mormon*** is found a page containing "The Testimony of the Three Witnesses" and "The Testimony of the Eight Witnesses." Although many of these witnesses became disaffected from the Church, they did not repudiate their testimony. Their lives have been studied in depth by historian **Richard L. Anderson.**

WOMEN, ROLES OF. In a large sense, Mormon women have experienced the same understanding of gender roles as the rest of American or Western society. The assumption was that most women would be wives and mothers. The idealized notion of "true womanhood"— woman as the refined, cultured, and religious influence in the home—was readily accepted by 19th-century Mormons. By the late 20th century, Mormon women enjoyed increased education, a higher percentage remained unmarried, **divorce** became more common, and paid work outside the home attracted (through desire or necessity) more and more women.

By comparison with some activists of the women's movement, certainly with those who disparage the role of wife and mother, Mormon women generally appear conservative. Those who know them, however, will acknowledge that they are articulate and talented. In the Church they occupy positions of leadership in the **Relief Society, Young Women,** and **Primary** organizations; serve as teachers in those organizations and in **Sunday School** and Church schools; and in many cases serve as full-time **missionaries**. They take the pulpit and deliver sermons at **sacrament** meetings and equal or surpass Mormon men in publicly bearing **testimony**. *See also* FEMINISM; RELIEF SOCIETY.

WOODRUFF, WILFORD (1807–1898). Missionary, apostle, **president** of the Church. One of the monumental achievements of Woodruff's life was his diary. Begun at the time of his conversion in 1834, this detailed record preserves many sermons of **Joseph Smith** and other early leaders, describes spiritual manifestations experienced by its author, and graphically conveys an abundance of concrete detail.

WORD OF WISDOM. Code of health announced by **Joseph Smith** in 1833 (*Doctrine and Covenants*, section 89). Not good for human consumption were alcohol, tobacco, and "hot drinks" (soon defined by **Hyrum Smith** as tea and coffee). Meat was to be used sparingly. Wholesome grains and fruits were recommended. The Word of Wisdom is "a principle with a promise." Consistent with the principle of caring for one's physical health, the lifestyle of Mormons includes cleanliness, physical exercise, recreation, abstinence from mind-altering drugs, regular medical examinations, and avoidance of excesses.

WORLD CONFERENCE ON RECORDS. Sponsored by the Utah Genealogical Society, the first World Conference on Records was held in Salt Lake City in 1969 and attracted nearly 3,000 participants from different countries. Its theme, addressed by many speakers in concurrent sessions, was "Records Protection in an Uncertain World." A second such conference was held in Salt Lake City in 1980. Emphasizing the compilation of pedigree charts and **family** histories, it attracted 11,500 registrants from many different countries. *See also* GENEALOGY.

WORLD RELIGIONS. In 1930, when the Church celebrated its hundredth year, **B. H. Roberts** insisted that it was not a narrow sect but a world movement. In her interpretation that Mormonism has the same relationship to historic **Christianity** that Christianity has to Judaism, historian Jan Shipps also comes close to granting the status of an incipient world religion. Sociologist Rodney Stark has advanced the possibility, based on his analysis of growth statistics, that in Mormonism we are seeing the emergence of another major world religion right before our eyes. Critics who emphasize its lack of correspondence to Christian orthodoxy at certain points tend to label it a **cult**, sect, or new religious movement. Even the Mormon self-definition is ambivalent. On the one hand, Mormons see themselves as a subset of Christianity; on the other hand, their claim to exclusivity, to being the only true church, sets them apart.

The traditional world religions include Christianity, Judaism, Islam, Buddhism, Jainism, and others. A **First Presidency** statement of 1978 reads, "The great religious leaders of the world such as Mohammed, Confucius, and the Reformers, as well as philosophers including Socrates, Plato, and others, received a portion of God's light. Moral truths were given to them by God to enlighten whole nations and to bring a higher level of understanding to individuals" (Palmer, *Mormons and Muslims*, 208). Appropriate in a period when Mormon **missionaries** are in all the inhabited continents, this general attitude was also expressed by **Joseph Smith** and other early Church leaders. *See also* CATHOLICISM; CHRISTIANITY; MEMBERSHIP; PROTESTANTISM.

WORTHINESS. A condition or status of moral uprightness considered essential for those performing certain Church functions or responsibilities. A general sincerity, while important, is not sufficient. Performance is expected. Regular attendance at meetings, payment of **tithing** and fast offering, observance of the **Word of Wisdom**, moral strictness, honesty in dealing with others, **sustaining** the Church leadership—these are among the determinants of worthiness. Mormons are under no illusion that ultimate salvation is determined only by a simple check-list. The heart must be right. But for determining minimal requirements for service in the Church on the earthly level, the concept of worthiness serves a useful purpose.

– Y –

YOUNG, BRIGHAM (1801–1877). Missionary, apostle, colonizer of the American West, and **president** of the Church. Versatile and strong of character, Young was able to hold the Church together and lead it to a new stability during crucial years. He died on 29 August 1877.

YOUNG, STEVE (1961–). Professional football player. Young participates in a variety of charitable causes. During the off-season he returned to **BYU** and earned a law degree.

YOUNG MEN. Auxiliary organization of the Church with programs to assist young male members develop socially, physically, and especially spiritually; formerly known as YMMIA. From the 1960s on, the organization came under direction of the **priesthood**, with activities revolving around the **quorums**. In 1977 the name was changed to Young Men. By age groups the young men meet on Sundays for religious instruction and on one evening during the week for scouting, service projects, sports, or career education. Joint activities, including social dances and the production of theatrical plays and skits, are also held with the **Young Women**.

YOUNG WOMEN. Starting in 1869 with a small organization founded by **Brigham Young** for his daughters, a Retrenchment Association expanded to include young women in the different **wards** of Salt Lake City, Utah. It replaced the Young Women's Mutual Improvement Association, which had replaced the YLMIA in 1934. Avoiding the expense and pretense of worldly fashions was one goal, but spiritual development, the study of literature, instruction in public speaking, and social projects were quickly added. From the 1960s on, the Young Women began to meet on Sundays at the same time as **priesthood** meetings were held for the **Young Men**. A meeting during the week allowed opportunities for recreation and social development. Sensitive to the inroads of secularism and temptation, leaders emphasized spiritual values.

YOUTH. In all human societies some kind of "coming of age" occurs. In 21st-century America, the stresses during this time of life have included experimentation with alcohol and drugs, sexual activity, teenage pregnancy, confusion over gender identity, and violence.

– Z –

ZION. (1) The pure in heart (*Doctrine and Covenants* 97:21). The expectations of an imminent **Millennium** explain the emphasis placed on definition 2 at the Church's beginning, while the doctrine of **gathering** explains the usage embodied in definition 4. The cessation of efforts to gather converts from foreign lands and the growth of the Church **membership** in all of the states and many foreign countries, especially emphatic in the latter half of the 20th century, help to explain the current emphasis on definitions 1 and 5.

ZION'S CAMP. An expedition of 1834 intending to come to the aid of persecuted Mormons in Missouri. Living in Ohio at the time, **Joseph Smith** responded to appeals from his Missouri followers by issuing a revelation (*Doctrine and Covenants*, section 103) commanding the organization of volunteers. Eventually about 200 men banded together, organized themselves into units, and trained as they made their way westward in May and June. After a journey of 600 or 700 miles, the army reached the trouble spot in western Missouri. Internal dissension, sickness, and the collapse of negotiations with the Missourians led to the disbanding of the expedition. Although it did not achieve its objective of restoring the Missouri Mormons to their property, Zion's Camp provided valuable experience in organization. Most of the **twelve apostles** named in 1835 had served in the expedition. **Brigham Young** and others later looked back upon it as a time of trial and seasoning. *See also* MISSOURI PERIOD.

Appendix 1

Church Presidents

Joseph Smith, 1832–1844
Brigham Young, 1847–1877
John Taylor, 1880–1887
Wilford Woodruff, 1889–1898
Lorenzo Snow, 1898–1901
Joseph F. Smith, 1901–1918
Heber J. Grant, 1918–1945
George Albert Smith, 1945–1951

David O. McKay, 1951–1970
Joseph Fielding Smith, 1970–1972
Harold B. Lee, 1972–1973
Spencer W. Kimball, 1973–1985
Ezra Taft Benson, 1985–1994
Howard W. Hunter, 1994–1995
Gordon B. Hinckley, 1995–2008
Thomas S. Monson, 2008–

Appendix 2

The Family: A Proclamation to the World

We, the First Presidency and the Council of the Twelve Apostles of the Church of Jesus Christ of Latter-day Saints, solemnly proclaim that marriage between a man and a woman is ordained of God and that the family is central to the Creator's plan for the eternal destiny of His children.

All human beings—male and female—are created in the image of God. Each is a beloved spirit son or daughter of heavenly parents, and, as such, each as a divine nature and destiny. Gender is an essential characteristic of individual pre-mortal, mortal, and eternal identity and purpose.

In the pre-mortal realm, spirit sons and daughters knew and worshiped God as their Eternal Father and accepted His plan by which His children could obtain a physical body and gain earthly experience to progress toward perfection and ultimately realize his or her divine destiny as an heir of eternal life. The divine plan of happiness enables family relationships to be perpetuated beyond the grave. Sacred ordinances and covenants available in holy temples make it possible for individuals to return to the presence of God and for families to be united eternally.

The first commandment that God gave to Adam and Eve pertained to their potential for parenthood as husband and wife. We declare that God's commandment for His children to multiply and replenish the earth remains in force. We further declare that God has commanded that the sacred powers of procreation are to be employed only between man and woman, lawfully wedded as husband and wife.

We declare the means by which mortal life is created to be divinely appointed. We affirm the sanctity of life and of its importance in God's eternal plan.

Husband and wife have a solemn responsibility to love and care for each other and for their children. "Children are an heritage of the Lord"

(Ps. 127:3). Parents have a sacred duty to rear their children in love and righteousness, to provide for their physical and spiritual needs, to teach them to love and serve one another, to observe the commandments of God and to be law-abiding citizens wherever they live. Husbands and wives—mothers and fathers—will be held accountable before God for the discharge of these obligations.

The family is ordained of God. Marriage between man and woman is essential to His eternal plan. Children are entitled to birth within the bonds of matrimony, and to be reared by a father and a mother who honor marital vows with complete fidelity. Happiness in family life is most likely to be achieved when founded upon the teachings of the Lord Jesus Christ. Successful marriages and families are established and maintained on principles of faith, prayer, repentance, forgiveness, respect, love, compassion, work, and wholesome recreational activities. By divine design, fathers are to preside over their families in love and righteousness and are responsible to provide the necessities of life and protection for their families. Mothers are primarily responsible for the nurture of their children. In these sacred responsibilities, fathers and mothers are obligated to help one another as equal partners. Disability, death, or other circumstances may necessitate individual adaptation. Extended families should lend support when needed.

We warn that individuals who violate covenants of chastity, who abuse spouse or offspring, or who fail to fulfill family responsibilities will one day stand accountable before God. Further, we warn that the disintegration of the family will bring upon individuals, communities, and nations the calamities foretold by ancient and modern prophets.

We call upon responsible citizens and officers of the government everywhere to promote those measures designed to maintain and strengthen the family as the fundamental unit of society.

—presented by President Gordon B. Hinckley at the
General Relief Society meeting, 23 September 1995

Appendix 3

Temples Dedicated through February 2008

Location	Dedication
Kirtland, Ohio	27 March 1836
Nauvoo, Illinois	30 April 1846
St. George, Utah	6 April 1877
Logan, Utah	17 May 1884
Manti, Utah	17 May 1884
Salt Lake City, Utah	6 April 1893
Laie, Oahu, Hawaii	27 November 1919
Cardston, Alberta, Canada	26 August 1923
Mesa, Arizona	23 October 1927
Idaho Falls, Idaho	23 September 1945
Zollikofen, Switzerland	11 September 1955
Los Angeles, California	11 March 1956
Hamilton, New Zealand	20 April 1958
Newchapel Surrey, England	7 September 1958
Oakland, California	17 November 1964
Ogden, Utah	18 January 1972
Provo, Utah	9 February 1972
Kensington, Maryland	19 November 1974
São Paulo, Brazil	30 October 1978
Tokyo, Japan	27 October 1980
Bellevue, Washington	17 November 1980
South Jordan, Utah	16 November 1981
Sandy Springs, Georgia	1 June 1983
Apia, Western Samoa	5 August 1983
Nuku'alofa, Tonga	9 August 1983
Santiago, Chile	15 September 1983
Pirae, Tahiti	17 October 1983
Mexico City, Mexico	2 December 1983

Boise Idaho	25 May 1984
Carlingford, Australia	20 September 1984
Quezon City, Philippines	25 September 1984
Dallas, Texas	19 October 1984
Taipei, Taiwan	17 November 1984
Guatemala City, Guatemala	14 December 1984
Freiberg, Germany	19 June 1985
Vasterhaninge, Sweden	1 July 1985
Glenview, Illinois	9 August 1985
Johannesburg, South Africa	24 August 1985
Seoul, Korea	14 December 1985
Lima, Peru	10 January 1986
Buenos Aires, Argentina	17 January 1986
Littleton, Colorado	24 October 1986
Friedrichsdorf, Germany	28 August 1987
Oswego, Oregon	19 August 1989
Las Vegas, Nevada	16 December 1989
Brampton, Ontario, Canada	25 August 1990
San Diego, California	25 April 1993
Orlando, Florida	9 October 1994
Bountiful, Utah	8 January 1995
Hong Kong	26 May 1996
American Fork, Utah	13 October 1996
St. Louis, Missouri	1 June 1997
Vernal, Utah	2 November 1997
Preston, England	7 June 1998
Monticello, Utah	26 July 1998
Anchorage, Alaska	9 January 1999
Colonia, Juarez, Chihuahua, Mexico	7 March 1999
Madrid, Spain	19 March 1999
Bogotá, Colombia	26 April 1999
Guayaquil, Ecuador	1 August 1999
Spokane, Washington	21 August 1999
Columbus, Ohio	4 September 1999
Bismarck, North Dakota	19 September 1999
Columbia, South Carolina	16 October 1999
Detroit, Michigan	23 October 1999
Halifax, Nova Scotia, Canada	14 November 1999

Regina, Saskatchewan, Canada	14 November 1999
Billings, Montana	20 November 1999
Edmonton, Alberta, Canada	11 December 1999
Raleigh, North Carolina	18 December 1999
St. Paul, Minnesota	9 January 2000
Kona, Hawaii	23 January 2000
Ciudad Juáraz, Mexico	26 February 2000
Hermosilla, Mexico	27 February 2000
Albuquerque, New Mexico	6 March 2000
Oaxaca, Mexico	11 March 2000
Tuxtla Gutiérrez, Mexico	12 March 2000
Louisville, Kentucky	19 March 2000
Palmyra, New York	6 April 2000
Fresno, California	9 April 2000
Medford, Oregon	16 April 2000
Memphis, Tennessee	23 April 2000
Reno, Nevada	23 April 2000
Cochabamba, Bolivia	30 April 2000
Tampico, Mexico	20 May 2000
Villahermosa, Mexico	21 May 2000
Nashville, Tennessee	21 May 2000
Montreal, Canada	4 June 2000
San José, Costa Rica	4 June 2000
Fukuoka, Japan	11 June 2000
Adelaide, Australia	15 June 2000
Melbourne, Australia	16 June 2000
Suva, Fiji	18 June 2000
Merida, Mexico	25 June 2000
Vera Cruz, Mexico	9 July 2000
Baton Rouge, Louisiana	16 July 2000
Yukon, Oklahoma	20 July 2000
Caracas, DC, Venezuela	20 August 2000
Klein, Texas	26 August 2000
Gardendale, Alabama	3 September 2000
Santo Domingo, Dominican Republic	17 September 2000
Belmont, Massachusetts	1 October 2000
Recife, Pernambuco, Brazil	15 December 2000
Porto Alegre, Rio Grande do Sul, Brazil	17 December 2000

Montevideo, Uruguay	18 March 2001
Winter Quarters, Nebraska	22 April 2001
Zapopan, Jalisco, Mexico	29 April 2001
Stirling, Western Australia	20 May 2001
Richland, Washington	18 November 2001
Snowflake, Arizona	3 March 2002
Lubbock, Texas	21 April 2002
Monterrey, Nuevo León, Mexico	28 April 2002
Campinas, Brazil	17 May 2002
Asunción, Paraguay	19 May 2002
Nauvoo, Illinois	27 June 2002
Zoetermeer, The Netherlands	8 September 2002
Kangaroo Point, Queensland, Australia	15 June 2003
Redlands, California	14 September 2003
Accra, Ghana	11 January 2004
Frederiksberg, Denmark	23 May 2004
New York City, New York	13 June 2004
San Antonio, Texas	22 May 2005
Aba, Abia, Nigeria	7 August 2005
Newport Beach, California	28 August 2005
Rancho Cordova, California	3 September 2006
Helsinki, Finland	22 October 2006
Rexburg, Idaho	10 February 2008

Appendix 4

The Living Christ: The Testimony of the Apostles of the Church of Jesus Christ of Latter-day Saints

As we commemorate the birth of Jesus Christ two millennia ago, we offer our testimony of the reality of His matchless life and the infinite virtue of His great atoning sacrifice. None other has had so profound an influence upon all who have lived and will yet live upon the earth.

He was the Great Jehovah of the Old Testament, the Messiah of the New. Under the direction of His Father, He was the creator of the earth. "All things were made by him; and without him was not any thing made that was made" (John 1:3). Though sinless, He was baptized to fulfill all righteousness. He "went about doing good" (Acts 10:38), yet was despised for it. His gospel was a message of peace and goodwill. He entreated all to follow His example. He walked the roads of Palestine, healing the sick, causing the blind to see, and raising the dead. He taught the truths of eternity, the reality of our premortal existence, the purpose of our life on earth, and the potential for the sons and daughters of God in the life to come.

He instituted the sacrament as a reminder of His great atoning sacrifice. He was arrested and condemned on spurious charges, convicted to satisfy a mob, and sentenced to die on Calvary's cross. He gave His life to atone for the sins of all mankind. His was a great vicarious gift in behalf of all who would ever live upon the earth.

We solemnly testify that His life, which is central to all human history, neither began in Bethlehem nor concluded on Calvary. He was the Firstborn of the Father, the Only Begotten Son in the flesh, the Redeemer of the world.

He rose from the grave to "become the firstfruits of them that slept" (1 Corinthians 15:20). As Risen Lord, He visited among those He had loved in life. He also ministered among His "other sheep" (John 10:16) in ancient America. In the modern world, He and His Father appeared to the boy Joseph Smith, ushering in the long-promised "dispensation of the fulness of times" (Ephesians 1:10). Of the Living Christ, the Prophet Joseph wrote:

> His eyes were as a flame of fire; the hair of his head was white like the pure snow; his countenance shone above the brightness of the sun; and his voice was as the sound of the rushing of great waters, even the voice of Jehovah, saying: "I am the first and the last; I am he who liveth, I am he who was slain; I am your advocate with the Father." (D&C 110:3–4)

Of Him the Prophet also declared:

> And now, after the many testimonies which have been given of him, this is the testimony, last of all, which we give of him: That he lives! For we saw him, even on the right hand of God; and we heard the voice bearing record that he is the Only Begotten of the Father—That by him, and through him, and of him, the worlds are and were created, and the inhabitants thereof are begotten sons and daughters unto God. (D&C 76:22–24)

We declare in words of solemnity that His priesthood and His Church have been restored upon the earth—"built upon the foundation of . . . apostles and prophets, Jesus Christ himself being the chief corner stone" (Ephesians 2:20).

We testify that He will someday return to earth. "And the glory of the Lord shall be revealed, and all flesh shall see it together" (Isaiah 40:5). He will rule as King of Kings and reign as Lord of Lords, and every knee shall bend and every tongue shall speak in worship before Him. Each of us will stand to be judged of Him according to our works and the desires of our hearts.

We bear testimony, as His duly ordained Apostles—that Jesus is the Living Christ, the immortal Son of God. He is the great King Immanuel, who stands today on the right hand of His Father. He is the light, the life, and the hope of the world. His way is the path that leads to happiness in this life and eternal life in the world to come. God be thanked for the matchless gift of His divine Son.

The First Presidency
The Quorum of the Twelve

Bibliography

INTRODUCTION

The selective list of titles offered here is sufficiently extensive to provide entry into the major phases of development and leading personalities of a religion that in some ways appears up to date, encouraging education and using the latest technology, while in other respects it may give the impression of stepping back into the past. Although 19th-century writings are used as source material by historians, they have been superseded by later scholarship. It was after the middle of the 20th century that historians and social scientists with professional training began to tackle the subject of Mormonism. Publications continue to proliferate. Mean-spirited attacks on one extreme and syrupy devotional literature on the other are excluded as not likely to satisfy the desire of the general reader for reliable information.

As an introduction to Mormonism and its history, readers will be well served by Leonard J. Arrington and Davis Bitton, *The Mormon Experience: A History of the Latter-day Saints* (1979, 2nd ed. 1992), and James B. Allen and Glen M. Leonard, *The Story of the Latter-day Saints* (1976, 2nd ed. 1992). A recent survey is Claudia L. Bushman and Richard L. Bushman, *Building the Kingdom: A History of Mormons in America* (2001). For an outsider's perspective, see Jan Shipps, *Mormonism: The Story of a New Religious Tradition* (1985), and Douglas J. Davies, *Introduction to Mormonism* (2005). With disarming frankness, Jana Rees and Christopher Kimball Bigelow convey much basic information in a sprightly way in *Mormonism for Dummies* (2005).

Biographies of founding prophet Joseph Smith range from the adoring George Q. Cannon, *Life of Joseph Smith the Prophet* (1889), to critical hatchet jobs and tortuous, speculative mind reading. Most accessible to non-Mormons since its appearance in 1945 has been Fawn Brodie, *No Man Knows My History*, whose naturalistic, psycho-biographical approach is persuasive to many readers. But she did not examine all the primary material available even at the time she wrote, and much has been uncovered in the past 50 years. A recent biographer following Brodie's basic approach, trying to patch together a convincing interpretation of Smith based on dreams and deductions from family relationships, is Dan Vogel, *Joseph Smith: The Making of a Prophet* (2004).

By all odds, the most important biography now available is Richard Bushman, *Joseph Smith: Rough Stone Rolling* (2005). Beautifully written and based on exhaustive research, it is a cultural biography that places its subject in the context of his time, noting parallels with contemporary figures but also important differences, not denying foibles and weaknesses but also demonstrating as no one has before the phenomenal achievement in doctrine and institution building of a young man who died before his 39th birthday.

The best introduction to the *Book of Mormon* and the different reactions to it, both attacks and defenses, is now Teryl Givens, *By the Hand of Mormon: The American Scripture That Launched a New World Religion* (2002).

For the dramatic expansion of Mormonism into England as well as insight into the extraordinary experiences of the twelve apostles, see James B. Allen, Ronald K. Esplin, and David J. Whittaker, *Men with a Mission, 1837–1841:*

The Quorum of the Twelve in the British Isles (1992). For the 19th century, especially the second half, the indispensable book is Leonard J. Arrington, *Great Basin Kingdom: An Economic History of the Latter-day Saints* (1958). Also recommended is Arrington's *Building the City of God* (1976), coauthored with Feramorz Y. Fox and Dean L. May, which treats cooperative programs and utopian communities among the Mormons.

For the epic story of crossing the plains as the Mormons sought a place of refuge in the West, Wallace Stegner, *The Gathering of Zion* (1981), is engagingly written and full of human interest. A more recent work is Richard Bennett, *We'll Find the Place: The Mormon Exodus, 1846–1848* (1997). The compelling saga of Scandinavian and British Latter-day Saints as they abandoned their homeland and traveled to their land of promise is told by William Mulder, *Homeward to Zion: The Mormon Migration from Scandinavia* (1957) and P. A. M. Taylor, *Expectations Westward: The Mormons and the Emigration of Their British Converts in the Nineteenth Century* (1965).

Richard S. Van Wagoner, *Mormon Polygamy: A History* (1989) lays out the essential facts about its subject. Greater depth and quantitative analysis can be found in Kathryn M. Daynes, *More Wives Than One: Transformation of the Mormon Marriage System, 1840–1910* (2001). Defenders of monogamy who worked tirelessly to bring a halt to the Mormon plural marriage practice are thoughtfully studied by Sarah Barringer Gordon, *The Mormon Question: Polygamy and Constitutional Conflict in Nineteenth Century America* (2002).

The completion of the transcontinental railroad ended the relative isolation of the Latter-day Saints in their mountain retreat. A fascinating study of the resulting tensions and a new schism is Ronald W. Walker, *Wayward Saints: The Godbeites and Brigham Young* (1998). In 1903, the election of monogamist Reed Smoot to the U. S. Senate led to drawn-out committee hearings in the nation's capital. Casting light on many details about the Church as it struggled to adjust to new conditions, these hearings have been thoughtfully studied by Kathleen Flake in *The Politics of American Religious Identity: The Seating of Senator Reed Smoot, Mormon Apostle* (2004).

With polygamy abandoned and the economic and political differences largely erased, Mormon history in the 20th century became less interesting to many people. Yet it was a century of important development and skyrocketing growth. Thomas G. Alexander, *Mormonism in Transition: A History of the Latter-day Saints, 1890–1930* (1986, 2nd ed. 1996), studies a wide range of issues, Mormon life, and institutional development early in the century.

A rewarding approach is through the biographies of leaders. Especially recommended are Gregory A. Prince and William Robert Wright, *David O. McKay and the Rise of Modern Mormonism* (2005); Edward L. Kimball and Andrew E. Kimball Jr., *Spencer W. Kimball* (1977); and Edward L. Kimball, *Lengthen*

Your Stride: The Presidency of Spencer W. Kimball (2005). Workmanlike studies that capture a good deal of human interest while giving a concrete sense of what was happening are Sheri L. Dew, *Ezra Taft Benson: A Biography* (1987); and Sheri L. Dew, *Go Forward with Faith: The Biography of Gordon B. Hinckley* (1996). Studies of earlier church leaders include Davis Bitton, *George Q. Cannon: A Biography* (1999), and Thomas G. Alexander, *Things in Heaven and Earth: The Life and Times of Wilford Woodruff, a Mormon Prophet* (1993).

Many different themes within Mormon history have been studied. Five book-length studies are recommended: Philip L. Barlow, *Mormons and the Bible* (1990); Edwin Brown Firmage and Richard Collin Mangrum, *Zion in the Courts: A Legal History of the Church of Jesus Christ of Latter-day Saints, 1830–1900* (1988); Lester E. Bush Jr., *Health and Medicine among the Latter-day Saints* (1993); Michael Hicks, *Mormonism and Music: A History* (1989); and Richard G. Oman and Robert O. Davis, *Images of Faith: Art of the Latter-day Saints* (1995).

Because of its smothering mass of detail, as well as a complex method of bunching citations that make evaluating its sources difficult, D. Michael Quinn, *The Mormon Hierarchy* in two volumes (1994, 1997), is probably not for general readers approaching the subject for the first time. Yet it contains a vast amount of data, and serious scholars will wish to consult it.

Collections

For the major collections of resources one starts, of course, with the Church's own library and archives in Salt Lake City, Utah. The Utah State Historical Society, the University of Utah library, and the Brigham Young University library preserve much source material. Utah State University already possessed some Mormon-related material when, in the 1990s, the S. George Ellsworth collection was donated there and subsequently the rich Leonard J. Arrington papers. Outside Utah the main collections are the Bancroft Library, Huntington Library, Community of Christ Archives, Princeton University, the Beinicke Library at Yale University, and the National Archives of the United States. A valuable survey of these and other collections, David J. Whittaker, ed., *Mormon Americana: A Guide to Sources and Collections in the United States* (1995), also includes bibliographical essays on published sources, material culture, emigration trails, folklore, literature, photoarchives, performing arts, visual arts, and others.

Chad Flake, *A Mormon Bibliography, 1830–1930* (1978), attempts to list all books about Mormons published between 1830 and 1930. Articles in newspapers and magazines as well as in scholarly journals are not included. Secondary studies, the historical and sociological scholarship, as well as a certain number of pieces that have some value as primary sources, are listed in James B. Allen,

Ronald W. Walker, and David J. Whittaker, *Studies in Mormon History, 1830–1997* (2000), also available online with updates. No one should pretend to be *au courant* on the state of scholarship without first examining this work.

Theology and Religion

This whole category of publications is often ignored by those interested primarily in history. The five-volume *Encyclopedia of Mormonism* (1992), available in many libraries, provides excellent introductions to theological, scriptural, and historical subjects. An illuminating discussion in a civil, respectful tone is Craig L. Blomberg and Stephen E. Robinson, *How Wide the Divide? A Mormon and an Evangelical in Conversation* (1997). Especially energetic in attempting to clarify the issues and develop amicable relations with other faiths has been Robert L. Millet, former dean of religious education at Brigham Young University. His works include *Mormon Faith: A New Look at Christianity* (1998), *Latter-day Christianity: Ten Basic Issues* (1998), *Getting at the Truth: Responding to Difficult Questions about LDS Beliefs* (2004), and *A Different Jesus? The Christ of the Latter-day Saints* (2005).

Websites

Of the hundreds of websites and blogs, varying widely in reliability, the following can be recommended:

lds.org. The official Church website is a portal to information on doctrine, history, and current programs. It allows examination of church magazines and conference addresses, thus providing direct access to what is being said and what is happening at present.

mormon.org. A site intended to assist nonmembers in answering their questions about the Church and its teachings under the headings Church, Families, Nature of God, Purpose of Life, Frequently Asked Questions.

cofchrist.org. Official site of the Community of Christ, previously known as the Reorganized Church of Jesus Christ of Latter Day Saints.

farms.byu.edu. Sponsored by the Neal A. Maxwell Institute for Religious Scholarship, this site allows access to research on the *Book of Mormon*, the *Pearl of Great Price*, and specific incidents in Church history. Its analytical book reviews show what criticisms are published and how Latter-day Saint scholars respond.

fairlds.org. Sponsored by the Foundation for Apologetic Information and Research, this site addresses literally hundreds of questions and provides links to other sites.

byustudies.byu.edu. Besides providing information about an important scholarly journal, this site contains a helpful FAQ (frequently asked questions) section. Under "Mormon Bibliography" users have access to the constantly expanding research on Mormon history.

jefflindsay.com. A private site maintained by an industrial scientist with wide interests in the world of Mormonism.

PERIODICALS AND YEARBOOKS

Brigham Young University Studies 1 (1959–).
Church News, 1943–. Weekly.
Conference Reports, 1880, 1897, 1899–.
Deseret News Church Almanac. Salt Lake City: Deseret News, 1973–
Deseret News, Church Section, 1931–1943.
Dialogue: A Journal of Mormon Thought 1 (1966–).
Ensign, 1971–. Monthly.
Exponent II, 1974–. Quarterly.
FARMS Review of Books 1 (1989–). Originally titled *Review of Books on the Book of Mormon*.
Improvement Era, 1897–1970. Monthly.
The John Whitmer Historical Association Journal 1 (1981–).
Journal of Book of Mormon Studies 1 (1992–).
Journal of Discourses 1–25 (1854–1884).
Relief Society Magazine 1–56 (1915–1970).
The Saints Herald 1 (1860–).
Sunstone 1 (1975–).

REFERENCE WORKS

Brown, S. Kent, Donald Q. Cannon, and Richard H. Jackson, eds. *Historical Atlas of Mormonism*. New York: Simon and Schuster, 1994.

Jenson, Andrew. *Church Chronology: A Record of Important Events*. 2nd ed. Salt Lake City: Deseret News Press, 1914.

——. *Encyclopedic History of the Church of Jesus Christ of Latter-day Saints*. Salt Lake City: Deseret News Press, 1941.

Ludlow, Daniel H., ed. *Encyclopedia of Mormonism*. 5 vols. New York: Macmillan, 1992.

Olpin, Robert S. *Dictionary of Utah Art*. Salt Lake City: Salt Lake Art Center, 1980.

Whittaker, David J. *Mormon Americana: A Guide to Sources and Collections in the United States*. Provo, UT: BYU Studies, 1995.

BIBLIOGRAPHIES

Alder, Douglas D. "Writing Southern Utah History: An Appraisal and a Bibliography." *Journal of Mormon History* 20 (Fall 1994): 156–78.

Alexander, Thomas G. "Historiography and the New Mormon History: A Historian's Perspective." *Dialogue: A Journal of Mormon Thought* 19 (Fall 1986): 25–49.

———. "Toward the New Mormon History: An Examination of the Literature on the Latter-day Saints in the Far West." In Michael P. Malone, ed., *Historians and the American West*. Lincoln: University of Nebraska Press, 1983.

Alexander, Thomas G., and James B. Allen, eds. "The Mormons in the Mountain West: A Selected Bibliography." *Arizona and the West* 9 (Winter 1967): 365–84.

Allen, James B., David J. Whittaker, and Ronald W. Walker. *Studies in Mormon History, 1830–1997: An Indexed Bibliography*. Urbana: University of Illinois Press, 2000.

Arrington, Leonard J. "Scholarly Studies of Mormonism in the Twentieth Century." *Dialogue: A Journal of Mormon Thought* 1 (Spring 1966): 15–32.

Baker, Sherry, and Daniel Stout. "Mormons and the Media, 1898–2003: A Selected, Annotated, and Indexed Bibliography." *Brigham Young University Studies* 42 (2003): 124–81.

Bitton, Davis. *Guide to Mormon Diaries and Autobiographies*. Provo, UT: Brigham Young University Press, 1977.

———. "Mormon Polygamy: A Review Article." *Journal of Mormon History* 4 (1977): 101–8.

Bringhurst, Newell G., and Lavina Fielding Anderson, eds. *Excavating Mormon Pasts: The New Historiography of the Last Half Century*. Salt Lake City: Greg Kofford Books, 2004.

Clement, Russell T. *Mormons in the Pacific: A Bibliography*. Laie, HI: Institute for Polynesian Studies, 1981.

Cowan, Richard O., and Frank A. Bruno. *Bibliography on Temples and Temple Work*. Provo, UT: Brigham Young University, 1982.

Crawley, Peter. "A Bibliography of the Church . . . in New York, Ohio, and Missouri." *Brigham Young University Studies* 12 (Summer 1972): 465–537.

———. *A Descriptive Bibliography of the Mormon Church*. Vol. 1, *1830–1847*. Provo, UT: Religious Studies Center, Brigham Young University, 1997.

Crawley, Peter, and David J. Whittaker. *Mormon Imprints in Great Britain and the Empire.* Provo, UT: Friends of the Brigham Young University Library, 1987.

Dennis, Ronald D. *Welsh Mormon Publications from 1844 to 1862: A Historical Bibliography.* Provo, UT: Religious Studies Center, Brigham Young University, 1988.

England, Eugene. "The Dawning of a Brighter Day: Mormon Literature after 150 Years." *Brigham Young University Studies* 22 (Spring 1982): 131–60.

Fales, Susan L. *An Addendum to Mormons and Mormonism in U.S. Government Documents: A Bibliography.* Provo, UT: N.p., 1989.

Fales, Susan L., and Chad J. Flake, comps. *Mormons and Mormonism in U.S. Government Documents: A Bibliography.* Salt Lake City: University of Utah Press, 1989.

Flake, Chad J., ed. *A Mormon Bibliography, 1830–1930.* Salt Lake City: University of Utah Press, 1978.

Flake, Chad J., and Larry Draper. *Supplement to* A Mormon Bibliography. Salt Lake City: University of Utah Press, 1989.

Frazier, Karen Purser. *Bibliography of Social Scientific, Historical, and Popular Writings about Mormon Women.* Provo, UT: Women's Research Institute, Brigham Young University, 1990.

Grover, Mark L. *The Mormon Church in Latin America: A Periodical Index, 1830–1976.* Provo, UT: Brigham Young University Press, 1977.

Hawkins, Chester Lee. "Selective Bibliography on African-Americans and Mormons, 1830–1890." *Dialogue: A Journal of Mormon Thought* 25 (Winter 1992): 113–31.

Hill, Marvin S. "The Historiography of Mormonism." *Church History* 28 (December 1959): 418–26.

Homer, Michael W. "The Church's Image in Italy from the 1840s to 1946: A Bibliographic Essay." *Brigham Young University Studies* 31 (Spring 1991): 83–114.

Laughlin, David L. "A Selective, Evaluative, and Annotated Bibliography on Mormonism." *Bulletin of Bibliography* 48 (June 1991): 75–101.

———. "It Began with a Book: A Didactically Annotated Bibliography on Mormonism." *Journal of Religious and Theological Information* 2 (1994): 45–94.

Launius, Roger D. "A Bibliographical Review of the Reorganized Church in the Nineteenth Century." *Mormon History Association Newsletter* 64 (January 1987): 5–8.

———. "A New Historiographical Frontier: The Reorganized Church in the Twentieth Century." *John Whitmer Historical Association Journal* 6 (1986): 53–63.

———. "The Reorganized Church in the Nineteenth Century: A Bibliographical Review." In Marjorie B. Troeh and Eileen M. Terril, eds., *Restoration Studies IV*, pp. 171–87. Independence, MO: Herald Publishing House, 1988.

Leonard, Glen M. "Recent Writing on Mormon Nauvoo." *Western Illinois Regional Studies* 11 (Fall 1988): 69–93.

Madsen, Carol Cornwall, and David J. Whittaker. "History's Sequel: A Source Essay on Women in Mormon History." *Journal of Mormon History* 6 (1979): 123–45.

Mauss, Armand L., and Jeffrey R. Franks. "Comprehensive Bibliography of Social Science Literature on the Mormons." *Review of Religious Research* 26 (September 1984): 73–115.

Paul, Rodman W. "The Mormons as a Theme in Western Historical Writing." *Journal of American History* 54 (December 1967): 511–23.

Poll, Richard D. "Nauvoo and the New Mormon History: A Bibliographical Survey." *Journal of Mormon History* 5 (1978): 105–23.

Saunders, Richard L. *Printing in Deseret: Mormons, Economy, Politics, and Utah's Incunabula, 1849–1851.* Salt Lake City: University of Utah Press, 2000.

Scott, Patricia Lyn. "Mormon Polygamy: A Bibliography, 1977–91." *Journal of Mormon History* 19 (Spring 1993): 133–55.

Shields, Steven L. *The Latter Day Saint Churches: An Annotated Bibliography.* New York/London: Garland Publishing, 1987.

Taylor, P. A. M. "Recent Writing on Utah and the Mormons." *Arizona and the West* 4 (Autumn 1962): 249–60.

Wahlquist, Wayne L. "A Review of Mormon Settlement Literature." *Utah Historical Quarterly* 45 (Winter 1977): 3–21.

Whittaker, David J. "Bibliography: LDS Missionary Work." *Mormon History Association Newsletter* 69 (July 1988): 5–8.

———. "History—Educational System of the LDS Church." *Mormon History Association Newsletter* 68 (April 1988): 2–5.

Whittaker, David J., ed. *Mormon Americana: A Guide to Sources and Collections in the United States.* Provo, UT: BYU Studies, 1995.

———. "Mormonism in Great Britain, 1837–1987." *Mormon History Association Newsletter* 66 (July 1987): 1–4.

———. "Mormons and Native Americans: A Historical and Bibliographical Introduction." *Dialogue: A Journal of Mormon Thought* 18 (Winter 1985): 33–64.

———. "Mormon Social History: A Selected Bibliography." *Mormon History Association Newsletter* 6 (April 1986): 2–5.

———. "Sources on Mormon Origins in New York and Pennsylvania." *Mormon History Association Newsletter* 43 (March 1980): 8–12.

Whittaker, David J., and Chris McClellan. *Mormon Missions and Missionaries: A Bibliographic Guide to Published and Manuscript Sources*. Provo, UT: Harold B. Lee Library, Brigham Young University, 1993.

Wilson, William A. "A Bibliography of Studies in Mormon Folklore." *Utah Historical Quarterly* 44 (Fall 1976): 389–94.

PUBLISHED PRIMARY SOURCES

Bagley, Will, ed. *Scoundrel's Tale: The Samuel Brannan Papers*. Vol. 3 of *Kingdom in the West: The Mormons and the American Frontier*. Spokane, WA: Arthur H. Clark Company, 1999.

Barney, Ronald O., ed. "Letters of a Missionary Apostle to His Wife: Brigham Young to Mary Ann Angell Young, 1839–1841." *Brigham Young University Studies* 38 (1999): 156–201.

Baugh, Alexander L. "Joseph Young's Affidavit of the Massacre at Haun's Mill." *Brigham Young University Studies* 38 (1999): 188–202.

Bigler, David L. *Fort Limhi: The Mormon Adventure in Oregon Territory, 1855–1858*. Vol. 6 of *Kingdom in the West: The Mormons and the American Frontier*. Spokane: WA: Arthur H. Clark Company, 2003.

The Book of Mormon. Salt Lake City: The Church of Jesus Christ of Latter-day Saints, 1981.

The Book of Mormon: A Reader's Edition. Ed. Grant Hardy. Urbana/Chicago: University of Illinois Press, 2003.

Buchanan, Frederick Stewart, ed. *A Good Time Coming: Mormon Letters to Scotland*. Salt Lake City: University of Utah Press, 1988.

Campbell, Eugene E., ed. *The Essential Brigham Young*. Salt Lake City: Signature Books, 1992.

Cannon, Donald Q., and Lyndon W. Cook, eds. *Far West Record: Minutes of the Church of Jesus Christ of Latter-day Saints, 1830–1844*. Salt Lake City: Deseret Book, 1983.

Clark, James R., ed. *Messages of the First Presidency of the Church of Jesus Christ of Latter-day Saints*. 6 vols. Salt Lake City: Bookcraft, 1971–1975.

Collier, Fred C., and William S. Hartwell, eds. *Kirtland Council Minute Book*. Salt Lake City: Collier's Publishing Co., 1996.

Cook, Lyndon W. "'Brother Joseph Is Truly a Wonderful Man, He Is All We Could Wish a Prophet to Be': Pre-1844 Letters of William Law." *Brigham Young University Studies* 20 (Winter 1980): 207–18.

Cook, Lyndon W., ed. *The Revelations of the Prophet Joseph Smith*. Provo, UT: Seventy's Mission Bookstore, 1981.

Cook, Lyndon W., and Milton V. Backman Jr., eds. *Kirtland Elders' Quorum Record, 1836–1841*. Provo, UT: Grandin Book Co., 1985.

Cook, Lyndon W., and Matthew K. Cook, eds. *David Whitmer Interviews: A Restoration Witness*. Orem, UT: Grandin Book Co., 1991.

Cracroft, Richard H., and Neal E. Lambert, eds. *A Believing People: Literature of the Latter-day Saints*. Provo, UT: Brigham Young University Press, 1974.

Crawley, Peter L., ed. *The Essential Parley P. Pratt*. Salt Lake City: Signature Books, 1990.

Dahl, Larry E., and Charles D. Tate Jr., eds. *The Lectures on Faith in Historical Perspective*. Provo, UT: Religious Studies Center, Brigham Young University, 1990.

Daughters of Utah Pioneers. *Chronicles of Courage*. 1– (1990–).

——. *An Enduring Legacy*. Vols. 1–12 (1978–1989).

——. *Heart Throbs of the West*. 12 vols. (1939–1951).

——. *Our Pioneer* Heritage. 20 vols. (1958–1977).

——. *Treasures of Pioneer History*. 6 vols. (1952–1957).

The Doctrine and Covenants. Salt Lake City: The Church of Jesus Christ of Latter-day Saints, 1981.

Durham, G. Homer, comp. *The Discourses of Wilford Woodruff*. Salt Lake City: Bookcraft, 1946.

Ehat, Andrew F., and Lyndon W. Cook, eds. *The Words of Joseph Smith*. Provo, UT: Religious Studies Center, Brigham Young University, 1980.

Ekins, Roger Robin, ed. *Defending Zion: George Q. Cannon and the California Mormon Newspaper Wars of 1856–1857*. Vol. 5 of *Kingdom in the West: The Mormons and the American Frontier*. Spokane, WA: Arthur H. Clark Co., 2002.

Ellsworth, Maria S., ed. *Mormon Odyssey: The Story of Ida Hunt Udall, Plural Wife*. Urbana: University of Illinois Press, 1992.

Ellsworth, S. George, ed. *Dear Ellen: Two Mormon Women and Their Letters*. Salt Lake City: Tanner Trust Fund, University of Utah Library, 1974.

Godfrey, Kenneth W., Audrey M. Godfrey, and Jill Mulvay Derr, eds. *Women's Voices: An Untold History of the Latter-day Saints*. Salt Lake City: Deseret Book, 1982.

Gospel Ideals: Selections from the Discourses of David O. McKay. Salt Lake City: Improvement Era, 1953.

Grant, Heber J. *Gospel Standards: Selections from the Sermons and Writings of Heber J. Grant*. Salt Lake City: Improvement Era, 1941.

Hansen, Jennifer Moulton, ed. *Letters of Catharine Cottam Romney, Plural Wife*. Urbana: University of Illinois Press, 1992.

Hardy, B. Carmon, ed. *Doing the Works of Abraham: Mormon Polygamy, Its Origin, Practice, and Demise*. Vol. 9 of *Kingdom in the West: The Mormons and the American Frontier*. Norman, OK: Arthur H. Clark Co., 2007.

Harris, James, ed. *The Essential James E. Talmage*. Salt Lake City: Signature Books, 1997.

Harwell, William S., ed. *Manuscript History of Brigham Young, 1847–1850*. Salt Lake City: Collier's Publishing Co., 1997. (See also Watson, Elden.)

Higbee, Marilyn. "'A Weary Traveler': The 1848–50 Diary of Zina D. H. Young." *Journal of Mormon History* 19 (Fall 1993): 86–125.

Hill, Marvin S., ed. *The Essential Joseph Smith*. Salt Lake City: Signature Books, 1995.

Holzapfel, Jeni Brobert, and Richad Neizel Holzapfel, eds. *A Woman's View: Helen Mar Whitney's Reminiscences of Early Church History*. Provo, UT: Religious Studies Center, Brigham Young University, 1997.

Homer, Michael W. *On the Way to Somewhere Else: European Sojourners in the Mormon West, 1834–1930*. Vol. 8 of *Kingdom in the West: Mormons and the American Frontier*. Spokane, WA: Arthur H. Clark, Co., 2006

Huntress, Keith C., ed. *Murder of an American Prophet*. San Francisco: Chandler Publishing Co., 1960.

Jessee, Dean C., ed. *Letters of Brigham Young to His Sons*. Salt Lake City: Deseret Book, 1974.

———. *The Papers of Joseph Smith*. Vols. 1–. Salt Lake City: Deseret Book Company, 1989–.

Johnson, Clark V., comp. *Mormon Redress Petitions: Documents of the 1833–1838 Missouri Conflict*. Religious Studies Center, Brigham Young University. Salt Lake City: Bookcraft, 1992.

Kimball, Edward L., ed. *The Teachings of Spencer W. Kimball*. Salt Lake City: Bookcraft, 1982.

Kirkham, Francis W. *A New Witness for Christ in America*. 2 vols. Independence, MO: Zion's Printing and Publishing, 1942, 1951.

Knight, Greg R., ed. *Thomas Bullock Nauvoo Journal*. Orem, UT: Grandin Book, 1994.

Larson, Stan. "A 'Meeting of the Brethren': The Discovery of Official Minutes of a 1902 Meeting of the First Presidency and Twelve Apostles." *Dialogue: A Journal of Mormon Thought* 31 (Summer 1998): 77–95.

———, ed. *Prisoner for Polygamy: The Memoirs and Letters of Rudger Clawson at the Utah Territorial Penitentiary, 1884–87*. Urbana: University of Illinois Press, 1993.

Lieber, Constance L. "'The Goose Hangs High': Excerpts from the Letters of Martha Hughes Cannon." *Utah Historical Quarterly* 48 (Winter 1980): 37–48.

Lieber, Constance L., and John Sillito, eds. *Letters from Exile: The Correspondence of Martha Hughes Cannon and Angus M. Cannon, 1886–1888.* Salt Lake City: Signature Books, 1989.

Madsen, Carol Cornwall. *In Their Own Words: Women and the Story of Nauvoo.* Salt Lake City: Deseret Book, 1994.

McKiernan, F. Mark, and Roger D. Launius, eds. *An Early Latter Day Saint History: The Book of John Whitmer.* Independence, MO: Herald Publishing House, 1980. (See also Westergren, Bruce.)

Millett, Robert L., ed. *Joseph Smith: Selected Sermons and Writings.* New York: Paulist Press, 1989.

Mulder, William, and A. Russell Mortensen, eds. *Among the Mormons: Historic Accounts by Contemporary Observers.* New York: Knopf, 1967.

Owens, Kenneth N. *Gold Rush Saints: California Mormons and the Great Rush for Riches.* Vol. 7 of *Kingdom in the West: The Mormons and the American Frontier.* Spokane, WA: Arthur H. Clark Co., 2004.

The Pearl of Great Price. Salt Lake City: The Church of Jesus Christ of Latter-day Saints, 1981.

Smith, Hyrum M., ed. *From Prophet to Son: Advice of Joseph F. Smith to His Missionary Sons.* Salt Lake City: Deseret Book, 1981.

Smith, Joseph. *History of the Church of Jesus Christ of Latter-day Saints.* 7 vols. Ed. B. H. Roberts. Salt Lake City: Deseret Book, 1902–1912.

Smith, Joseph F. *Gospel Doctrine.* 2nd ed. Salt Lake City: Deseret News, 1919.

Smith, Joseph Fielding, comp. *Teachings of the Prophet Joseph Smith.* Salt Lake City: Deseret Book, 1938.

Snow, Lorenzo. *The Teachings of Lorenzo Snow.* Comp. Clyde J. Williams. Salt Lake City: Bookcraft, 1984.

Taylor, John. *Gospel Kingdom: Selections from the Writings and Discourses of John Taylor.* Comp. G. Homer Durham. Salt Lake City: Bookcraft, 1943.

Van Orden, Bruce, ed. "Writing to Zion: The William W. Phelps Kirtland Letters (1835–1836)." *Brigham Young University Studies* 33 (1993): 542–93.

Vogel, Dan, ed. *Early Mormon Documents.* Vol. 1. Salt Lake City: Signature Books, 1995.

———. *Early Mormon Documents.* Vol. 2. Salt Lake City: Signature Books, 1998.

Watson, Elden J., ed. *Manuscript History of Brigham Young, 1846–1847.* Salt Lake City: Elden J. Watson, 1971. (See also Harwell, William.)

Welch, John W., ed. *Opening the Heavens: Accounts of Divine Manifestations, 1820–1844.* Provo, UT: Brigham Young University Press, and Salt Lake City: Deseret Book, 2005.

Westergren, Bruce N., and Julie J. Westergren, eds. *From Historian to Dissident: The Book of John Whitmer.* Salt Lake City: Signature Books, 1994. (See also McKiernan, Mark, above.)

Whittaker, David J., ed. *The Essential Orson Pratt.* Salt Lake City: Signature Books, 1991.

Woodruff, Wilford. *The Discourses of Wilford Woodruff.* Comp. G. Homer Durham. Salt Lake City: Bookcraft, 1946.

Young, Brigham. *Discourses of Brigham Young.* Comp. John A. Widtsoe. Salt Lake City: Deseret Book, 1925.

DIARIES AND AUTOBIOGRAPHIES

Allen, James B., and Thomas G. Alexander, eds. *Manchester Mormons: The Journal of William Clayton, 1840 to 1842.* Santa Barbara, CA/Salt Lake City: Peregrine Smith, 1974.

Anderson, Lavina Fielding, ed. *Lucy's Book: A Critical Edition of Lucy Mack Smith's Family Memoir.* Salt Lake City: Signature Books, 2000.

Archer, Patience Loader. *Recollections of Past Days: the Autobiography of Patience Loader Rozsa Archer.* Logan, UT: Utah State University Press, 2006.

Arrington, Leonard J. *Adventures of a Church Historian.* Urbana: University of Illinois Press, 1998.

——, ed. "Crusade against Theocracy: The Reminiscences of Judge Jacob Smith Boreman of Utah, 1872–1877." *Huntington Library Quarterly* 24 (November 1960): 1–45.

——, ed. "Oliver Cowdery's Kirtland, Ohio, 'Sketch Book.'" *Brigham Young University Studies* 12 (Summer 1972): 410–26.

Bagley, Will, ed. *Frontiersman: Abner Blackburn's Narrative.* Salt Lake City: University of Utah Press, 1992.

——. *The Pioneer Camp of the Saints: The 1846 and 1847 Mormon Trail Journals of Thomas Bullock.* Vol. 1 of *Kingdom in the West: The Mormons and the American Frontier.* Spokane, WA: Arthur H. Clark Co., 1997.

Barney, Ronald O., ed. *The Mormon Vanguard Brigade of 1847: Norton Jacob's Record.* Logan, UT: Utah State University Press, 2005.

Beecher, Maureen Ursenbach, ed. "'All Things Move in Order in the City': The Nauvoo Diary of Zina Diantha Huntington Jacobs." *Brigham Young University Studies* 19 (Spring 1979): 285–320.

——. "Eliza R. Snow's Nauvoo Journal." *Brigham Young University Studies* 15 (Summer 1975): 391–416.

——. "The Iowa Journal of Lorenzo Snow." *Brigham Young University Studies* 24 (Summer 1984): 261–73.

——. *The Personal Writings of Eliza Roxcy Snow*. Salt Lake City: University of Utah Press, 1995.

Bergera, Gary James, ed. *The Autobiography of B. H. Roberts*. Salt Lake City: Signature Books, 1990.

Bigler, David L., ed. *The Gold Discovery Journal of Azariah Smith*. Salt Lake City: University of Utah Press, 1990.

Bishop, William W., ed. *Mormonism Unveiled, or Life and Confession of John D. Lee*. Albuquerque, NM: Fierra Blanca, 2001

Brimhall, Sandra Dawn Allen, ed. *Journal of Isaiah Moses Coombs (1855–1856)*. Vol. 1. Salt Lake City: Privately published, 1993.

Brooks, Juanita, ed. *On the Mormon Frontier: The Diary of Hosea Stout, 1844–1861*. Salt Lake City: University of Utah Press, 1964.

——. *Quicksand and Cactus: A Memoir of the Southern Mormon Frontier*. Salt Lake City: Howe Brothers, 1982.

Buice, David. "'All Alone and None to Cheer Me': The Southern States Mission Diaries of J. Golden Kimball." *Dialogue: A Journal of Mormon Thought* 24 (Spring 1991): 35–54.

——. "Excerpts from the Diary of Teancum William Heward, Early Mormon Missionary to Georgia." *Georgia Historical Quarterly* 64 (Fall 1981): 317–25.

Bullock, Thomas. "Journal of Thomas Bullock, 31 August 1845 to 5 July 1846." *Brigham Young University Studies* 31 (Winter 1991): 15–75.

Busche, F. Enzio. *Yearning for the Living God: Reflections from the Life of F. Enzio Busche*. Salt Lake City: Deseret Book, 2004.

Cannon, M. Hamlin, ed. "The Prison Diary of a Mormon Apostle." *Pacific Historical Review* 16 (November 1947): 393–409.

Clayton, William. *William Clayton's Journal: A Daily Record of the Journey of the Original Company*. Salt Lake City: Clayton Family Association, 1921.

Cleland, Robert Glass, and Juanita Brooks, eds. *A Mormon Chronicle: The Diaries of John D. Lee*. 2 vols. San Marino, CA: Huntington Library, 1955.

Creer, Leland H., ed. "Journey to Zion: From the Journal of Erastus Snow." *Utah Humanities Review* 2 (April and July 1948): 107–28, 264–84.

Crookson, Douglas L. *Henry Ballard: The Story of a Courageous Pioneer*. N.p.: Privately published, 1994.

Egan, Howard R. *Pioneering the West, 1846–1878: Major Howard Egan's Diary*. Richmond, UT: Howard R. Egan Estate, 1917.

Ellsworth, Maria S., ed. *Mormon Odyssey: The Story of Ida Hunt Udall, Plural Wife*. Urbana/Chicago: University of Illinois Press, 1992.

Ellsworth, S. George, ed. *The History of Louisa Barnes Pratt: Being the Autobiography of a Mormon Missionary Widow and Pioneer*. Logan: Utah State University, 1998.

———. *The Journals of Addison Pratt*. Salt Lake City: University of Utah Press, 1990.

England, Eugene, ed. "George Laub's Nauvoo Journal." *Brigham Young University Studies* 18 (1978): 151–78.

Evans, Cleo H., comp. *Curtis Bolton: Pioneer Missionary*. N.p.: Privately published, 1968.

Firmage, Edwin Brown, ed. *An Abundant Life: The Memoirs of Hugh B. Brown*. Salt Lake City: Signature Books, 1988.

Garner, Hugh, ed. *A Mormon Rebel: The Life and Travels of Frederick Gardiner*. Salt Lake City: Signature Books, 1993.

Godfrey, Donald G., and Brigham Y. Card, eds. *The Diaries of Charles Ora Card: The Canadian Years, 1886–1903*. Salt Lake City: University of Utah Press, 1993.

Groberg, John H. *The Fire of Faith*. Salt Lake City: Bookcraft, 1996.

———. *In the Eye of the Storm*. Salt Lake City: Bookcraft, 1993.

Hart, Edward L. *Mormon in Motion: The Life and Journals of James H. Hart, 1825–1906*. Provo, UT: Windsor Books, 1978.

Hartley, William G. *My Best for the Kingdom: History and Autobiography of John Lowe Butler, a Mormon Frontiersman*. Salt Lake City: Aspen Books, 1993.

Hatch, Charles M., and Todd M. Compton, eds. *A Widow's Tale: The 1884–1896 Diary of Helen Mar Kimball Whitney*. Logan: Utah State University Press, 2003.

Heath, Harvard S., ed. *In the World: The Diaries of Reed Smoot*. Salt Lake City: Signature Books, 1994.

Holzapfel, Jeni Broberg, and Richard Neitzel Holzapfel. *A Woman"s View: Helen Mar Whitney's Reminiscences of Early Church History*. Provo, UT: Religious Studies Center, Brigham Young University, 1997.

Horne, Dennis B., ed. *An Apostle's Record: The Journals of Abraham H. Cannon*. Clearfield, UT: Gnolaum Books, 2004.

Jenson, Andrew. *Autobiography of Andrew Jenson, Assistant Historian of the Church*. Salt Lake City: Deseret News Press, 1938.

Jessee, Dean C., ed. "The John Taylor Nauvoo Journal." *Brigham Young University Studies* 23 (Summer 1983): 1–124.

———. "The Kirtland Diary of Wilford Woodruff." *Brigham Young University Studies* 12 (Summer 1972): 365–99.

Jessee, Dean C., et al., eds. "The Last Months of Mormonism in Missouri: The Albert Perry Rockwood Journal." *Brigham Young University Studies* 28 (1988): 5–41.

Johnson, Benjamin F. *My Life's Review: The Autobiography of Benjamin F. Johnson*. Provo, UT: Grandin Book Co., 1997.

Jones, Daniel W. *Forty Years among the Indians*. Salt Lake City: Juvenile Instructor Office, 1890.

Kenney, Scott G., ed. *Memories and Reflections: The Autobiography of E. E. Ericksen*. Salt Lake City: Signature Books, 1987.

———. *Wilford Woodruff's Journal*. 9 vols. Salt Lake City: Signature Books, 1983.

Kimball, Stanley B., ed. *On the Potter's Wheel: The Diaries of Heber C. Kimball*. Salt Lake City: Signature Books, 1987.

Krenkal, John H., ed. *The Life and Times of Joseph Fish, Mormon Pioneer*. Danville, IL: Interstate, 1970.

Landon, Michael N., ed. *The Journals of George Q. Cannon*. Vol 1, *To California in '49*. Salt Lake City: Deseret Book, 1999.

Larson, A. Karl, and Katherine Miles Larson, eds. *Diary of Charles Lowell Walker*. 2 vols. Logan: Utah State University Press, 1980.

Larson, Stan, ed. *A Ministry of Meetings: Diaries of Rudger Clawson*. Salt Lake City: Signature Books, 1993.

———. *Prisoner for Polygamy: The Memoirs and Letters of Rudger Clawson at the Utah Territorial Penitentiary, 1884–87*. Urbana/Chicago: University of Illinois Press, 1993.

Lee, George P. *Silent Courage, an Indian Story: The Autobiography of George P. Lee, a Navajo*. Salt Lake City: Deseret Book, 1987.

Lund, Anthon H. *Danish Apostle: The Diaries of Anthon H. Lund, 1890–1921*. Ed. John P. Hatch. Salt Lake City: Signature Books, 2006.

Madsen, Carol Cornwall, ed. *Journey to Zion: Voices from the Mormon Trail*. Salt Lake City: Deseret Book, 1997.

Martins, Helvecio. *The Autobiography of Elder Helvecio Martins*. Salt Lake City: Aspen Books, 1994.

McIntyre, Myron W., and Noel R. Barton, eds. *Christopher Layton: Colonizer, Statesman, Leader*. Salt Lake City: Christopher Layton Family Organization, 1966.

Neilsen, Reid L., ed. *The Japanese Missionary Journal of Elder Alma O. Taylor, 1901–10*. Provo, UT: BYU Studies, 2001.

Nixon, Loretta D. and L. Douglas Smoot. *Abraham Owen Smoot: A Testament of His Life*. Provo, UT: Brigham Young University Press, 1994.

Partridge, Scott H., ed. *Eliza Maria Partridge Journal*. Provo, UT: Grandin Book Co., 2003.

Pratt, Parley P., ed. *Autobiography of Parley Parker Pratt*. Salt Lake City: Deseret Book, 1961. (Orig. pub., 1874.)

Robertson, Frank C. *A Ram in the Thicket: The Story of a Roaming Homesteader Family on the Mormon Frontier*. Moscow, ID: University of Idaho Press, 1994.

Sessions, Gene A., ed. *Mormon Democrat: The Religious and Political Memoirs of James Henry Moyle*. Salt Lake City: James Moyle Genealogical and Historical Association, 1975.

Shipps, Jan. *Sojourner in the Promised Land: Forty Years among the Mormons*. Urbana/Chicago: University of Illinois Press, 2000.

Shipps, Jan, and John W. Welch, eds. *The Journals of William E. McLellan, 1831–1836*. Provo, UT: BYU Studies, and Urbana: University of Illinois Press, 1994.

Smart, Donna Toland, ed. *Exemplary Elder: The Life and Missionary Diaries of Perrigrine Sessions, 1814–1893*. Provo, UT: BYU Studies and Joseph Fielding Smith Institute for Latter-day Saint History, 2002.

———. *Mormon Midwife: The 1846–1888 Diaries of Patty Bartlett Sessions*. Vol. 2 of *Life Writings of Frontier Women*. Logan: Utah State University Press, 1997.

Smith, George D., ed. *An Intimate Chronicle: The Journals of William Clayton*. Salt Lake City: Signature Books, 1991.

Smith, Oliver R., ed. *Six Decades in the Early West: The Journal of Jesse Nathaniel Smith, 1834–1906*. Provo, UT: Jesse N. Smith Family Association, 1970.

Staker, Susan, ed. *Waiting for World's End: Diaries of Wilford Woodruff*. Salt Lake City: Signature Books, 1993.

Tanner, Annie Clark. *A Mormon Mother: An Autobiography*. Salt Lake City: Tanner Trust Fund, University of Utah Library, 1973.

Ward, Maurine Carr, ed. *Winter Quarters: The 1846–1848 Life Writings of Mary Haskin Parker Richards*. Logan: Utah State University Press, 1996.

Watson, Elden J., ed. *The Orson Pratt Journals*. Salt Lake City: Elden J. Watson, 1975.

Whitcomb, Elias W. "Reminiscences of a Pioneer: An Excerpt from the Diary of Elias W. Whitcomb." *Annals of Wyoming* 57 (Fall 1985): 21–32.

White, Jean Bickmore, ed. *Church, State, and Politics: The Diaries of John Henry Smith*. Salt Lake City: Signature Books, 1990.

BIOGRAPHIES

Alexander, Thomas G. *Things in Heaven and Earth: The Life and Times of Wilford Woodruff, a Mormon Prophet*. Salt Lake City: Signature Books, 1991.

Allen, James B. *Trials of Discipleship: The Story of William Clayton, a Mormon*. Urbana/Chicago: University of Illinois Press, 1987.

Anderson, Lavina Fielding. "A Ministry of Blessing: Nicholas Groesbeck Smith." *Dialogue: A Journal of Mormon Thought* 31 (Fall 1998): 59–78.

Anderson, Paul L. "William Henry Folsom: Pioneer Architect." *Utah Historical Quarterly* 43 (Summer 1975): 240–59.

Arrington, Harriet Horne. "Alice Merrill Horne, Art Promoter and Early Utah Legislator." *Utah Historical Quarterly* 58 (Summer 1990): 261–76.

Arrington, J. Earl. "William Weeks, Architect of the Nauvoo Temple." *Brigham Young University Studies* 19 (Spring 1979): 337–59.

Arrington, Leonard J. *Brigham Young: American Moses*. New York: Knopf, 1985.

———. *Charles C. Rich: Mormon General and Western Frontiersman*. Provo, UT: Brigham Young University Press, 1974.

———. *David Eccles: Pioneer Western Industrialist*. Logan: Utah State University Press, 1975.

———. *From Quaker to Latter-day Saint: Bishop Edwin D. Woolley*. Salt Lake City: Deseret Book, 1976.

———. *Harold F. Silver: Western Inventor, Businessman, and Civic Leader*. With John R. Alley Jr. Logan: Utah State University Press, 1992.

———. *Madelyn Cannon Stewart Silver: Poet, Teacher, Homemaker*. Salt Lake City, UT: Publishers Press, 1998.

———, ed. *The Presidents of the Church*. Salt Lake City: Deseret Book, 1986.

Arrington, Leonard J., and Davis Bitton. *Saints without Halos: The Human Side of Mormon History*. Salt Lake City: Signature Books, 1982.

Arrington, Leonard J., and Richard Jensen. "Pioneer Portraits: Lorenzo Hill Hatch." *Idaho Yesterdays* 17 (Summer 1973): 2–8.

Arrington, Leonard J., and Susan Arrington Madsen. *Mothers of the Prophets*. Salt Lake City: Deseret Book, 1987.

———. *Sunbonnet Sisters: The Stories of Mormon Women and Frontier Life*. Salt Lake City: Bookcraft, 1984.

Avery, Valeen Tippets. *From Mission to Madness: Last Son of the Mormon Prophet*. Urbana: University of Illinois Press, 1998.

———. "Sketches of the Sweet Singer: David Hyrum Smith, 1844–1904." *John Whitmer Historical Association Journal* 5 (1985): 3–15.

Avery, Valeen Tippetts, and Linda King Newell. "Lewis C. Bidamon, Stepchild of Mormondom." *Brigham Young University Studies* 19 (Spring 1979): 375–88.

———. "The Lion and the Lady: Brigham Young and Emma Smith." *Utah Historical Quarterly* 48 (Winter 1980): 81–97.

Backman, Milton V., Jr. *A Profile of Latter-day Saints of Kirtland, Ohio, and Members of Zion's Camp, 1830–1839*. Provo, UT: Brigham Young University Department of Church History and Doctrine, 1982.

Backus, Anna Jean. *Mountain Meadows Witness: The Life and Times of Bishop Philip Klingensmith*. Spokane, WA: Arthur H. Clark Co., 1995.

Barney, Ronald O. *One Side by Himself: The Life and Times of Lewis Barney, 1808–1894.* Logan: Utah State University Press, 2001.

Barron, Howard H. *Orson Hyde: Missionary, Apostle, Colonizer.* Bountiful, UT: Horizon, 1977.

Barton, Peggy Petersen. *Mark E. Petersen: A Biography.* Salt Lake City: Deseret Book, 1985.

Bates, Irene M. "Uncle John Smith, 1781–1854: Patriarchal Bridge." *Dialogue: A Journal of Mormon Thought* 20 (Fall 1987): 79–89.

Beecher, Maureen Ursenbach. "Each in Her Own Time: Four Zinas." *Dialogue: A Journal of Mormon Thought* 26 (Summer 1993): 119–35.

———. *Eliza and Her Sisters.* Salt Lake City: Aspen Books, 1991.

Bell, James P. *In the Strength of the Lord: The Life and Teachings of James E. Faust.* Salt Lake City: Deseret Book, 1999.

Bennion, Sherilyn Cox. "Lula Greene Richards: Utah's First Woman Editor." *Brigham Young University Studies* 21 (Spring 1981): 155–74.

Bergman, Ray L. *The Children Sang: The Life and Music of Evan Stephen.* Salt Lake City: Northwest Publishing, 1992.

Bishop, M. Guy. "After Sutter's Mill: The Life of Henry Bigler, 1848–1900." *Dialogue: A Journal of Mormon Thought* 20 (Spring 1987): 125–35.

———. "'A Great Little Saint': A Brief Look at the Life of Henry William Bigler." *Brigham Young University Studies* 30 (Fall 1990): 27–38.

———. *Henry William Bigler: Soldier, Gold Miner, Missionary, Chronicler, 1815–1900.* Logan: Utah State University Press, 1998.

Bitton, Davis. "Claude T. Barnes, Utah Naturalist." *Utah Historical Quarterly* 49 (Fall 1981): 316–30.

———. *George Q. Cannon: A Biography.* Salt Lake City: Deseret Book, 1999.

———. "'I'd Rather Have Some Roasting Ears': The Peregrinations of George Armstrong Hicks." *Utah Historical Quarterly* 68.3 (2000): 196–222.

———. *Images of the Prophet Joseph Smith.* Salt Lake City: Aspen Books, 1996.

———. *The Martyrdom Remembered.* Salt Lake City: Aspen Books, 1994.

———. *The Redoubtable John Pack.* Salt Lake City: Eden Hill, 1982.

Black, Susan Easton, and Larry C. Porter, eds. *Lion of the Lord: Essays on the Life and Service of Brigham Young.* Salt Lake City: Deseret Book, 1995.

Black, Susan Easton, and Charles D. Tate, Jr., eds. *Joseph Smith: The Prophet, the Man.* Provo, UT: Religious Studies Center, Brigham Young University, 1993.

Bradford, Mary Lythgoe. *Lowell L. Bennion: Teacher, Counselor, Humanitarian.* Salt Lake City: Dialogue Foundation, 1995.

Bradley, Martha Sonntag, and Mary Brown Firmage Woodward. *Four Zinas: A Story of Mothers and Daughters on the Mormon Frontier.* Salt Lake City: Signature Books, 2000.

Brady, Margaret K. *Mormon Healer and Folk Poet: Mary Susannah Fowler's Life of "Unselfish Usefulness."* Logan: Utah State University Press, 2000.

Bringhurst, Newell G. *Brigham Young and the Expanding American Frontier.* Boston: Little, Brown, 1986.

———. "The Private versus the Public David O. McKay: Profile of a Complex Personality." *Dialogue: A Journal of Mormon Thought* 31 (Fall 1998): 11–32.

Brodie, Fawn M. *No Man Knows My History: The Life of Joseph Smith, the Mormon Prophet.* New York: Knopf, 1945.

Brooks, Juanita. *Emma Lee.* Logan: Utah State University Press, 1984.

———. *Jacob Hamblin: Mormon Apostle to the Indians.* Salt Lake City: Westwater Press, 1980.

———. *John D. Lee: Zealot, Pioneer Builder, Scapegoat.* Rev. ed. Glendale, CA: Arthur H. Clark, 1972.

Buchanan, Frederick S. "Robert Lang Campbell: 'A Wise Scribe in Israel' and Schoolman to the Saints." *Brigham Young University Studies* 19 (Summer 1989): 5–27.

Burgess-Olson, Vicky D., ed. *Sister Saints.* Provo, UT: Brigham Young University Press, 1978.

Bush, Laura L. *Faithful Transgressions in the American West: Six Twentieth-Century Women's Autobiographical Acts.* Logan: Utah State University Press, 2004.

Bushman, Claudia, ed. *Mormon Sisters: Women in Early Utah.* 1st ed. Cambridge, MA, 1976. Rev. ed. Logan: Utah State University Press, 1997.

Bushman, Richard L. *Believing History: Latter-day Saint Essays.* New York: Columbia University Press, 2004.

———. *Joseph Smith and the Beginnings of Mormonism.* Urbana/Chicago: University of Illinois Press, 1984.

———. *Joseph Smith: Rough Stone Rolling.* New York: Knopf, 2005.

Campbell, Eugene E., and Poll, Richard D. *Hugh B. Brown: His Life and Thought.* Salt Lake City: Bookcraft, 1975.

Cannon, Kenneth L., II. "Brigham Bicknell Young, Musical Christian Scientist." *Utah Historical Quarterly* 50 (Spring 1982): 124–38.

Carmack, Noel A. "The Seven Ages of Thomas Lyne: A Tragedian among the Mormons." *John Whitmer Historical Association Journal* 14 (1994): 53–72.

Carmack, Noel A., and Karen Lynn Davidson, eds. *Out of the Black Patch: The Autobiography of Effie Marquess Carmack, Folk Musician, Artist, and Writer.* Logan: Utah State University Press.

Cheney, Thomas E. *The Golden Legacy: A Folk History of J. Golden Kimball.* Santa Barbara, CA/Salt Lake City: Peregrine Smith, 1974.

———. *Voices from the Bottom of the Bowl: A Folk History of Teton Valley, Idaho, 1823–1952.* Salt Lake City: University of Utah Press, 1991.

Christensen, Scott R. *Sagwitch: Shoshone Chieftain, Mormon Elder, 1822–1887.* Logan: Utah State University Press, 1999.

Condie, Spencer J. *Russell M. Nelson: Father, Surgeon, Apostle.* Salt Lake City: Deseret Book, 2003.

Cook, Lyndon W. "Isaac Galland—Mormon Benefactor." *Brigham Young University Studies* 19 (Spring 1979): 261–84.

———. *Joseph C. Kingsbury: A Biography.* Provo, UT: Grandin Book Co., 1985.

———. *William Law.* Orem, UT: Grandin Book Co., 1994.

———. "William Law, Nauvoo Dissenter." *Brigham Young University Studies* 22 (Winter 1982): 47–72.

Corbett, Pearson H. *Hyrum Smith, Patriarch.* Salt Lake City: Deseret Book, 1963.

Crawley, Peter. "Parley P. Pratt: Father of Mormon Pamphleteering." *Dialogue: A Journal of Mormon Thought* 15 (Autumn 1982): 13–26.

Davies, J. Kenneth. "Thomas Rhoads, Forgotten Mormon Pioneer of 1846." *Nebraska History* 64 (Spring 1983): 81–95.

Day, Kimberly. "Frederick Kesler, Utah Craftsman." *Utah Historical Quarterly* 56 (Winter 1988): 54–74.

Dew, Sheri L. *Ezra Taft Benson: A Biography.* Salt Lake City: Deseret Book, 1987.

———. *Go Forward with Faith: The Biography of Gordon B. Hinckley.* Salt Lake City: Deseret Book, 1996.

Durham, G. Homer. *N. Eldon Tanner: His Life and Service.* Salt Lake City: Deseret Book, 1982.

Edwards, Paul M. *The Chief: An Administrative Biography of Fred M. Smith.* Independence, MO: Herald Publishing House, 1988.

Ellsworth, S. George. *Samuel Claridge: Pioneering the Outposts of Zion.* Logan, UT: S. George Ellsworth, 1987.

England, Breck. *The Life and Thought of Orson Pratt.* Salt Lake City: University of Utah Press, 1985.

England, Eugene. *Brother Brigham.* Salt Lake City: Bookcraft, 1980.

Erekson, Arthur B. *A History of John Benbow.* Provo, UT: Author, 1987.

Erekson, Keith A., and Lloyd D. Newell, "The Conversion of Artemus Millet and His Call to Kirtland." *Brigham Young University Studies* 41 (2002): 76–115.

Euvrard, Christian. *Louis Auguste Bertrand (1808–1875): Journaliste Socialiste et Pionnier Mormon.* Paris: Privately published, 2005.

Evans, Richard L., Jr. *Richard L. Evans: The Man and the Message.* Salt Lake City: Bookcraft, 1973.

Flake, Lawrence R. *Mighty Men of Zion: General Authorities of the Last Dispensation*. Salt Lake City: Karl D. Butler, 1974.

Foster, Craig L. "From Temple Mormon to Anti-Mormon: The Ambivalent Odyssey of Increase Van Deusen." *Dialogue: A Journal of Mormon Thought* 27,3 (Fall 1994): 275–86.

Fox, Frank W. J. *Reuben Clark: The Public Years*. Provo, UT: Brigham Young University Press, 1980.

Gibbons, Francis M. *Brigham Young: Modern Moses, Prophet of God*. Salt Lake City: Deseret Book, 1981.

——. *George Albert Smith: Kind and Caring Christian, Prophet of God*. Salt Lake City: Deseret Book, 1990.

——. *Harold B. Lee: Man of Vision, Prophet of God*. Salt Lake City: Deseret Book, 1993.

——. *Heber J. Grant: Man of Steel, Prophet of God*. Salt Lake City: Deseret Book, 1979.

——. *John Taylor: Mormon Philosopher, Prophet of God*. Salt Lake City: Deseret Book, 1985.

——. *Joseph Smith: Martyr, Prophet of God*. Salt Lake City: Deseret Book, 1977.

——. *Joseph F. Smith: Patriarch and Preacher, Prophet of God*. Salt Lake City: Deseret Book, 1984.

——. *Lorenzo Snow: Spiritual Giant, Prophet of God*. Salt Lake City: Deseret Book, 1982.

——. *Spencer W. Kimball: Resolute Disciple, Prophet of God*. Salt Lake City: Deseret Book, 1995.

——. *Wilford Woodruff: Wondrous Worker, Prophet of God*. Salt Lake City: Deseret Book, 1988.

Goates, L. Brent. *Harold B. Lee: Prophet and Seer*. Salt Lake City: Bookcraft, 1985.

Godfrey, Donald G. "Zina Prescendia Young Williams Card: Brigham's Daughter, Cardston's First Lady." *Journal of Mormon History* 23 (Fall 1997): 107–27.

Godfrey, Kenneth W. "Charles S. Whitney: A Nineteenth-Century Salt Lake City Teenager's Life." *Journal of Mormon History* 27.2 (Fall 2001): 215–251.

Gregory, Thomas J. "Sidney Rigdon: Post Nauvoo." *Brigham Young University Studies* 21 (Winter 1981): 51–67.

Gunn, Stanley R. *Oliver Cowdery: Second Elder and Scribe*. Salt Lake City: Bookcraft, 1962.

Hafen, Bruce C. *A Disciple's Life: The Biography of Neal A. Maxwell*. Salt Lake City: Deseret Book, 2002.

Harris, Lynda W. "The Legend of Jessie Evans Smith." *Utah Historical Quarterly* 44 (Fall 1976): 351–64.

Hartley, William G. *Kindred Saints: The Mormon Immigrant Heritage of Alvin and Kathryne Christensen*. Salt Lake City: Eden Hill, 1982.

———. *My Best for the Kingdom: History and Biography of John Lowe Butler, Mormon Frontiersman*. Salt Lake City: Aspen Books, 1993.

———. *Stand by My Servant Joseph: The Story of the Joseph Knight Family and the Restoration*. Salt Lake City: Deseret Book, 2003.

———. *These Are My Friends: A History of the Joseph Knight Family, 1825–1850*. Provo, UT: Grandin Book Co., 1986.

Hatch, Jo Ann F. *Willing Hands: A Biography of Lorenzo Hill Hatch, 1826–1910*. Pinedale, AZ: Kymera Publishing Co., 1996.

Hefner, Loretta L. "From Apostle to Apostate: The Personal Struggle of Amasa Mason Lyman." *Dialogue: A Journal of Mormon Thought* 16 (Spring 1983): 90–104.

Hickman, Martin B. *David Matthew Kennedy: Banker, Statesman, Churchman*. Salt Lake City: Deseret Book, 1987.

Hiles, Norma Derry. *Gentle Monarch: The Presidency of Israel A. Smith*. Independence, MO: Herald Publishing House, 1991.

Hill, Donna. *Joseph Smith, the First Mormon*. New York: Doubleday, 1977.

Hinton, Wayne. "John D. T. McAllister: The Southern Utah Years, 1876–1910." *Journal of Mormon History* 29.2 (2003): 106–136.

Hoopes, David S., and Roy Hoopes. *The Making of a Mormon Apostle: The Story of Rudger Clawson*. Lanham, MD: Madison Books, 1990.

Howard, F. Burton. *Marion G. Romney: His Life and Faith*. Salt Lake City: Bookcraft, 1988.

Hunt, Larry E. *Fred M. Smith: Saint as Reformer*. Independence, MO: Herald Publishing House, 1982.

Hunter, Milton R. *Brigham Young the Colonizer*. 4th ed., rev. Santa Barbara, CA/Salt Lake City: Peregrine Smith, 1973.

Hyde, Myrtle Stevens. *Orson Hyde: The Olive Branch of Israel*. Salt Lake City: Agreka Books, 2000.

Hyde, Myrtle Stevens, and Everett L. Cooley. *The Life of Andrew Wood Cooley: A Story of Conviction*. Provo, UT: Andrew Wood Cooley Family Association, 1991.

Jenson, Andrew. *Latter-day Saint Biographical Encyclopedia*. 4 vols. Salt Lake City: Deseret News, 1901–1936.

Jessee, Dean C. "Brigham Young's Family: The Wilderness Years." *Brigham Young University Studies* 19 (Summer 1979): 474–500.

Johnson, Catherine M. "Emma Lucy Gates Bowen: Singer, Musician, Teacher." *Utah Historical Quarterly* 64 (Fall 1996): 344–55.

Johnson, Melvin C. *Polygamy on the Pedernales: Lyman Wight's Mormon Villages in Antebellum Texas, 1845 to 1858.* Logan: Utah State University Press, 2006.

Kimball, Edward L. *Lengthen Your Stride: The Presidency of Spencer W. Kimball.* Salt Lake City: Deseret Book, 2005.

Kimball, Edward L., and Andrew E. Kimball Jr. *Spencer W. Kimball.* Salt Lake City: Bookcraft, 1977.

———. *The Story of Spencer W. Kimball: A Short Man, a Long Stride.* Salt Lake City: Bookcraft, 1985.

Kimball, Edward L., and Caroline Eyring Miner. *Camilla: A Biography of Camilla Eyring Kimball.* Salt Lake City: Deseret Book, 1980.

Kimball, Stanley B. *Heber C. Kimball: Mormon Patriarch and Pioneer.* Urbana: University of Illinois Press, 1981.

Knowles, Eleanor. *Howard W. Hunter.* Salt Lake City: Deseret Book, 1994.

Larson, Andrew Karl. *Erastus Snow: The Life of a Missionary and Pioneer for the Early Mormon Church.* Salt Lake City: University of Utah Press, 1971.

Legg, Phillip R. *Oliver Cowdery: The Elusive Second Elder of the Restoration.* Independence, MO: Herald Publishing House, 1989.

Lund, Jennifer L. "Out of the Swan's Nest: The Ministry of Anthon H. Lund, Scandinavian Apostle." *Journal of Mormon History* 29.2 (Fall 2003): 77–105.

Lyman, Edward Leo. "The Alienation of an Apostle from His Quorum: The Moses Thatcher Case." *Dialogue: A Journal of Mormon Thought* 18 (Summer 1985): 67–91.

Lyon, T. Edgar, Jr. *John Lyon: The Life of a Pioneer Poet.* Provo, UT: Religious Studies Center, Brigham Young University, 1989.

———. *T. Edgar Lyon: A Teacher in Zion.* Provo, UT: Brigham Young University Press, 2002.

Macfarlane, L. W. *Yours Sincerely, John M. Macfarlane.* Salt Lake City: Privately published, 1980.

Madsen, Carol Cornwall. *An Advocate for Women: The Public Life of Emmeline B. Wells, 1870–1920.* Provo, UT: Brigham Young University Press and Salt Lake City: Deseret Book, 2006.

———. "Emmeline B. Wells: 'Am I Not a Woman and a Sister?'" *Brigham Young University Studies* 22 (Spring 1982): 161–78.

———. "Emmeline B. Wells: A Voice for Mormon Women." *John Whitmer Historical Association Journal* 2 (1982): 11–21.

Madsen, Truman G. *Defender of the Faith: The B. H. Roberts Story.* Salt Lake City: Bookcraft, 1980.

Maxwell, Bruce David. "George Careless, Pioneer Musician." *Utah Historical Quarterly* 53 (Spring 1985): 131–43.

McCloud, Susan Evans. *Not in Vain: The Inspiring Story of Ellis Shipp, Pioneer Woman Doctor*. Salt Lake City: Bookcraft, 1984.

McConkie, Joseph F. *The Bruce R. McConkie Story: Reflections of a Son*. Salt Lake City: Deseret Book, 2003.

——. *True and Faithful: The Life Story of Joseph Fielding Smith*. Salt Lake City: Bookcraft, 1971.

McConkie, Mark L., comp. *Remembering Joseph: Personal Recollections of Those Who Knew the Prophet Joseph Smith*. Salt Lake City: Deseret Book, 2003.

McKiernan, F. Mark. *The Voice of One Crying in the Wilderness: Sidney Rigdon, Religious Reformer, 1793–1876*. Lawrence, KS: Coronado Press, 1971.

Merrell, Kenneth W. *Scottish Shepherd: The Life and Times of John Murray Murdoch, Utah Pioneer*. Salt Lake City: University of Utah Press, 2006.

Merrill, Milton R. *Reed Smoot: Apostle in Politics*. Logan: Utah State University Press, 1990.

Milewski, Milessa Lambert, ed. *Before the Manifesto: The Life Writings of Mary Lois Walker Morris*. Logan: Utah State University Press, 2007.

Mortensen, Joann Follett. "King Follett: The Man behind the Discourse." *Journal of Mormon History* 32 (Summer 2005): 112–33.

Mullikin, Frances Hartman. *First Ladies of the Restoration*. Independence, MO: Herald Publishing House, 1985.

Newell, Linda King, and Valeen Tippetts Avery. *Mormon Enigma: Emma Hale Smith*. Garden City, NY: Doubleday, 1984.

Newton, Marjorie. *Hero or Traitor: A Biographical Study of Charles Wesley Wandell*. John Whitmer Association Monograph Series. Independence, MO: Independence Press, 1992.

Noord, Roger Van. *King of Beaver Island: The Life and Assassination of James Jesse Strang*. Urbana: University of Illinois Press, 1988.

O'Driscoll, Jefferey S. *Hyrum Smith: A Life of Integrity*. Salt Lake City: Deseret Book, 2003.

Olmstead, Jacob W., and Fred E. Woods. "'Give Me Any Situation Suitable': The Consecrated Life of the Multitalented Paul A. Schettler." *Brigham Young University Studies* 41 (2002): 108–26.

Oman, Richard G., and Richard L. Jensen. *C. C. A. Christensen, 1831–1912: Mormon Immigrant Artist*. Salt Lake City: Church of Jesus Christ of Latter-day Saints, 1984.

Parkinson, Benson Young. *S. Dilworth Young: General Authority, Scouter, Poet*. American Fork, UT: Covenant Publications, 1994.

Parrish, Alan K. *John A. Widtsoe: A Biography*. Salt Lake City: Deseret Book, 2003.

Petersen, Boyd Jay. *Hugh Nibley: A Consecrated Life*. Salt Lake City: Greg Kofford Books, 2002.

Peterson, Charles S. "'A Mighty Man Was Brother Lot': A Portrait of Lot Smith, Mormon Frontiersman." *Western Historical Quarterly* 1 (October 1970): 393–414.

Peterson, Janet, and LaRene Gaunt. *Elect Ladies: Presidents of the Relief Society*. Salt Lake City: Deseret Book, 1990.

———. *Keepers of the Flame: Presidents of the Young Women*. Salt Lake City: Deseret Book, 1993.

Peterson, Levi. *Juanita Brooks: Mormon Woman Historian*. Salt Lake City: University of Utah Press, 1988.

Peterson, Richard H. "Jesse Knight, Utah's Mormon Mining Mogul." *Utah Historical Quarterly* 57 (Summer 1989): 240–53.

Poll, Richard D. *Working the Divine Miracle: The Life of Apostle Henry D. Moyle*. Salt Lake City: Signature Books, 1999.

Porter, Larry C. "Reverend George Lane—Good 'Gifts,' Much 'Grace,' and Marked 'Usefulness.'" *Brigham Young University Studies* 9 (1970): 321–40.

Porter, Larry C., and Susan Easton Black, eds. *The Prophet Joseph: Essays on the Life and Meaning of Joseph Smith*. Salt Lake City: Deseret Book, 1988.

Pratt, Steven F. "Parley P. Pratt in Winter Quarters and the Trail West." *Brigham Young University Studies* 24 (Summer 1984): 373–88.

Prince, Gregory A., and William Robert Wright. *David O. McKay and the Rise of Modern Mormonism*. Salt Lake City: University of Utah Press, 2005.

Prince, Stephen L. "George Prince, Convert Out of Africa." *Journal of Mormon History* 28.2 (Fall 2002): 60–80.

Pusey, Merlo J. *Builders of the Kingdom: George A. Smith, John Henry Smith, George Albert Smith*. Provo, UT: Brigham Young University Press, 1981.

Quinn, D. Michael. *Elder Statesman: A Biography of J. Reuben Clark*. Salt Lake City: Signature Books, 2002.

———. "Jesse Gause: Joseph Smith's Little-Known Counselor." *Brigham Young University Studies* 17 (Summer 1984): 9–34.

———. *J. Reuben Clark: The Church Years*. Provo, UT: Brigham Young University Press, 1983.

Rollmann, Hans. "The Early Baptist Career of Sidney Rigdon in Warren, Ohio." *Brigham Young University Studies* 21 (Winter 1981): 37–50.

Romney, Thomas C. *Life Story of Miles Park Romney*. Salt Lake City: Zion's Printing and Publishing Co., 1948.

Rowley, Dennis. "Fishing on the Kennet: The Victorian Boyhood of James E. Talmage, 1862–1876." *Brigham Young University Studies* 33 (1993): 480–520.

Schindler, Harold. *Orrin Porter Rockwell: Man of God, Son of Thunder*. Salt Lake City: University of Utah Press, 1966.

Schlup, Leonard. "Utah Maverick: Frank J. Cannon and the Politics of Conscience in 1896." *Utah Historical Quarterly* 62.4 (Fall 1994): 335–48.

Schnibbe, Karl-Heinz. *The Price: The True Story of a Mormon Who Defied Hitler*. With Alan F. Keele and Douglas F. Tobler. Salt Lake City: Bookcraft, 1984.

Seegmiller, Janet Burton. *"Be Kind to the Poor": The Life Story of Robert Taylor Burton*. N.p.: Robert Taylor Burton Family Organization, 1988.

Seifrit, William C. "Charles Henry Wilcken: An Undervalued Saint." *Utah Historical Quarterly* 55 (Fall 1987): 308–21.

———. "The Prison Experience of Abraham H. Cannon." *Utah Historical Quarterly* 53 (Summer 1985): 223–36.

Sessions, Gene A. *Latter-day Patriots: Nine Mormon Families and Their Revolutionary War Heritage*. Salt Lake City: Deseret Book, 1975.

———, ed. *Mormon Democrat: The Religious and Political Memoirs of James Henry Moyle*. Salt Lake City: Signature Books, 1998.

———. *Mormon Thunder: A Documentary History of Jedediah Morgan Grant*. Urbana/Chicago: University of Illinois Press, 1982.

Smart, William B. "William H. Smart, Builder in the Basin." *Utah Historical Quarterly* 50 (Winter 1982): 59–67.

Smith, Andrew F. *The Saintly Scoundrel: The Life and Times of John C. Bennett*. Urbana: University of Illinois Press, 1997.

Smith, Henry A. *Matthew Cowley: Man of Faith*. Salt Lake City: Bookcraft, 1954.

Smith, Joseph Fielding. *Life of Joseph F. Smith*. Salt Lake City: Deseret Book, 1938.

Smith, Joseph Fielding, Jr., and John J. Stewart. *The Life of Joseph Fielding Smith, Tenth President of the Church*. Salt Lake City: Deseret Book, 1972.

Smith, Lucy Mack. *History of Joseph Smith by His Mother, Lucy Mack Smith*. Salt Lake City: Bookcraft, 1958. (Orig. pub., 1853.)

Sonne, Conway B. *Knight of the Kingdom: The Story of Richard Ballantyne*. Salt Lake City: Deseret Book, 1949.

———. *A Man Named Alma: The World of Alma Sonne*. Bountiful, UT: Horizon, 1988.

Speek, Vicky Cleverly. *"God Has Made Us a Kingdom": James J. Strang and the Midwest Mormons*. Salt Lake City: Signature Books, 2006.

Stott, G. St. John. "John Taylor's Religious Preparation." *Dialogue: A Journal of Mormon Thought* 19 (Spring 1986): 94–104.

Swetnam, Susan Hendricks. *Lives of the Saints in Southeast Idaho: An Introduction to Mormon Pioneer Life Story Writing*. Moscow, ID: University of Idaho Press, 1991.

Talmage, John R. *The Talmage Story: Life of James E. Talmage—Educator, Scientist, Apostle.* Salt Lake City: Bookcraft, 1972.

Tate, Lucile C. *Andrew B. Christenson: Mormon Educational Pioneer.* Provo, UT: Brigham Young University Press, 1981.

———. *David B. Haight: The Life of a Disciple.* Salt Lake City: Bookcraft, 1987.

———. *LeGrand Richards: Beloved Apostle.* Salt Lake City: Bookcraft, 1982.

Taylor, Samuel W. *The Kingdom or Nothing: The Life of John Taylor, Militant Mormon.* New York/London: Macmillan, 1976.

Taylor, Samuel W., and Raymond W. Taylor. *The John Taylor Papers: Records of the Last Utah Pioneer.* 2 vols. Redwood City, CA: Taylor Trust, 1984–1985.

Van Orden, Bruce A. *Prisoner for Conscience' Sake: The Life Story of George Reynolds.* Salt Lake City: Deseret Book, 1992.

Van Wagoner, Richard S. *Sidney Rigdon: A Portrait of Religious Excess.* Salt Lake City: Signature Books, 1994.

Van Wagoner, Richard S., and Mary C. Van Wagoner. "Orson Pratt, Jr.: Gifted Son of an Apostle and an Apostate." *Dialogue: A Journal of Mormon Thought* 21 (Spring 1988): 84–94.

Van Wagoner, Richard S., and Steven C. Walker. *A Book of Mormons.* Salt Lake City: Signature Books, 1982.

Vogel, Dan. *Joseph Smith: The Making of a Prophet.* Salt Lake City: Signature Books, 2004.

Walgren, Kent L. "James Adams: Early Springfield Mormon and Freemason." *Journal of the Illinois State Historical Society* 75 (Summer 1982): 121–36.

Walker, Ronald W. "Martin Harris: Mormonism's Early Convert." *Dialogue: A Journal of Mormon Thought* 19 (Winter 1986): 29–43.

———. "Mesquite and Sage: Spencer W. Kimball's Early Years." *Brigham Young University Studies* 25 (Fall 1985): 19–41.

———. *Qualities That Count: Heber J. Grant as Businessman, Missionary, and Apostle.* Provo, UT: Brigham Young University Press, 2004.

———. "Young 'Tony' Ivins: Dixie Frontiersman." *Brigham Young University Studies* 40 (2001): 105–31.

Ward, Margery W. *A Life Divided: The Biography of Joseph Marion Tanner, 1859–1927.* Salt Lake City: Publishers Press, 1980.

Welch, John W., ed. *The Worlds of Joseph Smith: A Bicentennial Conference at the Library of Congress. Brigham Young University Studies* 44.4 (2005). Special issue.

Welch, John W., and Larry E. Morris, eds. *Oliver Cowdery: Scribe, Elder, Witness.* Provo, UT: FARMS, 2006.

West, Franklin L. *Life of Franklin D. Richards.* Salt Lake City: Deseret News Press, 1924.

Whiting, Linda Shelley. *David W. Patten: Apostle and Martyr*. Springville, UT: Cedar Fort, 2003.

Widtsoe, John A. *Joseph Smith: Seeker after Truth, Prophet of God*. Salt Lake City: Deseret News Press, 1951.

Wight, Jermy Benton. *The Wild Ram of the Mountains: The Story of Lyman Wight*. Star Valley, WY: Afton Thrifty Print, 1996.

Williams, Frederick G., III. "Frederick Granger Williams of the First Presidency of the Church." *Brigham Young University Studies* 12 (Spring 1972): 243–61.

Wilson, Marian Robertson. *Leroy Robertson: Music Giant from the Rockies*. Salt Lake City, UT: Blue Ribbon Publications, 1996.

Winder, Michael K., comp. *Counselors to the Prophets*. Roy, UT: Eborn Books, 2001.

Winder, Michael K. *John R. Winder: Member of the First Presidency, Pioneer, Temple Builder, Dairyman*. Salt Lake City: Horizon, 1999.

Wixom, Hartt. *Edward Partridge: The First Bishop of the Church of Jesus Christ of Latter-day Saints*. Springville, UT: Cedar Fort, 1998.

Zobell, Albert L. *Sentinel in the East: A Biography of Thomas L. Kane*. Salt Lake City: Nicholas G. Morgan, 1965.

HISTORIES

General

Alexander, Thomas G., ed. *The Mormon People: Their Character and Traditions*. Provo, UT: Brigham Young University Press, 1980.

Alexander, Thomas G., and Jessie L. Embry, eds. *After 150 Years: The Latter-day Saints in Sesquicentennial Perspective*. Provo, UT: Charles Redd Center for Western Studies, 1983.

Allen, James B., and Jessie L. Embry. *Hearts Turned to the Fathers: A History of the Genealogical Society, 1894–1994*. Salt Lake City: Deseret Book, 1995.

Allen, James B., and Glen M. Leonard. *The Story of the Latter-day Saints*. 2nd ed., rev. Salt Lake City: Deseret Book, 1992.

Andrew, Laurel B. *The Early Temples of the Mormons*. Albany: State University of New York Press, 1978.

Arrington, Leonard J., and Bitton, Davis. *The Mormon Experience: A History of the Latter-day Saints*. New York: Knopf, 1979. 2nd ed., Urbana/Chicago: University of Illinois Press, 1992.

Barlow, Philip L. *Mormons and the Bible*. New York: Oxford University Press, 1990.

Barrett, Ivan J. *Joseph Smith and the Restoration: A History of the LDS Church to 1846*. Provo, UT: Brigham Young University Press, 1973.

Bartholomew, Rebecca. *Audacious Women: Early British Mormon Immigrants*. Salt Lake City: Signature Books, 1995.

Bates, Irene M., and E. Gary Smith. *Lost Legacy: The Mormon Office of Presiding Patriarch*. Urbana: University of Illinois Press, 1996.

Beecher, Maureen Ursenbach, and Lavina Fielding Anderson, eds. *Sisters in Spirit: Mormon Women in Historical and Cultural Perspective*. Urbana: University of Illinois Press, 1987.

Bergera, Gary James, and Ronald Priddis. *Brigham Young University: A House of Faith*. Salt Lake City: Signature Books, 1985.

Berrett, William E. *The Latter-day Saints: A Contemporary History of the Church of Jesus Christ of Latter-day Saints*. Salt Lake City: Deseret Book, 1985.

Bitton, Davis. *"The Ritualization of Mormon History," and Other Essays*. Urbana/Chicago: University of Illinois Press, 1994.

Bitton, Davis, and Leonard J. Arrington. *Mormons and Their Historians*. Salt Lake City: University of Utah Press, 1988.

Bitton, Davis, and Maureen Ursenbach Beecher, eds. *New Views of Mormon History: Essays in Honor of Leonard J. Arrington*. Salt Lake City: University of Utah Press, 1987.

Bradley, Martha Sonntag. "Seizing Sacred Space: Women's Engagement in Early Mormonism." *Dialogue: A Journal of Mormon Thought* 27 (Summer 1994): 57–70.

Bringhurst, Newell G. *Saints, Slaves, and Blacks: The Changing Place of Black People within Mormonism*. Westport, CT: Greenwood, 1981.

Britsch, R. Lanier. *Unto the Islands of the Sea: A History of the Latter-day Saints in the Pacific*. Salt Lake City: Deseret Book, 1986.

Brooke, John L. *The Refiner's Fire: The Making of Mormon Cosmology, 1644–1844*. Cambridge: Cambridge University Press, 1994.

Brunson, L. Madelon. *A History of the RLDS Women's Organizations, 1842–1983*. Independence, MO: Herald Publishing House, 1985.

Buerger, David John. *The Mysteries of Godliness: A History of Mormon Temple Worship*. Salt Lake City: Signature Books, 1994.

Bunker, Gary L., and Davis Bitton. *The Mormon Graphic Image, 1834–1914*. Salt Lake City: University of Utah Press, 1983.

Bush, Lester E., Jr. *Health and Medicine among the Latter-day Saints*. New York: Crossroad, 1993.

Bushman, Claudia L. *Contemporary Mormonism: The Latter-day Saints in Modern America*. Westport, CT: Praeger, 2006.

Bushman, Claudia L., and Richard L. Bushman. *Building the Kingdom: A History of the Mormons in America*. New York: Oxford University Press, 2001.

———. *Mormons in America*. New York: Oxford University Press, 1998.

Carter, Kate B. *Denominations That Base Their Beliefs on the Teachings of Joseph Smith*. Salt Lake City: Daughters of Utah Pioneers, 1969.

Cook, Lyndon W. *Joseph Smith and the Law of Consecration*. Provo, UT: Grandin Book Co., 1985.

Cooper, Rex Eugene. *Promises Made to the Fathers: Mormon Covenant Organization*. Salt Lake City: University of Utah Press, 1990.

Davies, Douglas J. *An Introduction to Mormonism*. Cambridge: Cambridge University Press, 2003.

Davis, David Brion. "The New England Origins of Mormonism." *New England Quarterly* 27 (June 1953): 148–53.

———. "Some Themes of Counter-Subversion: An Analysis of Anti-Masonic, Anti-Catholic, and Anti-Mormon Literature." *Mississippi Valley Historical Review* 47 (September 1970): 205–24.

De Pillis, Mario. "The Quest for Religious Authority and the Rise of Mormonism." *Dialogue: A Journal of Mormon Thought* 1 (Spring 1966): 68–88.

———. "The Social Forces of Mormonism." *Church History* 37 (March 1968): 50–79.

Derr, Jill Mulvay, Janath Russell Cannon, and Maureen Ursenbach Beecher. *Women of Covenant: The Story of Relief Society*. Salt Lake City: Deseret Book, 1992.

Divett, Robert J. *Medicine and the Mormons: An Introduction to the History of Latter-day Saint Health Care*. Bountiful, UT: Horizon Publishers, 1981.

Durham, Reed C., and Steven H. Heath. *Succession in the Church*. Salt Lake City: Bookcraft, 1970.

Edwards, Paul M. *Our Legacy of Faith: A Brief History of the Reorganized Church of Jesus Christ of Latter Day Saints*. Independence, MO: Herald Publishing House, 1991.

Embry, Jessie L. *Asian-American Mormons: Bridging Cultures*. Provo, UT: Charles Redd Center for Western Studies, 1999.

———. *Black Saints in a White Church: Contemporary African-American Mormons*. Salt Lake City: Signature Books, 1994.

———. *In His Own Language: Mormon Spanish-Speaking Congregations in the United States*. Provo, UT: Charles Redd Center for Western Studies, 1997.

Epperson, Steven. *Mormons and Jews: Early Mormon Theologies of Israel*. Salt Lake City: Signature Books, 1992.

Erickson, Dan. *As a Thief in the Night: The Mormon Quest for Millennial Deliverance*. Salt Lake City: Signature Books, 1998.

Firmage, Edwin Brown, and Mangrum, Richard Collin. *Zion in the Courts: A Legal History of the Church of Jesus Christ of Latter-day Saints, 1830–1900*. Urbana/Chicago: University of Illinois Press, 1988.

Foster, Lawrence. "New Paradigms for Understanding Mormonism and Mormon History." *Dialogue: A Journal of Mormon Thought* 27 (Spring 1994): 91–105.

——. *Religion and Sexuality: The Shakers, the Mormons, and the Oneida Community*. Urbana/Chicago: University of Illinois Press, 1984.

——. "Sex and Prophetic Power: A Comparison of John Humphrey Noyes, Founder of the Oneida Community, with Joseph Smith, the Mormon Prophet." *Dialogue: A Journal of Mormon Thought* 31 (Winter 1998): 65–83.

——. "Women and Utopia: Life among the Shakers, Oneidans, and Mormons." *Communities: Journal of Cooperative Living* 82 (Spring 1994): 53–56.

——. *Women, Family, and Utopia: Communal Experiments of the Shakers, the Oneida Community, and the Mormons*. Syracuse, NY: Syracuse University Press, 1992.

Givens, Terryl L. *The Viper on the Hearth: Mormons, Myths, and the Construction of Heresy*. New York: Oxford University Press, 1997.

Hansen, Klaus J. *Mormonism and the American Experience*. Chicago/London: University of Chicago Press, 1981.

——. *Quest for Empire: The Political Kingdom of God and the Council of Fifty in Mormon History*. East Lansing: Michigan State University Press, 1967.

Hardy, B. Carmon. *Solemn Covenant: The Mormon Polygamous Passage*. Urbana: University of Illinois Press, 1992.

Hicks, Michael. *Mormonism and Music: A History*. Urbana/Chicago: University of Illinois Press, 1989.

Hill, Marvin S. *Quest for Refuge: The Mormon Flight from American Pluralism*. Salt Lake City: Signature Books, 1989.

——. "The Shaping of the Mormon Mind in New England and New York." *Brigham Young University Studies* 9 (Spring 1969): 351–72

Hill, Marvin S., and James B. Allen, eds. *Mormonism and American Culture*. New York: Harper & Row, 1972.

Howard, Richard L. *The Church through the Years*. Vol. 1, *RLDS Beginnings to 1860*. Independence, MO: Herald Publishing House, 1992.

——. *The Church through the Years*. Vol. 2, *The Reorganization Comes of Age, 1860–1992*. Independence, MO: Herald Publishing House, 1993.

——. *Restoration Scriptures: A Study of Their Textual Development*. Independence, MO: Herald Publishing House, 1969.

Hughes, Dean. *The Mormon Church: A Basic History*. Salt Lake City: Deseret Book, 1986.

Launius, Roger D., and Linda Thatcher, eds. *Differing Visions: Dissenters in Mormon History*. Urbana/Chicago: University of Illinois Press, 1994.

Mangum, Garth L., and Bruce D. Blumell. *The Mormons' War on Poverty: A History of LDS Welfare, 1830–1990*. Salt Lake City: University of Utah Press, 1993.

Matthews, Robert J. *"A Plainer Translation": Joseph Smith's Translation of the Bible*. Provo, UT: Brigham Young University Press, 1975.

McKiernan, F. Mark, Alma Blair, and Paul M. Edwards, eds. *The Restoration Movement: Essays in Mormon History*. Lawrence, KS: Coronado Press, 1973.

Paul, Erich Robert. *Science, Religion, and Mormon Cosmology*. Urbana/Chicago: University of Illinois Press, 1992

Priddis, Ron, and Gary James Bergera. *The Lord's University: Inside BYU*. Salt Lake City: Signature Books, 1994.

Quinn, D. Michael. *Early Mormonism and the Magic World View*. Salt Lake City: Signature Books, 1987.

——. "LDS Church Finances from the 1830s to the 1990s." *Sunstone* 19 (June 1996): 17–29.

——. *The Mormon Hierarchy: Extensions of Power*. Salt Lake City: Signature Books, 1997.

——. *The Mormon Hierarchy: Origins of Power*. Salt Lake City: Signature Books, 1994.

——, ed. *The New Mormon History: Revisionist Essays on the Past*. Salt Lake City: Signature Books, 1992.

Riess, Jana, and Christopher Kimball Bigelow. *Mormonism for Dummies*. Hoboken, NJ: Wiley, 2005.

Roberts, B. H. *A Comprehensive History of the Church of Jesus Christ of Latter-day Saints*. 6 vols. Salt Lake City: The Church of Jesus Christ of Latter-day Saints, 1930.

Shepherd, Gordon, and Gary Shepherd. *A Kingdom Transformed: Themes in the Development of Mormonism*. Salt Lake City: University of Utah Press, 1984.

Shields, Steven L. *Divergent Paths of the Restoration: A History of the Latter-day Saint Movement*. Bountiful, UT: Restoration Research, 1982.

Shipps, Jan. *Mormonism: The Story of a New Religious Tradition*. Urbana/Chicago: University of Illinois Press, 1985.

Smith, George D., ed. *Faithful History: Essays in Writing Mormon History*. Salt Lake City: Signature Books, 1992.

Talbot, Wilburn D. *The Acts of the Modern Apostles*. Salt Lake City: Randall Books, 1985.

Tobler, Douglas F., and Nelson B. Wadsworth. *The History of the Mormons in Photographs and Text, 1830 to Present*. New York: Saint Martin's Press, 1987.

Todd, Jay M. *The Saga of the Book of Abraham*. Salt Lake City: Deseret Book, 1969.

Underwood, Grant. *The Millenarian World of Early Mormonism*. Urbana: University of Illinois Press, 1993.

Van Wagoner, Richard S. *Mormon Polygamy: A History*. Salt Lake City: Signature Books, 1989.

Walker, Ronald W. "Golden Memories: Remembering Life in a Mormon Village." *Brigham Young University Studies* 37 (1997–98): 191–218.

———. "Seeking the 'Remnant': The Native American during the Joseph Smith Period." *Journal of Mormon History* 19 (Spring 1993): 1–33.

Wilcox, Pearl. *Roots of the Reorganized Latter Day Saints in Southern Iowa*. Independence, MO: n.p., 1989.

Wilkinson, Ernest L., ed. *Brigham Young University: The First One Hundred Years*. 4 vols. Provo, UT: Brigham Young University Press, 1976–1976.

Wilkinson, Ernest L., and W. Cleon Skousen. *Brigham Young University: A School of Destiny*. Provo, UT: Brigham Young University Press, 1976.

Winn, Kenneth H. *Exiles in a Land of Liberty: Mormons in America, 1830–1846*. Chapel Hill/London: University of North Carolina Press, 1989.

Yorgason, Laurence M. "Preview on a Study of the Social and Geographical Origins of Early Mormon Converts, 1830–1845." *Brigham Young University Studies* 10 (Spring 1970): 279–82.

New York Period

Anderson, Richard Lloyd. *Investigating the Book of Mormon Witnesses*. Salt Lake City: Deseret Book, 1980.

———. *Joseph Smith's New England Heritage: Influences of Grandfathers Solomon Mack and Asael Smith*. Salt Lake City: Deseret Book, 1971.

———. "The Mature Joseph Smith and Treasure Searching." *Brigham Young University Studies* 24 (Fall 1984): 489–560.

Arrington, Leonard J. "Mormonism: From Its New York Beginnings." *New York History* 61 (October 1980): 387–410.

Backman, Milton V., Jr. *American Religions and the Rise of Mormonism*. Rev. ed. Salt Lake City: Deseret Book, 1970.

———. *Eyewitness Accounts of the Restoration*. Salt Lake City: Deseret Book, 1986.

———. *Joseph Smith's First Vision: Confirming Evidences and Contemporary Accounts*. 2nd ed. Salt Lake City: Bookcraft, 1980.

Hill, Marvin S. "The Rise of Mormonism in the Burned-over District: Another View." *New York History* 61 (October 1980): 411–30.

Madsen, Gordon A. "Joseph Smith's 1826 Trial: The Legal Setting." *Brigham Young University Studies* 30 (Spring 1990): 91–108.

Marquadt, H. Michael, and Wesley P. Walters. *Inventing Mormonism: Tradition and the Historical Record*. Salt Lake City: Signature Books, 1994.

Morris, Larry E. "Oliver Cowdery's Vermont Years and the Origins of Mormonism." *Brigham Young University Studies* 39 (2000): 106–129.

Paul, Robert. "Joseph Smith and the Manchester Library." *Brigham Young University Studies* 22 (Summer 1982): 333–56.

Perciaccante, Marianne. "Backlash against Formalism: Early Mormonism's Appeal in Jefferson County." *Journal of Mormon History* 19 (Fall 1993): 35–63.

Prince, Gregory A. *Having Authority: The Origins and Development of Priesthood during the Ministry of Joseph Smith*. Independence, MO: Independence Press, 1993.

———. *Power from On High: The Development of Mormon Priesthood*. Salt Lake City: Signature Books, 1995.

Quinn, D. Michael. "The First Months of Mormonism: A Contemporary View by Rev. Diedrich Willers." *New York History* 54 (July 1973): 317–33.

Underwood, Grant. "Early Mormon Millenarianism: Another Look." *Church History* 54 (June 1985): 215–29.

———. *The Millenarian World of Early Mormonism*. Urbana: University of Illinois Press, 1993

Vogel, Dan. "The Locations of Joseph Smith's Early Treasure Quests." *Dialogue: A Journal of Mormon Thought* 27 (Fall 1994): 197–231.

Walker, Ronald W. "Joseph Smith: The Palmyra Seer." *Brigham Young University Studies* 24 (Fall 1984): 461–72.

Ohio Period

Adams, Dale W. "Chartering the Kirtland Bank." *Brigham Young University Studies* 23 (Fall 1983): 467–82.

Alexander, Thomas G. "Wilford Woodruff and Zion's Camp: Baptism by Fire and the Spiritual Confirmation of a Future Prophet." *Brigham Young University Studies* 39 (2000): 130–46.

Anderson, Karl R. *Joseph Smith's Kirtland: Eyewitness Accounts*. Salt Lake City: Deseret Book, 1989.

Backman, Milton V., Jr. *The Heavens Resound: A History of the Latter-day Saints in Ohio, 1830–1838*. Salt Lake City: Deseret Book, 1983.

——. "The Quest for a Restoration: The Birth of Mormonism in Ohio." *Brigham Young University Studies* 12 (Summer 1972): 346–64.

Bitton, Davis. "Kirtland as a Center of Missionary Activity, 1830–1838." *Brigham Young University Studies* 11 (Summer 1971): 497–516.

Grandstaff, Mark R., and Milton V. Backman Jr. "The Social Origins of the Kirtland Mormons." *Brigham Young University Studies* 30 (Spring 1990): 47–66.

Hill, Marvin S. "Cultural Crisis in the Mormon Kingdom: A Reconsideration of the Causes of Kirtland Dissent." *Church History* 49 (September 1980): 286–97.

Hill, Marvin S., C. Keith Rooker, and Larry T. Wimmer. *The Kirtland Economy Revisited*. Provo, UT: Brigham Young University Press, 1977.

Launius, Roger D. "The Dream Shattered: The Abandonment of the Kirtland Temple, 1837–1862." *Restoration Studies* 5 (April 1986): 13–19.

——. *The Kirtland Temple: A Historical Narrative*. Independence, MO: Herald Publishing House, 1986.

——. "The Latter Day Saints in Ohio: Writing the History of Mormonism's Middle Period." *John Whitmer Historical Association Journal* 16 (1996): 31–56.

Layton, Robert L. "Kirtland: A Perspective on Time and Place." *Brigham Young University Studies* 11 (Summer 1971): 423–38.

Matthews, Robert J. "The 'New Translation' of the Bible, 1830–33: Doctrinal Development during the Kirtland Era." *Brigham Young University Studies* 11 (Summer 1971): 400–423.

McKiernan, F. Mark. "The Conversion of Sidney Rigdon to Mormonism." *Dialogue: A Journal of Mormon Thought* 5 (Summer 1970): 71–78.

Newell, Linda King, and Valeen Tippetts Avery. "Sweet Counsel and Seas of Tribulation: The Religious Life of the Women in Kirtland." *Brigham Young University Studies* 20 (Winter 1980): 151–62.

Parkin, Max H. "Mormon Political Involvement in Ohio." *Brigham Young University Studies* 9 (Summer 1969): 484–502.

Radke, Andrea G. "We Also Marched: The Women and Children of Zion's Camp, 1834." *Brigham Young University Studies* 39 (2000): 147–65.

Robison, Elwin C. *The First Mormon Temple: Design, Construction, and Historic Context of the Kirtland Temple*. Provo, UT: Brigham Young University Press, 1997.

Missouri Period

Anderson, Richard Lloyd. "Atchison's Letters and the Causes of Mormon Expulsion from Missouri." *Brigham Young University Studies* 26 (Summer 1986): 3–47.

——. "Jackson County in Early Mormon Descriptions." *Missouri Historical Review* 65 (April 1971): 270–93.

Arrington, Leonard J. "Early Mormon Communitarianism: The Law of Consecration and Stewardship." *Western Humanities Review* 7 (Autumn 1953): 341–69.

Baugh, Alexander L. *A Call to Arms: The 1838 Mormon Defense of Northern Missouri.* Provo, UT: Joseph Fielding Smith Institute for Latter-day Saint History/BYU Studies, 2000.

——. "Missouri Governor Lilburn W. Boggs and the Mormons." *John Whitmer Historical Association Journal* 16 (1998): 111–132.

Blair, Alma. "The Haun's Mill Massacre." *Brigham Young University Studies* 13 (Autumn 1972): 62–67.

Bushman, Richard L. "Mormon Persecution in Missouri, 1833." *Brigham Young University Studies* 3 (Autumn 1960): 11–20.

Crawley, Peter, and Richard L. Anderson. "The Political and Social Realities of Zion's Camp." *Brigham Young University Studies* 14 (Summer 1974): 406–20.

Durham, Reed C., Jr. "The Election Day Battle at Gallatin." *Brigham Young University Studies* 13 (Autumn 1972): 36–61.

Gentry, Leland H. "The Danite Band of 1838." *Brigham Young University Studies* 14 (Summer 1974): 421–50.

Hartley, William G. "'Almost Too Intolerable a Burthen': The Winter Exodus from Missouri, 1838–39." *Journal of Mormon History* 18 (Fall 1992): 6–40.

Jennings, Warren A. "The Army of Israel Marches into Missouri." *Missouri Historical Review* 62 (January 1968): 107–35.

——. "The Expulsion of the Mormons from Jackson County, Missouri." *Missouri Historical Review* 64 (October 1969): 41–63.

——. "Factors in the Destruction of the Mormon Press in Missouri, 1833." *Utah Historical Quarterly* 35 (Winter 1967): 56–76.

Johnson, Clark V. "The Missouri Redress Petitions: A Reappraisal of Mormon Persecutions in Missouri." *Brigham Young University Studies* 26 (Spring 1986): 31–44.

Launius, Roger. *Zion's Camp: Expedition to Missouri, 1834.* Independence, MO: Herald Publishing House, 1984.

LeSueur, Stephen C. *The 1838 Mormon War in Missouri.* Columbia: University of Missouri Press, 1987.

——. "The Danites Reconsidered: Were They Vigilantes or Just the Mormons' Version of the Elks Club?" *John Whitmer Historical Association Journal* 14 (1994): 35–51.

——. "High Treason and Murder: The Examination of Mormon Prisoners at Richmond, Missouri, in November 1838." *Brigham Young University Studies* 26 (Spring 1986): 3–30.

Lyon, T. Edgar. "Independence, Missouri, and the Mormons, 1827–1833." *Brigham Young University Studies* 13 (Autumn 1972): 10–19.

Madsen, Gordon A. "Joseph Smith and the Missouri Court of Inquiry: Austin A. King's Quest for Hostages." *Brigham Young University Studies* 43 (2004): 92–136.

Maynard, Gregory. "Alexander Doniphan: Man of Justice." *Brigham Young University Studies* 13 (Summer 1973): 462–72.

McKiernan, F. Mark. "Sidney Rigdon's Missouri Speeches." *Brigham Young University Studies* 11 (Autumn 1970): 90–92.

McLaws, Monte B. "The Attempted Assassination of Missouri's Ex-Governor, Lilburn W. Boggs." *Missouri Historical Review* 60 (October 1965): 50–62.

Richards, Paul C. "Missouri Persecutions: Petitions for Redress." *Brigham Young University Studies* 13 (Summer 1973): 520–43.

Roberts, B. H. *The Missouri Persecutions.* Salt Lake City: Bookcraft, 1965.

Illinois Period

Allen, James B., Ronald K. Esplin, and David J. Whittaker. *Men with a Mission: The Quorum of the Twelve Apostles in the British Isles, 1837–1841.* Salt Lake City: Deseret Book, 1992.

Bishop, M. Guy, et al. "Death at Mormon Nauvoo, 1843–1845." *Western Illinois Regional Studies* 9 (Fall 1986): 70–83.

———. "Sex Roles, Marriage and Childrearing at Mormon Nauvoo." *Western Illinois Regional Studies* 11 (Fall 1988): 30–45.

———. "'What Has Become of Our Fathers?' Baptism for the Dead at Nauvoo." *Dialogue: A Journal of Mormon Thought* 23 (Summer 1990): 85–97.

Bitton, Davis. "The Martyrdom of Joseph Smith in Early Mormon Writings." *John Whitmer Historical Association Journal* 3 (1983): 29–39. Revised as a chapter in Bitton, *The Martyrdom Remembered* (1994).

Black, Susan Easton. "How Large Was the Population of Nauvoo?" *Brigham Young University Studies* 35 (1995): 91–94.

Cannon, Janath. *Nauvoo Panorama: Views of Nauvoo before, during, and after Its Rise, Fall, and Restoration.* Salt Lake City: Nauvoo Restoration, 1991.

Clark, David L. "The Mormons of the Wisconsin Territory, 1835–1848." *Brigham Young University Studies* 37 (1997–98): 57–85.

Compton, Todd. *In Sacred Loneliness: The Plural Wives of Joseph Smith.* Salt Lake City: Signature Books, 1997.

Daynes, Kathryn M. "Family Ties: Belief and Practice in Nauvoo." *John Whitmer Historical Association Journal* 8 (1988): 63–75.

Ehat, Andrew F. "'It Seems Like Heaven Began on Earth': Joseph Smith and the Constitution of the Kingdom of God." *Brigham Young University Studies* 20 (Spring 1980): 253–79.

Ellsworth, Paul. "Mobocracy and the Rule of Law: American Press Reaction to the Murder of Joseph Smith." *Brigham Young University Studies* 20 (Fall 1979): 71–82.

Flanders, Robert B. *Nauvoo: Kingdom on the Mississippi*. Urbana/Chicago: University of Illinois Press, 1965.

Gardner, Hamilton. "The Nauvoo Legion, 1840–1845: A Unique Military Organization." *Journal of the Illinois State Historical Society* 65 (Summer 1961): 181–97.

Gayler, George R. "The 'Expositor' Affair: Prelude to the Downfall of Joseph Smith." *Northwest Missouri State College Studies* 25 (February 1961): 3–15.

———. "Governor Ford and the Death of Joseph and Hyrum Smith." *Journal of the Illinois State Historical Society* 50 (Winter 1957): 391–411.

———. "The Mormons and Politics in Illinois: 1839–1844." *Journal of the Illinois State Historical Society* 49 (Spring 1956): 48–66.

Givens, George W. *Old Nauvoo: Everyday Life in the City of Joseph*. Salt Lake City: Deseret Book, 1990.

Godfrey, Kenneth W. "Crime and Punishment in Mormon Nauvoo, 1839–1846." *Brigham Young University Studies* 32 (Winter/Spring 1992): 195–227.

———. "Non-Mormon Views of the Martyrdom: A Look at Some Early Published Accounts." *John Whitmer Historical Association Journal* 7 (1987): 12–20.

Hallwas, John E., and Roger D. Launius. *Cultures in Conflict: A Documentary History of the Mormon War in Illinois*. Logan: Utah State University Press, 1999.

Hamilton, Marshall. "From Assassination to Expulsion: Two Years of Distrust, Hostility, and Violence." *Brigham Young University Studies* 32 (Winter/Spring 1992): 229–48.

Hampshire, Annette P. *Mormonism in Conflict: The Nauvoo Years*. New York: Edwin Mellen Press, 1985.

———. "The Triumph of Mobocracy in Hancock County, 1844–1845." *Western Illinois Regional Studies* 5 (Spring 1982): 17–37.

Harrington, Virginia S. *Rediscovery of the Nauvoo Temple*. Salt Lake City: Nauvoo Restoration, 1971.

Hartley, William G. "Nauvoo Stake, Priesthood Quorums, and the Church's First Wards." *Brigham Young University Studies* 32 (Winter/Spring 1992): 57–80.

Holzapfel, Richard Netzel, and Jeni Broberg Holzapfel. *Women of Nauvoo*. Salt Lake City: Bookcraft, 1992.

Homer, Michael W. "'Similarity of Priesthood in Masonry': The Relationship between Freemasonry and Mormonism." *Dialogue: A Journal of Mormon Thought* 27 (Fall 1994): 1–113.

Jeffress, Melinda Evans. "Mapping Historic Nauvoo." *Brigham Young University Studies* 32 (Winter/Spring 1992): 269–75.

Jensen, Richard L. "Transplanted Zion: The Impact of British Latter-day Saint Immigration upon Nauvoo." *Brigham Young University Studies* 31 (Winter 1991): 76–87.

Jolley, Jerry C. "The Sting of the Wasp: Early Nauvoo Newspaper—April 1842 to April 1843." *Brigham Young University Studies* 22 (Fall 1982): 487–96.

Jorgensen, Lynne Watkins, et al. "The Mantle of the Prophet Joseph Passes to Brother Brigham: A Collective Spiritual Witness." *Brigham Young University Studies* 36 (1996–97): 125–204.

Kimball, James L., Jr. "The Nauvoo Charter: A Reinterpretation." *Journal of the Illinois State Historical Society* 64 (Spring 1971): 66–78.

———. "A Wall to Defend Zion: The Nauvoo Charter." *Brigham Young University Studies* 15 (Summer 1975): 491–97.

Kimball, Stanley B. "Heber C. Kimball and Family: The Nauvoo Years." *Brigham Young University Studies* 15 (Summer 1975): 447–79.

———. "The Mormons in Illinois, 1838–1846: A Special Introduction." *Journal of the Illinois State Historical Society* 64 (Spring 1971): 4–21.

Launius, Roger D. "The Murders in Carthage: Non-Mormon Reports of the Assassination of the Smith Brothers." *John Whitmer Historical Association Journal* 15 (1995): 17–34.

Launius, Roger D., and John E. Hallwas, eds. *Kingdom on the Mississippi Revisited: Nauvoo in Mormon History*. Urbana/Chicago: University of Illinois Press, 1996.

LeBaron, E. Dale. "Benjamin Franklin Johnson in Nauvoo: Friend, Confidant, and Defender of the Prophet." *Brigham Young University Studies* 32 (Winter/Spring 1992): 175–94.

Leonard, Glen M. "Letters Home: The Immigrant View from Nauvoo." *Brigham Young University Studies* 31 (Winter 1991): 89–100.

———. *Nauvoo: A Place of Peace, a People of Promise*. Salt Lake City: Deseret Book, and Provo, UT: Brigham Young University Press, 2002.

———. "Picturing the Nauvoo Legion." *Brigham Young University Studies* 35 (1995): 95–135.

Lyon, T. Edgar. "Doctrinal Development of the Church during the Nauvoo Sojourn, 1839–1846." *Brigham Young University Studies* 15 (Summer 1975): 435–46.

Miller, David E., and Della S. Miller. *Nauvoo: The City of Joseph*. Santa Barbara, CA/Salt Lake City: Peregrine Smith, 1974.

Mulder, William. "Nauvoo Observed." *Brigham Young University Studies* 32 (Winter/Spring 1992): 95–118.

Oaks, Dallin H. "The Suppression of the Nauvoo Expositor." *Utah Law Review* 9 (Winter 1965): 862–903.

Oaks, Dallin H., and Marvin S. Hill. *Carthage Conspiracy: The Trial of the Accused Assassins of Joseph Smith.* Urbana/Chicago: University of Illinois Press, 1975.

Poll, Richard D. "Joseph Smith and the Presidency, 1844." *Dialogue: A Journal of Mormon Thought* 3 (Autumn 1968): 17–21.

Porter, Larry C., and Milton V. Backman Jr. "Doctrine and the Temple in Nauvoo." *Brigham Young University Studies* 32 (Winter/Spring 1992): 41–56.

Quinn, D. Michael. "The Council of Fifty and Its Members, 1844 to 1945." *Brigham Young University Studies* 20 (Winter 1980): 163–97.

Robertson, Margaret C. "The Campaign the Kingdom: The Activities of the Electioneers in Joseph Smith's Presidential Campaign." *Brigham Young University Studies* 39 (2000): 147–180.

Rowley, Dennis. "The Mormon Experience in the Wisconsin Pineries, 1841–1845." *Brigham Young University Studies* 32 (Winter/Spring 1992): 119–48.

Rugh, Susan Sessions. "Conflict in the Countryside: The Mormon Settlement at Macedonia, Illinois." *Brigham Young University Studies* 32 (Winter/Spring 1992): 149–74.

Saunders, Richard L. "Officers and Arms: The 1843 General Return of the Nauvoo Legion's Second Cohort." *Brigham Young University Studies* 35 (1995): 138–51.

Smith, George D. "Nauvoo Roots of Mormon Polygamy, 1841–46: A Preliminary Demographic Report." *Dialogue: A Journal of Mormon Thought* 27 (Spring 1994): 1–72.

Tanner, Terence A. "The Mormon Press in Nauvoo, 1839–1846." *Western Illinois Regional Studies* 11 (Fall 1988): 5–29.

Van Orden, Bruce A. "William W. Phelps' Service in Nauvoo as Joseph Smith's Political Clerk." *Brigham Young University Studies* 32 (Winter/Spring 1992): 81–94.

Van Wagoner, Richard S. "The Making of a Mormon Myth: The 1844 Transfiguration of Brigham Young." *Dialogue: A Journal of Mormon Thought* 28 (Winter 1995): 1–24.

The Exodus

Bashore, Melvin L. "On the Heels of the Handcart Tragedy: Mormondom's Forgotten 1856 Wagon Companies." *Annals of Wyoming* 68 (Summer 1996): 38–49.

Beecher, Maureen Ursenbach. "Women in Winter Quarters." *Sunstone* 8 (July–August 1983): 11–19.

Bennett, Richard E. "Cousin Laman in the Wilderness: The Beginnings of Brigham Young's Indian Policy." *Nebraska History* 67 (Spring 1986): 68–82.

———. "Eastward to Eden: The Nauvoo Rescue Missions." *Dialogue: A Journal of Mormon Thought* 19 (Winter 1986): 100–108.

———. "Lamanism, Lymanism, and Cornfields." *Journal of Mormon History* 13 (1986–1987): 45–59.

———. *Mormons at the Missouri, 1846–52: "And Should We Die."* Norman: University of Oklahoma Press, 1987.

———. *We'll Find the Place: The Mormon Exodus, 1846–1848.* Salt Lake City: Deseret Book, 1997.

Bigler, David L., and Will Bagley, eds. *Army of Israel: Mormon Battalion Narratives.* Vol. 4 of *Kingdom in the West: The Mormons and the American Frontier.* Spokane: WA: Arthur H. Clark Co., 2000.

Bitton, Davis. "Mormons in Texas: The Ill-fated Lyman Wight Colony, 1844–1858." *Arizona and the West* 11 (Spring 1969): 5–26.

Black, Susan Easton, and William G. Hartley, eds. *The Iowa Mormon Trail: Legacy of Faith and Courage.* Orem, UT: Helix, 1997.

Brown, Joseph E. *The Mormon Trek West: The Journey of American Exiles.* Garden City, NY: Doubleday, 1980.

Bryson, Conrey. *Winter Quarters.* Salt Lake City: Deseret Book, 1986.

Campbell, Eugene. "Authority Conflicts in the Mormon Battalion." *Brigham Young University Studies* 8 (Winter 1968): 127–42.

Carter, Lyndia. "The Mormon Handcart Companies." *Overland Journal* 13 (1995): 2–18.

Christian, Lewis Clark. "Mormon Foreknowledge of the West." *Brigham Young University Studies* 21 (Fall 1981): 403–15.

Coates, Lawrence. "Cultural Conflict: Mormons and Indians in Nebraska." *Brigham Young University Studies* 24 (Summer 1983): 275–300.

———. "Refugees Meet: The Mormons and Indians in Iowa." *Brigham Young University Studies* 21 (Fall 1981): 491–514.

Crockett, David R. *Saints in Exile: A Day-by-Day Pioneer Experience, Nauvoo to Council Bluffs.* Tucson, AZ: LDS-Gems Press, 1996.

Gardner, Hamilton. "The Command and Staff of the Mormon Battalion in the Mexican War." *Utah Historical Quarterly* 29 (October 1952): 331–52.

Homer, Michael W. "After Winter Quarters and Council Bluffs: The Mormons in Nebraska Territory, 1854–1867." *Nebraska History* 65 (Winter 1984): 467–83.

Kimball, Stanley B. *Historic Sites and Markers along the Mormon and Other Great Western Trails.* Urbana/Chicago: University of Illinois Press, 1988.

——. "Mormon Trail Network in Nebraska, 1846–1868." *Brigham Young University Studies* 24 (Summer 1984): 321–36.

Kimball, Stanley B., and Hal Knight. *111 Days to Zion*. Salt Lake City: Deseret News Press, 1978.

King, Robert R. "The Enduring Significance of the Mormon Trek." *Dialogue: A Journal of Mormon Thought* 13 (Summer 1980): 102–7.

Melville, J. Keith. *Conflict and Compromise: The Mormons in Mid Nineteenth-Century American Politics*. Provo, UT: Brigham Young University Press, 1975.

Powell, A. Kent. *Mormon Battalion Trail Guide*. Salt Lake City: Utah State Historical Society, 1972.

Ricketts, Norma Baldwin. *The Mormon Battalion: United States Army of the West, 1846–1848*. Logan: Utah State University Press, 1996.

Stegner, Wallace. *The Gathering of Zion: The Story of the Mormon Trail*. New York: McGraw Hill, 1964; Salt Lake City: Westwater Press, 1981.

Tyler, Daniel. *A Concise History of the Mormon Battalion in the Mexican War, 1846–47*. N.p., 1881. Reprint, Chicago: Rio Grande Press, 1964.

Utah Period

Alexander, Thomas G. "Charles S. Zane, Apostle of the New Era." *Utah Historical Quarterly* 34 (Fall 1966): 290–314.

——. "Cooperation, Conflict, and Compromise: Women, Men, and the Environment in Salt Lake City, 1890–1930." *Brigham Young University Studies* 35 (1995): 7–39.

——. "An Experiment in Progressive Legislation: The Granting of Woman Suffrage in Utah in 1870." *Utah Historical Quarterly* 38 (Winter 1970): 20–30.

——. "Federal Authority versus Polygamic Theocracy: James B. McKean and the Mormons, 1870–1875." *Dialogue: A Journal of Mormon Thought* 1 (Autumn 1966): 85–100.

——. "Some Meanings of Utah History." *Utah Historical Quarterly* 64 (Spring 1996): 155–67.

——. "Utah's Constitution: A Reflection of the Territorial Experience." *Utah Historical Quarterly* 64 (Summer 1996): 264–81.

——. *Utah: The Right Place*. Salt Lake City: Gibbs Smith, 1995.

——. "Wilford Woodruff, Intellectual Progress, and the Growth of an Amateur Scientific and Technological Tradition in Early Territorial Utah." *Utah Historical Quarterly* 59 (Spring 1991): 164–88.

Allen, James B. "'Good Guys' vs. 'Good Guys': Rudger Clawson, John Sharp, and Civil Disobedience in Nineteenth-Century Utah." *Utah Historical Quarterly* 48 (Spring 1980): 148–74.

Anderson, Nels. *Desert Saints: The Mormon Frontier in Utah*. Chicago: University of Chicago Press, 1942.

Arrington, Leonard J. *Great Basin Kingdom: An Economic History of the Latter-day Saints*. Cambridge, MA: Harvard University Press, 1958.

——. "Rural Life Among Nineteenth-Century Mormons: The Woman's Experience." *Agricultural History* 58 (July 1984): 239–46.

Arrington, Leonard J., and Dean May. "'A Different Mode of Life': Irrigation and Society in Nineteenth-Century Utah." *Agricultural History* 49 (January 1975): 3–20.

Arrington, Leonard J., and Linda Wilcox. "From Subsistence to Golden Age: Cache Valley Agriculture, 1859–1900." *Utah Historical Quarterly* 57 (Fall 1989): 340–69.

Arrington, Leonard J., Dean May, and Feramorz Fox. *Building the City of God: Community and Cooperation among the Mormons*. Salt Lake City: Deseret Book, 1976.

Ashton, Wendell J. *Voice in the West: Biography of a Pioneer Newspaper*. New York: Duell, Sloan, & Pearce, 1950.

Bagley, Will. *Blood of the Prophets: Brigham Young and the Massacre at Mountain Meadows*. Norman: University of Oklahoma Press, 2002

Beecher, Maureen Ursenbach. "Women's Work on the Mormon Frontier." *Utah Historical Quarterly* 49 (Summer 1981): 276–90.

Bergera, Gary James. *Conflict in the Quorum: Orson Pratt, Brigham Young, Joseph Smith*. Salt Lake City: Signature Books, 2002.

Bigler, David L. *Forgotten Kingdom: The Mormon Theocracy in the American West, 1847–1896*. Spokane, WA: Arthur H. Clark, Co., 1998.

Bitton, Davis. "B. H. Roberts at the World Parliament of Religions." *Sunstone* 7 (January–February 1982): 46–51.

——. "The B. H. Roberts Case of 1898–1900." *Utah Historical Quarterly* 25 (January 1957): 27–46. Revised and reprinted in Bitton, *"The Ritualization of Mormon History," and Other Essays* (1994).

——. "'Strange Ramblings': The Ideal and Practice of Sermons in Early Mormonism." *Brigham Young University Studies* 41 (2002): 4–28.

——. "Zion's Rowdies: Growing up on the Mormon Frontier." *Utah Historical Quarterly* 50 (Spring 1982): 182–95. Reprinted in Bitton, *The Ritualization of Mormon History and Other Essays* (1994).

Bitton, Davis, and Linda P. Wilcox. "The Transformation of Utah's Agriculture, 1847–1900." In Thomas G. Alexander and John F. Bluth, eds., *The Twentieth Century American West*, pp. 57–83. Provo, UT: Charles Redd Center for Western Studies, 1983.

Brooks, Juanita. *The Mountain Meadows Massacre*. Norman: University of Oklahoma Press, 1962.

Buchanan, Frederick S. "Education Among the Mormons: Brigham Young and the Schools of Utah." *History of Education Quarterly* 22 (Winter 1982): 435–59.

Campbell, Eugene E. *Establishing Zion: The Mormon Church in the American West, 1847–69*. Salt Lake City: Signature Books, 1988.

Cannon, Kenneth L., II. "After the Manifesto: Mormon Polygamy, 1890–1906." *Sunstone* 8 (January–April 1983): 27–35.

———. "Mountain Common Law: The Extralegal Punishment of Seducers in Early Utah." *Utah Historical Quarterly* 51 (Fall 1983): 308–27.

Clayton, James L. "The Supreme Court, Polygamy and the Enforcement of Morals in Nineteenth Century America: An Analysis of *Reynolds v. United States*." *Dialogue: A Journal of Mormon Thought* 12 (Winter 1979): 46–61.

Cornwall, J. Spencer. *A Century of Singing: The Salt Lake Mormon Tabernacle Choir*. Salt Lake City: Deseret Book, 1958.

Cornwall, Rebecca, and Leonard J. Arrington. *Rescue of the 1856 Handcart Companies*. Provo, UT: Charles H. Redd Monographs in Western History, 1981.

Cowan, Richard O. "The Mormon Battalion and the Gadsden Purchase." *Brigham Young University Studies* 37 (1997–1998): 48–64.

Davies, J. Kenneth. *Mormon Gold: The Story of California's Mormon Argonauts*. Salt Lake City: Olympus Publishing, 1984.

Daynes, Kathryn M. *More Wives Than One: Transformation of the Mormon Marriage System, 1840–1910*. Urbana: University of Illinois Press, 2001.

———. "Single Men in a Polygamous Society: Male Marriage Patterns in Manti, Utah." *Journal of Mormon History* 24 (Spring 1998): 89–111.

Dwyer, Robert Joseph. *The Gentile Comes to Utah: A Study in Religious and Social Conflict, 1862–1890*. 2nd ed., rev. Salt Lake City: Western Epics, 1971.

Ekins, Roger Robin, ed. *Defending Zion: George Q. Cannon and the California Mormon Newspaper Wars of 1856–1857*. Spokane, WA: Arthur H. Clark Co., 2002.

Embry, Jessie L. "Burden or Pleasure? A Profile of LDS Polygamous Husbands." *Dialogue: A Journal of Mormon Thought* 20 (Winter 1987): 158–66.

———. "Effects of Polygamy on Mormon Women." *Frontiers* 7 (No. 3, 1984): 56–61.

———. "Little Berlin: Swiss Saints of the Logan Tenth Ward." *Utah Historical Quarterly* 56 (Summer 1988): 222–35.

———. *Mormon Polygamous Families: Life in the Principle*. Salt Lake City: University of Utah Press, 1987.

———. "Mormon Polygamy: Unconventional Practice or Adaptation to American Values?" *Journal of Unconventional History* 3 (1992): 42–56.

Embry, Jessie L., and Martha S. Bradley. "Mothers and Daughters in Polygamy." *Dialogue: A Journal of Mormon Thought* 18 (Fall 1985): 99–107.

Flake, Kathleen. *The Politics of American Religious Identity: The Seating of Senator Reed Smoot, Mormon Apostle.* Chapel Hill: University of North Carolina Press, 2004.

Furniss, Norman. *The Mormon Conflict, 1850–1859.* New Haven, CT: Yale University Press, 1960.

Godfrey, Kenneth W. "Charles W. Penrose and His Contributions to Utah Statehood." *Utah Historical Quarterly* 64 (Fall 1996): 356–71.

———. "Moses Thatcher in the Dock: His Trials, the Aftermath and His Last Days." *Journal of Mormon History* 24 (Spring 1998): 54–88.

Gordon, Sarah Barringer. *The Mormon Question: Polygamy and Constitutional Conflict in Nineteenth Century America.* Chapel Hill/London: University of North Carolina Press, 2002.

Grow, Stewart L. *A Tabernacle in the Desert.* Salt Lake City: Deseret Book, 1958.

Hafen, LeRoy R., and Ann W. Hafen. "Handcarts to Utah, 1856–1860." *Utah Historical Quarterly* 24 (October 1956): 309–17.

———. *Handcarts to Zion: The Story of a Unique Western Migration, 1856–1860.* Glendale, CA: Arthur H. Clark Co., 1960.

Hartley, William G. "Brigham Young's Overland Trails Revolution: The Creation of the 'Down-and-Back' Wagon-Train System." *Journal of Mormon History* 28.1 (Spring 2002): 1–30.

———. "The Priesthood Reorganization of 1877: Brigham Young's Last Achievement." *Brigham Young University Studies* 20 (Fall 1979): 3–36.

———. "The Seventies in the 1880s: Revelations and Reorganizing." *Dialogue: A Journal of Mormon Thought* 16 (Spring 1983): 62–88.

Heinerman, Joseph. "The Old Folks Day: A Unique Utah Tradition." *Utah Historical Quarterly* 53 (Spring 1985): 157–69.

Homer, Michael W. "The Judiciary and the Common Law in Utah Territory, 1850–61." *Dialogue: A Journal of Mormon Thought* 21 (Spring 1988): 97–108.

Howard, Richard P. "The Changing RLDS Response to Mormon Polygamy: A Preliminary Analysis." *John Whitmer Historical Association Journal* 3 (1983): 14–29.

Iversen, Joan Smyth. "A Debate on the American Home: The Antipolygamy Controversy, 1880–1890." *Journal of the History of Sexuality* 1.4 (April 1991): 585–602.

Johnson, Jeffery Ogden. "Determining and Defining 'Wife': The Brigham Young Households." *Dialogue: A Journal of Mormon Thought* 20 (Fall 1987): 57–70.

Larson, Gustive O. *The "Americanization" of Utah for Statehood*. San Marino, CA: Huntington Library, 1971.

———. "The Mormon Reformation." *Utah Historical Quarterly* 26 (January 1958): 45–63.

———. *Prelude to the Kingdom: Mormon Desert Conquest, a Chapter in American Cooperative Experience*. Francestown, NY: Marshall Jones Co., 1947.

Leonard, Glen M. "The Mormon Boundary Question in the 1849–50 Statehood Debates." *Journal of Mormon History* 18 (Spring 1992): 114–36.

———. "William Allen's Clients: A Socioeconomic Inquiry." *Utah Historical Quarterly* 54 (Winter 1986): 74–87.

Logue, Larry. *A Sermon in the Desert: Belief and Behavior in Early St. George, Utah*. Urbana: University of Illinois Press, 1988.

———. "Tabernacles for Waiting Spirits: Monogamous and Polygamous Fertility in a Mormon Town." *Journal of Family History* 10 (Spring 1985): 60–74.

Long, E. B. *The Saints and the Union: Utah Territory during the Civil War*. Champaign, IL: University of Illinois Press, 1981.

Lyman, E. Leo. "The Political Background of the Woodruff Manifesto." *Dialogue: A Journal of Mormon Thought* 24 (Fall 1991): 21–39.

———. *Political Deliverance: The Mormon Quest for Utah Statehood*. Urbana/Chicago: University of Illinois Press, 1986.

Madsen, Carol Cornwall. "'At Their Peril': Utah Law and the Case of Plural Wives, 1850–1900." *Western Historical Quarterly* 21 (November 1990): 425–43.

———. "Mormon Women and the Struggle for Definition: The Nineteenth-Century Church." *Sunstone* 6 (November–December 1981): 7–11.

Madsen, Carol Cornwall, and Susan Staker Oman. *Sisters and Little Saints: One Hundred Years of Primary*. Salt Lake City: Deseret Book, 1979.

May, Dean L. "People on the Mormon Frontier: Kanab's Families of 1874." *Journal of Family History* 1 (December 1976): 169–92.

———. *Three Frontiers: Family, Land, and Society in the American West, 1850–1900*. New York: Cambridge University Press, 1994.

———. *Utah: A People's History*. Salt Lake City: University of Utah Press, 1987.

———. "Utah Writ Small: Challenge and Change in Kane County's Past." *Utah Historical Quarterly* 53 (Spring 1985): 170–83.

McLaws, Monte B. *Spokesman for the Kingdom: Early Mormon Journalism and the Deseret News, 1830–1898*. Provo, UT: Brigham Young University Press, 1977.

Mehr, Kahlile. "Women's Response to Plural Marriage." *Dialogue: A Journal of Mormon Thought* 18 (Fall 1985): 84–97.

Miller, David S. *Hole-in-the-Rock: An Epic in the Colonization of the Great American West*. Salt Lake City: University of Utah Press, 1959.

Miller, Jeremy M. "A Critique of the Reynolds Decision." *Western State University Law Review* 11 (Spring 1984): 165–98.

Moorman, Donald R., and Gene A. Sessions. *Camp Floyd and the Mormons: The Utah War*. Salt Lake City: University of Utah Press, 1992.

Nelson, Lowry. *The Mormon Village: A Pattern and Techniques of Land Settlement*. Salt Lake City: University of Utah Press, 1952.

Pace, D. Gene. "Changing Patterns of Mormon Financial Administration: Traveling Bishops, Regional Bishops, and Bishop's Agents, 1851–88." *Brigham Young University Studies* 23 (Spring 1983): 183–95.

Peterson, Charles S. "The Hopis and the Mormons, 1858–1873." *Utah Historical Quarterly* 39 (Spring 1971): 179–93.

———. "Jacob Hamblin, Apostle to the Lamanites, and the Indian Mission." *Journal of Mormon History* 2 (1975): 21–34.

Poll, Richard D. "The Mormon Question Enters National Politics, 1850–1856." *Utah Historical Quarterly* 25 (April 1957): 117–31.

———. "The Legislative Antipolygamy Campaign." *Brigham Young University Studies* 26 (Fall 1986): 107–21.

———. "The Move South." *Brigham Young University Studies* 29 (Fall 1989): 65–88.

———. *Quixotic Mediator: Thomas L. Kane and the Utah War*. Ogden, UT: Weber State College Press, 1985.

Poll, Richard D. and William P. MacKinnon. "Causes of the Utah War Reconsidered." *Journal of Mormon History* 20 (Fall 1994): 16–44.

Polson, D. Michol. "The Swedes in Grantsville, Utah, 1860–1900." *Utah Historical Quarterly* 56 (Summer 1988): 208–21.

Quinn, D. Michael. "LDS Church Authority and New Plural Marriages, 1890–1904." *Dialogue: A Journal of Mormon Thought* 18 (Spring 1985): 9–105.

Ricks, Joel E. *Forms and Methods of Early Mormon Settlement in Utah and Surrounding Regions, 1847 to 1877*. Logan: Utah State University Press, 1974.

Sherlock, Richard. "Mormon Migration and Settlement after 1875." *Journal of Mormon History* 2 (1975): 53–68.

Shirts, Morris A., and Kathryn H. Shirts. *A Trial Furnace: Southern Utah's Iron Mission*. Provo, UT: Brigham Young University Press, 2001.

Simmonds, A. J. *The Gentile Comes to Cache Valley: A Study of the Logan Apostasies of 1874 and the Establishment of Non-Mormon Churches in Cache Valley, 1873–1913*. Logan: Utah State University Press, 1976.

Smart, Donna T. "Over the Rim to Red Rock Country: The Parley P. Pratt Exploring Company of 1849." *Utah Historical Quarterly* 62 (Spring 1994): 171–90.

Smart, William B., and Donna T. Smart, eds. *Over the Rim: The Parley P. Pratt Exploring Expedition to Southern Utah, 1849–50.* Logan: Utah State University Press, 1999.

Smith, Craig S. "The Curious Meet the Mormons: Images from Travel Narratives, 1850s and 1860s." *Journal of Mormon History* 24 (Fall 1998): 155–81.

———. "Wyoming, Nebraska Territory: Joseph W. Young and the Mormon Emigration of 1864." *Brigham Young University Studies* 39 (2000): 30–51.

Smith, E. Gary. "The Office of Presiding Patriarch: The Primacy Problem." *Journal of Mormon History* 14 (1988): 35–48.

Snow, Edwina Jo. "British Travelers View the Saints." *Brigham Young University Studies* 31 (Spring 1991): 63–81.

Stott, Clifford L. *Search for Sanctuary: Brigham Young and the White Mountain Expedition.* Salt Lake City: University of Utah Press, 1984.

Van Wagenen, Lola. "In Their Behalf: The Politicization of Mormon Women and the 1870 Franchise." *Dialogue: A Journal of Mormon Thought* 24 (Winter 1991): 31–43.

Walker, Ronald W. "B. H. Roberts and the Woodruff Manifesto." *Brigham Young University Studies* 22 (Summer 1982): 363–66.

———. "Brigham Young on the Social Order." *Brigham Young University Studies* 28 (Summer 1988): 37–52.

———. "Growing Up in Early Utah: The Wasatch Literary Association, 1874–1878." *Sunstone* 6 (November–December 1981): 44–51.

———. "Toward a Reconstruction of Mormon and Indian Relations, 1847–1877." *Brigham Young University Studies* 19 (Fall 1989): 23–42.

———. *Wayward Saints: The Godbeites and Brigham Young.* Urbana: University of Illinois Press, 1998.

———. "When the Spirits Did Abound: Nineteenth-Century Utah's Encounter with Free-Thought Radicalism." *Utah Historical Quarterly* 50 (Fall 1982): 304–24.

West, Ray B. *Kingdom of the Saints: The Story of Brigham Young and the Mormons.* New York: Viking, 1957.

Whittaker, David J. "The Bone in the Throat: Orson Pratt and the Public Announcement of Plural Marriage." *Western Historical Quarterly* 18 (July 1987): 293–314.

Woods, Fred E. "East to West through North and South: Mormon Immigration during the Civil War." *Brigham Young University Studies* 39 (2000): 7–29.

Twentieth Century

Alexander, Thomas G. *Mormonism in Transition: A History of the Latter-day Saints, 1890–1930*. Urbana/Chicago: University of Illinois Press, 1986.

———. "The Reconstruction of Mormon Doctrine: From Joseph Smith to Progressive Theology." *Sunstone* 5 (July–August 1980): 24–33.

———. "Reed Smoot, the LDS Church, and Progressive Legislation, 1903–1933." *Dialogue: A Journal of Mormon Thought* 7 (Spring 1972): 47–56.

Allen, James B. "On Becoming a Universal Church: Some Historical Perspectives." *Dialogue: A Journal of Mormon Thought* 25 (March 1992): 13–36.

Allen, James B., Jessie L. Embry, and Kahlile B. Mehr. *Hearts Turned to the Fathers: A History of the Genealogical Society of Utah, 1894–1994*. Provo, UT: BYU Studies, 1995.

Anderson, Paul. "Heroic Nostalgia: Enshrining the Mormon Past." *Sunstone* 5 (July–August 1980): 47–55.

Arrington, Leonard J. "The Founding of the LDS Institutes of Religion." *Dialogue: A Journal of Mormon Thought* 2 (Summer 1967): 137–47.

———. "Origin of the Welfare Plan of the Church." *Brigham Young University Studies* 5 (Winter 1964): 67–85.

Bennion, Lowell C. "Ben," and Lawrence A. Young. "The Uncertain Dynamics of LDS Expansion, 1950–2020." *Dialogue: A Journal of Mormon Thought* 29 (Spring 1996): 8–32.

Calman, Charles Jeffrey, and Kaufman, William I. *The Mormon Tabernacle Choir*. New York: Harper & Row, 1979.

Cannon, Brian Q., and Jacob W. Olmstead. "Scandalous Film: The Campaign to Suppress Anti-Mormon Motion Pictures, 1911–1912," *Journal of Mormon History* 29 (Fall 2003): 42–76

———. "What a Power We Will Be in This Land: The LDS Church, the Church Security Program, and the New Deal." *Journal of the West* 43 (Fall 2004): 63–75.

Christianson, James R., and Richard Cowan. *The International Church*. Provo, UT: Brigham Young University Publications, 1982.

Cowan, Richard O. *The Church in the Twentieth Century*. Salt Lake City: Bookcraft, 1985.

———. *Temples to Dot the Earth*. Salt Lake City: Bookcraft, 1989.

De Pillis, Mario S. "The Persistence of Mormon Community into the 1990s." *Sunstone* 15.4 (September 1991): 28–49.

Driggs, Ken. "Twentieth-Century Polygamy and Fundamentalist Mormons in Southern Utah." *Dialogue: A Journal of Mormon Thought* 24 (Winter 1991): 44–58.

Hartley, William G. "The Priesthood Reform Movement, 1908–1922." *Brigham Young University Studies* 13 (Winter 1973): 137–56.

Holsinger, M. Paul. "For God and the American Home: The Attempt to Unseat Senator Reed Smoot, 1903–1907." *Pacific Northwest Quarterly* 60 (July 1969): 154–60.

Jacobson, Cardell K. "Black Mormons in the 1980s: Pioneers in a White Church." *Review of Religious Research* 33 (December 1991): 146–52.

Kimball, Richard Ian. *Sports in Zion: Mormon Recreation, 1890–1940.* Urbana: University of Illinois Press, 2003.

Mauss, Armand L. *The Angel and the Beehive: The Mormon Struggle with Assimilation.* Urbana: University of Illinois Press, 1994.

———. *All Abraham's Children: Changing Mormon Conceptions of Race and Lineage.* Urbana: University of Illinois Press, 2003.

Mehr, Kahlile. "Area Supervision: Administration of the Worldwide Church." *Journal of Mormon History* 27.1 (Spring 2001): 192–214.

Ostling, Richard N., and Joan K. Ostling. *Mormon America: The Power and the Promise.* San Francisco: HarperSanFrancisco, 1999.

Palmer, Spencer J., ed. *The Expanding Church.* Salt Lake City: Deseret Book, 1978.

———. *Mormons and Muslims.* Provo, UT: Brigham Young University Press, 1983.

Peterson, Charles S. "Life in a Village Society, 1877–1920." *Utah Historical Quarterly* 49 (Winter 1981): 78–96.

Petersen, Gerald A. *More Than Music: The Mormon Tabernacle Choir.* Provo, UT: Brigham Young University Press, 1979.

Taber, Susan Buhler. *Mormon Lives: A Year in the Elkton Ward.* Urbana: University of Illinois Press, 1993.

Takagi, Shinji. "The Eagle and the Scattered Flock: LDS Church Beginnings in Occupied Japan, 1945–49." *Journal of Mormon History* 28.2 (Fall 2002): 104–138.

———. "Riding on the Eagle's Wings: The Japanese Mission under American Occupation,1948–52." *Journal of Mormon History* 29.1 (Spring 2003): 200–232.

Thorp, Malcolm R. "The British Government and the Mormon Question, 1910–1922." *Journal of Church and State* 21 (Spring 1979): 305–23.

Tullis, F. Lamond. *Mormonism: A Faith for All Cultures.* Provo, UT: Brigham Young University Press, 1978.

Local and Regional United States

Anderson, Lavina Fielding, ed. *Chesterfield: Mormon Outpost in Idaho.* Bancroft, ID: The Chesterfield Foundation, 1982.

Arrington, Leonard J. "A Mormon Apostle Visits the Umatilla and Nez Perce in 1885." *Idaho Yesterdays* 31 (Spring/Summer 1987): 47–54.

———. "The Mormon Settlement of Cassia County, Idaho, 1873–1921." *Idaho Yesterdays* 23 (Summer 1979): 36–46.

———. *The Mormons in Nevada.* Las Vegas, NV: Las Vegas Sun, 1979.

———. "The Promise of Eagle Rock: Idaho Falls, Idaho, 1863–1980." *Rendezvous* 18 (Spring 1983): 2–17.

Bagley, Will. "'Every Thing Is Favourable! And God Is on Our Side': Samuel Brannan and the Conquest of California." *Journal of Mormon History* 23 (Fall 1997): 185–209.

Bitton, Davis. "Peopling the Upper Snake: The Second Wave of Mormon Settlement in Idaho." *Idaho Yesterdays* 23 (Summer 1979): 47–52.

Boyce, Ronald R. "The Mormon Invasion and Settlement of the Upper Snake River Plain in the 1880s: The Case of Lewisville, Idaho." *Pacific Northwest Quarterly* 78 (January–April 1987): 50–58.

Britsch, R. Lanier. *Moramona: The Mormons in Hawaii.* Laie, HI: Institute for Polynesian Studies, 1989.

Buice, David. "When the Saints Come Marching In: The Mormon Experience in Antebellum New Orleans, 1840–1855." *Louisiana History* 23 (Summer 1982): 221–37.

Coates, Lawrence G., Peter G. Boag, Ronald L. Hatzenbuehler, and Merwin R. Swanson. "The Mormon Settlement of Southeastern Idaho, 1845–1900." *Journal of Mormon History* 20 (Fall 1994): 45–62.

Cowan, Richard, and William E. Homer. *California Saints: A 150-year Legacy in the Golden State.* Provo, UT: Religious Studies Center, Brigham Young University, 1996.

Durham, Michael S. *Deseret between the Mountains: Mormons, Miners, Padres, Mountain Men, and the Opening of the Great Basin, 1772–1869.* New York: Henry Holt, 1997.

Ellsworth, S. George. *Mormon Settlement on the Muddy.* Ogden, UT: Weber State College Press, 1987.

Grattan-Aiello, Carolyn. "New St. Joseph, Nevada: The Muddy Mission Experience Revisited." *Nevada Historical Society Quarterly* 29 (Spring 1986): 31–52.

Hatch, William Whitridge. *There Is No Law: A History of Mormon Civil Relations in the Southern States, 1865–1905.* New York: Vantage Press, 1968.

Kimball, Monique E. "A Matter of Faith: A Study of the Muddy Mission." *Nevada Historical Society Quarterly* 30 (Winter 1987): 291–303.

Larson, Andrew Karl. *"I Was Called to Dixie": The Virgin River Basin, Unique Experiences in Mormon Pioneering.* Salt Lake City: Deseret News Press, 1961.

Logue, Larry M. *A Sermon in the Desert: Belief and Behavior in Early St. George, Utah.* Urbana/Chicago: University of Illinois Press, 1988.

Lyman, Edward Leo. *San Bernardino: The Rise and Fall of a California Community.* Salt Lake City: Signature Books, 1996.

May, Dean L. "Star Valley in the Context of Western Settlement." *Snake River Echoes* 14 (Autumn 1985): 103–10.

———. *Three Frontiers: Land, Family, and Society in the American West, 1850–1900.* New York: Cambridge University Press, 1994

Miller, Mark E. "St. Johns's Saints: Interethnic Conflict in Northeastern Arizona, 1880–85." *Journal of Mormon History* 23 (Spring 1997): 66–99.

O'Brien, Robert. *Hands Across the Water: The Story of the Polynesian Cultural Center.* Laie, HI: Institute for Polynesian Studies, 1983.

Orton, Chad M. *More Faith Than Fear: The Los Angeles Stake Story.* Salt Lake City: Bookcraft, 1987.

Peterson, Charles S. *Take Up Your Mission: Mormon Colonizing along the Little Colorado River, 1870–1900.* Tucson: University of Arizona Press, 1973.

Rich, Russell R. *Land of the Sky-Blue Water: A History of the LDS Settlement of the Bear Lake Valley.* Provo, UT: Brigham Young University Press, 1963.

Ricks, Joel E., ed. *The History of a Valley: Cache Valley, Utah-Idaho.* Logan, UT: Utah State University Press, 1956.

Simmonds, A.J. "Southeast Idaho as a Pioneer Mormon Safety Valve." *Idaho Yesterdays* 23 (Winter 1980): 20–30.

Tullis, F. LaMond. "California and Chile in 1851 as Experienced by the Mormon Apostle Parley P. Pratt." *Southern California Quarterly* 67 (Fall 1985): 291–307.

Vogt, Evan Z., and Ethel M. Albert, eds. *People of Rimrock: A Study of Values in Five Cultures.* Cambridge, MA: Harvard University Press, 1966.

Wells, Merle W. *Anti-Mormonism in Idaho, 1872–1892.* Provo, UT: Brigham Young University Press, 1978.

Countries Outside the United States and Immigration

Acevedo A., Rodolfo. *Los Mormones en Chile.* Santiago, Chile: Impresos y Publicaciones Cumora, 1990.

Arrington, Leonard J. "Mormon Women in Nineteenth-Century Britain." *Brigham Young University Studies* 27 (Winter 1987): 67–83.

Baldridge, Steven W., and Rona, Marilyn M. *Grafting In: A History of the Latter-day Saints in the Holy Land.* Murray, UT: Roylance Publishing, 1989.

Bartholomew, Rebecca. *Audacious Women: Early British Mormon Immigrants.* Salt Lake City: Signature Books, 1995.

Beecher, Dale F. "Rey L. Pratt and the Mexican Mission." *Brigham Young University Studies* 15 (Spring 1975): 293–307.

Biddulph, Howard L. *The Morning Breaks: Stories of Conversion and Faith in the Former Soviet Union*. Salt Lake City: Deseret Book, 1996.

Bloxham, V. Ben, James R. Moss, and Larry C. Porter, eds. *Truth Will Prevail: The Rise of the Church . . . in the British Isles, 1837–1987*. Solihull, England: The Church of Jesus Christ of Latter-day Saints, 1987.

Britsch, R. Lanier. "Church Beginnings in China." *Brigham Young University Studies* 10 (Winter 1970): 161–72.

———. "The Closing of the Early Japan Mission." *Brigham Young University Studies* 15 (Winter 1975): 171–90.

———. *From the East: The History of the Latter-day Saints in Asia, 1851–1996*. Salt Lake City: Deseret Book, 1998.

———. "The Latter-day Mission to India, 1851–1856." *Brigham Young University Studies* 12 (Spring 1972): 262–77.

———. *Unto the Islands of the Sea: A History of the Latter-day Saints in the Pacific*. Salt Lake City: Deseret Book, 1986.

Browning, Gary L. "Out of Obscurity: The Emergence of the Church of Jesus Christ of Latter-day Saints in 'That Vast Empire' of Russia." *Brigham Young University Studies* 33 (1993): 674–89.

———. *Russia and the Restored Gospel*. Salt Lake City: Deseret Book, 1997.

Buchanan, Frederick S. "The Ebb and Flow of Mormonism in Scotland, 1840–1900." *Brigham Young University Studies* 17 (Spring 1987): 27–52.

Cannon, Donald Q. "George Q. Cannon and the British Mission." *Brigham Young University Studies* 27 (Winter 1987): 97–112.

Card, Brigham Y. "The Canadian Mormon Settlements, 1886–1925: A North-American Perspective." *Canadian Ethnic Studies* 26 (1994): 19–38.

Card, Brigham Y., et al., eds. *The Mormon Presence in Canada*. Logan: Utah State University Press, 1990.

Conkling, J. Christopher. "Members without a Church: Japanese Mormons in Japan from 1924 to 1948." *Brigham Young University Studies* 15 (Winter 1975): 191–214.

Cuthbert, Derek A. "Church Growth in the British Isles, 1937–1987." *Brigham Young University Studies* 27 (Spring 1987): 13–26.

———. *The Second Century: The Latter-day Saints in Great Britain, 1937–1987*. Cambridge, England: Cambridge University Press, 1987.

Davies, Douglas J. *Mormon Spirituality: Latter-day Saints in Wales and Zion*. Nottingham, England: University of Nottingham, 1987.

Davis, Garold N., and Norma S. Davis. "Behind the Iron Curtain: Recollections of Latter-day Saints in East Germany, 1945–1989." *Brigham Young University Studies* 35 (1995): 47–79.

Dennis, Ronald D. *The Call of Zion: The Story of the First Welsh Mormon Emigration*. Provo, UT: Religious Studies Center, Brigham Young University, 1987.

Dixon, Joseph F. "Mormons in the Third Reich, 1933–1945." *Dialogue: A Journal of Mormon Thought* 7 (Autumn–Winter 1971): 70–78.

Ellsworth, S. George, and Kathleen C. Perrin. *Seasons of Faith and Courage: The Church of Jesus Christ of Latter-day Saints in French Polynesia, 1843–1993*. Sandy, UT: Yves Perrin, 1994.

Evans, Richard L. *A Century of Mormonism in Great Britain*. Salt Lake City: Deseret News Press, 1937.

Folsom, Marjorie Wall. *Golden Harvest in Ghana*. Bountiful, UT: Horizon Publishers, 1989.

Geddes, Ross. "Before Stakehood: The Mission Years in Brisbane, Australia." *Journal of Mormon History* 22 (Fall 1996): 92–119.

———. "'A Storm in the Camp of Brighamism': LDS-RLDS Relations in Brisbane, Australia, 1901–1918." *John Whitmer Historical Association Journal* 11 (1991): 47–59.

Grover, Mark L. "Migration, Social Change, and Mormonism in Portugal." *Journal of Mormon History* 21 (Spring 1995): 65–79.

Harris, Claudia W. "Mormons on the Warfront: The Protestant Mormons and Catholic Mormons of Northern Ireland." *Brigham Young University Studies* 30 (Fall 1990): 7–19.

Harris, Jan G. "Mormons in Victorian Manchester." *Brigham Young University Studies* 17 (Winter 1987): 46–56.

Haslam, Gerald M. *Clash of Cultures: The Norwegian Experience with Mormonism, 1842–1920*. New York: Peter Lang, 1984.

Hatch, Nelle Spillsbury. *Colonia Juarez*. Salt Lake City: Deseret Book, 1954.

Heaton, Tim B., et al. "The Making of British Saints in Historical Perspective." *Brigham Young University Studies* 27 (Spring 1987): 119–35.

Jensen, Richard L., and Malcolm R. Thorp, eds. *Mormons in Early Victorian Britain*. Salt Lake City: University of Utah Press, 1989.

Jenson, Andrew. *History of the Scandinavian Mission*. Salt Lake City: Deseret News Press, 1927.

Katanuma, Seiji. "The Church in Japan." *Brigham Young University Studies* 14 (Autumn 1973): 16–28.

Kissi, Emmanuel Abu. *Walking in the Sand: A History of the Church of Jesus Christ of Latter-day Saints in Ghana*. Provo, UT: Brigham Young University Press, 2004.

Knowlton, David Clark. "Mormonism in Latin America: Towards the Twenty-first Century." *Dialogue: A Journal of Mormon Thought* 29 (Spring 1996): 159–76.

LeBaron, Dale E. *All Are Alike unto God*. Salt Lake City: Bookcraft, 1990.

Lemblé, Jean. *Dieu et les Francais: Les saints des derniers jours francophones*. Paris: Editions Liahona, 1986.

Louder, Dean R. "Canadian Mormons in Their North American Context: A Portrait." *Social Compass* 40 (1993): 271–90.

Lozano, Agricol. *Historia de la iglesia en Mexico*. Mexico, D.F.:N.p., 1980.

Mabey, Rendell N., and Gordon T. Allred. *Brother to Brother: The Story of Latter-day Saint Missionaries Who Took the Gospel to Black Africa*. Salt Lake City: Bookcraft, 1984

Marsh, Don W., comp. *"The Light of the Sun": Japan and the Saints*. Tokyo, Japan: Japan Mission, 1968.

Mehr, Kahlile. "Enduring Believers: Czechoslovakia and the LDS Church, 1884–1990." *Journal of Mormon History* 18 (Fall 1992): 111–54.

———. "Keeping Promises: The LDS Church Enters Bulgaria, 1990–1994." *Brigham Young University Studies* 36 (1996–97): 69–106.

———. *Mormon Missionaries Enter Eastern Europe*. Provo, UT: Brigham Young University Press, and Salt Lake City: Deseret Book, 2002.

Morrison, Alexander B. *The Dawning of a Brighter Day: The Church in Black Africa*. Salt Lake City: Deseret Book, 1990.

Moss, James R., et al. *The International Church*. Provo, UT: Brigham Young University Press, 1982.

Mulder, William. *Homeward to Zion: The Mormon Migration from Scandinavia*. Minneapolis: University of Minnesota Press, 1957.

Neilson, Reid L. and Van C. Gessel, eds. *Taking the Gospel to the Japanese, 1901–2002*. Provo, UT: BYU Studies.

Newton, Marjorie. "The Gathering of the Australian Saints in the 1850s." *Brigham Young University Studies* 27 (Spring 1987): 67–78.

———. *Southern Cross Saints: The Mormons in Australia*. Laie, HI: Institute for Polynesian Studies, 1991.

Palmer, Spencer J. *The Church Encounters Asia*. Salt Lake City: Deseret Book, 1970

Palmer, Spencer J., and Shirley H. Palmer, eds. *The Korean Saints: Personal Stories of Trial and Triumph, 1950–1980*. Provo, UT: Religious Studies Center, Brigham Young University, 1995.

Phillips, Andrew. "Mormons in Essex, 1850–1870." *Essex Journal* 18 (Winter 1983–1984): 57–65.

Romney, Thomas C. *The Mormon Colonies in Mexico*. Salt Lake City: Deseret Book, 1938.

Scharffs, Gilbert W. *Mormonism in Germany*. Salt Lake City: Deseret Book, 1970.

Schiele, Melani, ed. *In Ostdeutschland auf Mission: Erinnerungen, Tagebuchaufzeichnungen und Zeugnisse ehemaliger Missionare.* Leipzig, Germany: N.p., 2004.

Sonne, Conway B. *Saints on the Seas.* Salt Lake City: University of Utah Press, 1983.

————. *Ships, Saints and Mariners: A Maritime Encyclopedia of Mormon Migraiton, 1830–1890.* Salt Lake City: University of Utah Press, 1987.

Sorenson, John L. "Mormon World View and American Culture." *Dialogue: A Journal of Mormon Thought* 8 (Summer 1973): 17–29.

Tagg, Melvin S. *A History of the Mormon Church in Canada.* Lethbridge, Alberta: Lethbridge Herald Co., 1968.

Taylor, P. A. M. *Expectations Westward: The Mormons and the Emigration of Their British Converts in the Nineteenth Century.* Edinburgh and London: Oliver & Boyd, 1965, and Ithaca, NY: Cornell University Press, 1966.

Thorp, Malcolm R. "Sectarian Violence in Early Victorian Britain: The Mormon Experience, 1837–1860." *Bulletin of the John Rylands University Library* 70 (Autumn 1988): 135–47.

Tullis, F. LaMond. "Early Mormon Exploration and Missionary Activities in Mexico." *Brigham Young University Studies* 22 (Summer 1982): 289–310.

————. *Mormons in Mexico: The Dynamics of Faith and Culture.* Logan: Utah State University Press, 1987.

————. "Reopening the Mexican Mission in 1901." *Brigham Young University Studies* 22 (Fall 1982): 441–53.

————. "Three Myths about Mormons in Latin America." *Dialogue: A Journal of Mormon Thought* 7 (Spring 1972): 79–87.

Van Orden, Bruce A. "The Decline in Convert Baptisms and Member Emigration from the British Mission after 1870." *Brigham Young University Studies* 27 (Spring 1987): 97–105.

Walker, Ronald W. "Cradling Mormonism: The Rise of the Gospel in Early Victorian England." *Brigham Young University Studies* 17 (Winter 1987): 25–36.

Williams, Frederick S., and Williams, Frederick G. *From Acorn to Oak Tree: A Personal History of the Establishment and First Quarter Development of the South American Missions.* Fullerton, CA: Etcetera, 1987.

Zobell, Albert L., Jr. *Under the Midnight Sun: Centennial History of the Scandinavian Missions.* Salt Lake City: Deseret Book, 1950.

SOCIAL SCIENCE

Albrecht, Stan L., and Tim B. Heaton. "Secularization, Higher Education, and Religiosity." *Review of Religious Research* 26 (September 1984): 43–58.

Alston, Jon P., and David Johnson. "A Cross-Cultural Analysis of Mormon Missionary Success." *Measuring Mormonism* 5 (Fall 1979): 1–17.

Bahr, Howard M., and Renata Tonks Forste. "Towards a Social Science of Contemporary Mormonism." *Brigham Young University Studies* 26 (1986): 73–121.

Bush, Lester E. "Birth Control among the Mormons: Introduction to an Insistent Question." *Dialogue: A Journal of Mormon Thought* 10 (Autumn 1976): 12–44.

Christensen, Harold T. "Mormon Sexuality in Cross-cultural Perspective." *Dialogue: A Journal of Mormon Thought* 10 (Autumn 1976): 62–75.

———. "The Persistence of Chastity: A Built-in Resistance within Mormon Culture to Secular Trends." *Sunstone* 7 (March–April 1982): 7–14.

Corcoran, Brent, ed. *Multiply and Replenish: Mormon Essays on Sex and Family*. Salt Lake City: Signature Books, 1994.

Cornwall, Marie, Tim B. Heaton, and Lawrence A. Young, eds. *Contemporary Mormonism: Social Science* Perspectives. Urbana: University of Illinois Press, 1994.

Leone, Mark P. *Roots of Modern Mormonism*. Cambridge, MA/London: Harvard University Press, 1979.

Mauss, Armand L. "The Mormon Struggle with Assimilation and Identity: Trends and Developments since Midcentury." *Dialogue: A Journal of Mormon Thought* 27 (Spring 1994): 129–49.

———. "Sociological Perspectives on the Mormon Subculture." *Annual Review of Sociology* 10 (1984): 437–60.

O'Dea, Thomas F. *The Mormons*. Chicago: University of Chicago Press, 1957.

Peck, Granger C. "The Religiosity of Mormon Academicians." *Measuring Mormonism* 5 (Fall 1979): 18–41.

Schow, Ron, Wayne Schow, and Marybeth Raines, eds. *Peculiar People: Mormons and Same-Sex Orientation*. Salt Lake City: Signature Books, 1995.

Shepherd, Gary, and Gordon Shepherd. *Mormon Passage: A Missionary Chronicle*. Urbana: University of Illinois Press, 1998.

Sorenson, John L. *Mormon Culture: Four Decades of Essays on Mormon Society and Personality*. Salt Lake City: New Sage Books, 1997.

Toney, Michael B., et al. "Mormon and Non-Mormon Migration in and out of Utah." *Review of Religious Research* 25 (December 1983): 114–26.

Vernon, Glenn M. *Research on Mormonism: A Collection of Readings*. Salt Lake City: Association for the Study of Religion, 1974.

———. *Sociology of Mormonism: A Preliminary Analysis*. Salt Lake City: Author, 1975.

Vernon, Glenn M., and Charles E. Waddell. "Dying as Social Behavior: Mormon Behavior through Half a Century." *Omega* 5 (Fall 1974): 199–206.

PHILOSOPHY

Edwards, Paul M. *Preface to Faith: A Philosophical Inquiry into RLDS Beliefs*. Midvale, UT: Signature Books, 1984.

McMurrin, Sterling M. *The Theological Foundations of the Mormon Religion*. Salt Lake City: University of Utah Press, 1965.

Ostler, Blake T. *Exploring Mormon Thought: The Attributes of God*. Salt Lake City: Kofford Books, 2001.

———. *Exploring Mormon Thought: The Problems of Theism and the Love of God*. Salt Lake City: Kofford Books, 2006.

FOLKLORE

Cheney, Thomas E., ed. *Lore of Faith and Folly*. Salt Lake City: University of Utah Press, 1971.

Eliason, Eric A. "Toward the Folkloristic Study of Latter-day Saint Conversion Narratives." *Brigham Young University Studies* 38 (1999): 137–50.

Fife, Austin, and Alta Fife. *Saints of Sage and Saddle: Folklore among the Mormons*. Bloomington: Indiana University Press, 1956.

Wilson, William A. "Mormon Folklore: Cut from the Marrow of Everyday Experience." *Brigham Young University Studies* 33 (1993): 521–40.

———. "Mormon Folklore: Faith or Folly?" *Brigham Young Magazine* 49 (May 1995): 47–54.

PERSONAL ESSAYS

Barlow, Philip L., ed. *A Thoughtful Faith: Essays on Belief by Mormon Scholars*. Centerville, UT: Canon Press, 1986.

Black, Susan Easton, ed. *Expressions of Faith: Testimonies of Latter-day Saint Scholars*. Salt Lake City: Deseret Book Company, and Provo, UT: FARMS, 1996.

Bradford, Mary Lythgoe, ed. *Mormon Women Speak: A Collection of Essays*. Salt Lake City: Olympus Publishing Co., 1982.

Christensen, Parley A. *All in a Teacher's Day: Essays of a Mormon Professor*. Salt Lake City: Author, 1948.

———. *Of a Number of Things*. Salt Lake City: University of Utah Press, 1962.

England, Eugene. *Dialogues with Myself: Personal Essays on Mormon Experience*. Salt Lake City: Orion Books, 1984.

———. *The Quality of Mercy: Personal Essays on Mormon Experience*. Salt Lake City: Bookcraft, 1992.

———. *Why the Church Is as True as the Gospel: Personal Essays on Mormon Experience*. Salt Lake City: Bookcraft, 1986.

Geary, Edward A. *Goodbye to Poplarhaven: Recollections of a Utah Boyhood*. Salt Lake City: University of Utah Press, 1985.

King, Arthur Henry. *The Abundance of the Heart*. Salt Lake City: Bookcraft, 1986. Revised, expanded edition entitled *Arm the Children: Faith's Response to a Violent World*. Provo, UT: Brigham Young University Press, 1998.

Newton, Marjorie. "My Family, My Friends, My Faith." *Brigham Young University Studies* 41 (2002): 141–46.

Poll, Richard D. *History and Faith: Reflections of a Mormon Historian*. Salt Lake City: Signature Books, 1989.

Rasmussen, Dennis. *The Lord's Question: Thoughts on the Life of Response*. Provo, UT: Keter Foundation, 1985.

DOCTRINAL AND APOLOGETIC

Alexander, Thomas G. "The Reconstruction of Mormon Doctrine: From Joseph Smith to Progressive Theology." *Sunstone* 5 (July–August 1980): 24–33.

———. "The Word of Wisdom: From Principle to Requirement." *Dialogue* 14 (Fall 1981): 78–88.

Bennion, Lowell L. *Religion and the Pursuit of Truth*. Salt Lake City: Deseret Book, 1968.

———. *The Religion of the Latter-day Saints*. Salt Lake City: LDS Department of Education, 1940.

Blomberg, Craig L., and Stephen E. Robinson. *How Wide the Divide? A Mormon and an Evangelical in Conversation*. Downers Grove, IL: InterVarsity Press, 1997.

Clark, David L., ed. *Of Heaven and Earth: Reconciling Scientific Thought with LDS Theology*. Salt Lake City: Deseret Book, 1998.

England, Eugene, ed. *Converted to Christ through the* Book of Mormon. Salt Lake City: Deseret Book, 1989.

Eyring, Henry. *The Faith of a Scientist*. Salt Lake City: Bookcraft, 1967.

Hafen, Bruce C. *The Believing Heart: Nourishing the Seed of Faith*. 2nd ed. Salt Lake City: Deseret Book, 1986.

———. *The Broken Heart: Applying the Atonement to Life's Experiences*. Salt Lake City: Deseret Book, 1989.

Jackson, Kent P., et al., eds. *Studies in Scripture*. 8 vols. Salt Lake City: Randall Book Co., 1984–1985, and Deseret Book, 1986–1989.

Keller, Roger R. *Reformed Christians and Mormon Christians: Let's Talk*. N.p.: Pryor Pettengill, 1986.

Lee, Rex E. *What Do Mormons Believe?* Salt Lake City: Deseret Book, 1992.

Ludlow, Victor L. *Principles and Practices of the Restored Gospel*. Salt Lake City: Deseret Book, 1992.

Madsen, Truman G., ed. *Reflections on Mormonism: Judaeo-Christian Parallels*. Provo, UT: Religious Studies Center, Brigham Young University, 1978.

Matthews, Robert J. *"A Plainer Translation": Joseph Smith's Translation of the Bible*. Provo, UT: Brigham Young University Press, 1975.

McConkie, Bruce R. *Mormon Doctrine*. 2nd ed. Salt Lake City: Bookcraft, 1966.

———. *A New Witness for the Articles of Faith*. Salt Lake City: Deseret Book, 1985.

McConkie, Mark L., ed. *Doctrines of the Restoration: Sermons and Writings of Bruce R. McConkie*. Salt Lake City: Bookcraft, 1989.

Millet, Robert L. *Alive in Christ: The Miracle of Spiritual Rebirth*. Salt Lake City: Deseret Book, 1997.

———. *By Grace Are We Saved*. Salt Lake City: Deseret Book, 1989.

———. *A Different Jesus: The Christ of the Latter-day Saints*. Grand Rapids, MI: Eerdmans, 2005.

———. *An Eye Single to the Glory of God*. Salt Lake City: Deseret Book, 1991.

———. *Getting at the Truth: Responding to Difficult Questions about LDS Beliefs*. Salt Lake City: Deseret Book, 2004.

———. *Latter-day Christianity: Ten Basic Issues*. Salt Lake City: Covenant Communications, 1998.

———. *The Mormon Faith: A New Look at Christianity*. Salt Lake City: Shadow Mountain, 1998.

Nibley, Hugh. *The Collected Works of Hugh Nibley*. 13 vols. Salt Lake City: Deseret Book, 1986–1992. (This multivolume work by Mormonism's most erudite defender of the late 20th century includes studies of the Old Testament, ancient history, the *Pearl of Great Price*, early Christianity, the *Book of Mormon*, and early Mormon history.)

Palmer, Spencer J., and Keller, Roger R. *Religions of the World: A Latter-day Saint View*. Provo, UT: Brigham Young University Press, 1989.

Peterson, Daniel C., and Stephen D. Ricks. *Offenders for a Word: How Anti-Mormons Play Word Games to Attack the Latter-day Saints*. Salt Lake City: Aspen Books, 1992.

Peterson, H. Donl. *The* Pearl of Great Price: *A History and Commentary*. Salt Lake City: Deseret Book, 1987.

Rector, Hartman, and Connie Rector. *No More Strangers.* 4 vols. Salt Lake City: Bookcraft, 1971–1990.

Reynolds, Noel, ed. Book of Mormon *Authorship Revisited: The Evidence for Ancient Origins.* Provo, UT: FARMS, 1997.

Richards, LeGrand. *A Marvelous Work and a Wonder.* Salt Lake City: Deseret Book, 1950.

Roberts, B. H. *The Falling Away.* Salt Lake City: Deseret Book, 1931.

———. *The Truth, the Way, the Life: An Elementary Treatise on Theology.* Ed. John W. Welch. Provo, UT: BYU Studies, 1994.

———. *The Truth, the Way, the Life: An Elementary Treatise on Theology: The Masterwork of B. H. Roberts.* Ed. Stan Larson. San Francisco: Smith Research Associates, 1994. (These two editions, published simultaneously, follow different but defensible editorial procedures. The former edition has the advantage of 12 essays by different scholars analyzing and evaluating different aspects of Roberts's work.)

Robinson, Stephen E. *Are Mormons Christians?* Salt Lake City: Bookcraft, 1991.

Sessions, Gene A., and Craig J. Oberg, eds. *The Search for Harmony: Essays on Science and Mormonism.* Salt Lake City: Signature Books, 1993.

Shipps, Jan. "Is Mormonism Christian? Reflections on a Complicated Question." *Brigham Young University Studies* 33 (1993): 438–65.

Sorenson, John L. *An Ancient American Setting for the Book of Mormon.* Salt Lake City: Deseret Book, 1985.

———. *Images of Ancient America: Visualizing Book of Mormon Life.* Provo, UT: Research Press, FARMS, 1998.

Sorenson, John L., and Thorne, Melvin J., eds. *Rediscovering the* Book of Mormon. Salt Lake City: Deseret Book, and Provo: FARMS, 1991.

A Sure Foundation: Answers to Difficult Gospel Questions. Salt Lake City: Deseret Book, 1988.

Talmage, James E. *The Articles of Faith.* Salt Lake City: Deseret News, 1899.

———. *The Great Apostasy.* Salt Lake City: Deseret News, 1909.

———. *The House of the Lord: A Study of Holy Sanctuaries, Ancient and Modern.* Salt Lake City: Deseret News, 1912.

———. *Jesus the Christ: A Study of the Messiah and His Mission According to Holy Scriptures Both Ancient and Modern.* Salt Lake City: Deseret Book, 1915.

Taylor, John. *The Mediation and Atonement of Our Lord and Savior Jesus Christ.* Salt Lake City: Deseret News, 1882.

Welch, John W., ed. *Reexploring the* Book of Mormon. Salt Lake City: Deseret Book, 1992.

———. *The Sermon at the Temple and the Sermon on the Mount.* Salt Lake City: Deseret Book, 1990.

Widtsoe, John A. *Evidences and Reconciliations.* Salt Lake City: Bookcraft, 1960.

———. *Priesthood and Church Government.* Rev. ed. Salt Lake City: Deseret Book, 1939.

———. *A Rational Theology.* Salt Lake City: General Priesthood Committee, 1915.

Widtsoe, John A., and Leah D. Widtsoe. *The Word of Wisdom: A Modern Interpretation.* Salt Lake City: Deseret Book, 1937.

LITERATURE AND ART

Anderson, Lavina Fielding, and Eugene England, eds. *Tending the Garden: Essays on Mormon Literature.* Salt Lake City: Signature Books, 1996.

Bell, Shane, ed. *Washed By a Wave of Wind: Science Fiction from the Corridor.* Salt Lake City: Signature Books, 1993.

Card, Orson Scott. *A Storyteller in Zion: Essays and Speeches.* Salt Lake City: Bookcraft, 1993.

England, Eugene, ed. *Bright Angels and Familiars: Contemporary Mormon Stories.* Salt Lake City: Signature Books, 1992.

Hamilton, C. Mark. *Nineteenth-Century Mormon Architecture and City Planning.* New York: Oxford University Press, 1995.

Howe, Susan Elizabeth, and Sheree Maxwell Bench, eds. *Discoveries: Two Centuries of Poems by Mormon Women.* Provo, UT: BYU Studies, 2004.

Jackson, Richard W. *Places of Worship: 150 Years of LDS Architecture.* Provo, UT: Religious Studies Center, Brigham Young University, 2003.

Mulder, William. "Telling It Slant: Aiming for Truth in Contemporary Mormon Literature." *Dialogue: A Journal of Mormon Thought* 26 (Summer 1993): 155–69.

Oman, Richard G., and Robert O. Davis. *Images of Faith: Art of the Latter-day Saints.* Salt Lake City: Deseret Book, 1995.

Swanson, Vern G., Robert S. Olpin, and William C. Seifrit. *Utah Painting and Sculpture.* Layton, UT: Gibbs Smith, 1997.

About the Authors

Davis Bitton was emeritus professor of history at the University of Utah. He received his B.A. degree from Brigham Young University and both his M.A. and Ph.D. from Princeton University. As a specialist in early modern European history, he published *The French Nobility in Crisis, 1560–1640*. He held faculty appointments at the University of Texas and the University of California at Santa Barbara. He had an interest in Mormon history for many years and was a charter member and past president of the Mormon History Association. He conducted oral history interviews with many participants in Mormon history at the end of the 20th century. His extensive publications include *Guide to Mormon Diaries and Autobiographies* (1977), *The Mormon Experience: A History of the Latter-day Saints* (1978), and *George Q. Cannon: A Biography* (1999).

Thomas G. Alexander is the Lemuel Hardison Redd Jr. professor emeritus of western American history at Brigham Young University. His B.S. and M.S. degrees are from Utah State University and he received the Ph.D. from the University of California at Berkeley. A specialist in U.S. history with an emphasis on the American West and American environmental history, he has authored, coauthored, edited, or coedited 24 books and monographs and more than 125 articles. Among his books are *A Clash of Interests: Interior Department and Mountain West, 1863–96* (1977), *Mormons and Gentiles: A History of Salt Lake City* (1984, with James B. Allen), *Mormonism in Transition: A History of the Latter-day Saints, 1890-1930* (1986, 2nd ed. 1996), *Things in Heaven and Earth: The Life and Times of Wilford Woodruff, a Mormon Prophet* (1991, 2nd ed. 1996), *Utah, the Right Place* (1995, rev. eds. 1996 and 2003), and *Grace and Grandeur: A History of Salt Lake City* (2002). He is one of the founders and a past president of the Mormon History Association.